P9-CSH-739

THE ROUGH GUIDE TO

The Best Music You've Never Heard

**ROUGH
GUIDES**

www.roughguides.com

Credits

Rough Guides Reference

Reference Director: Andrew Lockett
Editors: Peter Buckley, Tracy Hopkins,
Sean Mahoney, Matthew Milton,
Joe Staines and Ruth Tidball

The Rough Guide to the Best Music You've Never Heard

Editor: Matthew Milton
Design and layout: Peter Buckley, Andrew Clare, Dan May
and Matthew Milton
Proofreading: Kate Berens
Cover: Diana Jarvis and Chloë Roberts
Production: Vicky Baldwin and Rebecca Short
Contributors: David Smyth and Robert Webb
Additional contributors: Roger Bardon, Chris Brook, Geoff
Colquitt, Neil Foxlee, Rhodri Marsden, Matthew Milton, Peter
Moyse and Joe Staines

Publishing Information

This first edition published October 2008 by
Rough Guides Ltd, 80 Strand, London WC2R 0RL
345 Hudson St, 4th Floor, New York 10014, USA
Email: mail@roughguides.com

Distributed by the Penguin Group:
Penguin Books Ltd, 80 Strand, London WC2R 0RL
Penguin Putnam, Inc., 375 Hudson Street, NY 10014, USA
Penguin Group (Australia), 250 Camberwell Road, Camberwell,
Victoria 3124, Australia
Penguin Books Canada Ltd, 90 Eglinton Avenue East, Toronto,
Ontario, Canada M4P 2YE
Penguin Group (New Zealand), Cnr Rosedale and Airborne
Roads, Albany, Auckland, New Zealand

Printed in China

Typeset in Chaparral, Helvetica Neue, Myriad and OCE A Std

The publishers and authors have done their best to ensure the
accuracy and currency of all information in *The Rough Guide to
the Best Music You've Never Heard*; however, they can accept no
responsibility for any loss or inconvenience sustained by any
reader as a result of its information or advice.

No part of this book may be reproduced in any form without
permission from the publisher except for the quotation of brief
passages in reviews.

© Rough Guides, 2008

288 pages; includes index

A catalogue record for this book is available from the British
Library

ISBN: 978-1-84836-003-7

1 3 5 7 9 8 6 4 2

THE ROUGH GUIDE TO

The Best Music You've Never Heard

by

Nigel Williamson

with additional material by
David Smyth and Robert Webb

Contents

I write the songs
they had singer-songwriter stamped in their passport   1

Strictly indie
alt.rock heroes of the bedsit   **29**

Lonesome highways
alternative Americana   **57**

Lost soul
fraught funk and wronged R&B   75

Prog and proud
keyboard solos and concept albums   95

Bluesmen and bawlers
the Delta and elsewhere

Let there be rock
the amps that went up to 11

Forgotten folk
taking the finger out the ear

Blips, beats and glitches
techno-heads, MCs and electro-geeks 155

Psychedelic relics
the troubadours of tie-dye 173

Not for export
world, reggae and more   191

The art school
conceptualists, bohemians and the too-clever-by-half   209

Conservatoires and cocktail bars
classical misfits, jazz hepcats and the pioneers in between   223

Outsiders
the musicians that never fitted in   **243**

Introduction

This book is in effect an alternative history of music, a collection of signposts to great albums that most people don't know about. But although many of the artists featured are obscure, it is not a book devoted to obscurity for the sake of it. We feel that all the music championed in these pages deserves to be heard, and we try to explain why these records – buried deep in the bargain bins, or left to moulder in the vaults of the world's record companies – warrant your attention. We also tell the fascinating and sometimes tragic stories behind the neglected geniuses who made them.

Some of the names here will be familiar. Nick Drake has over recent years become a cult figure, name-checked by every nascent singer-songwriter and every cool new indie band on the block as a "seminal influence". We included him because in many ways he is the patron saint of this book. The first of popular music's Van Gogh figures, he was an artist who sold virtually no records in his lifetime and died in obscurity, but he is now recognized as a toweringly influential figure. Since Drake's critical rehabilitation, the catalogue of numerous other artists, such as Judee Sill, Karen Dalton and David Ackles, who never achieved commercial success in their lifetimes, has undergone a similar process of favourable reappraisal. More happily, others, such as Vashti Bunyan and Bill Fay, are still around to belatedly enjoy having found an appreciative audience for music that the record-buying public ignored at the time of its original release.

You will also find in this book familiar names such as Bob Dylan and the Rolling Stones – but in a less familiar context. We examine the more obscure corners of their back catalogue and reclaim as lost classics unpopular and derided albums such as *Self Portrait* and *Their Satanic Majesties Request*.

Ultimately, whether you recognize the names or not, *The Rough Guide to the Best Music You've Never Heard* is a book of great stories. The reasons why the musicians featured in this book didn't become household names are many and often complex.

Sometimes it was down to the flawed characters of the artists involved. In this guide, you will meet the mad, the bad and the dangerous to know. Sometimes the music was genuinely ahead of its time. Sometimes it simply failed to find an audience due to the stupidity and/or venality of record companies, managers, and other hangers-on.

But in each case, the result was the same – great music didn't get the exposure or sales it deserved at the time. Enjoy the voyage of discovery we hope this book will take you on, and please write to us with your own examples of lost classics and overlooked genius. We'll try to include the most interesting in the next edition.

Nigel Williamson

Acknowledgements

I would like to thank Magali for 33 years of extraordinary patience and my two adult sons Adam and Piers for constantly reminding me that music did not come to an end the day Jimi Hendrix died. Thanks to all the other writers who have contributed a section or two of the book (see credits) especially David Smyth, Robert Webb, Rhodri Marsden, Matt Milton and Joe Staines, and of course Andy Partridge of XTC and Natasha Khan of Bat For Lashes. The initials of writers (including my own) are given at the end of each article.

Author profiles

Nigel Williamson is a former news editor of *The Times*, one-time editor of *Tribune*, and a respected rock writer and journalist. His music writing has been featured in numerous newspapers and magazines, including *Uncut*, *Billboard* and *Songlines*, and he spent five years as a judge for the Mercury Music Prize. His books include *Journey Through the Past: the Stories Behind the Classic Songs of Neil Young* (2002), *The Rough Guide to Bob Dylan* (2004) and *The Rough Guide to the Blues* (2007).

David Smyth is the *London Evening Standard*'s rock and pop critic, and has also written for *Q*, *The New Statesman* and *The Daily Telegraph*. He lives in London, where he goes to more gigs than is strictly good for him.

Robert Webb is a freelance music journalist and book editor and has contributed to BBC radio, *Time Out*, *Mojo* and the *Independent*, for which he currently writes the regular "Cult Classics" and "Story of the Song" columns.

Finding music online

Reading this book, you are sure to come across many intriguing artists that you will want to hear… perhaps just the once, but you'll want to hear them nonetheless. To get a free "streaming" taster of many thousands of artists, the best places to start are MySpace.com (where even many long-dead musicians have a presence) and YouTube.com (where you'll get to see, as well as hear, your new discovery). As for downloading songs to keep, some artists on MySpace do make songs available to download from their pages as MP3s (either for free or at a cost), though to get whole albums legally in digital form you are going to have to visit a download store. At the time of writing, the most popular and well-stocked is Apple's iTunes Store, which is accessed through the iTunes software, not via the web (find out more at apple.com/itunes). As for good old-fashioned records and CDs, Google will make quick work of directing you to a plethora of specialized online mail-order services, though you may well have better luck looking for that one special item by regularly dropping by eBay. Happy hunting…

I WRITE THE SONGS
they had singer-songwriter
stamped in their passport

David Ackles

When David Ackles died in almost total obscurity in 1999, even the normally conservative Reuters news agency was moved to note that "he could have been another Leonard Cohen or Randy Newman."

Between 1968 and 1974, Ackles released four albums without ever bothering the charts. Yet the handful who did buy his records included an impressive coterie of fellow singer-songwriters who couldn't quite understand how they had made it huge while Ackles remained unknown.

Elton John was one who believed that Ackles was a genius. "He was Elton's favourite songwriter," recalls Elektra boss Jac Holzman. "When Elton first appeared in America at the Troubadour in LA in August 1970, he saw David Ackles was on the same bill and thought he was opening for him. He couldn't believe it was actually the other way around."

With California's music biz elite in the audience, the concert launched Elton on the path to superstardom. Ackles, by contrast, was dumped straight back into obscurity. Some felt the industry anointed the wrong man that night. One person who might agree is Phil Collins, who chose Ackles' "Down River" (but nothing by Elton) among his "Desert Island Discs". Another is Elvis Costello, who says he's mystified at the public's indifference to Ackles' wonderful songs.

Born in Rock Island, Illinois, in 1937, Ackles was a child actor, a teenage jailbird, a student of Old English at Edinburgh University and a private detective before he turned to music. He originally came to Elektra as a non-performing songwriter, touting a song called "Blue Ribbons", which he'd written with Cher in mind (although she never recorded it). When Elektra had no luck placing his songs with other artists, he recorded them himself. His solemn, cerebral compositions and mournful baritone were teamed by Elektra with an unlikely backing band of acid-rockers, mostly drawn from label stablemates Rhinoceros.

The result was 1967's *David Ackles*, a collection of songs that were masterful and mature – he was already thirty. They were populated by stoical characters in various stages of desolation and presented with an understated melodrama (if there is such a thing) which music critic John Mulvey summed up as a fusion of the folk-romantic fatalism of Tim Buckley and Leonard Cohen with the more theatrical craftsmanship of Jimmy Webb and Randy Newman.

Ackles' voice and keyboards were allowed plenty of space but the band complemented him brilliantly, particularly on opener "The Road to Cairo" (Ackles' best-known song after it was covered by Julie Driscoll as the follow-up to "This Wheel's On Fire") and "Down River". The latter is a truly extraordinary piece of narrative songwriting in which the singer meets his old girlfriend after being released from prison and gently chides her for not staying in touch. Gradually it emerges that she's living with his best friend. Although the song's lyrics are a conversation, we only ever get to hear the words from one side. The brilliance of his singing lies in the way he bottles up the anguish but by the end cannot quite keep it all in.

"His Name Is Andrew" is even bleaker, the story of a depressive who works in a canning factory, loses his Christian faith and chooses "to wait alone for this life to end". The drama is intense, as it is in a quite different way on the jaunty, vagrant's anthem "Laissez-Faire", which resembles something from Kurt Weill's *The Threepenny Opera*.

Two years later came *Subway to the Country* (1969), on which Ackles' debt to Weill and Brecht was even more evident and the subject matter even less mainstream. "Candy Man", for example, is a harrowing tale about a child molester – a crippled war veteran whose sick behaviour is a warped act of vengeance on society. In many ways it was a stepping stone to 1973's *American Gothic*, produced by Elton John's lyricist Bernie Taupin. It's hardly a rock record at all – more an extended piece of orchestrated musical art-theatre which Taupin has described as "almost Wagnerian", and which features strings by Nick Drake's arranger, Robert Kirby. On tracks such as the ten-minute "Montana Song", the clear influence of Aaron Copeland and George Gershwin can also be heard.

American Gothic got powerfully good reviews. Its moving but never sentimental vignettes of lonely, broken people looking for connections even led one critic to call Ackles "the John Updike of popular song". Yet it sold no more than his previous releases and Elektra dropped him. He moved to Columbia for *Five & Dime* (1973), another distinctive collection of songs that included "Aberfan", a characteristically bleak mini-suite about the disaster that destroyed a school and most of its pupils in a Welsh mining village in 1966. Yet after the ambition and achievement of *American Gothic*, it sounded like a retreat. *Five & Dime* was treated by the record-buying public with even greater indifference than his previous three albums, and Ackles abandoned his recording career.

As Elton John noted, "Some people don't get hyped enough. People like David Ackles. He's one of the best that America had to offer."

NW

playlist:

1 Down River *from* David Ackles
Has anguish ever sounded so understated – and yet so utterly convincing? Elton's right: he and Bernie never wrote anything as emotionally powerful as this.

2 The Road to Cairo *from* David Ackles
"I can't walk down this road to Cairo/They're better thinkin' I'm dead" – the abandoned journey in this song in many ways mirrors Ackles' musical career.

3 His Name Is Andrew *from* David Ackles
Violated innocence, alienation and lost faith; whoever said it was like a six-minute Harold Pinter play in song really wasn't far off the mark.

4 Be My Friend *from* David Ackles
No, he wasn't predicting the arrival of MySpace. He's never sounded as elegiacally lovely as on this closing track from his debut album.

5 The Grave of God *from* There Is A River: The Elektra Recordings
This powerful but doomy outtake from the late 1960s is a hard one to track down: it's only on a Rhino Records retrospective that never made it to the shops.

6 Candy Man *from* Subway to the Country
Controversial, chilling and shocking in its dealing with cycles of abuse, even Cohen or Dylan would have shied away from writing a song as uncompromising as this.

7 Another Friday Night *from* American Gothic
A piano ballad of muted resignation, it swells miraculously into a defiant country-gospel finale.

8 One Night Stand *from* American Gothic
If Sondheim had written this as a show tune, it surely would have been acclaimed a Broadway masterpiece.

9 Waiting for the Moving Van *from* American Gothic
One of the most touching songs in Ackles' canon. Hanging on in quiet desperation is the American way, too, it seems.

10 Montana Song *from* American Gothic
An astonishing new direction that he sadly never pursued, the alternatively austere and fulsome strings of the London Symphony Orchestra perfectly underscore Ackles' epic tale of his forefathers.

Joseph Arthur

S ometimes it seems the singers most admired by their fellow musicians are the ones least able to make their mark on the wider world. Ohio-born Joseph Arthur was discovered working in a guitar shop by Peter Gabriel, and his world-weary ballad "In the Sun" has been covered as a duet by REM's Michael Stipe and Coldplay's Chris Martin, who called it "the greatest song ever written".

His music is classic American singer-songwriter stuff, his songs are dusty panoramas reminiscent of Tom Petty, Neil Young, the Stones, Bob Dylan and the Waterboys. Yet they're skewed by occasional unlikely vocal mannerisms and electronic touches that suggest a late-1970s Bowie influence, with nods in the direction of The Cure and Beck.

On his 2008 song "King of the Pavement" he oddly recalls Echo & the Bunnymen, sounding unnervingly like Ian

Ripe for rediscovery:
Paul McCartney's
McCartney II

In the summer of 1979, following the release of what turned out to be Wings' final album, *Back to the Egg*, McCartney retreated to his Scottish farmhouse and began working on new material in solitary fashion. Writing, performing, singing, recording and producing everything himself, the first track he cut was merely a test for his new electronic equipment and so was titled "Check My Machine". By the time he'd finished, he had recorded more than twenty songs and instrumentals.

The material was then put to one side while he toured with Wings. When the group arrived in Tokyo in January 1980, however, a search of McCartney's luggage revealed 219 grammes of marijuana. He was immediately arrested and the tour cancelled. After spending nine days in a Japanese jail, on his release he returned to Scotland and, while he contemplated his future, re-evaluated the recordings from the previous summer and decided to release them as the belated follow-up to his solo debut a decade earlier.

On the release of *McCartney II* in April 1980, many were puzzled by the record's unfinished sound and experimental, synth-based wisps of tunes. Most critics were scathing. *Rolling Stone* dismissed it as "an album of aural doodles designed for the amusement of very young children" on which the vocals sounded like "a cross between an insect and a wind-up toy". That didn't prevent the album from going to number one in Britain and number three in America, but it has since been routinely dismissed as the weakest album in the former Beatle's canon.

More discerning McCartney watchers, however, have come to regard it as a misunderstood – if flawed – classic. Far better, they argue, to have Macca in such an adventurous state of mind than producing the kind of formulaic pop we all know he can churn out in his sleep.

The opener, "Coming Up", is one of the album's more conventional moments. "Temporary Secretary" is more experimental, based on an atonal, hypnotic keyboard rhythm which can be seen as a forerunner of today's techno. "On the Way" is a classic McCartney ballad, but given a cosmic feel by the reverb on his voice and his double-tracked electric guitar. "Waterfalls" has an acoustic simplicity that recalls Beatles songs such as "Blackbird" or "Martha My Dear". The synthesizer instrumentals "Front Parlour", "Summer's Day Song" and "Frozen Jap" are full of hypnotic little hooks and a bizarre charm. "Bogey Music" is another electronic experiment, with clever echo effects and multi-tracked vocals, before McCartney brilliantly refocuses on his more traditional songwriting strengths with the closing track, "One of These Days".

It doesn't all work. But at the very least it has to go down as one of the bravest and most fascinating experiments in Paul McCartney's long and illustrious career.

NW

McCulloch. But his music is not difficult to listen to, and he is not short on tunes. So it's hard to explain exactly why he is not a big success.

Perhaps it is that Arthur is too dedicated to following his wayward muse to worry about matching the commercial appeal of his famous fans. Having parted with Gabriel's Real World label after three albums, the songs on his fourth and finest, *Our Shadows Will Remain*, came to him after he had put his New York possessions in storage and wandered to New Orleans with just a suitcase and a guitar. "It was accidental Buddhism," he said.

In concert he has generally performed alone, building up layers of sound using looping effects pedals, and spending as much time painting onstage as he does singing. The distorted heads and abstract splashes that fill his canvases are as accomplished as his songs – his only Grammy nomination to date has been for album artwork. "When your conscious brain is focusing on singing, your unconscious is freer to express itself. It gave me a different kind of energy, electric and live."

Prolific in both his music and his visual art, when he acquired his first backing band, The Lonely Astronauts, in 2007, they recorded eighty songs in three weeks. The masses wouldn't be keen on most of them but to a man who lives only for his art, that's hardly worth worrying about.

DS

Gary Farr

Gary Farr was the son of the heavyweight boxer Tommy Farr – the "Tonypandy Terror", who famously survived fifteen rounds with the World Champion Joe Louis in 1937. Gary preferred R&B to pugilism, however, and, along with many of his generation, was swept up by the British beat boom of the early 1960s, forming his own band, the T-Bones. They had the same manager as the Yardbirds, Giorgio Gomelsky, and in 1964 they settled into a weekly residency at London's Marquee, taking over from the Yardbirds as the club's Friday night draw.

The T-Bones were something of an act to catch and, as the British invasion got underway, even played on American TV, on the show *Shindig Goes to London*, alongside the Animals, the Moody Blues and Rod Stewart. But while his compatriots began to sign deals and have hits, Farr and his band struggled to replicate their energetic live reputation on vinyl. To make matters worse, when their *T-Bones* EP

The T-Bones, with Gary Farr (centre).

appeared in France, it was mistakenly packaged with a photograph of the Yardbirds.

Suffering from a constantly shifting line-up – Keith Emerson briefly tinkled the ivories for them, on his way to The Nice and ELP – Farr took to gigging as a solo artist, urged on by his brother, the future Isle of Wight Festival promoter Rikki Farr. He released his debut album, *Take Something With You*, on Gomelsky's Marmalade label, in 1969. Farr's new direction was as a thoughtful troubadour with a moody edge, in the style of the three late-1960s Tims: Hardin, Rose and Buckley.

Farr's second, and best, album, *Strange Fruit*, was issued in 1970. Augmented by the psychedelic band Mighty Baby, it also featured the talents of a greenhorn Richard Thompson (the bassist's first session beyond Joe Boyd's Witchseason stable), with string arrangements by the Womble-to-be Mike Batt. *Addressed to the Censors of Love* (1973), recorded at Alabama's Muscle Shoals studio and co-produced by Jerry Wexler, completed a trilogy of albums which, despite some sterling performances from all involved, failed to make Farr a name to remember. "I've been told I'm too commercial, and I can't be used because I'm not folk," he commented at the time. "But I am doing what I feel are really valid songs for today."

Ultimately, Farr was lost in the shuffle of early 1970s rock. Emigrating to Los Angeles in the middle of the decade, he hooked up with Little Feat's latter-day guitarist Fred Tackett, in a short-lived R&B band, Jumping Dogs, and cut some home recordings. The music failed to pay the rent, however, and Farr switched to making a living from still photography and fine carpentry.

RW

Great lost albums: Elton John's Thom Bell album

In the mid-1970s Elton John fell so in love with the sweet Philadelphia soul of the Stylistics, Harold Melvin, the O'Jays and the Spinners that he couldn't wait to work with the man who had produced their records. He knew that Thom Bell insisted on controlling every aspect of the recording process, but as a fan he was so besotted with Bell's signature sound that he was more than prepared to sacrifice his own hard-won creative independence in return for a little of the Philly magic.

He approached the producer via the Spinners backstage at one of their London concerts and he arrived at Bell's new studio – which was not in Philadelphia at all by then, but in Seattle – to begin work on 14 October 1977. Over four days, they recorded six tracks. On the first two days, Bell's usual crack team of session musicians laid down the instrumentals. On days three and four John added his vocals. Later at Philadelphia's Sigma Sound Studios, Bell added strings, horns and backing vocals by the Spinners.

It was quite clear that Bell was totally in charge and only two of the songs were even co-compositions by Elton. "Nice and Slow", a lighthearted melody with sexually suggestive lyrics, was a co-write with Bernie Taupin and Bell. "Shine On Through" was written with lyricist Gary Osborne. Bell and his session guitarist Casey James penned three more, "Mama Can't Buy You Love", "Three Way Love Affair" and "Are You Ready for Love", and they also recorded "Country Love Song".

The tracks are notable for a new development in John's vocal style, as Bell coaxed a more masculine-sounding tenor out of him. "He was the first person that ever taught me about my voice," John later admitted. "He said, 'You don't use your lower register enough and you don't breathe properly'. I thought 'Oh fabulous, we're going to get on really well.' But he was right."

He was less convinced about other aspects of Bell's production, however. When he got the final mixes, the Elton ego really couldn't cope with what Bell had done to "Are You Ready for Love", on which he was left singing a single verse while the Spinners did the rest. He cancelled the planned second session in 1978, intended to complete the album, and told Bell he was putting the already recorded tracks on hold because they were "too saccharine".

Eventually, in 1979, John remixed the three songs written by Bell and James, reducing their sugariness and removing much of the Spinners' contribution to "Are You Ready for Love", with the help of Clive Franks. All three were issued on an EP called *The Thom Bell Sessions* and the other three tracks eventually surfaced a decade later in 1989. What a full-blown Bell-produced Elton album might have sounded like, however, we shall now never know.

NW

Bill Fay

Until his albums were reissued in 1998, few had heard of Bill Fay. His music turned out to be one of the great lost treasures of British rock. Fay's songs were either tiny epics or grandiose gems, full of tender compassion, quasi-mysticism and strong arrangements. *Bill Fay* and *Time of the Last Persecution* had been off-radar for 27 years when the record label owner Colin Miles excavated the two albums from his collection and, with Fay's blessing, bundled them together on a two-for-one CD. Word got around and with the help of savvy reviewers and fans such as Wilco and the producer Jim O'Rourke, Fay's career – he claims it was a "non-career" – was resuscitated. In 2007 he even took to the stage for the first time in thirty years, with Wilco, to sing a duet of his song "Be Not So Fearful".

It had been a long and rather quiet road from his days as just another singer-songwriter signing. Decca first offered Fay a contract in 1967, for a three-year deal. A single failed to chart, but two albums appeared as the decade turned. Sales were slender and, like his contemporary Nick Drake, he was reluctant to help things along by playing live. Musical tastes soon shifted and his contract expired. Fay and his band – the guitarist Ray Russell and drummer Alan Rushton – ploughed on in the studio working up demos, while Terry Noon, his manager, tried in vain to secure another contract. Some of the recordings made during these years have now surfaced on the album *From the Bottom of an Old Grandfather Clock*.

At the end of the 1970s, he teamed up with a trio, including the guitarist Gary Smith, and over a couple of years in studios and back rooms gathered enough material for a third album, but with no great ambitions to make it happen. But until the twenty-first century, there would be no more from Bill Fay and he became a virtual recluse. Eventually his late-1970s work saw daylight as the extraordinarily beautiful *Tomorrow, Tomorrow and Tomorrow*, released on the back of the Fay revival in 2004. These days, Bill is philosophical about his time at Decca and grateful that his long-lost albums are once more being listened to, despite only ever having had a half-hearted commitment to the process of making records. "I am naturally a songwriter – that's always been the case," he says. "It's not something that's done for necessarily ulterior motives. It's done for the sake of the music. That is satisfying enough in itself."

RW

playlist:

1 Goodnight Stan *from* Bill Fay
Bittersweet strings accompany an old gardener on his way home from his allotment, as the sun dips behind the beanpoles.

2 Pictures of Adolf Again *from* Time of the Last Persecution
Fay in cautionary mood. It was later covered by Jim O'Rourke and Glenn Kotche of Wilco.

3 Cosmic Boxer *from* Tomorrow, Tomorrow and Tomorrow
Championed by Marc Almond, this is taken from the much-delayed third album, recorded in 1978–81 and issued 25 years later. "It took that amount of time for the right people to come along," says Fay.

4 Strange Stairway *from* Tomorrow, Tomorrow and Tomorrow
Backed by the Acme Quartet (actually a trio), this gem from Fay's third album is a true lost treasure of early 1980s pop.

The Free Design

The Free Design, as with many acts whose legacy has sadly been forgotten, were unfortunate to have a sound that fell midway between two genres: on one side there were the close-harmony, sunshine pop groups such as The Association ("Never My Love") and Fifth Dimension ("Up Up and Away") and, on the other, the more cerebral, intricate compositions associated with bands like Love and *Pet Sounds*-era Beach Boys, and composers such as Harry Nilsson and Burt Bacharach.

The group never enjoyed significant commercial success, but their well-forged alliance of the two styles created a wonderful series of almost clinically precise pop tunes, and would become an inspiration for modern independent artists such as Stereolab and Cornelius. New Yorker Chris Dedrick, a classically trained musician, formed the group in the mid-1960s, along with his brother Bruce and his sister Sandy. Over six years they released seven albums, characterized by obsessively detailed musical arrangements and luscious vocal harmonies. Where they did manage to rein things in, however, was in the emotion department. While the songs of their contemporaries might tearfully recount the breakdown of a relationship, The Free Design were singing of the joys of personal space, chirping merrily: "You be you and I'll be me ... Distance, freedom, turn me on."

So, did this put off a record-buying public who were used to their sugary pop being overrun with schmaltz? It would seem so: The Free Design had a noticeable lack of chart success. They acknowledged this disappointing fact in typically detached fashion in "A Hit Song" asking "How can this hit miss?", complaining "We've done it all right and sealed it with a kiss". By 1972 Dedrick had decided to call it a day. He went on to record a solo album – which didn't see the light of day until some 25 years later – and embarked on a career in music production and soundtrack composition. But some recognition was to arrive, eventually; reissues in the last decade have brought the Dedricks' work to a wider audience, and they reformed for 2001's *Cosmic Peekaboo* – a record which showed them to have lost none of their instinct for harmony, even if modern production techniques did add an almost unbearable layer of extra gloss. For the group at their meticulous best, check out their debut, *Kites Are Fun*, or 1969's *Heaven/Earth*.

RM

Ripe for rediscovery:
John Phillips'
The Wolfking of L.A.

Divorce is sometimes for the best. When the Mamas and the Papas separated in a listless haze of drug habits and fatigue, their principal patriarch, John Phillips – by then the wrong side of thirty – went solo. He'd already penned hits such as "California Dreamin'", "Monday Monday" and, for Scott Mackenzie, "San Francisco (Be Sure to Wear Flowers in Your Hair)". Papa John was undoubtedly a prodigious songwriting talent.

So was it record label shortcomings or shifting musical trends that were to blame for the commercial failure of his solitary solo album, 1970's *The Wolfking of L.A.*?

As his wife Michelle, also of the Mamas and the Papas, has pointed out, it contains some of his strongest material.

There are sour country-rockers and laments to Michelle, who had left Phillips shortly before the album was released, as well as tender tributes to his new belle and soon-to-be second wife, Genevieve Waite.

Amongst the album's strongest cuts are the soft-focus opener "April Anne" and "Let it Bleed, Genevieve". "Someone's Sleeping" is based on a trip to Morocco that Phillips made with Michelle. Elvis Presley loved it and even covered one track, the upbeat "Mississippi".

The Wolfking of L.A. came packaged in photos of Phillips dressed like a shaggy beach-bum and acquired a cult reputation, despite its poor ranking in the charts and swift deletion in the early 1970s. And the title? "I called him 'Wolfking' because of his big coat," said Waite. "And he would howl at the moon sometimes for me."

RW

Fred Neil

You might know the name – perhaps as the man who wrote "Everybody's Talkin'", the song taken to the movies by Harry Nilsson as the theme to *Midnight Cowboy* and later a UK hit for the Beautiful South. Or maybe you've seen Fred's name next to "The Dolphins", the oceanic classic covered by Beth Orton, Billy Bragg and Tim Buckley. He's been admirably covered, but Fred Neil's own records have been unfairly overlooked. An erratic output, total lack of ambition and his subsequent disappearance from the music scene have done little justice to one of the great American voices. For a brief time in the 1960s, Neil's booming, bottomless baritone carried a song like no other.

His biography is rife with mystery, rumour and contradiction. He was born in Florida on 1 January 1937 – that much seems certain. Stories have abounded that he was a child star who once appeared on the *Grand Ole Opry*; that he once wrote a song for Buddy Holly; that he worked on a Florida dolphin farm; and that he was a relative of the hillbilly superstar, Jimmie Rodgers. The Buddy Holly song is likely to be "Modern Don Juan", penned by Bob Neal, not Fred Neil. But the rest may well be true.

By the mid-1950s, Fred was in New York, working as a staff writer in the legendary Brill Building, the home of post-war American popular songwriting. After a shot at stardom as a recording artist, which failed to ignite interest in the teen market of the day, he resigned himself to achieving fame either via his writing or as a café folk singer. Roy Orbison covered his Brill composition "Candy Man", which earned him some royalties. From 1961 he was in and out of Greenwich Village folk joints such as Café Wha? and the Gaslight, inspiring a very young Bob Dylan – who on at least one occasion even accompanied Neil on harmonica – and grabbing the attention of David Crosby and Stephen Stills.

Neil was making an impression and was tipped for great things – far beyond his local Village reputation. Labels began to take notice and eventually he signed to Elektra in 1964, not as a solo artist, but as the second half of a "hootenanny" folk duo called Martin & Neil. Fred had teamed up with the folk singer and guitarist Vincent Marcellino, who had

anglicized his name in preparation for stardom. Neil would eventually make it – just – but Martin was destined for musical backwaters. Of the artists appearing on the duo's only album, *Tear Down the Walls*, it would be their backing musicians, John Sebastian and Felix Pappalardi, who would achieve the real fame, with The Lovin' Spoonful and Mountain respectively.

Nevertheless, *Tear Down the Walls* contained an alluring mixture of co-written numbers and arrangements from the traditional songbook, notably "Red Flowers" and "Morning Dew" – although Martin's mid-range struggles to match Neil's languorous, nicotine-stained blues moan. Righting their error, Elektra converted the deal to a solo contract and Neil made the next one, *Bleecker & MacDougal*, without Martin. He came into his own with this album, cutting his own version of the Orbison hit "Candy Man", alongside other self-penned numbers such as "Little Bit of Rain" and the almost Johnny Cash-like "The Other Side of Life". His work appealed to the burgeoning acid-folk scene of the mid-1960s, and began to feature in the repertoires of up-and-coming names, such as Jefferson Airplane and Tim Buckley, as well as more staid acts like Peter, Paul and Mary. Even Gram Parsons, it later emerged, used Neil's songs on his early demos.

Recorded in the winter of 1966 under the stewardship of Nik Venet, who had tempted the freckle-faced Neil over to the Capitol label, Fred's third album was simply titled *Fred Neil* and marked another new beginning. Moving from all-acoustic, folk-club arrangements to a fully electric sound, it's his equivalent of *Bringing It All Back Home*. At the time it seemed the first proper step on a path to long-term commercial success for Neil. It turned out, in rock stardom terms, to be a blind alley. Friends of his, such as Tom Rush and Judy Henske, have said Neil was a great and talented writer and player, but one who didn't have an ambitious bone in his body.

The next effort, 1967's *Sessions*, consisted of seven imperfect songs fleshed out with studio chatter, and seemed to confirm this. After a third and final album for Elektra in 1971, which gathered together live versions and studio outtakes, Neil mysteriously vanished, almost overnight. Much of his next thirty years were apparently spent in the shade of Florida's Coconut Grove, where he avoided recording studios, shunned any kind of publicity or media attention and emerged only very occasionally to play a gig for friends. Until his death was announced in 2001, few knew if this half-forgotten genius was even still alive.

RW

playlist:

1 Baby *from* Tear Down the Walls
Neil sings from the bottom of a well, over wailing harp and an almost raga-like drone. Martin and Neil at their best.

2 Little Bit of Rain *from* Bleecker & MacDougal
A blueprint for what would follow on tracks such as "The Dolphins". Shimmering guitar, more deep-chested vocals and a tearful tale to tell.

3 Everybody's Talkin' *from* Fred Neil
The original – and, some might say, the best – version of the song John Schlesinger appropriated for *Midnight Cowboy*.

4 The Dolphins *from* Fred Neil
Tim Buckley made it famous, bringing Neil's name to the attention of record buyers.

5 Faretheewell *from* Fred Neil
Subtitled "Fred's Tune", this is the blues by any other name. The saddest of sad goodbyes.

Knocking on heaven's door:
talents that died too young

Mozart shuffled off this mortal coil at 35. Robert Johnson handed in his dinner pail at just 27. But it's rock'n'roll that has romanticized early death with its "too fast to live, too young to die" fetish. From Buddy Holly, Eddie Cochran and Otis Redding through Jimi Hendrix, Janis Joplin and Nick Drake on to Marc Bolan, Ian Curtis and Kurt Cobain, there's a tragic track record several generations deep of rock stars dying before they made it out of their twenties. The musicians mentioned here left some tantalizingly great music behind, and some had barely started. But all of them, you suspect, were capable of even greater things. The single track recommended here in each case is merely the tip of the iceberg of what these artists had to offer.

Johnny Ace (1929–54)

Ace's cracking R&B ballads made him a huge draw in America's black community in the early 1950s and a prototype rock'n'roll star. Backstage, following a performance at Houston's City Auditorium on Christmas Day 1954, he played a game of Russian roulette; he blew his brains out with the sole bullet in the gun's chamber.

Pledging My Love *from* The Best of Johnny Ace

Pig Pen (1946–73)

Ron "Pig Pen" McKernan played organ with the Grateful Dead from 1965 to 72 and sang in a gritty and rasping voice that provided the band's acid-rock a much needed harder R&B edge. Although he eschewed the psychedelic drugs favoured by the rest of the band, he had a problem with alcoholism, which eventually proved fatal. Keith Godchaux, Brent Mydland and Vince Welnick, also keyboard players for the Grateful Dead, all died young.

Turn on Your Love Light *from* Live Dead

Richard Farina (1937–66)

A close buddy of Bob Dylan and the husband of Joan Baez's younger sister Mimi, Farina recorded two classic albums as a folk duo with his wife. He died in a motorcycle crash in California on his way home from a party jointly celebrating her 21st birthday and the publication of his first novel.

Pack Up Your Sorrows *from* The Best of the Vanguard Years

Gram Parsons (1946–73)

Parsons almost single-handedly invented country-rock with the Byrds and the Flying Burrito Brothers. He turned Keith Richards on to country music and introduced Emmylou Harris to the world. Despite this glittering CV, he had still only begun to explore the full extent of his talent when he died after consuming a fatal quantity of alcohol and morphine in the Californian desert.

She *from* GP

Sandy Denny (1947–78)

Denny's pure, nuanced voice graced Fairport Convention, Fotheringay and a quartet of superb solo albums. She died at 31, after lapsing into a coma following a fall down a flight of stairs. Already the greatest female folk singer of her generation and a peerless songwriter, you only have to look at the career of Norma Waterson to realize what she might have gone on to achieve.

Who Knows Where the Time Goes *from* Unhalfbricking

Paul Kossoff (1950–76)

Kossoff achieved immortality when still a teenager with his guitar solo on Free's "All Right Now". But when he died of drug-induced heart failure, he was only 25. Had he been able to overcome his problems, he could have given Clapton, Beck and Page a serious run for their money as the finest British blues guitarist of them all.

Tuesday Morning *from* Back Street Crawler

Tim Buckley (1947–75) & Jeff Buckley (1966–97)

Tim Buckley recorded prolifically in his short life, releasing nine classic albums in eight years before his death from a heroin overdose at 28. In many ways the death of his son Jeff was even more tragic, for in his lifetime he released just one hugely influential full-length album, before drowning, aged thirty, while swimming in a Memphis river.

Buzzin Fly *from* Happy/Sad

Hallelujah *from* Grace

Matthew Jay (1978–2003)

Jay was raised in the Welsh valleys and was signed by EMI on the strength of a demo of his wonderfully sensitive and insightful songs, when he was just twenty years old. His debut album, *Draw*, appeared in 2000 and had reviewers comparing him to Nick Drake and Elliott Smith. While working on the songs for his second album in 2002, he died after a mysterious fall from the window of an apartment block in London. An inquest recorded an open verdict.

Please Don't Send Me Away *from* Draw

NW

Great lost albums: Neil Young's Homegrown

The art of predicting what Neil Young will do next has never been easy – indeed, the man himself has often appeared not to know until the last minute. During the 1970s in particular, he was inclined to plan, record, alter and scrap albums almost on a whim. In 1974, *Tonight's the Night* was shelved to put out *On the Beach*. The following year, *Homegrown* was shelved in order to ressurect *Tonight's the Night*. Other albums during this chaotically creative period that never materialized were titled *Ride My Llama* and *Chrome Dreams*. It was typical of Young's perversity that in 2007 he released an album called *Chrome Dreams II*, even though we had never officially heard *Chrome Dreams I*.

The world of illicit bootleg recordings is littered with various attempts to reconstruct these discarded albums, the most legendary of which is *Homegrown*. Recorded in late 1974 and early 1975, the album was so close to release that a cover was designed featuring Young smoking a corncob pipe.

One night, shortly before it was due to hit record stores, he played the record to a bunch of friends that included Rick Danko and Levon Helm of The Band at his Californian home on Zuma beach. At the same time, he also played them the unreleased 1973 recordings of *Tonight's the Night*. Fuelled by copious quantities of alcohol (and who knows what else), the assembled throng told him that he should put out *Tonight's the Night*.

Had he stuck with *Homegrown*, it would surely have been his most commercial release since *Harvest*. Many of the songs were solo performances on guitar and harmonica, and dealt with the collapse of his relationship with the actress Carrie Snodgrass, the mother of his first son, Zeke. In truth, he didn't need much persuading not to release the album that drunken evening, for he has hinted several times that he found many of the songs painfully over-personal with their agenda of loss, hopelessness and emotional numbness.

The exact track list is uncertain and quite possibly Young had not taken a final decision when he scrapped the album, but more than two dozen songs have been cited as contenders. About a third of them subsequently surfaced on other albums, either in the original or re-recorded versions. Several more, including "Traces", "Separate Ways", "Kansas", "Love/Art Blues", "Homefires", "Give Me Strength," "Try" and "Mexico" have at different times been performed in concert.

Others, such as the bleak "Frozen Man", the stoned blues vamp "We Don't Smoke It", "Vacancy", "Florida", "Hawaiian Sunrise", "Daughters", "Four Walls" and "Barefoot Floors", have only been heard in bootleg form or, in some cases, not at all. The story may become clearer when he releases his long-awaited multi-disc *Archives* set, which he has hinted may include several of his "lost" albums in their originally intended form.

NW

Harry Nilsson

I n 1968, at the press conference held to announce the launch of Apple, Lennon and McCartney were asked by one journalist for their favourite American artist. They gave a one-word reply: "Nilsson". These days, Harry Nilsson's best-known four minutes might be a lofty 1970s cover of the morbid "Without You", one of the biggest hits in pop history. Or perhaps it is his wistful take on Fred Neil's classic "world go away" number, "Everybody's Talkin'".

Back in 1968, things were beginning to look rosy for the struggling singer-songwriter. After The Beatles name-drop, the phone, as he put it, started jumping off the hook. With an impressive three-octave range, Nilsson not only had one of the great pop voices, but he was also a prodigious composer of quirky and romantic songs. In the mid-1960s, he was jobbing as a songwriter when he wasn't working the night shift at an LA bank. He'd had a couple of moderate successes, notably in collaboration with Phil Spector, but nothing to write home about. He was renting a space with a piano in an office block of music publishers. One night he came up with three exceptional songs: "Don't Leave Me", the autobiographical "1941", and an extraordinary love ballad, "Without Her".

Nilsson was convinced he would never write another bad song. One publisher asked for a demo, an octave down, telling Nilsson never to go for the high notes. "Without Her" wound up with Glen Campbell. It was perfect for his subterranean tenor. Bolstered by the success, Nilsson ignored that publisher's advice and set about hitting the high notes himself. He signed to RCA for a run of albums, beginning with the wonderful *Pandemonium Shadow Show* (1967) and *Aerial Ballet* (1968). Over the dozen or so that followed, Nilsson tackled everything from the sentimental to the downright trite, although the expletives on "You're Breaking My Heart" had the album *Son of Schmilsson* banned in the US. He reached a commercial peak with *Nilsson Schmilsson*, the album which spawned "Without You". He even narrated a children's story, *The Point!*. In 1973 he triumphantly tackled the Great American Songbook on *A Little Touch of Schmilsson in the Night*. The flippant album titles hardly did justice to the depth of the recordings.

He covered "Without You", from the Apple signing Badfinger, and he developed a lifelong friendship with Lennon, which resulted in the 1974 duet album *Pussy Cats*. Taking time out from making his rock'n'roll album of 1950s covers during his infamous, year-long "lost weekend", Lennon took to a restless round of LA socializing with Nilsson, fuelled by an endless stream of Brandy Alexanders. "We're wasting time here," Lennon reportedly told him. "We might as well put all this energy into work." As the sessions drew to a close, Lennon's past caught up with him. On 28 March 1974, Paul McCartney dropped by and in a historic jam with Nilsson and Stevie Wonder, the ex-Beatles cut the last tracks they would make together.

Pussy Cats (Nilsson's label rejected his suggestion to title the joint effort "Strange Pussies") finally emerged as a sort of little brother to Lennon's *Rock'n'Roll*. The Macca-Lennon-Wonder tracks were omitted.

Nilsson ruptured his vocal cords during the recording of *Pussy Cats* and never made a great album again. The following year's *Duit on Mon Dei* (as in "do it on Monday") has its moments, but the high notes were stubbornly out of reach. Nilsson projects rose and fell with dispiriting alacrity. His 1973 movie *Son of Dracula*, backed by Ringo Starr, swiftly sank like a stone, as did a later musical, *Zapata*, which managed just one performance. His recording career was also swerving off the rails. The clumsily titled *Knnillssonn* appeared a month before Elvis Presley's death in 1977, and with RCA preoccupied on the Presley back catalogue, there was zero promotion for the album. His next effort, *Flash Harry*, wasn't even released in the US. Misfortune, it seemed, was becoming Nilsson's watchword. Worst of all, in 1978, the Who's drummer Keith Moon was found dead in Nilsson's London flat. (It was the second death at what must be rock's most unlucky address: four years earlier, Mama Cass Elliott suffered heart failure there in her sleep.)

When Lennon was shot dead in 1980, Nilsson diverted his energies into the Coalition to Stop Gun Violence. Despite the onset of diabetes and depression – exacerbated by the revelation that all his earnings had been embezzled by a financial advisor – he contributed a joyful "Zip-a-Dee-Doo-Dah" to Hal Willner's 1988 compilation of Disney covers. It was his last decent recording opportunity. On Valentine's Day 1993 he suffered a massive heart attack. Seemingly recovered, he resumed recording a new album, the release of which was abandoned after his death in January 1994. In 2008, Ringo recorded "Harry's Song" about his friend.

RW

playlist:

1 Without Her *from* Pandemonium Shadow Show
The real Nilsson classic – first covered by Glen Campbell.

2 All I Think About is You *from* Knnillssonn
A gorgeous, plaintive love song – the romantic side of Nilsson in a nutshell.

3 Moonbeam Song *from* Nilsson Schmilsson
Few got past the ubiquitous "Without You", but this cute number is one of the album's hidden treasures.

4 Many Rivers to Cross *from* Pussy Cats
Nilsson and Lennon get to grips with Jimmy Cliff's reggae classic. Nilsson tore his vocal cords on this recording, and it shows.

5 Salmon Fall *from* Duit on Mon Dei
Produced by Van Dyke Parks, this is surely the greatest song about the life cycle of the salmon ever to be recorded.

6 As Time Goes By *from* A Little Touch of Schmilsson in the Night
Nilsson's voice was never in better shape than during the recording of his American Songbook collection in 1973. The closing track was his moving rendition of Herman Hupfield's nostalgic standard.

7 Who Done It? *from* Knnillssonn
An Abbott and Costello film provided the title and a lifelong interest in gothic thrillers and black humour inspired this dramatic murder ballad. The lights go out and, one by one, the occupants of a creaky old house are found dead.

You know the songs, now check out the originals

Tim Rose

Hey Joe *from* Tim Rose
Considerable confusion surrounds the authorship of "Hey Joe", generally attributed to the obscure Billy Roberts. The earliest known recording was by The Leaves in 1965 and it was swiftly covered by Love and The Byrds. But it was Tim Rose's atmospheric, slowed-down arrangement that inspired the best-known version by the Jimi Hendrix Experience, after the guitarist had heard him singing it at the Café Wha? in New York in 1966. Rose claimed it to be a traditional song when it appeared on his debut album.

Tim Hardin

Reason to Believe *from* Tim Hardin 1
Covered by everyone from Bobby Darin to the Carpenters but most closely associated with Rod Stewart, "Reason to Believe" was written by Tim Hardin in 1965. A brilliant singer-songwriter who should have been up there in the troubadour hierarchy alongside the likes of James Taylor and Jackson Browne, he also wrote "If I Were a Carpenter", but his career imploded due to his heroin addiction, and he died in 1980 at the age of 39. Hardin's version of "Reason to Believe" eventually reached a wider audience when it was heard in the film *The Wonder Boys,* resulting in some film fans wondering who it was "singing that Rod Stewart song".

Tom Rush

No Regrets *from* The Circle Game
A hit single for Scott Walker and the Walker Brothers, and a song also covered by Robbie Williams among others, none can touch the elegant simplicity of the folk arrangement heard on the original 1968 recording of "No Regrets" by the song's writer, Tom Rush. Rush's own version appeared on an album called *The Circle Game,* named after a cover of a Joni Mitchell song. The same LP also found him giving early exposure to songs by the then little-known Jackson Browne and James Taylor.

Crazy Horse

I Don't Want to Talk About It *from* Crazy Horse
Rod Stewart's ear for a good song has never been surpassed by his eye for a leggy blonde, and he had a number-one hit in 1977 with this heart-rending tune written by Danny Whitten for his band Crazy Horse. Sadly, Whitten was not around to enjoy the royalties from Rod's multi-platinum seller. He died of a heroin overdose in 1972 at the age of 29, which was the subject of Neil Young's song "The Needle and the Damage Done".

Warren Zevon

Poor Poor Pitiful Me *from* Warren Zevon
Linda Ronstadt plundered Zevon's song book several times and scored a hit single with her version of this song in 1977. Listen to Zevon's original boozing, brawling, caustic take on "Poor Poor Pitiful Me", however, and you will barely recognize it as the same song.

Jackie De Shannon

When You Walk in the Room *from* The Best of Jackie De Shannon
The underrated De Shannon was arguably the first significant female singer-songwriter of the 1960s and her original version of "When You Walk in the Room" competed unsuccessfully in the charts against the hit cover by The Searchers. Her career then intersected with many of pop's biggest names without her ever quite becoming a household name herself: she toured with The Beatles in 1964, contributed a song to The Byrds' debut album, dated Elvis Presley, collaborated with Jimmy Page in writing a top-ten hit for Marianne Faithfull, and duetted with Van Morrison.

Mac Davis

In the Ghetto *from* Mac Davis: Greatest Hits
The tale of a young boy who grows up in the ghetto, falls into a life of crime and is eventually shot and killed presented unlikely subject matter for Elvis Presley, but he loved the song and ignored those who warned him it was too controversial. He was proved right when it returned him to the top ten in 1969 after a four-year absence. The song was written by Mac Davis, who three years later had his own number one with "Baby Don't Get Hooked on Me". Presley recorded several other Davis compositions, including "A Little Less Conversation".

John Stewart

Daydream Believer *from* The Lonesome Picker Rides Again
A number-one hit for The Monkees in 1967, "Daydream Believer" was written by folk singer John Stewart when he was still a member of the clean-cut Kingston Trio. Shortly after, he grew his hair, donned a stone-washed denim shirt and a cowboy hat and launched a solo career. A cult figure in the development of country-rock, his 1969 album *California Bloodlines* is considered his masterpiece.

Badfinger

Without You *from* No Dice
Best known for the histrionic 1972 version by Nillson, "Without You" was written by Pete Ham and Tom Evans of Badfinger in 1970. One of the first signings to The Beatles' Apple label, great things were expected of them but it never quite happened. In a horribly ironic twist on the song's "I can't live..." hook, Ham hung himself in 1975 and Evans committed suicide in similar fashion eight years later.

NW

Van Dyke Parks

In 1966, Brian Wilson engaged a bespectacled, Carnegie Institute graduate to help out on an ambitious new Beach Boys project. The *Smile* album was to be the follow-up to *Pet Sounds* and Van Dyke Parks was Wilson's idiosyncratic choice as lyricist. The pair clearly shared a vision, although they failed to see eye to eye with the other Beach Boys. Mike Love famously derided the surreal lyrics he was asked to sing on epic numbers such as "Surf's Up". Although *Smile* was destined to be, for forty years, rock's famous lost album, it opened the door for one of the most erratic and eccentric solo careers in popular music.

Parks comes from a musical family and, as a teen chorster in 1950s Princeton, even had the distinction of accompanying an elderly Albert Einstein as he scraped on violin. Making his stamp as an LA session player, songwriter and arranger in the mid-1960s, he gained an early commission sorting out the strings and wind on "The Bare Necessities" for the soundtrack to Disney's *The Jungle Book*.

Signing to Warner Bros in 1966, Parks brought to the label a peculiarly curatorial grasp of Americana, with a fondness for pre-rock'n'roll styles. He filtered his conventional background through a sonic kaleidoscope of psychedelia, as befitted the times, for his debut release, *Song Cycle* – in 1968, this was one of the most expensive albums ever made. It fared well in reviews, although punters were less keen on its marshmallow-sky take on America's musical heritage. Sales were ultimately so poor that the label resorted to giving away copies to anyone who asked.

Drawing on such "anti-rock" trends as calypso, crooning and pre-war parlour jazz, Parks' subsequent releases contain some of his most alluring arrangements, especially 1972's *Discover America*, his tour of the Gulf of Mexico, which continued to knock the soil from his country's musical roots. Parks produced other acts such as the calypso singer Mighty Sparrow and such novelties as a single by Goldie Hawn covering, unusually, a classic ska song by Ernie Smith. The partnership with Wilson was revived on 1995's excellent *Orange Crate Art*, and Parks remains an arranger and producer-in-demand for the likes of Randy Newman, Scissor Sisters and Rufus Wainwright. He has retained a low profile as a solo performer, however, returning to acting (he was a child television star in

the 1950s), for a bit-part in David Lynch's surreal 1990s TV soap *Twin Peaks*. As the new millennium dawned, he played a rare concert in London, backed by Parks devotees and Beach Boys acolytes The High Llamas. "I want to ensure that [music] is discerning, that it is anxious, that it flies nervously, and not with its grip on the joystick of preordained method," Parks once explained. He's doing a good job.

RW

playlist:

1 The All Golden *from* Song Cycle
The ambitious, eccentric *Song Cycle* is best sampled with this track, in which Parks announces that "nowadays a Yankee dread not take his time to wend to sea".

2 The Four Mills Brothers *from* Discover America
Parks' brother Carson wrote for the Mills Brothers vocal quartet. Honouring the old-timers, this track sits neatly alongside the album's likeminded tributes to Jack Palance and Bing Crosby.

3 Manzanar *from* Tokyo Rose
"The theme is stolen goods" said Parks of his exotica album, rooted in wartime American popular music's appropriation of South Pacific sounds. This Japanese-flavoured track is a classic Parks arrangement.

4 Orange Crate Art *from* Orange Crate Art
After the debacle over the Beach Boys' *Smile* album in the late 1960s, Parks was reunited with Brian Wilson for this 90s album, an overlooked gem in the catalogue and, as it turned out, the perfect vehicle for both collaborators.

5 Jump! *from* Moonlighting: Live at the Ash Grove
Parks' 1984 studio album *Jump*, a reading of the Uncle Remus stories, was really designed for the stage, so the best place to hear the title track, as well as "Hominy Grove", is on this live set, recorded in 1996.

Giving up the day job...
or not

There's a popular joke in the circles that rock'n'roll bands move in that goes like this. What do you call a drummer without a girl-friend? Homeless. Popular mythology has it that when musicians aren't being adored and worshipped on stage, they're a bunch of feckless layabouts and wastrels totally unable to fend for themselves. Yet there are some who have bucked the trend.

Writer

Making a living as a novelist is probably even harder than being a professional musician, but that hasn't prevented several from trying. Wesley Stace, an English singer-songwriter based in the US, records under the name John Wesley Harding. He's heavily influenced by Bob Dylan (fairly unsurprisingly), Springsteen and Phil Ochs. But he has also published several novels under his real name, and in 2005 managed to have both his novel, *Misfortune*, and his album, *Songs from Misfortune*, in two best-of-the-year top-tens. Willy Vlautin, frontman with acclaimed alt.country outfit Richmond Fontaine, has also published a brace of novels, while Max Décharné, lead singer of bequiffed garage rockers The Flaming Stars, has written several books documenting such subjects as 1950s slang, film noir and the history of the Kings Road. That he is a former drummer for Gallon Drunk should probably come as no surprise.

Lawyer

Given that rock bands seem to get routinely ripped off by a long queue of dishonest promoters, agents, managers and record labels, Barry Melton may just be the smartest man in rock. Once the guitarist for San Francisco/Woodstock favourites Country Joe & The Fish, he retrained as an attorney and has spent more than twenty years as a criminal defence lawyer. He currently serves as the Public Defender in Yolo County, California. Check out his playing on "Silver and Gold", from the 1970 album *CJ Fish*, for one of the finest acid-rock lead guitar solos ever.

Floor layer

Kurt Wagner, singer and songwriter with alt.country pioneers Lambchop, kept his day job laying and sanding wooden floors until shortly before the release of the band's acclaimed fifth album, *Nixon* (2000). Even then he claimed the main reason for "retiring" was that his knees had started to go. There's a certain irony in the fact that many of those who employed him in their expensive mansions were the very people who ran the Nashville record industry that kept his band out in the cold.

Cook

Plenty of would-be rock stars have no doubt done a brief teen-age turn flipping burgers but few have shown the staying power of Flaming Lips leader Wayne Coyne. The eleven years he spent as a fry cook at Long John Silver's, the American fast-food fish-and-chips chain, was longer than The Beatles' entire recording career.

Teacher

Sting's famous stint as a junior maths teacher was low-grade stuff. Drew Daniel, one half of the electronic experimental duo Matmos, is an assistant English professor at Johns Hopkins University in Baltimore. The academic prize, however, goes to Greg Graffin, the singer with punk rock veterans Bad Religion. He received a PhD in zoology for his dissertation "Monism, Athe-ism and the Naturalist Worldview: Perspectives from Evolutionary Biology" and now has a successful second career teaching life sciences at UCLA.

Boxer

There have been some notable rock'n'roll punch-ups over the years but it's the guys in the blues corner you should look out for. Johnny Copeland and Champion Jack Dupree were both noted professional pugilists but our heavyweight golden gloves champion has to be Willie Dixon, who gave up pro-fighting to write songs such as "Hoochie Coochie Man", "I Just Want to Make Love to You", "Spoonful" and "Little Red Rooster" for the likes of Muddy Waters and Howlin' Wolf.

Politician

There are plenty of musicians out there who have swapped rec-ord sales to seek votes at the ballot box. Sonny Bono became mayor of Palm Springs and a Republican congressman, while the late, great Ali Farka Touré was also mayor of his village in Mali. Peter Garrett, one-time singer with Midnight Oil, is the min-ister for environment, heritage and arts in the Australian govern-ment led by Kevin Rudd, and Gilberto Gil, imprisoned and exiled by Brazil's military government in the 1970s, is now the country's minister for culture. But our favourite muso-politicos have to be Scottish stalwarts Runrig, who fell out not over who got the best groupies or snorted the last of the cocaine, but over home rule. Keyboardist Pete Wishart became a Scottish Nationalist MP while lead singer Donnie Munro stood for parliament for the pro-union British Labour Party. After losing the 1997 general election to future Lib-Dem party leader Charles Kennedy, he resumed a solo singing career.

NW

Ripe for rediscovery:
Bob Dylan's Self Portrait

"What is this shit?" wrote Greil Marcus in the opening line of his review in *Rolling Stone*, one of the most savagely withering demolitions in the history of rock journalism. At the time he spoke for most Dylan fans, who were feeling perplexed, angry, betrayed and demoralized by the album.

Over the years, the record has remained an object of ridicule. But Ryan Adams began a modest rehabilitation in 2002 when he pronounced it a "great album" and several have since argued that were *Self Portrait* to be released now, many of the songs would be regarded as modern Americana classics, and that the record's simple verities and absence of ego seem far more in tune today with the spirit of our times.

There is some "shit", particularly on tracks such as "Blue Moon" and "Let It Be Me", which are buried in syrupy strings overdubbed in Nashville and straitjacketed by trite pop arrangements. One of the main objections at the time of release was the absence of new material from the man who, over the previous decade, had proved himself to be the greatest songwriter of the age.

Yet even here, Dylan was knowingly laughing up his sleeve. On the opening track, he repeated a single line over and over again: "All the tired horses in the sun/How'm I s'posed to get any ridin' done?". Or was that "writin'"? But the versions of such trad staples as "Little Sadie", "Living the Blues", "Copper Kettle" and "Alberta" are superb, looking forward to his two fine 1990s albums of similar material, *World Gone Wrong* and *Good As I Been to You*.

True, on one level the two discs lack any sense of internal coherence. On the other hand, Dylan had just been infuriated by becoming the subject of the world's first ever bootleg, 1969's *Great White Wonder*, a ragbag of unreleased live recordings and practice tapes assembled from different sources. *Self Portrait* was his response. "I just figured I'd put all this stuff together and put it out – my own bootleg records, so to speak," he said in 1985.

What he was doing, in effect, was putting out a record that deliberately eroded his own myth. He was exhausted by being the new messiah – playing the role had almost killed him on his world tour in 1966 – and by 1970 he wanted to be allowed to be "just a singer making music", as he put it. Today, *Self Portrait* can finally be appreciated for what it is: a personal, witty and high revealing scrapbook of the music that provided the backdrop to the evolution of Dylan's genius, not unlike his recent *Theme Time* radio shows, which have earned him some of the best reviews of his career.

NW

Graham Parker

He could've been... Elvis Costello?

Graham Parker came roaring out of the suburbs of Surrey in the mid-1970s with a sizeable chip on his shoulder, enough aggression to fuel a small army, a gritty R&B voice and an enviable songwriting talent to match. It was hard to see how he could fail. Backed by The Rumour (made up of former members of Brinsley Schwarz), he was one of the earliest signings to the ultra-hip Stiff Records, and his 1976 debut, *Howlin' Wind*, was produced by Nick Lowe. It was an album of startling freshness that fizzed with energy, attitude and imagination, with instantly memorable songs such as "White Honey", "Silly Thing", "Soul Shoes" and "Don't Ask Me Questions" appearing to join up the dots between soul, rockabilly, blues, pop, ska, R&B, rock and gospel in a way that nobody else at the time, with the possible exception of Van Morrison, was even attempting.

The single "Hold Back the Night" took him into the charts and even led to a couple of appearances on *Top of the Pops*. Then along came punk. Parker may not have had the safety-pins or bondage trousers, but he had all the requisite fire and aggression to keep up with the Bromley contingent and their cousins up and down the country. But as a product of London's pub-rock scene – which the majority of the punk scene loathed and despised for its alleged lack of ambition and its adherence to the old-fashioned values of songcraft and musicianship – he was immediately suspect, and the likes of Elvis Costello stole his thunder. Bob Geldof, at the time a gobby member of the punk hordes as singer with The Boomtown Rats, came to lament this situation many years later: "Punk laid waste all behind it and one of its victims was the superb Graham Parker. There were newer kids around and he got subsumed."

Hindsight is a fine thing, but in 2004 Geldof included Parker's "You Can't Be Too Strong" alongside tracks by Bob Dylan and Leonard Cohen on an *Under the Influence* compilation of his favourite songs. "It is a huge performance," he wrote in the liner notes. "The voice drips with pain, sorrow, despair, disdain, contempt and devastating pity and sadness. Where is Graham Parker and why are we not listening to a man who can write like this, and sing like that?"

The cream of Parker's work remains his prolific set of early studio albums with The Rumour. After his superb debut came equally strong sets in the form of *Heat Treatment*, *Stick To Me*, *Squeezing Out Sparks* and *The Up Escalator*. After that The Rumour broke up and Parker moved to New York, where he has continued to make fine but neglected records. He consistently upholds the uncompromising attitude towards the music industry that has ensured he never quite became the superstar his talent deserved.

NW

Ripe for rediscovery:

Dennis Wilson's Pacific Ocean Blue

Most trivia buffs know that Dennis Wilson was the only Beach Boy who could actually surf but hardly anyone, including his bandmates, had him pegged as much of a musical talent. He was originally simply the drummer in the band, installed alongside brothers Brian and Carl at the insistence of his mother; in the early days, he enjoyed the lifestyle that the music gave him but had little to do with its composition.

Then, after Brian suffered a mental breakdown during the production of the great lost Beach Boys album, 1967's *Smile*, the other band members were required to make a greater creative contribution. Dennis acquitted himself remarkably well, with four fine contributions to *Sunflower* in 1970, and soon the group's party king had the confidence to create what would become the first album by a solo Beach Boy. In the late 1970s, de facto Beach Boys leader Mike Love was plugging a sound that heavily referenced the sunshine, cars and girls sound of their early days. While the title of Dennis's album – *Pacific Ocean Blue* – may have been very Beach Boys, the album was something else indeed. Rich and multilayered, with complex song structures, a gospel choir and Dennis's rough, mournful singing voice, tracks such as "Farewell My Friend" and "Thoughts of You" were exquisite.

Dennis drowned at the age of 39, before he could finish a mooted follow-up, *Bamboo*, which he had talked up as his real masterpiece. The unreleased material, coupled with the fact that *Pacific Ocean Blue* was inexplicably out of print for many years, gave Dennis's solo work a semi-mythical status that placed it close to, if not on quite the same level as, *Smile*. When Dennis's music got a proper CD release in May 2008 the world finally got to hear something that was a lot more than just a diversion from the tortured Beach Boys tale. It might not have been a work of genius, but it was a colourful and inventive slab of West Coast psychedelic rock-soul – a great album by anyone's standards.

DS

Terry Reid

Terry Reid is better known for the things he hasn't done than those he has. His resume is littered with almosts and should-haves, his career hampered by missed opportunities and plain old bad luck. Back in 1968, after a stint with Peter Jay and the Jaywalkers, the 19-year-old singer was newly signed to Mickie Most's management roster and tipped for stardom. His first album, *Bang Bang, You're Terry Reid*, earned him the nickname "Superlungs" and prompted Aretha Franklin, of all people, to proclaim, "There are only three things happening in London: The Beatles, the Rolling Stones and Terry Reid." His was a truly magnificent voice for one so young, arguably eclipsing the best of the rest – Rod Stewart, Steve Marriott and Paul Rodgers.

It was no surprise, therefore, that when Jimmy Page began piecing together his post-Yardbirds outfit, initially called the New Yardbirds but soon to morph into Led Zeppelin, his finger fell on Reid's phone number. But with a promising solo career down the road and a slot opening for the Rolling Stones on an American tour, Reid was reluctant. "I don't want to be the one to tell Keith I'm not going: you'll have to call him," Reid told Page. Instead, he suggested Page try out a flaxen-haired singer he'd just seen gigging in Buxton, Derbyshire. And so, on Reid's tip-off, Robert Plant joined Led Zeppelin and Reid completed his Rolling Stones tour. He maintained his A-list credentials, playing at Mick Jagger's wedding, hanging out with Keith Richards and entertaining a few hundred hippies at the first Glastonbury Festival in 1970.

As the decade turned, Reid started work on a third album (in the meantime turning down another invitation, this time to front Deep Purple). By now, he was on a different course to his blues-rock contemporaries. Signed to Atlantic Records Reid began the album which would become *River*. When his band fell apart, Atlantic's Ahmet Ertegun tempted him over to the US to record with the legendary producer Tom Dowd. Relocated in the States, Reid resumed work on the album, with Dowd and the Latin percussionist Willie Bobo tethered to the sessions. Under Dowd's guidance, Reid swerved off into new areas: jazz, folk and Brazilian rhythms. Recording was slow and it wasn't until 1973 that *River* finally hit the stores, appearing in a sleeve that depicted a pastoral river scene – actually the Colorado, although Reid claims that the waterway which inspired the album was the Ouse, near his childhood home in Cambridgeshire.

It had been four years since Reid had last been heard by the record-buying public. Musical tastes had moved on and he was all but forgotten. It was issued with tentative backing from Atlantic, who were unsure

what to make of their investment. Ertegun had considered putting it out on Cotillion, a jazz label, but there was too much rock'n'roll on it. No one knew what to make of tracks like "River", "Dream" and "Milestones". What worked against it in 1973 is precisely what's appealing about it today: its beautifully haunting mix of folk-rock, soul-funk and Latin grooves. In its day it was a commercial flop. The critics were tentatively approving, but it was too little, too late. Ertegun tore up Reid's contract, releasing him without further obligation.

Another long sabbatical followed. He eventually re-emerged in 1976 with *Seed of Memory*, produced by an old friend from England, Graham Nash. It included some of Reid's strongest material, in particular "Faith To Arise", "To Be Treated Rite", "Brave Awakening" and "The Frame". These days, the album might be considered a career high, but in the 1970s it flopped as its label, ABC, folded.

Thereafter, Terry Reid's career truly lost momentum. *Rogue Waves* slipped out on Capitol in 1979, largely unnoticed. After ten years and five albums on almost as many labels, Reid all but abandoned recording, making a rare appearance in 1991 with a fresh set, *The Driver*. Reid claims nobody asked him to record, but conceded that during the 1980s and 90s, his family took precedence. How different might the rock landscape be today had he accepted Page's invitation in 1968 – or even just spent a little more time in the studio.

RW

playlist:

1 Stay With Me Baby *from* Superlungs
A powerful cover of the Lorraine Ellison screamer and as good an example of Terry Reid's early tonsil twiddling as you'll find.

2 C'mon Mary *from* Live at the Isle of Wight
Reid is at his best in the live environment. This is typical of the kind of rollicking country honk which Rod Stewart also aimed for on his early albums, but which Reid manages with much more panache.

3 River *from* River
Willie Bobo sets a gentle pace while Reid meanders through a watery tale of rolling down the Colorado. Or is it fishing in the Ouse?

4 To Be Treated Rite *from* Seed of Memory
A cautionary tale, rooted in a sorry chapter of American history: the story of how sixteenth-century Spanish missionaries travelled the Camino Real, converting the locals as they worked their way from Santa Fe down to Mexico City.

5 Brave Awakening *from* Seed of Memory
A soulful letter to Reid's grandmother about the North of England's dwindling coal mining industry. Strings, pedal steel and harmonies of the Crosby, Stills & Nash school calm Reid's troubled waters.

Paul Siebel

"The music industry is a cruel and shallow money-trench," Hunter S. Thompson wrote. "A long plastic hallway where thieves and pimps run free and good men die like dogs. There is also a negative side." Paul Siebel didn't see it quite so philosophically. After two near-perfect but almost totally ignored albums released over a twelve-month period in 1970 and 1971, the American singer-songwriter Paul Siebel realized that the way the music industry swallowed up and destroyed good people totally sucked. He didn't quite walk away, for he remained on the road as a performer for several years. But without a record deal, he fell into depression and drugs and gradually lost touch with his songwriting impulse. "I just sort of petered out," he later admitted.

It was, by any reckoning, one of the most criminal wastes of talent in the history of songwriting. Had he been nurtured and encouraged to persist in the way he should have been, Siebel could have rivalled Jackson Browne and James Taylor as a troubadour for our times. "I wasn't getting anywhere, so I stopped," he explained in an interview in 1996, by which time he had become a baker, satisfied that the public that had ignored his records was at least buying his bread. Eight years later, when his two flawless LPs were eventually reissued as a single CD, it was reported that he had become a park keeper.

Born in Buffalo, New York, in 1937 into a European family, Siebel studied classical violin and grew up hearing Strauss waltzes. Called up in 1959, three years' military service meant he missed the start of the folk boom but on his discharge in 1962 he began playing clubs around Buffalo. It wasn't until 1965 that he migrated to Greenwich Village, following in the footsteps of Dylan, whom he acknowledges as a major inspiration. An equally significant inspiration, however, was Hank Williams; there was a strong country tinge in his music long before Gram Parsons made it fashionable. "Those two were constantly in the forefront of my creativity. That's what I was drawing on and was inspiring me," he recalls. "But I always fluff it and say it was the era when that was just happening; all these new ideas flying around."

Initially, his repertoire was standard folk club fare – traditional songs like "Black Is the Colour of My True Love's Hair" and "Come All Ye Fair and Tender Maidens". Slowly he began adding more of his own compositions until by 1968 that's all he was singing. One of his first songs was "Louise", a tale inspired by the brothels he'd seen in his army days. Jerry Jeff Walker was the first of many to cover the song in 1968 and it helped bring Siebel to the attention of Elektra Records, whose founder Jac Holzman came to check him out in a Greenwich Village coffeehouse. A set of demos recorded in 1969 with David Bromberg helped to clinch him a deal and Elektra allowed him twelve hours studio time to record his debut, 1970's *Woodsmoke and Oranges*.

Elektra's promotional budget was minimal and, despite some wondrous songs, the record failed to sell. The follow-up *Jack-Knife Gypsy* (1971) was recorded with a cracking support

was nobody's fault but his own. "I made my own mess and wallowed in it," he says. Yet you can't help blaming that old "cruel and shallow money-trench" for the casual indifference that allowed such a colossal talent to wither on the vine.

NW

playlist:

1 Louise *from* Woodsmoke and Oranges
Much-covered it may be, but nobody has ever sung it as achingly as Siebel.

2 The Ballad of Honest Sam *from* Woodsmoke and Oranges
A ramblin', gamblin' country ballad to match anything the Eagles conjured on *Desperado*.

3 Long Afternoons *from* Woodsmoke and Oranges
Siebel at his sweetest, melodic best: the sort of song Don McLean or John Denver might have taken to the top of the charts.

4 Hillbilly Child *from* Jack-Knife Gypsy
"You should see her dance the sneaky boogaloo", Paul tantalizingly admonishes on this song inspired by his great friend and supporter Linda Ronstadt.

5 Jack-Knife Gypsy *from* Jack-Knife Gypsy
A wonderful, rootsy, mid-tempo rocker that wouldn't have sounded out of place on one of The Band's albums or, at a pinch, even on Exile on Main Street.

band that included the Byrds' guitarist Clarence White and future Eagle Bernie Leadon. It was a finely crafted and cultured set of country-rock songs, full of emotional resonance, powerful narrative and gimlet-eyed observation. Yet despite a growing band of fans among his fellow musicans, including Linda Ronstadt, Bonnie Raitt, John Sebastian and Kris Kristofferson (who later tipped his hat to Siebel in his song "The Pilgrim"), once again the record failed to bring about the hoped-for commercial breakthrough.

"They were just a cult thing," Siebel observed on the reissue of the two albums more than thirty years later. "It just didn't seem to work. That led to some depression and some bad habits and the usual self-destructive stuff." He insists it

Clifford T. Ward

Unfashionably middle-class, Clifford T. Ward has a story that's more slippers, tea and biscuits than sex, drugs and rock'n'roll. His albums give you a firm handshake, with genteel songs about the Open University and being stuck in traffic, and tales of coat hangers and cellophane.

Ward was born in 1944, near Kidderminster. He got married at seventeen and began writing songs, often for his wife Pat. A demo tape found its way to Led Zeppelin's Jimmy Page, then working as the in-house producer for Andrew Loog Oldham's Immediate label. Page liked what he heard and, although a deal couldn't be reached, Ward was given the encouragement he needed. He formed a band with some local musicians; the name changed from the Cruisers to the Secrets, and finally to Simon's Secrets. Some singles were made for CBS and a nationwide tour followed, but the Secrets were just a little too well kept and the singles all flopped. On a tour of France he wrote what would, years later, become his big hello: "Home Thoughts from Abroad", a song shaped for distant lovers, based on Robert Browning's verse, and famously cited by many as the only pop song to mention Worcestershire, where Ward was from.

With a young family to support, gigging was becoming difficult and Ward needed a day job. He took a teaching post at a secondary school (where his pupils included a twelve-year-old Karl Hyde, later of the dance act Underworld), continuing to play and write when he wasn't marking homework. By the early 1970s he was ready to try again. Championed by Clive Selwood of the Dandelion label, Ward was signed up for the album *Singer/Songwriter*. The self-explanatory title neatly summed up Clifford T. Ward's unpretentious art.

A switch to Charisma resulted in a trio of splendid releases, notably *Home Thoughts*. Although he reluctantly appeared on television to promote the slow-burn hit "Gaye", in summer 1973, and its domestic follow-up, "Scullery", Ward was less at home in front of an audience than he had been a classroom. As a result, his career began to flounder. After six more albums on almost as many labels, one released only in Ireland, he announced in the late 1980s that he was suffering from multiple sclerosis. Yet he recorded several more albums, the last of which he was forced to complete crawling on all fours around his home studio. MS eventually claimed his life in 2001.

Despite his English reserve, Ward was one of the great composers of modern love songs, his poetic turn of phrase always ensuring he stayed just the right side of twee. He had a mix of the breezy and the philosophical not unlike Paul McCartney, and his songs have been covered by dozens, including Colin Blunstone, Judy Collins and Art Garfunkel.

RW

playlist:

1 Scullery *from* Mantle Pieces
Written for his wife Pat, refreshingly straightforward and entirely lacking in irony: "We used to live in a lovely old Worcestershire farmhouse and it had a scullery," informs Ward.

2 Home Thoughts from Abroad *from* Home Thoughts
Ward, away from his beloved, enquires poignantly if the cistern is still leaking and if she still keeps the TV on to send her to sleep.

3 Up in the World *from* No More Rock'n'Roll
Covered by both Cliff Richard, who declared it to be amongst the best ballads he had ever been given to sing, and Art Garfunkel, who cut a breathy version on his superb *Scissors Cut* album.

4 Someone I Know *from* New England Days
As the title suggests, *New England Days* was Ward's American album, recorded with a Massachusetts backing band and including this elegant but unsuccessful single.

5 Jayne from Andromeda Spiral *from* No More Rock 'n' Roll
Written after Ward saw Patrick Moore talking about our closest galaxy on television's *The Sky at Night*. "It seems it's very probable life exists there," commented Ward. "Well, you know, I'd love to meet someone from another planet."

Jesse Winchester

Draft dodgers in 1960s America often wound up north of the border. In 1967, the Memphis-raised Jesse Winchester avoided the call-up by escaping to Montreal. From childhood he had always played music, mostly backing up other singers. The French-speaking city had a thriving music scene and Winchester set about trying to make it as a singer. Taking a job in a coffee house, he settled in amongst Montreal's poets and beatniks: it became clear that if he was to be successful on the city's folk circuit, he needed to write his own material.

Through a mutual friend he came to the attention of Robbie Robertson of The Band and signed with Robertson's manager, the entrepreneurial Albert Grossman. In 1969, Robertson produced a selection of Winchester's best songs (one of which, "Snow", Robertson also co-wrote), the backing provided by a band featuring the Canadian guitarist Bob Boucher and The Band's Levon Helm. *Jesse Winchester*, an alluring mix of country ballads and gingham-edged rockers, appeared in 1970 on the tiny Ampex label.

The album was a slow burner, but over time his songs got around. "The Brand New Tennessee Waltz", a bittersweet love song, was picked up by the Everley Brothers. The randy rocker "Payday" found a natural home in Elvis Costello's repertoire and the languid "Biloxi", perhaps Winchester's best song, caught the ear of Ted Hawkins. Others from the Winchester songbook have been covered by Reba McEntire and Sweethearts of the Rodeo.

As a draft dodger, Winchester was prevented from touring the US for years, although the ban was eventually lifted, and he relocated back to Memphis before settling in Virginia. (One of Winchester's songs, "Mississippi You're On My Mind", even received an award from the State Legislature of Mississippi.) Despite some fine albums, such as *Learn to Love It*, *Let the Rough Side Drag* and *Third Down, 110 to Go*, Winchester's profile as a performer and recording artist has been as low as the cello drone on his eerie "Skip Rope Song". This is mainly due to the ban on US touring, which hindered his most creative years. "I don't believe I ever made any money from my own records," he once said, his income mainly coming from songwriting royalties and tours of Canada. "I just don't sell a whole lot of records. I'm sorry about that."

playlist:

1 Mississippi You're on My Mind *from* Learn to Love It
One of Winchester's biggest successes, albeit via a cover by the country singer Stoney Edwards.

2 Biloxi *from* Jesse Winchester
Ted Hawkins covered it on *The Next Hundred Years*, but nothing beats the dreamy, languorous original from Winchester's much overlooked debut.

3 Silly Heart *from* Third Down, 110 to Go
From the album titled after a football scoreline and produced by Todd Rundgren, this is Winchester at his breezy best.

4 My Songbird *from* Nothing But a Breeze
Winchester's invisibility in the US hampered album sales, but he was pardoned in 1977 and returned to the States for his fifth album. Emmylou Harris soon took notice of this track.

5 Brand New Tennessee Waltz *from* Jesse Winchester
Winchester admitted his early bluegrass number was "kinda cryptic", although he knew who it was about. "It was stream of consciousness writing, which was in fashion in those days," he said.

RW

STRICTLY INDIE
alt.rock heroes of the bedsit

Baby Dee

She plays the harp, like Joanna Newsom, and her appearance is sexually ambiguous, like her former musical collaborator Antony Hegarty (of Antony and the Johnsons). But Baby Dee is as unique as musicians get. A fifty-something transsexual, Dee has spent time working as a church organist, a tree surgeon and as the star of a Coney Island freak show. Her belated musical breakthrough only came once she quit the tree business after accidentally felling one right onto someone's house.

Her early musical work back in the 1970s included a stint as a street performer in New York. She played the harp wearing a bear costume and rode a specially built tricycle. But she also took musical study seriously, fascinated by Gregorian chant and Renaissance music. Her interests led to her settling down for a decade as organist and musical director of a large Catholic church in the South Bronx. "Then I realized I was a tranny," she explained, deciding that to live as a woman, and eventually to undergo a sex change, was incompatible with this career. Her feelings about God today are outlined in the piano ballad "Fresh Out of Candles": "The light got dark and stayed that way".

Work among New York's performance artists in the 1990s came to a halt when she returned to her family's Cleveland home to look after her sick father, but she passed time by writing songs and sending them to her friend Antony Hegarty, a Mercury Music Prize winner with Antony and the Johnsons, with the idea that he'd cover them. Instead, Hegarty helped her recordings to get a limited release as the albums *Little Window* and *Love's Small Song*.

They garnered a small amount of attention, but she would have carried on her then career as a tree surgeon had she not had her little accident and smashed someone's roof. In desperation, she emailed past contacts in the music business, and a valuable introduction led to work with the eminent singer-songwriter Will Oldham. He encouraged her to expand her horizons beyond solo harp work and co-produced *Safe Inside the Day*, her first album to gain worldwide attention.

This was down to a fascinating new sound that mixed showtune jauntiness, Tom Waits-style growling and choirboy falsetto in songs that were simultaneously beautiful and gruesome. Tracks such as "A Christmas Jig for a Three-Legged Cat" and "Big Titty Bee Girl (From Dino Town)" displayed the kind of imagination you'd expect of a character who has led a life significantly more colourful than most. So it seems we have the wind to thank for an album unlike anything else around and the unveiling, at last, of a truly original talent.

DS

where to start:

1 The Dance of Diminishing Possibilities *from* Safe Inside the Day
A colourful tale about childhood neighbours destroying a piano, yet failing to damage the strings inside provides both an explanation for the singer's instrument of choice and a neat metaphor for her own transformation: "There's a harp in that piano/There's a girl inside that boy".

2 The Only Bones that Show *from* Safe Inside the Day
A bouncy swing number with a dark core, Dee makes the act of smiling sound like the most sinister thing imaginable, with her hissed chorus "Teeth are the only bones that show".

Side projects:
Robert Smith, Cult Hero and The Glove

The career of The Cure's Robert Smith, now spanning more than thirty years, has tended to be characterized by bursts of frenetic activity followed by grim periods of dissatisfaction and introspection. Indeed, it's tough to find many references to Robert Smith being happy in his work – but when he was, it seemed to be when he was able to shrug off the shackles of The Cure and just have a bit of fun.

In 1979 The Cure were shifting from their spiky, wiry, post-punk origins to a more gloomy, expansive sound; as an experiment, various past and present members of the band slung together a single called "I'm a Cult Hero" – under the name Cult Hero – with their local postman, Frank Bell, on deadpan lead vocals. The record itself is a largely forgettable two-chord rant, but they did make one solitary live appearance in March 1980, supporting The Passions, where they played a set of covers of the top ten from the equivalent week's chart in 1973. Smith uncharacteristically described the gig as a "great night".

A more substantial project took shape in 1983, when the task of churning out bleak songs of hopelessness to crowds of dead-eyed goths had become all a bit much for Smith. While he tried to decide whether The Cure should become a fully-fledged pop group or not (producing singles such as "Let's Go To Bed" and "The Walk"), he was spending nights holed up in a studio with Siouxsie and the Banshees' bass player Steve Severin, working on a psychedelic project called The Glove. News of this got to the boss of The Cure's label, Fiction, who reminded Smith that he was contractually barred from singing on any non-Cure releases; they compromised on allowing him to sing on two songs, neither of which could come out as singles. The rest of the album featured the voice of Jeanette Landray, girlfriend of Banshees' drummer Budgie, who had never sung in a studio before.

The resulting album, *Blue Sunshine*, is a gloriously loopy piece of work that probably steered Smith in the direction he was to take with The Cure's 1984 album, *The Top*: a hotch-potch of instruments and ideas, thrown together with some magnificent melodies and nightmarish subject matter. A recent reissue,

featuring Smith's original demos, shows how the album might have sounded had contractual wrangles not got in the way – but Smith himself only has fond memories of it. "It'll always be a special album," he says on the reissue's sleeve notes, "a souvenir of a long, hot psychedelic winter."

RM

BARDO

In many ways, Bardo Pond are a band stuck in the wrong time: even compared to other contemporary noise-rock acts, such as Mogwai and Earth, their sound, approach and aesthetic seem tantalizingly out of step with most contemporary music. In fact, on hearing almost any of the recordings from the band's vast catalogue, you might be forgiven for thinking that you had in fact stumbled upon some long lost Krautrock gem – perhaps a little-known Faust side project or obscure Amon Duul recording.

And yet such comparisons are misleading, since perhaps Bardo Pond's most intriguing virtue is an ability to remodel their sound, either subtly or wholeheartedly, for each subsequent release. The result is a canon that serves to redefine and blur the edges of what in some quarters might be called acid rock, psychedelic rock or post-rock, and elsewhere would be labelled noise or improvisation. Their music is undeniably out-there, and no one would be naïve enough as to deny that there is an unapologetic druggy vibe to the sound – a vibe also implicit in many of the band's album titles.

The group's loose genesis can be traced back to Philadelphia, 1989, and two brothers named Michael and John Gibbons. Within a couple of years the line-up had expanded to include vocalist and flautist Isobel Sollenberger, whose gravel-over-velvet vocals and puffs of silvery flute would become a near-constant hallmark of the shifting, jamming sound of Bardo Pond. The band by now had swollen to include Clint Takeda on bass and Joe Culver on drums (the latter was in turn replaced within the year by new drummer Ed Farnsworth). After a trickle of seven-inch singles and self-released recordings, the group's first album proper appeared on the label Drunken Fish in 1995.

Entitled *Bufo Alvarius Amen 29:15*, the set opens with a slow, chant-accompanied guitar riff drenched in a warm fog of distortion. The feel is noisy and loose – very loose – and leaves the listener in no doubt that these recordings were the result of semi-improvised jam sessions. The CD's final statement of intent was the epic "Amen", which weighs in at just under half an hour and comes pretty damn close to simulating the sensation of slowly falling asleep, drunk, after attending a very loud gig.

It was clear from the start that Bardo Pond were going to be an acquired taste, were never going to receive mainstream recognition and, to a considerable degree, were only really there to make music for themselves. From this point of view, few would have been surprised if Bardo Pond had thrown forth a couple more records and then disappeared off the face of the planet. And yet they soon found themselves signed to Matador Records, one of the bigger players among the independent labels of the time. For Matador they produced a string of critically well-received albums around the turn of the century – *Amanita*, *Lapsed*, *Set and Setting* and *Dilate* – all of which continued to tinker with the formula of extended, churning guitar pieces with the scope of cinematic soundtracks. By this point, the group's catalogue was also straining at the seams from the increasing number of limited edition gig-only recordings, side projects and solo works that were emerging. But this glut of material was not simply falling into a void: the band's solid fanbase lapped it up, whilst increasingly improvisational live shows were well-attended, though arguably inferior to the consistently extraordinary material that appeared on record.

One of the most interesting things about the band, however, has been the way they have encouraged fans to record their shows. This has done much to bolster the online community that surrounds the group's activities, with many such live recordings being easily tracked down as free downloads. Some of the best can be found on the group's own site, Hummingbird Mountain, while others require a little more digging.

POND

In more recent years, Bardo Pond have settled on the All Tomorrow's Parties label (after appearing, at Thurston Moore's behest, at an ATP festival in 2001 programmed by Sonic Youth). Under this roof, the group have so far produced two stunning releases. Both 2003's *On the Ellipse* and 2006's *Ticket Crystals*, for example, have introduced a sense of restraint and composure to the music that had previously been either completely missing or subservient to the mountainous cloud-swells of wah and noise.

On a press release from the time of *Ticket Crystals*, guitarist Michael Gibbons pointed out that "On this album we really investigated the dynamics between acoustic sound and heavy electrics." It perfectly sums up the band's current direction while also hinting at the fact that the improved

recording techniques they use today, compared to the lo-fi aesthetic of earlier releases, have allowed them to use bells, percussion and electronics in a far more subtle, detailed way. Or, perhaps, they are mellowing just a little with age and experience. Either way, the explorations of Bardo Pond are consistently compelling and, hopefully, won't come to an end any time soon.

PM

playlist:

1 On a Side Street *from* Bufo Alvarius Amen 29:15
Behind the guitar skree and twisted wah-wah of this seven-minute-plus track, a gentle, almost delicate guitar line ticks throughout. As with so many of the band's numbers, it's this collision of the fragile and the apocalyptic that makes the music so special.

2 Call the Doctor *from* Tribute to Spacemen 3
This 1998 release found Bardo Pond paying tribute to space rock pioneers Spacemen 3 alongside fellow sonic architects such as Mogwai, Low, Bowery Electric and Piano Magic. The whole set is pretty impressive, though Bardo Pond's offering is of particular interest for its use of driving drum machine and explosive feedback. This is one of the few BP songs you could (kinda) dance to.

3 Every Man *from* On the Ellipse
Michael Gibbons has stated that "On the Ellipse was really influenced by the post 9/11 vibe". Whatever demons that evoked, they are working to full effect here. This track has one of the most delicate openings of anything in the band's canon, but also one of the most blistering and sudden changes of weather when the guitars kick in. Listen to this one loud.

4 Isle *from* Ticket Crystals
This eight-minute delight starts off softer than a lullaby, a beguiling flute melody toppling over an acoustic guitar lick. It doesn't take long, however, for the rest of the group to find their pews, plug in and start to build the mantra. By the time of the closing minutes the growl of guitars is as fierce as a pack of hungry dogs.

5 Cry Baby Cry *from* Ticket Crystals
This re-imagining of the Beatles classic from *The White Album* first appeared as a BBC broadcast recorded to commemorate the 25th anniversary of John Lennon's death. The cut starts off innocently enough, but soon explodes into a shower of guitar shrapnel and heavy doom sludge.

Ripe for rediscovery:
The Flaming Lips' Zaireeka

Surround sound is common in plenty of living rooms these days, but when Flaming Lips mastermind Wayne Coyne began experimenting with the medium, he saw possibilities far more exciting than merely DVD movies with more realistic explosions.

Prior to his Oklahoma band's current status as the mainstream's favourite cuddly alt.rock freaks, Coyne had just one hit single to his name, 1993's ode to eating

Vaseline for breakfast, "She Don't Use Jelly". On the back of this minor success, he had persuaded major label Warner Bros to fund confusing sonic exploration rather than more chart-friendly novelties. First there were the *Parking Lot Experiments* of 1996 – up to fifty cars in a covered garage simultaneously playing different cassettes of Coyne's devising. He called the resulting music "random-precision tape deck performance ... a kind of mutated symphony".

The experience inspired *Zaireeka*, a four-disc album that would create a similar surround-sound world in the listener's home, with the aid of four separate CD players and four arms to press play on each one at the same time. Eight songs combined deliberately disorientating sound frequencies, funereal organ, long guitar solos and barking dogs. In Coyne's own words, they generated "music that was both clear and confusing, music in which rhythms fought each other, where time signatures were simple but unpredictable ... music that would be unfamiliar even after a thousand listens."

He encouraged playing with the separate volume, bass and treble controls, starting discs at different points and even leaving out discs altogether. The Flaming Lips would later become known for psychedelic pop ditties and fancy dress performances, but they never sounded more unique than on this delightfully impractical slice of conceptual aural madness.

DS

British Sea Power

If you could earn a Boy Scout badge for rock music, then British Sea Power would no longer have any space left on their caps. Indeed, so industrious are the plucky BSP that, during the passage of this book from conception to printed copy, they have actually become a band too popular to justify their place here. They now have several top-selling CDs under their (utility) belts – you've probably heard of them. Such are their idiosyncrasies, however, that their tale warrants telling.

Indie rock has a core set of influences – The Clash, the Pixies, the Stooges and so on – rarely does a band dare to stray from the canon. But in 2003, Brighton's British Sea Power came yomping through the shrubbery in chunky jumpers and puttees, bringing a bizarre alternative rock ethos with them. They sold T-shirts at gigs emblazoned with the legend "Heron Addict", a reflection of their love of birdwatching and rambling. They decorated their stages with foliage and stuffed owls, and if a journalist should want to meet them, he or she would be given Ordnance Survey grid references as directions.

This evocation of a simpler England, amusing though it was, was no mere affectation – or at least, if it was, it was one they took very seriously. The band's admiration for the poetry of John Betjeman ran so deep that in 2006 they performed at Betjeman centenary concerts in both London and Cornwall, on bills that also featured cosy personalities Prunella Scales, Joanna Lumley and Ronnie Corbett.

Musically they have been generally more orthodox, generating a rough-edged rock sound similar to any number of dark-hearted post-punk bands, and perhaps hampering their commercial potential with songs such as "Apologies to Insect Life", a frantic stomp that features the line, "Oh Theodore you are the most attractive man" screamed over and over. Usually it's their lyrics that fascinate the most, their subject matter covering such topics as the Larsen B ice shelf ("Oh Larsen B"), light pollution ("Lights Out for Darker Skies"), insomnia remedies ("To Get to Sleep") and the 1942 assassination of Nazi SS chief Reinhard Heydrich in Prague ("A Lovely Day Tomorrow").

They are only becoming more wordy, too, as the epic liner notes to their third album, *Do You Like Rock Music?*, demonstrate. The pages of dense type include references to igneous rock formations, the 1930s actress Hedy Lamarr, tick-borne encephalitis, Brazilian football coach Dunga, and badgers.

Yet despite the left-field choice of Efrim Menuck from neo-classical post-rockers Godspeed You! Black Emperor as producer, the songs became more welcoming. A huge, widescreen guitar sound and catchier tunes, and even an unlikely revival of "Easy! Easy!", the chant of 1980s wrestler Big Daddy, all added up to their best chance yet for a commercial breakthrough. It paid off and BSP suddenly found themselves with a hit album.

Their big sound and vintage togs have meant some now have them pegged as a UK version of Arcade Fire, but until the Canadians take up hiking and start munching Kendal Mint Cake, British Sea Power will always be in a field of their own.

DS

where to start:

1 **Remember Me** *from* The Decline of British Sea Power
The strongest tune on the band's debut album sidelines smart lyrics in favour of crashing drums and a soaring lead guitar line, proving that sometimes there's no harm in a simple, thrilling rock song.

2 **Waving Flags** *from* Do You Like Rock Music?
A crowd-pleasing anthem in praise of the influx of immigrants to Britain from Eastern Europe, with a non-PC and, one assumes, tongue-in-cheek respect for their ability to hold their drink: "You are astronomical fans of alcohol, so welcome in".

CHROME

In the late 1970s Damon Edge and Helios Creed created some of the most freaked-out music of their – or any other – time. Under the name Chrome, they invented post-rock some fifteen years before anyone got around to using the term. Inspired by a twin obsession with sci-fi movies and warping sound, it was perhaps fitting that they hailed from San Francisco, the spiritual home of psychedelia. Yet the apocalyptic intensity of their dense and vivid sci-fi epics travelled way beyond anything imagined by even the most audacious of the 1960s acid-rock bands. They produced an awesome fantasia of dense, mechanical noise, flanged and phased guitars and twisted voices drawing on such influences as Neu! and Suicide as well as Pink Floyd and Hendrix. It was memorably described by one critic as "like the Stooges playing Can in cyberspace".

Formed by Edge in 1975, Chrome's debut *The Visitation* was a relatively conventional West Coast rock album. All that changed with the arrival of Helios Creed for 1977's *Alien Soundtracks*. Seldom can an album have been so aptly titled. A concept album that purported to be the music for a strip show set in a space-age totalitarian state, this was Aldous Huxley's *Brave New World* painted by Salvador Dali and set to music. "ST37" was about sexual intercourse with an android, but if you want to taste their sonic manipulation at its most breathtaking, "Nova Feedback" is the quintessential track.

Alien Soundtracks probably remains Chrome's finest hour and it certainly defined their sound. However, its follow-up, *Half Machine Lip Moves*, another slab of LSD-inspired metallic otherworldliness driven by Creed's scary FX-laden guitar and Edge's eerie synth and vocals, is arguably as good. In 1990, the Jesus Lizard released the single "Chrome", a compressed medley cover of the entire album.

Over four further releases, the Chrome sound changed little apart from taking on a more industrial clang, and Edge and Creed parted company after *Raining Milk* (1983). Edge continued releasing less experimental records with a new band formed in Europe under the Chrome moniker. Many of them were frankly unworthy of the name and served only to dilute the potency of the Chrome legend. By the time Edge died in LA in 1995 he had become a reclusive figure. It's a measure of how isolated he was that when he died, his body lay undiscovered in his apartment for a month. Since his old colleague's death, Creed has resumed using the Chrome name, continuing his self-professed quest to replicate the sound he heard in his head while "listening to Black Sabbath on LSD on headphones when [he] was a teenager".

NW

"R2-D2, getting into punk, would have chosen Chrome over the Pistols every time because you could dance to them. Regular humans such as myself always wore oven gloves when handling their discs for fear of death via some hitherto unknown space disease."

Julian Cope on Chrome

Felt

According to his own self-mythologizing, Lawrence Hayward formed Felt as a band of, for and defined by the decade of the 1980s. Influenced by the glam and punk of the previous decade, and Tom Verlaine and Lou Reed in particular, the group released ten albums and ten singles in the ten years between 1979 and 1989. They then proudly disappeared, Hayward adhering strictly to a manifesto he had dreamed up in 1980: that Felt were a band built for posterity with a planned obsolescence right from the start.

During those ten years Felt made some extraordinarily diverse music, although Hayward's morosely ascetic yet acutely volatile personality often became the main story. From the get-go he conducted himself like a bona fide indie rock legend, one out of proportion with Felt's actual record sales. He capriciously sacked his first drummer, Tony Race, for having curly hair and, according to rumour, turned up to play at Glastonbury demanding to know where his on-site bungalow was sited. On at least one occasion, Felt performed as a duo because the despotic Hayward had so alienated the rest of the band that they refused to take the stage with him. His relationships with other group members were presumably not helped by his self-promotion as a "new puritan" who disapproved of drink, drugs and smoking – or his Howard Hughes-like obsession with hygiene and cleanliness.

But what about the music? Felt's first single "Index", from 1979, was a solo piece of crude minimalism recorded on a cassette in his bedroom. The following year he put a band together and Felt's early sound owed much to the intricate, jangling guitar playing of the classically trained Maurice Deebank, whose partnership with Hayward fuelled suggestions that the band were a West Midlands version of The Smiths, with a Morrissey-and-Marr-style duo at their heart, "mixing self-pity, self-aggrandisement and provincial melancholy with an aesthete's reinterpretation of indie-rock manners." The pinnacle of the Deebank period came on 1985's *Ignite the Seven Cannons*, produced by Robin Guthrie and featuring backing vocals from his Cocteau Twins partner Elizabeth Fraser.

By then future Primal Scream keyboardist Martin Duffy had joined but Deebank departed soon after. Switching to Alan McGee's Creation label, Felt released *Forever Breathes the Lonely Word* in 1986. It's the album regarded by many fans as Felt's masterpiece, a lush, opulently melancholic set smeared with classic pop harmonies. The group's penultimate release, *Train Above the City*, came out in 1988. It was, perversely, a collection of tinkling cocktail jazz piano instrumentals composed by Duffy, to which Hayward's only contribution was to name the track titles. They then signed off brilliantly with *Me and a Monkey on the Moon* in 1989, a cycle of inspired songs about growing up in the 1970s.

In many ways it was a signpost to Hayward's next project. After disbanding Felt, he immersed himself in 1970s nostalgia, forming the glam/synth-pop novelty band Denim. He managed to recruit the rhythm section of The Glitter Band to back him up, and the album *Back in Denim* turned out to be a hell of a lot more fun than it should have been – a great lost pop album that indisputedly would have been a smash hit, were it not for the insurmountable hindrance of it not having been released twenty years earlier.

NW

Gavin Friday

He could have been Bono. Well, perhaps not quite – for Gavin Friday isn't on a personal mission to save the world and doesn't keep company with presidents and popes. But he was born just a few blocks from the U2 singer in Dublin; the two were in the same year at school; and they were both part of the same close-knit musical community, out of which Bono formed U2 and Friday created the Virgin Prunes. At that point their careers took somewhat different turns, although Friday and Bono have remained close friends and occasional collaborators. While U2 set about fashioning a stadium-filling rock sound, Friday and the Virgin Prunes explored the confrontational aesthetic of punk, performing savage, cathartic gigs that became notorious for Friday's shock-rock tactics, involving on-stage nudity, simulated sex acts and gothic theatricals.

They were signed to Rough Trade, but the Virgin Prunes never quite captured the anarchic, Dadaist edge of their live shows in the studio. As a result they never enjoyed more than a cult following and the best representation of their uncompromising style on record is to be found on the 1987 live album *The Hidden Lie*. By the time of its release, Friday (real name Fionnain Hanvey) had already left the band, briefly abandoning music to concentrate on his painting. Within a year he had returned to performing and started a Dublin cabaret spot called the Blue Jaysus. It was here that he met the pianist Maurice Roycroft – whom he promptly renamed The Man Seezer – and the pair landed a recording deal with Island in 1988.

Their debut, *Each Man Kills the Thing He Loves*, came out the following year. Produced by Hal Wilner, it was a masterpiece, and Friday claimed with some justification that the record articulated everything he hadn't been able to say in the Virgin Prunes. Exploring themes of love, death and sex and his growing interest in such European singers and songwriters as Edith Piaf, Bertolt Brecht, Kurt Weill and Jacques Brel – whose vicious satire "Next" is covered on the album – Friday sings in a voice that sounds like a more menacing David Bowie. Behind him is a darkly compelling sonic tapestry created by a wonderful supporting cast assembled by Wilner, among them the endlessly inventive guitarists Bill Frisell and Marc Ribot.

The follow-up, 1992's *Adam 'N' Eves*, was a more conventional rock record, balancing Friday's adolescent passion for the trash-glam of T-Rex et al with more "serious" influences ranging from Satie to Bacharach. Sadly, instead of sounding like a brave and inspired marriage, the results were merely confused and rather camp. Better was to come the following year when Friday and Seezer composed three songs with Bono for the soundtrack of Jim Sheridan's film *In the Name of the Father*, with Bono and Friday sharing the vocals on two of them.

Shag Tobacco was described by Friday as a "science fiction cabaret" and was another fine record – a sultry, cinematic take on the world of sex that combined the dark, European carnival of his solo debut with 1990s dance tropes. Since then Friday has involved himself in a variety of projects. These have included several film scores, such as a partnership with Quincy Jones on the 50 Cent biopic *Get Rich or Die Trying*; 2001's *Ich Liebe Dich*, a musical theatre tribute to Kurt Weill; a new arrangement of Prokofiev's *Peter and the Wolf* (released in a luxury box-set, with artwork by Bono); an autobiographical one-man show called *I Didn't Come up the Liffey in a Bubble*; a movie cameo as a sexually ambiguous rocker in Neil Jordan's *Breakfast on Pluto*; and a collaboration with the composer Gavin Bryars and the Royal Shakespeare Company on a series of musical settings of Shakespeare's sonnets.

His music is often erratic, frequently difficult and at times far too self-important – more shades of Bono there. But his work offers the endless fascination of an artist whose creative impulses are always born of a desire to challenge rather than to conform.

NW

playlist:

1 Each Man Kills the Thing He Loves *from* Each Man Kills the Thing He Loves
Friday does Oscar Wilde.

2 Next *from* Each Man Kills the Thing He Loves
Brilliant cover of Brel's bitter protest about standing in line.

3 In the Name of the Father *from* In the Name of the Father OST
One of two rather good duets from the film with St Bono.

4 Caruso *from* Shag Tobacco
"Oh my Lord, I'm so bored, what's on the TV? Do we really need these pissy pop stars when there's not enough of me" Jealous? Moi?

5 A Pagan Lovesong *from* The Hidden Lie
The power and the passion of the Virgin Prunes at their best.

The La's

They could've been... Oasis?

Noel Gallagher once said that Oasis existed "to finish what The La's started". Certainly The La's themselves never finished much at all, due to the obsessive perfectionism of their maverick leader Lee Mavers. The band only ever released one album – and that took four years, seven studios, two producers and numerous abandoned sessions. Even then, the band's exasperated record label Go! Discs had to employ Steve Lillywhite to piece together an album from the hordes of scrapped recordings, fearing that otherwise Mavers would never deliver a finished record. The resulting album, *The La's,* was a classic, reviving the breezy, Beatles-esque glory of 1960s jangly pop and including the magical, majestic, euphoric rush of "There She Goes", a hit single three times in the last two decades and one of the most glorious sounds in modern pop.

Mavers grumbled to the music press disconsolately, complaining that the tracks were shoddy demos with guide vocals only which never should have been released. He then announced that he was going to spend the next eight years producing The La's' "perfect" second album. At the time of writing, some eighteen years have passed without any sign of it.

The La's' story dates back to 1983, but only gets really interesting three years later when Mavers replaced founder Mike Badger, who had coined the name – a Liverpudlian abbreviation of "lad". At the time, British pop music was floundering in over-produced, synthetic pap but Mavers was determined to revive the classic sounds of The Beatles, The Kinks and The Who with a post-modern lyrical twist. "There She Goes" first appeared as a single in 1988 but, from the outset, the band's record company had difficulty in coaxing finished product out of Mavers.

Obsessed with retaining the "purity" of his music, he spoke at length of his search for the perfect studio and a mixing desk with "original 60s dust". He seemed unable to find it. Songs were recorded over and over again and scrapped until in 1990 the record company lost patience and stuck the album out anyway.

By 1992 bassist John Power had left in exasperation to form Cast and rumours were rife that Mavers was addicted to heroin. Asked in 1995 if the lyrics of "There She Goes" were a coded paean to the drug, rather than to a girl, he replied: "I don't know. Truth is, I don't wanna know. Drugs and madness go hand in hand."

With Mavers hors de combat, Oasis emerged to steal the La's melodic thunder as the inheritors of The Beatles' mantle, but at least acknowledged their debt: at the height of their success in 1997, the Mancunians took to the stage at their sell-out arena shows to the strains of "There She Goes".

In 1998 it was reported that Mavers had forty new songs. A decade later he's still working away on them, 45 years old and with a 22-year "career" behind him that has produced one sole album, and even that he claims was an unfinished work. The sad truth is that it is probably now way too late – if new material does ever see the light of day, it can only dilute the potency of the myth behind one of the most perplexing enigmas in modern pop.

NW

Godspeed You! Black Emperor

Named after a 1970s documentary about a Japanese biker gang, Godspeed You! Black Emperor's place in this book was probably cemented when they titled their debut release, in 1994, *All Lights Fucked On The Hairy Amp Drooling* and released it in a limited cassette-only edition of just 33 copies.

Few have ever heard that first obscure set, but on their more widely available albums, Godspeed! have mapped out an apocalyptic vision of a society in moral collapse, a thunderous musical amalgam of paranoid fantasy, social dissent and desolation. Their epic soundscapes are further enlivened with sampled monologues from such diverse sources as street preachers, gas station announcements and crackly, short wave radio broadcasts.

Formed in 1994 in Mile End, Québec, Godspeed! initially consisted of Efrim Menuck (guitar/keyboards) and Mauro Pezzente (bass), who came together playing underground bring-a-bottle shows in defiance of the pay-to-play policy operated by local club owners. It was this duo that recorded *All Lights Fucked* at a poky studio-cum-venue called Hotel2Tango. Titles on the tape – reportedly even more chaotic than their later releases – included "Perfumed Pink Corpses From the Lips of Ms Celine Dion" and "Loose the Idiot Dogs."

The line-up has since expanded and changed frequently, with David Bryant (guitar), Thierry Amar (bass), Aidan Girt and Bruce Cawdron (drums/percussion), Sophie Trudeau (violin), Norsola Johnson (cello) and Roger-Tellier Craig (guitar), and they are occasionally augmented by other instruments such as glockenspiel, French horn and bagpipes. However, the group has deliberately courted anonymity, insisting the focus should be on their music rather than their personalities. When the band were made reluctant cover stars by *NME* in 1999, Menuck volleyed questions by saying: "If I want to have an awkward conversation with people about things I hold to be self-evident, I'll go to my parents' place for the holidays."

Their full debut, irritatingly titled *F# A# Infinity*, appeared in 1997 as a limited-edition vinyl LP on Constellation Records, sumptuously packaged with individually assembled covers featuring pasted photographs of urban skylines and old locomotives and including an old coin flattened on the rail tracks behind their Hotel2Tango base.

When it was released with additional material on CD the following year, the artwork was bleaker – a single, grainy image of three lonely antennas and a blurred signpost, dwarfed by a stormy sky. The music was even more striking: a collection of cinematic drones, guitar twangs, swooping strings, fierce crescendos and found monologues; not so much songs in the conventional sense as sound sculptures, conjuring an intense post-rock vision of beauty, anger, mystery and classicism quite unlike anything else to be heard in the musical firmament of the time.

The 1999 EP *Slow Riot for New Zero Kanada* built a denser sound and was followed in 2000 by *Levez Vos Skinny Fists Comme Antennas to Heaven*, a masterful and epic double CD that defined their hallmark sound. To the surprise of some, they then turned to noted rock producer Steve Albini to helm 2002's *Yanqui U.X.O.*, which vacillated between explosions of thunder and quiet melancholy in the course of its characteristically elongated and meandering five tracks.

In recent years the band has been on an indefinite hiatus, its members busy with various side projects. One of them, A Silver Mount Zion, has rather threatened to overshadow Godspeed! itself. Sometimes labouring under the rather unwieldy name Thee Silver Mt. Zion Memorial Orchestra & Tra-La-La Band, they are comprised of the trio of Menuck, Amar and Trudeau, and in 2000 they recorded the wonderful, piano-led *He Has Left Us Alone but Shafts of Light Sometimes Grace the Corners of Our Rooms*.

Operating as a leaderless collective, Godspeed! apparently hold an annual meeting and vote on whether to reconvene – and on every occasion so far since 2003 have voted against doing so, although the band's website insists they have not disbanded. Several band members are anarchists and a potent strand of radical politics runs through much of their work. Indeed, on an American tour in 2003 the group were detained by police and questioned by the FBI as suspected terrorists in Ardmore, Oklahoma – an incident later recorded in Michael Moore's book, *Dude, Where's My Country?*

NW

playlist:

Godspeed You! Black Emperor

1 Dead Flag Blues *from* F# A# Infinity
As the opening cut of the group's first album proper, this was most certainly a
challenging statement of intent. The scene of this epic fifteen-minute track is set
by a gravel-voiced spoken-word evocation of desolation and the end of capital-
ism. From there things slowly build and churn into a cacophony of slide guitar,
atmospherics and molten strings. Powerful stuff indeed.

2 Broken Windows, Locks of Love Part III *from* Leves Vos Skinny
Fists Comme Antennas to Heaven
Another colossal, cinematic selection. This time the momentum pushes and
pushes through as the overdriven guitars become ever more frantic and blistered,
finally giving way to a mellower metronomic passage with bells and delicate
chord progressions. As you might expect, everything takes off again before the
track is put to rest ... and even after all that you'll still be none the wiser about
the title.

A Silver Mount Zion

1 13 Angels Standing Guard Round the Side of Your Bed
from He Has Left Us Alone but Shafts of Light Sometimes Grace the Corners
of Our Rooms
More amazing track and album titles here and, with regard to the music, arguably the band's most beautiful moment. If this exquisite progression of strings
and synth doesn't bring a lump to your throat, then you must either be made
of stone or the kind of person who likes drowning kittens.

2 God Bless Our Dead Marines *from* **Horses in the Sky**
Horses in the Sky saw A Silver Mount Zion fully embrace more traditional song
structures for the first time, though still set within a frame of expanded, shifting
compositions. Lyrically this is at face value an anti-war song, but listen more
carefully and you'll discover some of the most stunning lyrical constructions
and images of any band's work in recent years.

A Silver Mount Zion

Lightspeed Champion

O n the cover of *Falling Off the Lavender Bridge*, his debut album under the name Lightspeed Champion, Devonte Hynes sports a bright red cardigan, yellow bow tie and thick geeky spectacles, looking like the world's most miserable clown. Ever contrary, in his career to date he has always made it difficult to tell when he is joking.

Which is the real Hynes? The dayglo-clad screamer in the ridiculously named trio Test Icicles? Their ramshackle blend of martial electronica and abrasive guitars was so unpalatable that when they announced their disbanding after just one album, even they admitted they didn't like their music. Or is he the sensitive balladeer he became as Lightspeed Champion? Even here, ostensibly more conventional songs were characterized by confrontational titles such as "All to Shit" and "Let the Bitches Die", and lyrics about being sick in someone else's mouth.

Born in Houston, Texas, but a London resident from the age of four, Hynes first emerged as one of the freshest faces of east London's overly fashionable social scene. He was a flatmate of Simon Taylor-Davis from Klaxons, but Test Icicles's harsh mash-up of guitars and electronics preceded Klaxons' huge success in making rave music for indie kids – and was a good deal more musically adventurous to boot. Test Icicles' sole album was an early job for producer James Ford, who went on to have more success with Arctic Monkeys and Klaxons. That album, *For Screening Purposes Only*, was the sound of a trio who had already tired of making music together. Of the songs, Hynes said, "We never worked on them – a lot were made up on the spot."

"A grim old din," concluded *The Guardian*'s reviewer, although the single "Circle Square Triangle" did manage to capture something of the energy and spirit of the indie disco. They played a final gig after they announced their split at London's Astoria in April 2006, which should have been the last we heard of these briefly cool chancers.

Given his past, the sound of Hynes's 2008 comeback as Lightspeed Champion could not have been more surprising. Recorded in Omaha, Nebraska, the home of acclaimed American troubadour Bright Eyes, *Falling Off the Lavender Bridge* has a similar offbeat folk feel to his US peer. A great pal of Peaches Geldof, Hynes enlisted Alex Turner from Arctic Monkeys and folk hipster Emmy the Great among his backing musicians. There are twanging country guitars, lush strings, winsome backing vocals from Emmy, and Hynes sings with a sensitivity previously undetected. Next time maybe he'll go hip-hop, but currently his place in the musical firmament is well worth visiting.

DS

where to start:

1 Circle Square Triangle *from* For Screening Purposes Only
House beats and a funky bass groove coupled with shouted lyrics and noisily ringing guitars, this is the most accessible moment from Test Icicles' brief racket. To cement its appeal to the kids, it's about PlayStations.

2 Everyone I Know is Listening to Crunk *from* Falling Off the Lavender Bridge
Hynes successfully distances himself from current trends by writing a song about the latest hip-hop craze which sounds like a jaunty country ballad from the mid-1970s.

Other versions:
unsung covers
of great songs

Once, cover versions were virtually all there was, as singers who didn't write songs themselves concentrated on putting their stamp on an array of different standards. Today the cover is marginalized and frequently dismissed as a novelty, but it can be a great source of pleasure if handled correctly.

Currently the chief promulgator of the idea of the cover as something re-evaluative and often ironic is Radio 1 DJ Jo Whiley, whose show's "Live Lounge" segment mostly encourages indie bands to tackle pop songs in a rather superior manner. There are now two *Live Lounge* compilations, which feature the likes of Arctic Monkeys beefing up Girls Aloud's "Love Machine", Franz Ferdinand rocking up Gwen Stefani's "What You Waiting For" and Biffy Clyro attempting Rihanna's "Umbrella". More fun than this pair, however, are the two *Crazy Covers* collections, compiled by DJ Tom Middleton, upon which you're as likely to find Hayseed Dixie's yeehawing bluegrass version of "Walk This Way" as the Algerian Raï singer Rachid Taha playing The Clash's "Rock the Casbah".

Singer-songwriter Ben Folds is probably the man who puts the most effort into the ironic cover. His sensitive interpretation of Dr Dre's "Bitches Ain't Shit" (from Folds' *Supersunnyspeedgraphic* album of 2006) turns an astonishingly foul-mouthed hip-hop track into a gorgeous piano ballad, and his take on Pulp's "Common People", with Star Trek's William Shatner on spoken vocals, is a masterpiece of the bizarre you can hear on Shatner's *Has Been* album of 2004.

The cover can be an effective calling card, a short cut to understanding where a musician is coming from. Think Oasis roaring through "I Am The Walrus" – or the covers album *Rock 'n' Roll* by their mentor, John Lennon. The White Stripes emphasized their roots in country and blues by covering Dolly Parton's "Jolene" and Robert Johnson's "Stop Breaking Down" on their "Dead Leaves and the Dirty Ground" single, before wrongfooting everybody with Corky Robbins's 1950s matador anthem "Conquest" on their *Icky Thump* album. Rufus Wainwright signalled his deep love for the showtunes of Judy Garland by recreating her legendary Carnegie Hall concert with a series of shows, a DVD and a double album entitled *Rufus Does Judy at Carnegie Hall* (2007).

Taking a familiar song and making it fully your own can also produce powerful results. Tori Amos's 2001 album *Strange Little Girls* saw her singing songs written by men and giving them a new female perspective, including Eminem's "97 Bonnie & Clyde" and The Beatles' "Happiness Is A Warm Gun". Cat Power has now made two albums of dark, almost completely unrecognizable cover versions – *The Covers Record* and *Jukebox* – while French band Nouvelle Vague have carved a surprisingly successful career out of giving a sunny bossa nova swing to punk and new wave anthems, such as "Love Will Tear Us Apart" and "Teenage Kicks". The many Latin-style covers of 1960s classics by the blind Puerto Rican guitarist José Feliciano are of great kitsch value, while another 1960s curiosity – Ray Charles' soulful excursion into country entitled *Modern Sounds in Country and Western Music* – proved to be a great success despite looking like a disaster on paper. The alien, bass-heavy version of "(I Can't Get No) Satisfaction" by the 1980s synth irritants Devo effectively demonstrated how little the new wave geeks had in common with classic rock.

Some covers are so well done they effectively change the ownership of the song, such as Jeff Buckley's career-defining take on Leonard Cohen's "Hallelujah" or Johnny Cash's heart-stopping version of "Hurt" by Nine Inch Nails. Soft Cell's "Tainted Love" was originally a northern soul stomper sung by Gloria Jones in 1964, but is now known principally for its iconic bleeps, while Tiffany's 1980s pop classic "I Think We're Alone Now" started out as a 1967 guitar number by Tommy James & The Shondells.

Country singer Willie Nelson became a real star thanks to cover versions. His 1978 album of standards, *Stardust*, turned out to be the biggest seller of his career. DJ and producer Mark Ronson has made covers his business in the present day, scooping a Brit Award for his *Version* album of horn-packed takes on Coldplay, The Smiths and Britney Spears.

For the greatest wealth of cover versions in one place, however, we must look to reggae. The sound's precursor, ska, began when Jamaican musicians started copying the American R&B hits they heard on the radio, and as a result thousands of American songs of the 1950s and 60s have a bouncy Caribbean twin. Fans of the greats of rock'n'roll should treat themselves to the compilation *All Shook Up: A Reggae Tribute to the King* or any of the dozens of Beatles covers albums. More off the beaten track is *Kung Fu! Reggae Vs The Martial Arts*, including Lloyd Parks's version of "Kung Fu Fighting", or *Studio One Soul*, with its takes on Aretha and Cat Stevens. But for real quirkiness look to the Easy Star All-Stars, who to date have given the entire albums *Dark Side of the Moon* and *OK Computer* an irresistible reggae lilt.

DS

The Sound of
Young Scotland:
Postcard and post-punk

Who would have imagined that a country in the throes of 1970s industrial decline would spawn a music scene so vibrant, life-affirming and strangely romantic that it would alter the entire direction of independent music in the 1980s and beyond? The phrase "The Sound of Young Scotland" has often been used in conjunction with Postcard Records – the label that coined it and proudly printed it on their releases – but it could equally be applied to acts who never actually signed to Postcard. And, indeed, bands that didn't even form until after the label had ceased trading. All of them share a common spirit, and some – such as Altered Images in the 1980s and Franz Ferdinand today – went on to achieve mainstream pop success.

Scottish post-punk bands knew that they stood little chance of persuading A&R scouts from major record labels to get on the train and come and see them play. But a label from Edinburgh, Fast Product, put out singles by the Gang Of Four, The Human League and The Mekons. When The Mekons' record was made *NME*'s single of the week by Tony Parsons, the UK's curiosity was piqued. Might something be going on north of the border?

Alan Horne, a nineteen-year-old upstart with entrepreneurial flair and the gift of the gab, launched Postcard Records from his tiny flat and put out the single "Falling and Laughing" by Orange Juice in April 1980 to critical acclaim. And, whether intentional or not, it provided a blueprint for dozens of Scottish acts. While fiercely independent, they also in many ways represented

The Fire Engines

Orange Juice

Falling and Laughing *from* You Can't Hide Your Love Forever
It's been said that Orange Juice's first gig – on 20 April, 1979 – kickstarted the whole movement. The truth is probably not quite as straightforward, but there's no doubt that this slice of haphazard, crooning indie funk, slotted neatly into its Postcard sleeve, had a effect on all who heard it disproportionate to the economy of its package.

Aztec Camera

Mattress of Wire *from* Mattress of Wire single
Swapping the clanging electric guitars for lushly strummed chords, this song was, as far as anyone remembers, the final Postcard release, and marked the end of an era. Roddy Frame went on to bigger-budget, quasi-stadium rock productions, but this is a wonderful reminder of what a fantastic songwriter of the old school he was – albeit one slightly obscured by the lo-fi Postcard production.

Josef K

Sorry for Laughing *from* Sorry for Laughing
You couldn't give it many marks for rhythmic precision, but the relentless guitarwork and Paul Haig's mournful vocal made for a unique take on the Scottish post-punk sound. It's worth checking out an extraordinary version by the German act Propaganda on their debut album on ZTT, if only to hear what the song might have sounded like if Josef K had had a hotshot producer behind them.

Fire Engines

Discord *from* Lubricate Your Living Room
No philosophical issues debated here, and no winsome, lovelorn poetry. Just a circular riff repeated for seven glorious minutes, accompanied by scratching, fizzing guitar chords, Davy Henderson's barking vocals and, of course, that omnipresent cowbell. Franz Ferdinand went on to cover the song, but could never match this for its sheer exuberance.

The Associates

Kitchen Person *from* Fourth Drawer Down
Most people are familiar with "Party Fears Two", The Associates' breakthrough single that got Billy Mackenzie's extraordinary voice heard on *Top of the Pops* for the first time. But delve back into their earlier work, and you'll find such fabulously unhinged moments as this, an exhilarating mixture of xylophones and drum machines underpinned by an almost gothically atonal riff.

the antithesis of punk rock aggression. Guitars were brittle and jangling, with no distortion, as if they were just hotwired straight into the mixing desk with a minimum of messing about. There was also a sense of joyous optimism about the records, a boundless energy that, again, stood in contrast to dour acts from England such as The Fall and Joy Division. But above all, there was an almost fey, foppish intelligence that many would never have expected to emerge from a city such as Glasgow, with its hard-man reputation.

There was clear evidence of an East-West, Edinburgh-Glasgow rivalry. The Edinburgh band Josef K was viewed by the Glaswegians as somewhat pretentious, while the Fire Engines, also from Edinburgh, seemed to be operating in their own freakish, discordant, riff-driven bubble. But it was the collective V-sign that the whole scene flicked at a haughty London music scene that went on to inspire artists not just from Scotland, but across the UK, America and beyond. While there have been noisier bands, more extreme bands and ruder bands, none of them encapsulated that spirit of independence quite like "The Sound of Young Scotland".

RM

Pavement

I t is famously said that few people bought the Velvet Underground's records at the time, but that most of those who did went on to form their own bands. If there's a 1990s equivalent it might just be Pavement, who enjoyed only modest sales for the five albums they released between 1992 and 1999, but have since become the spiritual godfathers of an entire school of skewed, post-millennial American indie bands from Modest Mouse to The Shins. Their influence crossed the Atlantic, too: when Blur moved away from Britpop in the late 1990s, they let it be known that Pavement were prominent among the influences on their new sound.

When Seattle grunge was drowning out everything else in the early 1990s, Pavement showed that there was another way for American rock music with clattering, off-kilter beats, lo-fi fuzzy melodicism and fractured experimentalism. They did so with a sloppy charm, an enthralling sense of adventure and an indefinable feeling that anything was possible. As the critic John Mulvey put it, Pavement contrived to sound like a band that was "entertainingly heading in the same direction by accident". Since the group's demise, erstwhile leader Stephen Malkmus has attained senior status as an alternative-rock guru, treading a similarly engaging sidewalk on four further albums of cerebral but fluent maverick guitar-rock, either solo or with his new band, the Jicks.

Formed in Stockton, California in 1989 by Malkmus and guitarist Scott Kannberg (known originally only as "S.M." and "Spiral Stairs"), Pavement announced themselves with a series of EPs recorded at Louder Than You Think, the home studio of ageing local hippie Gary Young, who also filled in on drums. Their early sound – and Malkmus's singing style in particular – owed a lot to The Fall. Rather too much for the liking of Mark E. Smith, who loudly complained that the American upstarts were ripping him off.

With the addition of extra percussionist Bob Nastanovich to help the erratically flailing Young to keep time, and Mark Ibold on bass, their first full-length release, *Slanted and Enchanted*, appeared in 1992. Despite seeing the light of day initially in a roughly edited, un-marketed cassette version, it remains one of the finest debuts by a rock band in the last twenty years, the

music drawing gloriously on classic indie influences such as the Pixies, Sonic Youth, the Replacements and, of course, The Fall. It ranged from nuggets of melody to storms of experimental noise, all given individuality and character by Malkmus's emerging skills as a songwriter. John Peel adopted them as favourites and the critics loved them, especially as they came with a good story in the strange Keith Moon-style behaviour of Young, who during the band's live performances liked to run around the venue doing handstands and was prone to falling drunkenly off his drum stool when he resumed his place on stage. At one point he also allegedly pulled a gun on Malkmus. Keith Moon got away with similarly manic behaviour because he was a great drummer. Young wasn't, and it was no surprise when he was sacked at the end of their first European tour in 1993, to be replaced by Steve West.

Pavement's step was steadier without him, as they showed on *Crooked Rain, Crooked Rain* (1994) and *Wowee Zowee* (1995), a brace of wonderful, starry-eyed albums with a breadth, depth and eclecticism that was at times dazzling, ranging from ferocious garage punk to rock of a languid poignancy.

After 1997's *Brighten the Corners*, cracks began to appear in the band and both Kannberg and Malkmus played a series of solo gigs. When 1999's *Twilight Terror* contained no material by Kannberg, it was obvious that Pavement had come to the end of the road. Kannberg went on to release two intermittently interesting albums as Preston School of Industry, but it's Malkmus who has won most of the plaudits and produced the most interesting work, most recently on 2008's *Real Emotional Trash*.

NW

playlist:

1 Trigger Cut *from* Slanted and Enchanted
The most melodic cut to poke its way out of the deliberately murky undergrowth that gave their debut its signature sound.

2 Cut Your Hair *from* Crooked Rain, Crooked Rain
Flawless post-pop – the nearest Pavement ever came to a mainstream hit.

3 Range Life *from* Crooked Rain, Crooked Rain
Its infamous lyric attacking alt.rock superstars was the source of a long-running spat between Malkmus and Smashing Pumpkins' Billy Corgan.

4 Grounded *from* Wowee Zowee
Pavement take to the freeway on this majestic epic.

5 Father to a Sister of Thought *from* Wowee Zowee
Poignant balladry with a pedal-steel guitar to ache, weep and die for.

Pavement's Stephen Malkmus (left) and Mark Ibold (right).

Slint

Slint's own website describes the band from Louisville, Kentucky, as "impossibly influential and somewhat mysterious". Mysterious certainly, for after just two albums that were largely ignored at the time, they split up in 1991 amid dark rumours that some, if not all of the band, had committed themselves to a psychi-atric institution. Impossibly influential is also a cap that fits, for they have since assumed almost legendary status as one of the most innovative bands of their all-too-brief time, who inspired much of what happened in American alternative rock over the next decade.

They reformed for live shows in 2005 and regrouped once

its entirety at a series of shows across Europe and America. At the same time they debuted a new composition, "King's Approach", sparking hopes of a more reunion and a new album. Slint trace their origins back to 1981 when guitarist Brian McMahan and drummer Britt Walford began playing together in Louisville while still in their pre-teens. Despite their youth, before long they were playing gigs at the Café Dog in Louisville and by the mid-1980s had formed Squirrel Bait, with the addition of vocalist Peter Searcy, guitarist David Grubbs and bassist Ethan Buckler. Playing a metal-flavoured hardcore influenced by Hüsker Dü and Black Flag, they recorded two albums of ferocious teen punk described by one commentator as "the missing link between The Replacements and Nirvana", and which earned the personal endorsement of Hüsker Dü's Bob Mould.

Squirrel Bait splintered into myriad different groups and its various members went on over the years to play in Bastro, Palace Brothers, Evergreen, King Kong, Big Wheel and Gastr del Sol. By far the most significant of Squirrel Bait's progeny, however, was Slint, featuring McMahan, Walford, Buckler and new recruit Dave Pajo, a nineteen-year-old Texas-born guitarist whose family had moved to Louisville when he was a child. Another key player in the story was Steve Albini, at the time playing with Big Black and starting to make his name as a heavyweight producer. Having produced Squirrel Bait's first album he was a natural choice for Slint's 1987 debut, *Tweez*. Together they came up with an idiosyncratic, almost schizophrenic record that was like almost nothing else in American rock at the time. In parts it was dense and dark. In other places it was playful and light-hearted, its bright poppiness bubbling up through Albini's brooding sludge-rock production of metal guitars and booming drums.

Released on vinyl, the two sides of the album were titled "Bemis" and "Gerber" after the brand name of a toilet manufacturer, while the largely instrumental tracks were named after the parents of various band members (and the drummer's dog). Where there were vocals, they were snatches of dialogue, used like sound-effects and sounding as if they had been recorded in one of Bemis-Gerber's closets. At the time few took any notice and it was almost four years before Slint got to record the follow-up, by which time

Albini had given way in the control booth to Brian Paulson and Buckler had been replaced on bass by Todd Brasher. By now grizzled veterans in their early twenties, Slint set about creating their masterpiece. Recorded over two weekends because they were all holding down day-jobs, *Spiderland* (1991) was a far more deft, warm, sophisticated and spacious work. The album's six tracks swung wildly in volume and tempo, from thundering to murmuring, often in the space of the same song.

Today, the record is revered as the foundation stone of that peculiarly American invention "math rock" (although it also influenced British musicians such as Blur's Graham Coxon and Radiohead's Thom Yorke). *Spiderland* was also the making of Paulson. "I was thinking 'I've never heard anything like this. I'm really digging this but it's really fucking weird'," he recalled. "We knocked that record out in four days ... And then the phone started ringing."

The record's impact on the band was less positive. The rumours of some sort of collective mental breakdown may or may not be true but they swiftly disintegrated as *Spiderland* got lost in the crush of Seattle grunge. A posthumous EP of old Slint material appeared in 1994, by which time Pajo had gone back to art college. He later joined the band Tortoise, reunited with McMahan as the irritatingly named The For Carnation and also worked solo as Papa M. Other members populated various interesting Midwest bands, including Will Oldham's long-running Palace Brothers aggregate.

NL

playlist:

1 Kent *from* Tweez
Dark, brooding alt.rock that points the way to emo. Which isn't their fault.

2 Breadcrumb Trail *from* Spiderland
Wonderfully chiming guitars are set beautifully against McMahan's odd, compelling narrative.

3 Don, a man *from* Spiderland
Moody, whispered lyrics and laid-back strumming builds and builds unbearably: the soundtrack to a nervous breakdown.

4 Washer *from* Spiderland
Quasi-religious lyrics – "Wash yourself in your tears, and build your church on the strength of your faith" – helped make this the most yearning Slint ever sounded.

5 Good Morning, Captain *from* Spiderland
Intense, emotional and dramatic, complete with explosive screams of "I miss you!

Smoosh

The pop world is all too full of child stars, grinning adorably in blissful ignorance of an adulthood of psychological torment to come. Children who are cult heroes of the indie underground, however, are a bizarre rarity. Smoosh are Seattle sisters who released their 2005 debut album when singer and keyboardist Asya was 13 and drummer Chloe was just 11. These days an even

mature voice, a fully grown, wavering thing that captures an adult kind of hurt on tracks such as "Make It Through" and "It's Cold". Childlike spirit comes through on exuberant raps such as "Rad" ("Go play/Maybe football, maybe soccer/Get on a soccer team/You can help them") but these moments of acting their age are rare.

The girls' musical career began when a trip to Seattle's Trading Musician store to buy Chloe a violin ended in a chance encounter with drum teacher Jason McGerr, and the purchase of a $600 drum kit instead. McGerr, who happened to be the drummer in cult rock band Death Cab For Cutie, agreed to give Chloe lessons. It was this connection that would lend the girls their instant indie cred.

When Asya revealed to McGerr that she had been writing songs on her keyboard, he was struck by her natural ability and encouraged the girls to play together. "When we see youth having so much effortless fun creating songs, it rekindles our initial feelings of love for music," he said. A hastily built website and a few scratchy demos later and the gig invitations started to arrive.

Now managed by their refreshingly unpushy parents, a physician and an academic, as they grow older their novelty value is wearing off and all that's left is excellent songs. For now, though, they're still the only group around who think that the coolest thing about rock music is "when you stay in a hotel that has a swimming pool".

DS

younger sibling, Maia, joins their tours on bass. It would be easy to dismiss them as cutesy novelties until you peruse the list of alternative rock luminaries they have supported in concert – Pearl Jam, Cat Power, Bloc Party and Rilo Kiley, to name a few.

These hipsters approve because that album, *She Like Electric*, sounds great even without making allowances for the youth of its composers. Fourteen minimal, warped pop songs that could seem basic are given weight by Asya's

where to start:

1 Massive Cure *from* She Like Electric
The opening track on the girls' debut album immediately proves that these are not just kids messing about. Asya's rough-edged keyboard riffs almost sound like an electric guitar while Chloe pounds primitive drums like a young Meg White.

2 Make It Through *from* She Like Electric
An ice-cold, hypnotic ballad on which Asya manages to channel all the pain and frustration of a struggling love affair, despite not being old enough to have a boyfriend.

Ripe for rediscovery:
The Magnetic Fields'
69 Love Songs

Like the professional gambler's suggestion, "Why don't we make this a bit more interesting?", merely writing a song isn't enough for the endlessly prolific composer Stephin Merritt, a man whose music is as idiosyncratic as the spelling of his forename. Under his Magnetic Fields pseudonym, the New York-based Harvard graduate has written albums on which every track title began with the letter i, and albums on which every instrument, including piano and accordion, gave off noisy feedback. However, he may never trump his greatest self-imposed challenge: the triple-album *69 Love Songs*, an epic collection of odes both for and against romance.

Having received little attention for the music he wrote under the names The Gothic Archies, The 6ths and Future Bible Heroes, Merritt's original plan was to put together one hundred love songs as a gigantic calling card for a possible career in writing musicals. In the end he stopped at a figure arguably more appropriate to the subject matter. Which was still a remarkable feat of large-scale creativity.

For an album by one man on one subject, *69 Love Songs* is incredibly varied. Merritt plays almost 100 instruments (including omnichord, penny whistle and "chicken shakers") and the styles he adopts include country, electronica, reggae and showtunes. There are minute-long throwaway novelties ("The Cactus where your Heart should Be" and "How Fucking Romantic"), there are genuinely moving ballads ("Come Back from San Francisco" and "How To Say Goodbye") and a great deal of humour ("Let's Pretend We're Bunny Rabbits").

Merritt's low, cavernous voice is not for everyone – although fellow vocalists Claudia Gonson and Shirley Simms offer numerous sweeter turns – and his lo-fi, defiantly odd sound takes a little getting used to. But once you're absorbed, exploring this album's many twists and turns is time very well spent.

DS

Spacemen 3

To read their press cuttings, you might imagine that the only interesting thing about Spacemen 3 was their drug consumption. It's an understandable reaction: an early band logo was a syringe and founder member Pete Kember for a time went under the nickname "Mainliner". But while many great bands have been destroyed by drugs, for a time at least, the narcotics fired and fuelled Spacemen 3: without the illegal substances it's unlikely that their hypnotic, shimmering noise could have reached such heights of creativity. A collection of their early demos was titled *Taking Drugs to Make Music to Take Drugs to* and hardcore fans still maintain their music is best listened to in a chemically altered state, although it sounds pretty fine when you are straight, too.

They were inspired by a potent cocktail that ranged from the garage sounds of MC5, the 13th Floor Elevators and the Stooges to the out-there weirdness of Captain Beefheart, Sun Ra and the Silver Apples – with the spectre of the Velvet Underground also looming large. Spacemen 3's droning guitars, feedback, narcoticized vocals and pounding, monolithic rhythms were never going to bring them great commercial success, but they went on to be a huge influence on the entire, vast musical landscape that has loosely come to be termed post-rock.

Formed in 1982 by art students and fellow guitarists Pete Kember and Jason Pierce (or Sonic Boom and J Spaceman, as they preferred to style themselves), the band's line-up changed frequently over the years, and has included Pete Bain, Natty Brooker, Sterling Roswell, Will Carruthers and Jonny Mattock. Spacemen 3 initially struggled to make much impact outside their West Midlands base but they gradually became notorious for the distorted, coma-inducing noise of their live shows, during which they sat on chairs to play, accompanied by a budget light show. Their debut album, *Sound of Confusion*, surfaced in 1986, a blistering assault of pulsating, primal psychedelic rock, laced with a strange but compelling bleakness that led one critic to call it the music of "unlit rooms, unpaid debts and unfeigned terror".

But it was their second album, *The Perfect Prescription*, that established their claim to greatness. Combining a trancey, dream-like quality with their brain-frying guitar noise, the record seemed to replicate the hedonistic drug experience of rush, peak, plateau and crash with uncanny effect on tracks such as "Walking With Jesus", "Feels So Good", "Transparent Radiation", "Take Me to the Other Side" and "Call the Doctor".

By the time of 1989's third album, *Playing with Fire*, the psychedelic drones had grown spacier and more elliptical. Fans are divided over whether this or *The Perfect Prescription* represents their finest hour. *Playing with Fire* is certainly the more unsettling, particularly on "Suicide" – a ten-minute squall of beats and guitars – and on the plaintive cry for salvation of "Lord Can You Hear Me". Then there was "Revolution", Kember's manifesto for drug legalization, which was later covered by Mudhoney, who altered the lyrics to parody Spacemen 3's own drug usage. It was music that was minimalist yet bottomless, angry yet passive, volcanic and yet trance-like at the same time. It was also pretty much the end for Spacemen 3 as a coherent unit.

With the relationship between Pierce and Kember rapidly disintegrating, the group's final album, 1991's *Recurring*, was effectively two different records. On one side, Kember set out the experimental, electronic template for his future solo projects, while on the other Pierce's "Hypnotized" and "Feel So Sad" toyed with the cosmic, orchestral-gospel fantasies he was to pursue with Spiritualized. Pierce has had a higher public profile since Spacemen 3 disintegrated, and several of the albums he has recorded with his band Spiritualized, such as

Lazer Guided Memories, *Ladies and Gentlemen We Are Floating in Space* and *Let it Come Down*, have been commercial successes. *Ladies and Gentlemen...* was the first of his albums to feature a gospel choir, and the core of Spiritualized's appeal resides in the seamless way Pierce integrates the sounds of black American blues and soul with the mesmerism of post-Velvet Underground drone-rock.

Kember's projects, however, have increasingly focused on instrumental electronic music. While his first releases under the Spectrum moniker were recognizably cut from the same cloth as Spacemen 3 – 1960s-style dreamy pop with wall-of-sound production – his recent work has gathered up and extended the threads left by more experimental practitioners of psychedelic electronic music. Kember has collaborated with Eddie Prévost, percussionist and mainstay of AMM, on an album put out under the name EAR (Experimental Audio Research), which also featured Kevin Martin (former member of the band God, better known these days as The Bug) and My Bloody Valentine's guitarist Kevin Shields. The group lived up to its name, their sound a dense, detailed, drone-based noise that followed its own logic.

Kember also made music with Delia Derbyshire, rekindling the public's interest in the former BBC Radiophonic Workshop's extraordinary music. He even played himself in a charming dramatization for radio about the last years of Derbyshire's life. And one of his recent musical collaborations has been with Jim Dickinson (trading under the name Captain Memphis), a legendary American record producer responsible for some classic albums by Screamin' Jay Hawkins and Alex Chilton. Their album, *Indian Giver*, is the bluesiest thing Boom's done, featuring such menacing sub-aquatic boogie as "The Lonesome Death of Johnny Ace", in which 1960s cosmic electronics complement a harmonica-led stomp.

During Spacemen 3's lifespan, their peers and near-contemporaries in the so-called shoegazing scene – such as Slowdive, Ride, the Telescopes and the Pale Saints – all owed them a huge debt. Since their demise, the band's influence has continued to grow. A 1998 tribute album featured the likes of Mogwai and Low, and there has been a steady stream of archival releases, featuring demos and live recordings. The most interesting of them is *Forged Prescriptions*, a two-disc collection from *The Perfect Prescription* sessions, featuring alternate versions of the songs with additional layers of guitars, removed from the original release because the sound could not be reproduced on stage.

It's a long time now since Messrs Boom and Spaceman went their separate ways, but both of their subsequent output has stayed true to the underlying power of pullulating drones and spacey repetition, illuminating the hidden wiring between earthy blues and the music of the spheres.

NW

playlist:

1 Walking With Jesus *from* The Perfect Prescription
Minimal percussion and spatial atmospherics: darkly, disturbingly beautiful.

2 Transparent Radiation *from* The Perfect Prescription
Glistening, textured cover of a Red Krayola classic.

3 Suicide *from* Playing With Fire
Kember once described Spacemen 3's music as the sound of "slashing your wrists and life draining out of you", although this track could also be a tribute to the band of the same name.

4 Revolution *from* Playing With Fire
"I'm so tired of the lot of people in a lot of high places/Who don't want you and me to enjoy ourselves": the Spacemen 3 legalization manifesto.

5 Hypnotized *from* Recurring
The sound of J Spaceman's space-gospel future.

6 An Evening of Contemporary Sitar Music *from* Dreamweapon
Recorded live in 1988, these forty disorientating minutes of drones 'n' tones with the occasional fragmented melody pretty much sum up their performing aesthetic.

Blogger rock:
PR and pioneers

In the 1980s there was College Rock, a quirky, lo-fi strain of music that flourished away from the mainstream thanks to the enthusiasm of American university radio stations, and ultimately made stars of bands such as REM and the Lemonheads. Today a similar alternative musical universe is being created by a handful of passionate amateurs – a universe of Blogger Rock.

We all know what blogging is by now: the practice of telling the world about the monotony of your daily routine via an easily created online diary. So far, so tedious. But around 2003 the first audio blogs appeared: regularly updated websites that raved about music new and old and, most importantly, gave away free MP3 files of songs to download for yourself.

There are now thousands of them out there, mostly in America, and their combined buzz is capable of launching a new band high into the charts. Acts such as Arcade Fire, Arctic Monkeys and Lily Allen owe much of their success to the evangelistic sharing of their early material on blogs such as Stereogum, Fluxblog and Gorilla vs Bear. And while the bloggers' custom of giving away songs is essentially illegal, bloggers generally delete songs a few days later and their readerships are small enough that, for the most part, record companies prefer to encourage their enthusiasm, collaborating in generating early hype for their artists rather than shutting them down.

It's an insular world in which bands can appear to be globally famous long before even the NME has had a sniff at them, where the quirky is celebrated and the mainstream sneered at. Here,

Samuel Beam, aka Iron & Wine

Clap Your Hands Say Yeah

madcap singer-songwriter Sufjan Stevens is a fantasy number one every week, cult artists such as M.I.A., Beirut and Spank Rock are huge stars, and the more inventive British chart pop by Girls Aloud or Rachel Stevens is appreciated by Americans for its musical daring rather than the amount of flesh the performers display.

Some bloggers, such as Said The Gramophone, trade in florid, expressionistic posts that call to mind music journalism's supposed "golden age" of the 1970s, when writers such as Lester Bangs and Nick Kent could cover their favourite bands at vast, self-indulgent length, praising or dismissing with no regard to the power of advertisers. They write differently from today's music journalists because audio blogs don't need to impart the same kind of information. When your readers can listen to the music at the same time as they read your thoughts on it, why bother describing what it sounds like?

On the downside, others barely bother writing anything, simply offering up free music and dashing on to the next thing. It accelerates the discovery of new bands but also the backlash – it's something that Brooklyn's Clap Your Hands Say Yeah discovered. They went from posting their debut album out in the mail themselves in 2005, to finding that their Talking Heads-inspired indie rock was suddenly the hottest sound in the world. Then, astonishingly, there was barely any interest in their second album, *Some Loud Thunder*, less than two years later.

New Yorker Matthew Perpetua, whose excellent Fluxblog is one of the originals, has complained that "a lot of bloggers now don't seem to want to be writers", suggesting that "It's almost like they're trying out for PR jobs." Chris Cantalini, the Dallas-based radio DJ behind Gorilla vs Bear, one of the liveliest blogs on the scene, has given it a more positive slant: "It's become more of a fan-based medium, as opposed to a critical one, which isn't necessarily a bad thing."

Cold War Kids, Californians whose debut album *Robbers & Cowards* featured quality, angsty rock that lived up to the early hype, are gods on the web but rather less famous in the real world, a position they share with Deerhoof, Animal Collective and Of Montreal, whose varied styles, disjointed rhythms and breakneck gear changes are typical of the oddness bloggers like in their rockers. Iron & Wine and Beirut have been heavily blogged, both of them bringing some left-field cool to old-fashioned folk. Just occasionally, major sales figures and blogger love can overlap – Radiohead are adored in this universe even more than they are in the offline world.

For those who want to bypass the amateur ramblings and get straight to the music (ie the majority of us) there are "aggregators", such as Elbo.ws and the Hype Machine, sites which automatically trawl all the blogs and link to them whenever they put up new music. The Hype Machine in particular is an incredible starting point for leaping into this overwhelming world, allowing you see which artists are getting the most attention, or to search for a particular band and then play every song that has been put online in the form of a pseudo-radio station.

Deerhoof

So the fans get a varied, vibrant, consistently fascinating source of new music, the bloggers get an ego-swelling opportunity to have a hand in discovering the next big thing, and the record companies get a cheap way to generate a genuine grassroots fanbase worldwide. If dodgy writing is the only catch, this really may be the future of music.

DS

Yo La Tengo

The mean streets of Hoboken, New Jersey, have made two great contributions to the history of popular music, first as the birthplace of Frank Sinatra and more recently as the home base of Yo La Tengo. They are one of the most influential avant-rock bands of the last twenty years, a fact recognized by the film director Hal Hartley, who has regularly slipped their songs – and even concert posters – into his pictures.

The band was formed by the husband-and-wife team of Ira Kaplan (guitar/vocals) and Georgia Hubley (drums/vocals) in 1984. The name means "I got it!" in Spanish and it's a phrase steeped in American baseball history – in particular an incident during a New York Mets game in 1962. As several of the team only spoke Spanish, "yo la tengo" became the cry used to avoid collisions between fielders going for a catch on the outfield. On this particular occasion it failed to work and after a horrible crashing of heads, one player was left on the deck demanding, "What the hell is a yellow tango?"

Guitarist Dave Schramm and bass player Mike Lewis augmented the line-up on the band's 1986 debut album *Ride the Tiger,* but left soon after. With the arrival of Stephan Wichnewski on bass, Kaplan switched to lead guitar for *New Wave Hot Dogs* (1987) and *President Yo La Tengo* (1989), two critically acclaimed but commercially ignored albums, as the group's trademark sound coalesced around Kaplan's atonal guitar playing and slow, unearthly and mysteriously whispered boho ballads. This early sound was perhaps best captured on "Five Cornered Drone (Crispy Duck)", which appeared on the 1991 mini-album *This Is Yo La Tengo* and has since become a band anthem. The arrival of new bass player James McNew added fresh impetus to their sound, which moved hazily in the direction of My Bloody Valentine's dream-pop on albums such as *Electr-O-Pura* (1995), *Genius+Love=Yo La Tengo* (1997) and *Painful* (2003).

Also worth checking out is McNew's work with his side-project Dump on *A Plea For Tenderness* (1998), a wonderfully idiosyncratic home-recorded mix of camp cover versions, big-band samples and introspective despair. More than two decades on from their debut, Kaplan and Hubley are still making some of the most literate and satisfying music in modern pop, with the continued support of McNew. *And Then Nothing Turned Itself Inside Out* (2000) and *Summer Sun* (2003), a sun-dappled mix of summer pop, bossa nova and dreamy retro-electronica, are as good as anything in their entire career.

The band has also become famous for its huge repertoire of cover songs. Every year they play live for a charity fundraising marathon on the New Jersey radio station WFMU, and in 2006 they released a compilation of the performances entitled *Yo La Tengo Is Murdering the Classics.* Recent covers have included Bob Dylan's "I Wanna Be Your Lover" and "Fourth Time Around", both of which were included on the soundtrack album to the Dylan biopic *I'm Not There.*

NW

LONESOME HIGHWAYS
alternative Americana

Vic Chesnutt

Two events have shaped Vic Chesnutt's life and his music. In 1983, at the age of eighteen, he was playing keyboards in a band called the La De Das. One night he was behind the wheel of his car when drunk and crashed at speed into a ditch. The accident left him confined to a wheelchair and forced a switch from keyboards to guitar, which he learned to play with a pick attached to his arm.

"One hand is paralysed, and the other has big problems so it affects the notes I play and how I play 'em. I'm physically impaired, so I've got to be a little wily," he has said. Strumming simple chords on an acoustic with his newly acquired technique, he began playing and singing solo in the clubs around Athens, Georgia, where Michael Stipe saw him one night at the 40 Watt club. The REM singer was so impressed with Chesnutt's songs and their thrilling juxtaposition of wit, charm and idealism with darker themes of alienation, guilt and remorse, that he suggested recording them and offered to produce.

Recorded in a single day in 1988 at REM's headquarters, the album took two years to find a record company willing to release it, even with the heavyweight backing of Stipe. Titled *Little*, the album was somewhat overshadowed by REM's own contemporaneous blockbuster *Out of Time*, but discerning listeners immediately recognized that Chesnutt was an extraordinary songwriter whose highly literary influences ranged from Lewis Carroll to Franz Kafka via Flannery O'Connor. One song, "Rabbit Box", recalled catching a rabbit and a possum in his childhood and feeling guilty until he set them free. Another, "Mr Riley", told the story of Joan, a newspaper girl who hanged herself. "They found her by the frozen lake/But it wasn't frozen enough to skate," Chesnutt sang unforgettably, in his unsteady voice, "but by the look on her face it must have been awful tempting."

Stipe also produced the follow-up, 1992's *West of Rome*, which was a collection of challenging and nakedly honest songs. The subject matter ranged from jealousy ("Where Were You") to self-loathing ("Stupid Preoccupation"). Chesnutt's idiosyncratic journey continued on 1994's *Drunk*. Its title was due to the fact that Chesnutt was sloshed throughout the recording process and the album included "Dodge", which dealt with his self-destructive tendencies, and several other songs that referenced his accident. "I've gained insights into the human condition from the way I am now, from the times in the hospital and being relegated to handicapped parking spaces," he says. "But I've been writing songs my whole life, even before I was in a wheelchair, so I still think about the same things I did before."

He's continued to record prolifically, and has to date released a dozen albums. A bit part in Billy Bob Thornton's 1995 film *Slingblade* and a tribute album, on which Madonna, Smashing Pumpkins, Garbage and REM performed his songs, raised his profile, and in 2000 Georgia's House of Representatives passed a resolution honouring his "off-beat musical genius". He remains rather *too* off-beat for the mainstream (his 1995 album *Is The Actor Happy?* recently appeared in a list of "twenty critics' favourites that the public hates"), but he deservedly boasts one of the most devoted followings in the labyrinthine backwaters of cultdom.

NW

Classic compilations:
the field recordings of Alan Lomax

Folk music is typically at its best when played by small groups or solo performers – unadorned and not too polished. But the raw power of the songs brought to light by the musicologist Alan Lomax are something else entirely. Keeping it simple has rarely resulted in such potent, beautiful music that is simultaneously so alien and yet so familiar.

From the 1930s onwards, Lomax lugged his 350-pound recording machine across highways and state lines, preserving an extraordinary body of music. First travelling America's deep south with his folklorist father John, and later recording traditional, ancient music as far afield as Ireland, Spain, Italy and India, he captured five thousand hours of ordinary people singing songs that had never been written down – folk sounds that might otherwise have been lost forever.

In the course of their travels he and his father uncovered world-class talent such as the blues singers Leadbelly, Muddy Waters, Jelly Roll Morton and Mississippi Fred MacDowell, as well as Bob Dylan's chief inspiration, Woody Guthrie. Even more impressive was his dedication to the task – he stood in the cotton plantation at the Mississippi State Penitentiary, recording prisoners hollering with only the sound of their tools hitting the dirt for accompaniment. He kept the true identities of many of his discoveries secret for years, because their horrifying tales of abuse by white employers, both spoken and sung, could have got them killed. And occasionally he found himself looking down the barrel of a gun.

Along with fellow American Harry Smith, and Britain's Cecil Sharp and Maud Karpeles, Lomax played a vital role in the preservation of unknown music by ordinary people. Dozens of fine collections of his recordings are available today. Head for the extensive selection of recent reissues by Rounder Records, or Atlantic's four-CD box set *Sounds of the South*.

DS

ALAN LOMAX

Authority on American Folk-Lore . . . Archivist to the Library of Congress . . . Commentator and Artist on "Columbia's School of the Air"

John Fahey

"**I** was creating for myself an imaginary, beautiful world and pretending that I lived there," said the American guitarist John Fahey in one of his last interviews before his death in 2001. It was a world in which country, blues, folk, ragtime, hillbilly, jazz, Episcopal hymns and twentieth-century classical forms were uniquely corralled into a finger-picking style that led to the application of such soubriquets as "the guitarist's guitarist" and "the original American primitive" to Mr Fahey.

Wordless and serene, his music was a meditative elegy for another time and place, the "old weird America" so often vaunted today, which gave his recordings an eerie, haunted quality. Performing his iconoclastic, genre-defying compositions on a steel-string acoustic, his style was unique, although he denied his music was as complex and unusual as it sounded. "It wasn't really that weird from a harmonic, rhythmic standpoint," he said. "It would just touch on these deeper, darker emotions. I wouldn't call myself a great guitar player but I'm an awfully deep one. I play best when my unconscious is altered."

Born in Takoma Park, Maryland, in 1939, he bought his first guitar at the age of fourteen and fell in love with the ghostly sound of the pre-war acoustic blues after a friend played him a Blind Willie Johnson record. It was a moment of epiphany. "I started to feel nauseated so I made him take it off," he later admitted. "But it kept going through my head so I had to hear it again. The second time, I started to cry."

Fahey began collecting old blues 78s, making trips to the South to seek them out. His debut album, *Blind Joe Death*, came out in 1959, purporting to be a collection of lost 78s by an old bluesman, with Fahey's name on one side and that of his fictional creation on the other. He could afford to press only 100 copies. Five got broken in transit and it took him two years to shift the remaining 95. He sold a few, gave others away, placed copies surreptitiously in the racks of local record shops and sent some to folk music scholars, several of whom were reputedly fooled into thinking that there really was an ancient blues singer called Blind Joe Death. His debut was later described by *Rolling Stone* magazine as "the most famous obscure album of recent times". He subsequently re-recorded the album and reprised the character on 1965's *The Transfiguration of Blind Joe Death* and 1987's *I Remember Blind Joe Death*.

Further albums, such as *Death Chants, Breakdowns and Military Waltzes*, *The Great San Bernardino Birthday Party and Other Excursions* and *The Voice of the Turtle* drew not only on the blues but on a wider set of musical influences, including the work of composers such as Bartok, Vaughan Williams and Charles Ives, as he built mantra-like pieces based on his highly unusual guitar tunings. One piece, "Stomping Tonight on the Pennsylvania/Alabama Border", he described as starting with elements of the last movement of Vaughan Williams' "Sixth Symphony", before moving into a Gregorian chant via a Skip James motif.

His albums came accompanied by striking artwork and rambling liner notes, full of stories in which it was hard to disentangle fact from fiction. Such self-mythologizing helped to make Fahey a full-blown, if obscure, cult figure. Inevitably, the only person ever to play him on the radio was John Peel.

As startling a performer as he was, Fahey was also a lot more than that. He wrote a master's thesis on Charley Patton, reviving interest in the forgotten work of Booker "Bukka" White and rediscovering Skip James. Hovering on the fringes of the psychedelic rock scene, he worked with members of Red Crayola, Canned Heat and Spirit and was heard on the soundtrack to the film *Zabriskie Point*. On albums such as *Requia* and *The Yellow Princess*, both recorded for Vanguard in the late 1960s, he built sound collages from such diverse elements as gamelan orchestras, Tibetan chants, animal cries, birdsong and found sounds, such as a singing bridge. He also had some success with his own label Takoma, releasing material by fellow guitar innovators Leo

Kottke and Robbie Basho, although he was forced to sell the label in 1979.

In later years he suffered from ill health and personal problems and by the early 1990s he had allegedly pawned his guitars. A spate of reissues and his championing by such alt.rock luminaries as Sonic Youth and Jim O'Rourke revived interest in his oeuvre and he resumed recording. He also used an inheritance that he received on the death of his father to start Revenant Records, on which he released old blues and other obscure material, including a Grammy-winning seven-disc retrospective of Charley Patton and his contemporaries. His record label had a fitting name: Fahey's entire life's work seemed to be the persistent bringing back of forgotten strains, in strange and haunting forms.

NW

playlist:

1 In Christ There Is No East or West *from* The Legend of Blind Joe Death

2 Give Me Cornbread When I'm Hungry *from* The Dance of Death and Other Plantation Favourites

3 Stomping Tonight on the Pennsylvania/ Alabama Border *from* Death Chants, Breakdowns and Military Waltzes

4 Sunflower River Blues *from* Death Chants, Breakdowns and Military Waltzes

5 Dance of the Inhabitants of the Palace of King Phillip XIV of Spain *from* Death Chants, Breakdowns and Military Waltzes

6 Fare Forward Voyagers *from* Fare Forward Voyagers

Handsome Family

There are few starker and more compelling contemporary exponents of what Greil Marcus called the "old, weird America" than the Handsome Family, whose Southern gothic backwoods music has created an entire sub-genre of alt.country that is all their own. They are endlessly fascinated by the precarious mystery of

Rennie, a sometime fiction writer from Long Island, is one half of the Family. The other is her husband Brett Sparks, who hails from Texas, where he studied music and had a spell working on oil rigs. They've been married for over twenty years and started making music together in the early 1990s, when Brett persuaded Rennie to write some lyrics for him. The result was their 1995 debut album, *Odessa*, recorded in the front parlour of their Chicago home. Rockier than any of their subsequent outings, it made little impact, apart from a radio ban on a typically dark murder ballad about a woman who gets bludgeoned to death. The follow-up *Milk and Scissors* was more rooted in traditional country and old-time folk music and led to a tour with Wilco and their first visit to Europe. Their progress, however, was slowed when Brett suffered a breakdown and was diagnosed as a manic-depressive and hospitalized. *Through the Trees* (1998) was written and recorded during his recovery, an intense set of songs that laid bare the misery of the human condition with Rennie's intimately raw and emotional lyrics delivered by Brett in a deadpan, fatalistic baritone. Despite – or perhaps because of – its morose tone, it was their breakthrough album, enabling them both to give up their day jobs and focus on music full time. *In the Air* (2000) had a lighter, more spacious sound with Rennie's lyrics growing ever more surreal. The couple then moved to Albuquerque, New Mexico, where they have continued to craft their uniquely unruffled, paradoxically graceful music, and the splendidly titled *Last Days of Wonder*, from 2006, had

mortality – for them, the worst is always yet to come. That's not to say that their stark, dark and lowering music is not flecked with flashes of breathtaking beauty. It's just that, in the words of lyricist Rennie Sparks: "if you are going to believe that there is some inherent order to the universe, you have to accept that this order includes not only rainbows and kittens but also gas chambers and the Black Death."

a strange and dreadful beauty.

Steeped in magic realism, the Handsome Family claim angels can he heard "whispering inside potatoes and from the curling leaves of blooming plants". Their songs inhabit a world that is enchantingly bizarre; their stories are eerie, haunting, dark and elemental.

NW

Holy Modal Rounders

Many of the acts in this book missed out on mainstream fame due to bad luck, being ahead of their time, or because their record company failed to understand or promote them. The Holy Modal Rounders never enjoyed commercial success because their brand of dippy psychedelic folk was simply too weird, eccentric and out-there to appeal to anyone other than a cult audience of similarly off-the-wall oddballs and outsiders. What's more, they were proud to be freaks and boasted that their approach to music-making was "really bent". They were also capable of making a quite glorious racket, even if they are still something of an acquired taste. A listen to the only Rounders song ever to escape the underground – that's them singing "Bird Song" on the *Easy Rider* soundtrack – gives you an idea of their flavour.

It might all have been even odder. The group's first name was the Total Quintessence Stomach Pumpers, followed by the Temporal Worth High Steppers, before they settled on the Total Modal Rounders. When they were stoned one day, the name got accidentally twisted into the Holy Modal Rounders. It was, as founder member and driving force Peter Stampfel noted, a very "practical way to get named".

The band came out of New York's fertile Greenwich Village scene when Stampfel got together in 1963 with Steve Weber. From the outset their intention was to give the folk revival – which in the hands of Pete Seeger and his buddies could be somewhat po-faced – a subversive twist. The duo's weapons ranged from the strange and surreal to the plain silly. They didn't really care, as long as they got under the skin of the old guard.

The Rounders' self-titled 1964 debut album is famous for the first use of the term "psychedelic" in popular music: "Got my psycho-delic feet, in my psycho-delic shoes, I believe lordy mama got the psycho-delic blues" they sang on "Hesitation Blues". Stampfel explained his cavalier attitude to traditional song in the liner notes: "I made up new words to it because it was easier than listening to the tape and writing the words down." How he must have enjoyed imagining Pete Seeger turning puce with rage when he wrote that.

Following the release of their second album in 1965, Stampfel and Weber briefly hooked up with Ed Sanders and Tuli Kupferberg in The Fugs, who were on a similar mission to subvert the rock world by letting their freak flag fly (try "Kill For Peace" or "Group Grope"). The Fugs recorded a couple of the Rounders' outré songs – Weber's "Boobs a Lot" and Stampfel's "New Amphetamine Shriek" – but the pair soon re-formed the Rounders with new members Lee Crabtree and playwright Sam Shepard on drums, the line-up which recorded the wonderfully chaotic *Indian War Whoop* in 1967.

At this point, Jac Holzman took the gamble of signing them to Elektra. If he imagined that he could sell them to the folk mainstream, he had underestimated their perversity. True to form they turned in the totally outlandish *The Moray Eels Eat the Holy Modal Rounders*. Holzman's one commercial success was to sell "Bird Song" (basically Ray Price's "You Done Me Wrong" with lysergically altered lyrics) to the makers of *Easy Rider*. But drug-addled ramblings such as "The Mind Capsized" and "The STP Song" ensured that the album failed to reach a mass audience and that was the end of the Rounders' brief association with Elektra.

There were still a few more bizarre twists to come in the Rounders' tale, though, including the wonderfully titled *Good Taste Is Timeless*, engineered in Nashville by Sun Records legend Scotty Moore, who played guitar on "That's All Right", improbably providing a link between Elvis Presley and The Fugs and making the Holy Modal Rounders the answer to the ultimate pop trivia quiz question.

NW

playlist:

1 The Bird Song *from* The Moray Eels Eat the Holy Modal Rounders
Mad, bad and irresistible acid folk.

2 The STP Song *from* The Moray Eels Eat the Holy Modal Rounders
And it didn't have anything to do with motor oil.

3 Boobs a Lot *from* Good Taste Is Timeless
"Do you like boobs a lot? Yes, I like boobs a lot, boobs a lot, boobs a lot. You gotta like boobs a lot." I think we get the point.

4 New Amphetamine Shriek *from* Virgin Fugs
Not a Motörhead song – but perhaps it should have been.

5 Hesitation Blues *from* Holy Modal Rounders
"Hear song, forget song, try to remember song while adding your personal wrinkles – bingo!" wrote Stampfel in the sleeve notes. Which perhaps explains how the term "psychedelic" ended up in a song published in 1915.

Great lost albums:
The Beach Boys' Adult/Child

Had this book been published five years ago, this page would undoubtedly have been devoted to *Smile*, at the time the most famous unfinished and unreleased album in rock history. Then in 2004, Brian Wilson teamed up with original collaborator Van Dyke Parks to complete the project and the re-recorded *Brian Wilson Presents Smile* appeared, receiving almost universal five-star reviews. Yet the Beach Boys' history is smeared with unreleased and discarded records and after *Smile*, perhaps the most sought-after is 1977's *Adult/Child*.

More a Brian Wilson solo project than a full-scale Beach Boys album, by 1976 the band's troubled genius had rediscovered his appetite for the recording studio and by the end of the year had completed almost enough material for two new albums. *The Beach Boys Love You* (originally titled *Brian Loves You*) appeared in May 1977, by which time Wilson was already back in the studio working on an album called *Adult/Child*, a title reportedly dreamed up by the controversial psychiatrist Gene Landy (who Wilson thanked on his debut solo album for saving his life). Four of the tracks were recycled from the surfeit of material the previous year. Another, "Shortenin' Bread" with Brian on bass vocal and brother Carl on lead, came from 1973. The rest was newly recorded. Several tracks were in a big band style with arrangements by Dick Reynolds, who had done the same job on the Beach Boys' 1964 *Christmas Album*.

A number were covers ("Deep Purple", "My Diane", "On Broadway" and "You've Lost That Loving Feeling") but there are some extraordinary Wilson originals too, including "H.E.L.P. Is On the Way" (which includes the line "doughy lumps, stomach pumps, enemas too/That's what you get when you eat that way"), "Hey Little Tomboy" ("Little tomboy, sit here on my lap"), "Life Is for the Living" ("don't sit around on your ass smoking grass") and "Still I Dream of It". The last was written by Wilson either for Elvis Presley or Stevie Wonder – he's claimed both at different times – but neither ever recorded it. The album was widely publicized as the next Beach Boys release, but fell foul first of a serious group fall-out over the big band tracks and was then rejected anyway by Reprise as "too erratic". It's easy to hear why they reached that conclusion, but more than three decades on it has a quirky charm and goofy unpredictability that perfectly reflects the album's title and presents a fascinating – if slightly painful – picture of the rather strange place Brian Wilson was at in the 1970s.

NW

Ripe for rediscovery:
Neil Young's
Tonight's the Night

After mainstream success with Crosby, Stills, Nash & Young, and a number one solo album in the shape of 1972's *Harvest*, Neil Young famously noted that when you find yourself travelling in the middle of the road, it's time to head for the ditch. He duly followed *Harvest* with the totally uncommercial *Time Fades Away* and then planned to unleash an even darker exploration of the twilight of his soul called *Tonight's the Night*. His horrified record company told him he was chucking his career onto the bonfire and persuaded him to release *On the Beach* instead.

Tonight's the Night would not be denied, however, and it eventually appeared in 1975, two years after it was recorded. A stark and startling expression of his grief following the death from heroin overdoses of Crazy Horse guitarist Danny Whitten and roadie Bruce Berry, critics and fans alike were shocked by the album's nakedness and emotional honesty. The album's dozen tracks found Young sounding alternately abrasive, manic, strung-out and "too wasted" to write his own tune, as he admitted in the lyrics of "Borrowed Tune", set to the melody of the Rolling Stones' "Lady Jane". On "Mellow My Mind", his voice cracks and breaks and wanders hopelessly off key. Instead of sounding embarrassing, the effect is utterly transfixing.

Yet the album is more than a moving wake for two friends who died from overdoses. It becomes an epitaph for an America that has lost its moral compass in the killing fields of Vietnam and on the mean streets of its own inner cities. Described by Young affectionately as "the black sheep" in his musical family, *Tonight's the Night* was the least commercially successful release of his early career. But it's also one of the edgiest and most absorbing records he ever made.

NW

Albert Lee

When it comes to compiling lists – that favourite occupation of male rock'n'roll fans of a certain age – any reckoning of the best British electric guitarists usually begins with Clapton, Page and Beck, followed perhaps by Green, Kossoff and Keith Richards. Suggest that the list should include Albert Lee and it's as likely as not that you will be asked if you mean Alvin Lee, plank-spanker for the band Ten Years After. It's a confusion that has dogged Albert for much of his career, with Alvin even being erroneously credited on albums that his near-namesake played on.

But many of his fellow musicians will tell you that Albert Lee is the most talented British axeman of them all, the ultimate guitarist's guitar-player, and a man often known simply as "Mr Telecaster" for his expertise on his chosen instrument. Lee's numerous music-celeb fans include Eric Clapton, in whose band he played for five years. Emmylou Harris once said the following: "When St Peter asks me to chronicle my time down here on earth, I'll be able to say – with pride if that's allowed – that for a while I played rhythm guitar in a band with Albert Lee."

So why is he not a household name? First, perhaps, because he's essentially a country guitarist, whereas most of the other top British names in the field have tended to work in the blues idiom. Secondly, he is famously said to be the only lead guitarist in rock music without an ego. And thirdly, living in America since the 1970s, much of his finest work has been as a sideman, bringing his immaculate licks and peerless tone to the records of others – although he has of course also produced some cracking albums with his own bands, particularly the influential but neglected early-1970s country rockers Head, Hands & Feet.

Born in 1943, Albert Lee grew up in south London and studied piano before switching to guitar in 1958. After a decade on the circuit playing with Chris Farlowe and The Thunderbirds, among others, he formed Head, Hands & Feet, a pioneering British country-rock band. Their debut album included "Country Boy", an extraordinary showcase for Lee's breakneck technique which inspired a generation of Nashville pickers. It also impressed Emmylou Harris enough for her to ask him to replace James Burton in her Hot Band.

After that came a half-decade tenure with Clapton, a gig as the Everly Brothers' musical director and sessions with everyone from bluegrass legend Earl Scruggs to the superstar diva of country, Dolly Parton. Not bad for a country boy from London SE3.

NW

"The clever one in the woolly hat..."

Michael Nesmith

After leaving the world's first manufactured boy band, former Monkee Mike Nesmith reinvented himself as a cosmic cowboy and a pioneer of country-rock. The trilogy of albums he recorded with the First National Band are rated as highly by the critics today as anything that the more credible Gram Parsons created. At the time it seemed such an improbable reinvention that many were not even prepared to listen, let alone forgive Nesmith his bubblegum past. There was one infamous early FNB gig in 1970, supporting the Flying Burrito Brothers. The two bands actually had a lot in common but, rather than discovering any kind of musical camaraderie, the Burritos laughed out loud at them.

With the benefit of hindsight, it's easy to see that Nesmith never quite fitted into the Monkees. The clever one in the woolly hat, he never really played the pop game as the group's Hollywood puppet masters demanded, and it was Nesmith who blew the whistle on the fact that the band were not allowed to play any instruments on their early records. He contributed more songs than the others to the hit Monkees albums but musically he was always the outsider. "There was no reception within the Monkees for my music at all," he recalled in 2008. "My songs, my singing, were perceived as liabilities in the effort to create pop records." The two songs he managed to smuggle onto the Monkees' 1966 debut album, "Papa Gene's Blues" and "Sweet Young Thing" showed him already trying to forge a pre-Gram Parsons country-rock hybrid.

In 1968, around the time the Byrds were cutting *Sweetheart of the Rodeo,* Nesmith recorded an album's worth of songs in Nashville with the cream of country's top session players. He was still a member of the Monkees at the time, and most of the tracks remained unreleased until the 1990s. But when you listen to Nesmith's 1960s songs you hear what could have been a great, pioneering early country-rock album.

When he finally left the Monkees in 1970, Nesmith formed the First National Band with drummer John Ware, bassist John London and pedal-steel supremo Red Rhodes. The band stayed together for little more than a year but in that time they recorded and released three classic albums. *Magnetic South* was a brilliant debut, combining honky-tonk ballads, country-pop, southern soul and much more besides; *Loose Salute* was even more adventurous. By *Nevada Fighter,*

however, the FNB was on the point of falling apart. Side one featured some of the band's strongest moments, on the title track, "Propinquity" and "Grand Ennui". Side two featured Nesmith backed by Elvis Presley sidemen, some of whom went on to join him in the Second National Band, who recorded the excellent *Tantamount to Treason* in 1972. Sadly, there was nobody listening and the records sold pitifully. Nesmith simply couldn't get the Monkees off his back, as it were. "The National Band was ignored. I don't recall any compliment or encouragement," he says today, without bitterness but with an understandable regret. By the 1980s his recordings had become increasingly sporadic and idiosyncratic. Nevertheless, his work with the FNB continues to stand as some of the finest, most inventive and criminally underrated country-rock ever recorded.

NW

Great lost albums:
Bruce Springsteen's
The Ties That Bind

After hitting pay-dirt in 1975 with *Born to Run*, a protracted legal battle with his first manager Mike Appel meant that it took Bruce Springsteen three years to get the follow-up, 1978's *Darkness On the Edge of Town*, into record stores. During that time he was writing prolifically and, once *Darkness* eventually appeared, Springsteen found himself with a backlog of great songs that hadn't made the cut, including "Independence Day", "Point Blank", "Ramrod" and "Sherry Darling". He resolved that after the long, enforced silence he was going to rush out his next album as quickly as was possible, and called in The E Street Band for sessions in May 1979, at which he worked up a bunch of songs in double-quick time, many of them in a classic, upbeat, three-minute-jukebox-single style. By September that year, an album titled *The Ties That Bind* had been mixed and mastered and was ready to go. The tight, peppy set included ten songs: "The Ties That Bind", "Cindy", "Hungry Heart", "Stolen Car", "Be True", "The River", "You Can Look (But You Better Not Touch)", "The Price You Pay", "I Wanna Marry You" and "Loose Ends".

At the last minute Springsteen got cold feet, believing that the album was too poppy and lightweight, even frivolous. According to biographer Dave Marsh, the feeling was fuelled

by an appearance at the anti-nuclear Musicians United for Safe Energy concert at New York's Madison Square Garden in late September. Hit by the weighty issues behind the concert, he decided he needed to make a bigger statement, and went back into the studio, eventually emerging a year later with the sprawling double album, *The River*.

Some of the songs from *The Ties That Bind* were re-recorded for the double album but bootlegs show that several of the original versions are almost unrecognizable from the songs that eventually turned up on *The River*. "You Can Look", for example, was originally recorded as a screaming rockabilly number and "Stolen Car" had an appealing folk-rock feel. Other changes were less radical but still fundamentally altered the tone: the version of the haunting "Price You Pay" on *The River* lost a verse and the vocal on the re-recorded "The Ties That Bind" conveyed a quite different atmosphere and mood. Other songs such as "Be True", "Loose Ends" and the wonderful, jangling romance of "Cindy" were lost in the shuffle. Several of the cast-offs were later released as part of the box set *Tracks*. But if he hadn't gone and got all serious on us, *The Ties That Bind* could easily have been one of the most joyous in Springsteen's entire canon, one that could have best lived up to his own definition of rock'n'roll as "this joy, this certain happiness that is in its way the most beautiful thing in life."

NW

Will Oldham

Will Oldham remains one of the most mysterious figures in contemporary American music. He rarely grants interviews and strongly resents the intrusion of the outside world into his life. "What are interviews for?" he complained during one rare encounter with the media. "They have nothing to do with the music. It's usually people asking a bunch of weird questions like, 'Why are the songs so slow?' Well, maybe because they are. Because that's how we play them. Because I wrote them at a less rapid pace. It's always why, why, why?"

Under a series of different names – Palace, Palace Music, Palace Songs and Bonnie Prince Billy – he's recorded a dozen albums over the last fifteen years. The various pseudonyms, he insists, are not to throw us off his scent but to "allow both the audience and the performer to have a relationship with the performed that is valid and unbreakable."

Born in Louisville, Kentucky, in 1970, as a youth he attended drama classes and enjoyed a teenage career as a film actor – although "enjoyed" is hardly the right word. He walked off the set one day and never went back, writing his agent a letter saying he'd quit. He next turned up in Czechoslovakia, where he had some kind of mental breakdown. When he'd recovered, he began a new career making a kind of deathless American music that manages to sound new and startling in its emotional intensity while drawing deep on a vernacular tradition of murder ballads, stern, unforgiving gospel, demonic blues, dust-blown folk and old, weird country.

His early albums, *There Is No-One what will Take Care of You* and *Days in the Wake*, were credited to Palace Brothers, and sound fragile and ramshackle, like they were made in a backwoods shed. Perhaps they were: the first cost a grand total of $950 to record and the second just $350. The third, *Viva Last Blues* (1995), released under the name Palace Music, was produced by Steve Albini. Louder and more electrified, it was fevered and raucous but at the same time dark, intimate and claustrophobic. "He doesn't rehearse," Albini later noted of Oldham's methods. "He chooses the people he's going to play with shortly before the session, so everyone is playing by the seat of their pants, and the music is at constant risk, subject to the weaknesses of whoever's in the room."

The oddball *Arise Therefore* was released under the abbreviated name Palace in 1996, and it included such "love songs" as "You Have Cum in Your Hair" and "Your Dick Is Hanging Out". Oldham then abandoned his various Palace guises and adopted the persona of Bonnie Prince Billy. Since then he's pursued a singular path as an outsider, an auteur of American song who has taken such timeless themes as death and despair, spiritual decay and carnal sin and refashioned them for the modern world. His first release as Bonnie Prince Billy, 1999's *I See a Darkness*, was an astonishing record of gentle, trembling awe and haunted, lonely beauty: it's a measure of the album's gravity that Johnny Cash later covered the title track. *Ease Down the Road*, from 2001, was less foreboding, and Oldham sounded almost jaunty in places on a set of songs about infidelity and lust. "She likes to go down on me/And I like to go down on her too," he croaked on "A King at Night". *Master and Everyone* was Will back at his starkest and most disarmingly beautiful, a 35-minute masterful set of parables about love and fear.

Collaborations with Matt Sweeney and Tortoise gave him the wiggle room to experiment before he delivered another masterpiece in 2006's *The Letting Go*, a lusher set recorded in Iceland and backed in places by a string quartet. Then, with characteristic perversity, came a quixotic set of covers entitled *Ask Forgiveness* in 2007. It documented his improbable takes on songs by such outré talents as R. Kelly and Björk, among others, with Oldham taking their pulse and then pumping his own blood and soul into them.

NW

playlist:

1 I See a Darkness *from* I See a Darkness
Whether you prefer Oldham's original version or Johnny Cash's splendid cover, this is spellbinding stuff.

2 Ain't You Wealthy, Ain't You Wise? *from* Master and Everyone
A duet with Marty Slayton that recalls the glory days of Gram and Emmylou.

3 The Brute Choir *from* Viva Last Blues
Oldham at his warmest, with improbable help from Steve Albini.

4 No Bad News *from* The Letting Go
A classic modern-day folk song inspired by the devastating tsunami of Boxing Day, 2004.

5 Then The Letting Go *from* The Letting Go
Another exquisite duet, featuring the lovely voice of Faun Fables' Dawn McCarthy.

Doug Sahm

At the age of eleven in 1952, "Little" Doug Sahm sat on the knee of Hank Williams in what turned out to be the last concert the "drifting cowboy" played. Already proficient on steel guitar, mandolin and violin, he'd also made his first country record, *A Real American Joe*. Yet it was as the leader of the "British invasion" beat group the Sir Douglas Quintet in the mid-1960s that he first tasted major success with the top twenty single "She's about a Mover".

The Quintet weren't really British, of course. But at the time real American Joes couldn't buy their way into the US charts and so the deft change of nationality was dreamed up by the band's label to capitalize on the mania for British groups in the wake of The Beatles. Inevitably the scam was soon exposed – whether Sahm's Texan accent or the fact that two-fifths of the Quintet were Mexican was the biggest giveaway is a moot point. Early publicity photos attempted to obscure questions of ethnic origin by showing the band in silhouette.

Surprisingly, there was little backlash against the deception: the "joke" was taken by fans and the industry in good part and, after moving to San Francisco, Sahm and the Quintet had another hit with the contagious, country-tinged psych-pop of "Mendicino".

Ironically, it would have been hard for any musician to be closer to his lone star roots than Sahm. A Texan born and bred, he grew up in San Antone and had absorbed every kind of Southern American music, including not only country, but Western swing, honky-tonk, blues, roadhouse R&B, Cajun and Mexican styles. In 1971, he returned to Texas and began to fuse them all into a wonderful melange that today tends to get branded as country-rock but was actually much more than that.

His 1973 album, *Doug Sahm and Friends*, was a relaxed but near-perfect distillation of Texan musical forms, lifted up by the presence of Dr John, the legendary Tex-Mex accordion player Flaco Jimenez and Bob Dylan, who even gave him the unreleased song "Wallflower" and duetted with him on it. Sahm continued making great but underrated records right up until his death in New Mexico in 1999. Just a glance at his album titles – *Texas Rock for Country Rollers* and *Juke Box Music*, for instance – will give you an idea of their flavour. In 1990 he teamed up with Freddy Fender, Jimenez and former Sir Douglas keyboardist Augie Meyer in the roots music supergroup The Texas Tornados. Not bad for a fake Brit from Dixie.

NW

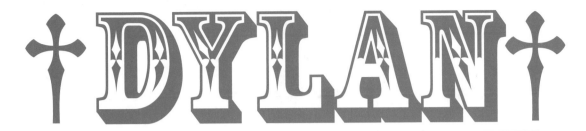

Great lost albums:
Bob Dylan and Johnny Cash's Nashville duets

Many hardcore Bob Dylan fans didn't quite know what to make of it when he recorded *Nashville Skyline*. In hip rock'n'roll circles at the time, country was seen as the music of rednecks and bigots, so what was Dylan doing making a country album? Was it a sell-out, a cop-out, a contemptuous disowning of his old fans – or actually a sincere engagement with music that he loved? Had the album of duets with Johnny Cash he recorded around the same time ever been released, then fans might have been even more bemused.

Dylan and Cash had first met in 1963 and at the Newport Folk Festival of 1964 they had spent a night in a hotel room trading songs with each other. Cash was moved enough to ceremonially give Dylan his guitar when dawn broke. Yet it was not until 17 February 1969, on the third day of the *Nashville Skyline* sessions, that they got to record together. As they were sharing adjoining studios at Columbia's Music Row studios, Cash decided to gatecrash Dylan's session. The Man in Black and his band, featuring rockabilly pioneer Carl Perkins, sat in for two days and together they cut more than twenty tracks, including such Cash classics as "Big River", "I Walk the Line" and "Ring of Fire", Carl Perkins's "Matchbox" and Dylan's "Don't Think Twice It's All Right", "One Too Many Mornings" and "Girl from the North Country". Despite planning to release a duets album, only the last song has ever officially seen the light of day when it appeared on *Nashville Skyline*, to which Cash also contributed the liner notes.

So why was the album shelved? The answer appears to be that the expectations raised by such an epochal summit were unrealistically high and, on playing back the tapes, Dylan and Cash concluded that fans would be disappointed by the results. Listening to one of the many available bootlegs of the sessions induces mixed reactions. The recordings are loose to the point where at times they fall apart. After an attempt at "Just a Closer Walk With Thee" peters out, Cash turns to Dylan and asks: "What's one you know, Bob?" At the same time, some of the playing sounds stiff and stilted, the Nashville session crew running through familiar by-the-numbers routines. Dylan and Cash also sound cautious, as if they're afraid of treading on each other's toes.

On the other hand, it's a unique and historic moment. Kris Kristofferson likens it to two forks of lightning meeting: a flawed but fascinating portrait of two friends who just happened to be among the giants of twentieth-century popular song trying to figure each other out.

NW

Sparklehorse

Not so much a band as something that happens in Mark Linkous's head, everything in Sparklehorse's career seems to have occurred by chance. As a teenager, Linkous formed his first band, Dancing Hoods, and left his home in Richmond, Virginia, for Los Angeles with dreams of punk-rock stardom in his head. He swiftly decided he hated the music industry and everything that went with it. "I was as bored as shit with the idea of trying to make a rock record and getting signed," he later recalled. "And then somebody played me a Tom Waits record."

That was enough to persuade him to return to Virginia, where he joined a band which he says played nothing but "300-year-old Irish songs" and discarded everything he thought he knew about music. "That period was about abandoning a lot of things and just starting from scratch and learning how to write again," he says.

His ideas started to coalesce when friend and former Camper Van Beethoven frontman David Lowery left his eight-track recorder at Linkous's home while he went on tour with Cracker. Linkous started playing around with the equipment, taught himself how to record, and when Lowery came back to collect his gear two years later, Sparklehorse had been born.

When Linkous signed to Capitol he was working as a chimney-sweep and a house-painter. His recording deal happened by chance when a girl at the record company played his demo to the president of the company. He recorded the debut album at his Static King home studio on his rented Virginia farm, the sound of the cows in the neighbouring field frequently prompting unscheduled halts in the recording process. When the lowing herd had finally allowed him to finish the record, he decided to call it *vivadixiesubmarinetransmissionplot* and it was released in 1995.

Thom Yorke heard the album, loved its ragged beauty and invited Linkous to support Radiohead on tour. On the London date, demonstrating a characteristic ability to snatch disaster from the jaws of victory, he followed up the concert by accidentally overdosing on a combination of anti-depressants, sleeping pills, heroin and alcohol in his hotel room. He was not discovered until fourteen hours later, unconscious and with his legs pinned underneath him, the circulation cut off. When medics attempted to straighten his legs, the procedure triggered a heart attack.

Doctors initially told him amputation would be necessary but after a three-month stay in hospital and seven operations, they were saved. Unable to walk, for a time he performed from a wheelchair. Later he graduated to leg braces but he spent two years on morphine medication. His near-death experience, of course, provided him with some great material for his second album *Good Morning Spider*. The distorted, melancholic beauty and the tortured power of his songs, not to mention the poignancy of his life's experiences, brought him to the attention of the likes of P.J. Harvey, Tom Waits and the Cardigans' Nina Persson, all of whom volunteered their services for his third album, *It's A Wonderful Life*.

Like his first two albums, it failed to sell and he lost his record deal. Disillusioned and depressed, he lost the desire to

perform and announced that he'd given up music. His mental state continued to fray and he sank back into drug addiction until concerned friends decided that only a major intervention could save him from himself. They relocated him to a rural property in North Carolina where there were no drug dealers and the idea of recording again slowly returned. Finally, after a five-year hiatus, came *Dreamt for Light Years in the Belly of a Mountain*, produced by Brian "Danger Mouse" Burton, of Gnarls Barkley fame.

Given his fragile equilibrium, you get the impression that success and its accompanying celebrity would only add to Linkous's well-documented problems. He seems to know it, too. When he was supporting REM, the band offered encouragement by telling him that if he stuck at it he could be as big as they were. When he thought about it, he realized that he hated the idea. Fortunately for him, Sparklehorse's admirers remain a private members club.

NW

playlist:

1 Someday I Will Treat You Good *from* vivadixiesubmarinetransmissionplot
Tortured, powerful and unforgettable.

2 Pig *from* Good Morning Spider
Linkous rocks out in frustration at his post-accident predicament.

3 Sick of Goodbyes *from* Good Morning Spider
The song was co-written by Linkous and originally recorded by the band Cracker, but this Sparklehorse version is the definitive one.

4 Gold Day *from* It's a Wonderful Life
Lovely, childlike Beatles-esque psychedelia.

5 Piano Fire *from* It's a Wonderful Life
The Tom Waits collaboration on the third album is disappointing, but there's compensation in this fantastic duet with P.J. Harvey, which, despite the title, is full of distorted guitars and subtle electronics.

Gillian Welch

"Gillian writes with what at first seems to be childlike simplicity, but on closer listening, you realize you are in the presence of an old soul, one who knows the blue highways of the heart... it is a gift to all of us who need music to be more than just background noise."

Emmylou Harris on Gillian Welch

Y ou will probably find Gillian Welch filed in your local record store alongside Shania Twain in the rack marked "Country". In reality, the two inhabit completely different universes. Welch's records sound like they belong to an era when records were made of shellac and played on a wind-up gramophone.

With her Depression-era gingham cotton dresses and drawn-back hair, she looks like she's escaped from an Appalachian back porch or a Carter Family sepia portrait of the 1930s. Yet in many ways she's an unlikely champion of old-time country music and down-home hillbilly values. For Welch is a born-and-bred city girl who has never roped a steer in her life.

Born in New York City and adopted at birth (a subject she has often referred to in songs such as "Orphan Girl" and "No-One Knows My Name"), she was raised in Los Angeles, where her adoptive parents worked as the musical directors of the 1970s TV programme *The Carol Burnett Show*. She was given a guitar for her eighth birthday and began taking lessons, but it was not until she went to college to study photography that she first heard bluegrass. It was a band called the Harmony Grits that was her epiphany, leading her onto the music of the Carter Family, the Stanley Brothers and bluegrass king Bill Monroe.

She moved to Boston, to study at Berklee School of Music, and there she met the phenomenal guitarist David Rawlings. His style, while recognizably that of an accomplished country and bluegrass picker, is full of unusual dissonances and sophisticated turns. Welch has played with him ever since, and the pair moved to Nashville in 1992. Her 1996 debut, the aptly titled *Revival*, was a quiet masterpiece. The songs were mostly originals, but they found their inspiration in pre-World War II subject matter such as rural poverty, illicit moonshine stills and the most god-fearing kind of Christianity. Yet she never sounded fake or affected.

When it came to the soundtrack of the Coen Brothers' time-warped 1997 film *O Brother Where Art Thou?*, Welch was a shoo-in. She contributed "Didn't Leave Nobody But the Baby" and "I'll Fly Away" and ended up making a cameo

appearance. On a series of albums since then her music has just gone on getting sharper. Sepulchral bluegrass balladry may be their trademark but Welch and Rawlings have extended their art into Patsy Cline-like shuffles, sultry country-rock and homages to Elvis. Her spare, keening voice, unadorned honesty and dark and sombre songs render utterly irrelevant the doubts of the folk purists who have questioned her "authenticity".

NW

LOST SOUL
fraught funk and wronged R&B

Terry Callier

Other singers from Chicago's housing projects, such as Terry Callier's childhood friend Curtis Mayfield, set out to reshape contemporary soul by blending music with social comment. Callier, however, was initially less certain of his musical direction. At seventeen he signed first with Chess Records, for one single, then switched to Prestige and finished an album. While he waited for it to be pressed, his producer, the legendary Samuel Charters, went walkabout with the master tapes. It took four years for *The New Folk Sound of Terry Callier*, a mix of covers and traditional American folk songs, to appear. It was barely noticed by record buyers.

An infatuation with the hallowed jazz of John Coltrane gave Callier new impetus and, now signed to Chess offshoot Cadet Concept, he set about making a follow-up to *The New Folk Sound*. The shamefully neglected 1972 album *Occasional Rain* and its equally overlooked companion *What Color Is Love?*, with its seductive cover, were a revelation: this was rich, sophisticated and spiritual music. "Dancing Girl", the epic, nine-minute opener for *What Color Is Love?* took Callier's music into the stratosphere.

But his "boogie, bop or boogaloo", to quote one of his lines, failed to excite buyers and he parted company with Cadet in the mid-1970s. In 1983 he was granted custody of his twelve-year-old daughter and her welfare became his main priority. Anxious for a regular income and paid vacations, he abandoned his recording career for a job in computers at the University of Chicago. His albums had never sold too well, often falling between the twin stools of jazz and soul, and, despite belated acclaim for a handful of releases,

he refused to return to the music. The calls from record companies soon tailed off.

Eventually his past caught up with him. Britain's Acid Jazz label (and scene) was founded on obscure soul and jazz back catalogues and new acts influenced by them: an obvious place to look was Terry Callier. In 1989, one song in particular, "I Don't Want to See Myself (Without You)" was all over the London dance floors. A remix appeared in the spring of 1990; gradually the royalties resumed and the phone started ringing again. Callier was, once more, a name to check. His comeback was confirmed in 1998 with a much lauded album on Verve entitled *TimePeace*. Callier remains a reluctant soul man, however. "Since I walked out of the music business," he explained in the late 1990s, "I have not been knocking on too many doors trying to get back in."

Callier's guitar playing was never flashy – sophisticated and restrained, it had a poise that set it apart from both the folk pickers and the soul-jazz musos. But his voice was another thing entirely, a unique and androgenous instrument that somehow manages to summon Nina Simone, Josh White, John Martyn and Paul Robeson all into the same space. It's hardly surprising that he could never be slotted into a marketing-friendly commercial niche. And his music was all the better for it.

RW

playlist:

1 Dancing Girl *from* What Color Is Love?
The wonderful, impressionistic opener to Callier's best album swells from vibes and chimes to explode into a lush, downbeat epic, courtesy of arranger Charles "Rotary Connection" Stepney.

2 Trance on Sedgewick Street *from* Occasional Rain
The upbeat "Ordinary Joe" was the almost-hit, but this track better captures Callier's spiritual hybrid of jazz, folk and soul.

3 What Color Is Love? *from* What Color Is Love?
The title track to his 1972 masterpiece remains an undisputed supper-club classic, yet gracefully avoids all the clichés that might imply.

4 Lazarus Man *from* TimePeace
Callier's rebirth into music had the perfect soundtrack with this song, from the 1998 comeback album. Accompanied by a soulfully picked guitar, Callier relaxes into a nine-minute tale of tribulation and redemption.

Ripe for rediscovery:
Marvin Gaye's Here My Dear

There's a popular myth that, when ordered to hand over all the royalties from his next record to his ex-wife as part of a divorce settlement, Marvin Gaye deliberately recorded a wretched album designed to sell poorly. The story is false on one count at least, for although *Here My Dear* was Gaye's worst-selling record, it's not the dud it's often made out to be, but a fascinating "concept album" that chronicles the fallout from their mutilated relationship in voyeuristically compelling fashion.

Gaye had married Anna Gordy, the sister of Motown founder Berry Gordy, in 1962, but they separated in 1973 amid mutual accusations of infidelities. Divorce proceedings dragged out over two years as Gaye spent as much of his fortune as he could on extravagant living until there was little left for his wife's alimony. When the cash was almost all gone, the court eventually ruled that Anna would have to be paid from the royalties earned by Gaye's next album.

"At first, I figured I'd just do a quickie record – nothing heavy, nothing even good," Gaye later admitted. "Why should I break my neck when Anna was going to wind up with the money?" He swiftly decided, however, that there was a better way to extract revenge than turning in a worthless record: "I'll give her my next album but it'll be something she won't want to play and it'll be something she won't want the world to hear because I'm gonna tell the truth."

The result was a record full of bold ideas and sophisticated music ranging from soul-jazz to disco-funk that cut extremely close to the emotional quick. "I Met a Little Girl" told the story of their meeting and falling in love. "When Did You Stop Loving Me, When Did I Stop Loving You" appeared three times in different forms and mused philosophically on the nature of love. Elsewhere he accused her of preventing him from seeing their son and lying to God. His rage was palpable, but he also knew what it was doing to him as he sang lyrics such as "Anger ... can make you old ... can make you sick ... destroys your soul." The record failed to sell and when he died in 1984 he still owed his ex-wife $300,000. But it was certainly not because he had made a wilfully bad album.

NW

Billie Davis

I n 1963, an unknown seventeen-year-old called Billie Davis shot to brief stardom when "Tell Him", a contagious slice of early Tin-Pan-Alley Britpop taken at a whirling, pizzicato gallop, raced into the British top ten. Davis was the original English "dolly bird", a bob-haired bombshell dressed in kinky boots and a leather mini-skirt with a sexy, rough and ready R&B voice to match. When she shared the bill with The Beatles at the London Palladium, a clearly smitten John Lennon tried to chat her up. She politely declined his advances.

If there were any justice, she would be remembered alongside the likes of Dusty Springfield, Lulu and Sandie Shaw as one of the great British female singers of the era. Yet, despite a 2005 anthology of material from her 1960s heyday, which provoked a favourable reassessment in the "serious" music magazines, she remains an obscure figure to all but a handful of pop connoisseurs.

The reason why can probably be dated to a fateful day in September 1963. While returning from a concert in Worcester, the car she was travelling in with her lover, former Shadows bass player Jet Harris, crashed into a bus. She suffered a broken jaw and was unable to sing for months on end while her jaw was wired. Worse, the crash exposed her affair with Harris, who was a married man – in those prurient times she was "shamed" in the press as "the scarlet woman of pop". Her career never really recovered.

Born Carol Hedges in Woking, Surrey, in 1945, her stage name – given to her by the impresario Robert Stigwood – was taken from Billie Holiday and Sammy Davis Jr. When she left school she became a secretary but, after winning a talent contest, she came under Stigwood's wing, cutting some demos with Joe Meek and recording a duet with Mike Sarne before charting with her infectious cover of "Tell Him", originally written for the Exciters by Bert Berns. It was followed by the lesser hit "He's The One". Then came the accident.

Once her broken jaw had mended, bad luck seemed to dog her every move. Her exquisite 1967 version of Chip Taylor's "Angel of the Morning" missed out in the charts to an inferior version by P.P. Arnold (who, ironically, sang backing vocals on Davis's version). The following year, she released the great soul-stomping "I Want You to Be My Baby", which would have been a hit, had it not been for a strike at the record pressing plant.

At least it never stopped her performing. Her commitment to song is beyond question, and she is still singing as "Miss Billie Davis" to this day. Hers is a voice, however, that you can't help feel deserves substantially more exposure than the nostalgia circuit she works. NW

Defunkt

Defunkt came on like a hi-NRG Sly and the Family Stone for the 1980s. When they played live, funk, punk and jazz collided in a dazzling coruscation, the walls ran with sweat and tracks like "Avoid the Funk" and "Strangling Me With Your Love" tore the roof off. The multiracial, mixed-gender collective formed in 1978 in New York around mainstays Joe Bowie on vocals/trombone and bassist Kim Clarke. Bowie, born in 1953 and the more wayward younger brother of jazz trumpeter Lester Bowie, had loose connections with the Big Apple's No Wave scene of the late 1970s. No Wave was an eclectic scene that injected avant-garde music with the aggression of punk, and was centered on acts such as James White and the Blacks, a band Bowie played with, and from which Defunkt were born. They borrowed as much from the free-jazz playing of Ornette Coleman as they did from the JBs' disciplined dance grooves.

Defunkt were just as happy opening for The Clash (as they did on their Sandinista US tour) as they were for James Brown or Larry Graham. Their frenetic stage act was captured in the studio on their debut album, *Defunkt*, and its follow-up, the just as feverish *Thermonuclear Sweat*. The releases took the heavyweight "skunk funk" of horn-blowing brothers Michael and Randy Brecker and married it to the sounds of early rap and the strutting disco grooves of outfits such as Brass Construction and the Ohio Players. With musicians such as the soon-to-be Living Colour guitarist Vernon Reid amongst their ever-shifting line-up, and lyrics that edged towards the thought-provoking and political, Defunkt showed the way for many hip-hop and rock acts which followed.

Their albums expanded the fanbase, but failed to shift enough copies to keep the band together and, in 1983, they took the advice of one of their own songs – "Avoid the Funk" – by splitting up. But a mere three years later, they were back for more albums and a tour of Europe, and they have been an on-off working entity ever since. More recently Bowie fronted the Defunkt Big Band, updating a 1940s format for the new millennium, but rarely venturing far from New York. The band's ultimate failure to cross over to the mainstream, Bowie claims, has been a blessing, allowing them to stay grounded and, as he puts it, draw energy and inspiration from the experiences of all people.

RW

Ripe for rediscovery: Stevie Wonder's Journey Through the Secret Life of Plants

Few musicians have ever managed the kind of prolific period Wonder enjoyed in the mid-1970s. From 1972's *Music of My Mind* through *Talking Book*, *Inner Visions* and *Fulfillingness First Finale* to 1976's *Songs in the Key of Life*, he was an irresistible force, taking soul and R&B out of the singles market and into the albums arena with a series of records of breathtaking eloquency and invention. Most of them won him Grammy awards for album of the year and such was his dominance that when Paul Simon won the award in 1975 for *Still Crazy After All These Years*, the first person he thanked in his acceptance speech was Wonder – for not releasing an album that year.

After this run, a three-year gap ensued, following *Songs in the Key of Life*, before Wonder returned in 1979 with *Journey Through the Secret Life of Plants*. The soundtrack to a documentary film of the same name, there were no obvious singles, the record-buying public was bewildered and reviews of the double-album were the worst of his career. To be sure, there were a few disasters, including "Venus Flytrap and the Bug", a jazz-comedy piece in which Wonder played the part of the bug. In retrospect, however, the album is ripe for reassessment as a neglected classic, a bold attempt to try something radically different from his Grammy-garlanded clavier-funk. In many ways the record's atmospheric instrumentals and world music chants can be seen as paving the way for the genre that subsequently became known as New Age. Though it's *so* much better than that.

NW

ESG

You might have heard of a band called The Shaggs. Three sisters from New Hampshire were bought instruments by their parents in the late 1960s and encouraged to play together in a band; their father's enthusiasm, combined with the sisters' lack of cohesion (and, some might say, talent), resulted in one of the more extraordinary albums ever made, *Philosophy of the World*. It came to be regarded as a landmark of outsider art. Ten years later and 250 miles south, in New York, the mother of sisters Deborah, Renee, Marie and Valerie Scroggins bought some instruments to keep her daughters busy and out of trouble. Together they formed a group called ESG, and set about trying to learn some Rolling Stones songs.

Crucially, their mother couldn't afford any kind of music lessons, and this proved – as with The Shaggs – to be the single most important contribution to their success. But unlike The Shaggs, there would be no giggling behind hands at their untutored efforts: ESG's sound – based upon heavy, repetitive grooves – happened to fit perfectly with the emerging sound of new wave. These sisters from the Bronx suddenly found themselves a seemingly anomalous presence on bills with post-punk luminaries such as PiL and A Certain Ratio, and were fêted by such influential characters as Tony Wilson from Factory Records.

Their debut EP, featuring the songs "You're No Good", "Moody" and "UFO", is probably their best-known release. While its sparse sound and funk-inspired beats are up there with the best records of that era by PiL, The Pop Group and The Slits, the sisters stood apart from the scene. They had no punk background; they didn't feel the need to prove themselves as aloof and artistic, or talk themselves up to the press. They were just making music at a time when people were most receptive to it – the happiest of coincidences. Their distance from the music business machine meant that ESG never burned themselves out, as many of their contemporaries did. They took things at their own pace, releasing a debut album in 1983, then lying dormant for a few years (during which much of their work was heavily sampled by artists such as Wu-Tang Clan and the Beastie Boys) before returning in 1993, and again in 2002, with a similarly hard-edged sound. They're one of the few bands who can claim never to have sold out. In fact, the notion has probably never once occurred to them.

RM

Wanda Jackson

She could've been... Elvis?

The world of early rock'n'roll was no place for a lady, but thanks to the chaperoning abilities of Wanda Jackson's father and manager Tom, the pioneering singer seems to have emerged from a relationship with Elvis Presley with honour intact.

"Our dating amounted to what we could do on the road," she said of the 1955–56 country package tour of the American South, on which she shared the bill and the occasional milkshake with a bequiffed young man on the cusp of major fame. "If we got in town early, we might take in a matinee movie. Then after shows we could go places with his band – and my dad, of course."

It was Elvis who suggested to his belle, already a promising country singer who had had her own Oklahoma radio show while still at school, that she break free of country's staid traditions and try her hand at something a little livelier. The King thus had a hand in creating the Queen of Rockabilly, the first woman with the vocal power to sing that riotous new sound.

Rock'n'roll was hardly bursting with songs written from a female perspective, so Jackson penned a few of her own, including the man-baiting boogie "Mean Mean Man". On this and other originals such as "Rock Your Baby", her voice found a scratchy, crude roughness that was worlds away from her original country yodel.

No stranger to novelty, she recorded the track "Fujiyama Mama", a bouncy rock'n'roll number that, in extremely dubious taste, likened the force of the singer's anger to the nuclear attacks on Hiroshima and Nagasaki. Incredibly, the song went on to be number one in Japan for six months.

The rock'n'roll didn't last long after she lost touch with Elvis. In the 1960s she retreated back to country music, recording schmaltzier hits such as "Tears Will Be the Chaser For Your Wine". In 1971 she and her husband (and new manager) Wendell Goodman became born-again Christians, and Jackson left her early sound even further behind by only performing gospel music in churches for many years.

It wasn't until 1995 that a Wanda Jackson revival began, when country singer Rosie Flores produced a covers album called *Rockabilly Filly* and persuaded Jackson to sing a duet and join her on tour. Since then, Jackson has continued to tour for a new generation of rockabilly fans. A 2003 album, *Heart Trouble*, even featured guests such as the other Elvis (Mr Costello) and The Cramps. The King may be long gone, but his female equivalent is still cookin'.

DS

where to start:

1 Let's Have A Party *from* Wanda Jackson
Jackson's biggest rockabilly hit has all the key ingredients: stop-start rhythms, pounding piano, twanging guitar and one of her rawest vocals.

2 I Gotta Know *from* Rockin' With Wanda
The two sides of her personality come together in this charming oddity, which flits between slow-motion country fiddle and attitude-packed rock'n'roll, while Wanda demands commitment from a no-good suitor.

Candie Payne

She could've been... Amy Winehouse?

"I couldn't even get a manager before Amy Winehouse and Lily Allen took off," admitted Liverpudlian songbird Candie Payne in 2007. "Now it's a completely different story." At the time she was promoting her debut album, *I Wish I Could Have Loved You More*. No article written about Payne managed to avoid mentioning Winehouse, whose extraordinary success showed that the British and American public had a voracious appetite for retro soul pop – a hunger that her anointed successor could surely help to satisfy.

Payne had hipper credentials than her near peer. Signed to Deltasonic, the indie label that is home to successful rock band The Coral, she also had brothers in both The Zutons and the less successful Liverpool group The Stands. Having worked in a vintage clothes store in her hometown, she had an old-school look far classier than Amy's beehive, looking like she could have stepped out of a David Bailey photoshoot.

Whereas Winehouse had Brit Award winner Mark Ronson making sure her horns parped in just the right places, Payne had her own respected backroom boffin in Simon Dine. He had been buffing up dusty 1960s sounds on his laptop for years before Ronson's arrival on the scene, having made over four albums with his own band, Noonday Underground.

Nevertheless, the charts remained a stranger to Miss Payne's charms. Perhaps it's down to the fact that, whereas Winehouse channelled the self-destructive spirit of Billie Holiday, Payne had chosen to resurrect the more wholesome swinging sounds of Dusty Springfield and Petula Clark. Given her geographical background, it was not surprising that comparisons were even made to 1960s Cilla Black. One reviewer called her music "painstakingly crafted but curiously emotionless – like laboratory soul". Still crueller was pointing out that the last singer to take a musical turn down Carnaby Street had been Spice Girl Emma Bunton.

"One More Chance" was supposed to be Payne's trump card, the one on which the production reins were handed over to Ronson in a bid to add some extra sheen and produce that elusive hit. But his golden touch didn't do the trick. The most successful man in British pop in 2007 spent part of that year making a single that limped into the chart at 122.

All of this does disservice to an album that thrills the listener with the funky drums and squalling organ of its title track, revisits the Northern Soul dance floor on "Take Me", and on "One More Chance" comes up with a yearning break-up anthem stuffed with church bells, violins and a chorus that whooshes skyward.

DS

where to start:

1 One More Chance *from* I Wish I Could Have Loved You More
How could it fail, sounding like Phil Spector's wall of sound rebuilt, boasting Payne's strongest vocal as she begs a former lover for forgiveness? Yet fail it did, even with Midas Mark Ronson on board.

2 By Tomorrow *from* I Wish I Could Have Loved You More
Racing bass, echoing horns and a shimmying, irresistible beat, here Payne sounds like she's having more fun than anywhere else on her album.

Classic black gospel

While nearly everybody knows "Oh Happy Day" and has at least heard of Mahalia Jackson, gospel has never broken out of the ghetto of its black Christian constituency and gained its rightful recognition as a great popular American artform. Although lip service is customarily paid to the role of black gospel as a kind of preparatory school for soul singers, few people bother to explore the music that the likes of Sam Cooke and Aretha Franklin grew up singing. The reason is obvious: religious lyrics. Get over this psychological hurdle, however, and you're opened up to a rich variety of music unmatched for its vocal expressiveness and sheer emotional power.

Of gospel's many incarnations, the first worthy of note is that of the guitar evangelists. If you've seen the film *Amélie*, you may recall a wonderful piece of archive footage showing an unidentified guitar-toting gospel-singing mama rocking the house. That was rock'n'roll pioneer Sister Rosetta Tharpe, whose recordings encompassed bluesy solo work, big bands, R&B, marvellous duets with her mother and Marie Knight, and even her own (paying) public wedding concert. A real trouper, Tharpe sometimes sported mink and carried on performing even after a stroke led to the amputation of a leg.

In 1944, meanwhile, a tradition of thrillingly primitive electric-guitar evangelism was launched by the Rev. Utah Smith with his recording of "I Want Two Wings" – a number he allegedly went on to perform wearing two giant angel's wings, playing his guitar behind his head or between his knees. This tradition was continued in the 1950s by Elder Anderson Johnson and in the 1970s by the gravel-voiced Rev. Charlie Jackson.

Also worth exploring are gospel quartets. Here, the term "quartet" refers to four-part harmony male vocal groups, rather than the number of singers – hence the original Five Blind Boys of Alabama and Five Blind Boys of Mississippi. Both epitomized the school of "hard" gospel, with lead singers – Clarence Fountain and Archie Brownlee respectively – whose screaming vocals drove audiences wild. The first gospel quartet recordings date as far back as 1908 but, until the mid-1930s, quartet singing – in the close-harmony "jubilee" style – tended to be rather stiff and formal. In 1937, however, the Golden Gate Quartet blew the cobwebs away, wowing audiences with superb a capella arrangements. Equally adept at performing "rhythmic spirituals", novelty numbers ("Stalin Wasn't Stallin'") and deeper gospel songs, the Golden Gates also imitated instruments with their voices and practised an embryonic form of rap. *Rock My Soul* (Acrobat) provides a perfect single-disc introduction to their astonishing vocal artistry.

One of the best-known quartets, thanks to soul giant Sam Cooke's tenure with the group, is the legendary Soul Stirrers. Led by the hugely influential R.H. Harris, the pre-Cooke incarnation of the Soul Stirrers revolutionized quartet singing by introducing a second lead singer to help create tension and added excitement.

Like Sam Cooke, family gospel group the Staple Singers made their greatest impact in the secular field. Other leading groups included the Caravans, the Davis Sisters – whose lead singer Ruth Davis was a match for most of her male counterparts – and the mixed-gender Roberta Martin Singers. Pride of place, however, must be reserved for the gripping and gritty Dorothy Love Coates & the Original Gospel Harmonettes, and the spectacular Ward Singers, led by Aretha's idol Clara Ward and featuring the great Marion Williams. One of the genre's many superb solo singers, Williams was a gospel earth mother who has since been hailed by the *Rolling Stone Album Guide* as "the greatest singer ever". As for leading male soloists, search out the flamboyant Alex Bradford, who partnered Williams in the gospel musical *Black Nativity*; and Brother Joe May, a powerhouse performer who was perhaps the greatest male singer in any genre outside opera.

Arguably the most evocative form of gospel is that practiced by choirs. It is hard not to be moved, for example, by Aretha Franklin's stunning *Amazing Grace* album, recorded live in church with the Southern California Choir. It's a record that leans heavily on the arranging skills of Rev. James Cleveland – a powerful but rough-hewn singer himself and the godfather of modern gospel and the mass choir sound. His groundbreaking *Peace Be Still* album of 1962, recorded with the Angelic Choir, sold a phenomenal 800,000 copies.

NF

playlist:

The Golden Gate Quartet

1 Jezebel *from* Rock My Soul
Astonishingly intricate and propulsive 1941 a capella performances with a proto-rap lead. The acme of the "rhythmic spiritual".

The Roberta Martin Singers

2 Yield Not to Temptation *from* V/A: When Gospel Was Gospel
The original 78 is hissy and the style quaint, but lead singer Delois Barrett has high notes that are out of this world.

Sister Rosetta Tharpe & Marie Knight

3 Up Above My Head *from* Up Above My Head
Tharpe was a great solo performer, but the incredible vocal interplay on this 1947 duet with Marie Knight adds an extra touch of magic.

The Soul Stirrers & R.H. Harris

4 By and By *from* Shine on Me
An example of the "switch lead" technique pioneered by Harris, partnered here by Paul Foster in 1950: the emotion of this quartet piece just builds and builds.

Elder A. Johnson

5 God Don't Like It *from* 1950s Gospel Classics
Breathtaking bottleneck guitar on Johnson's superior first version of this familiar warning against drinking moonshine. Only one copy of the original 78rpm record from 1953 survives.

Brother Joe May

6 Have Mercy Lord *from* When Gospel Was Gospel
The "Thunderbolt of the Middle West" was simply the greatest male gospel soloist ever, with a dynamic tenor that ranged from a whisper to a roar, as demonstrated on this tantalizingly truncated 1954 live recording.

Sister Wynona Carr

7 Our Father *from* Dragnet for Jesus
Carr's speciality was novelty numbers, but this fragmented live 1954 take on the Lord's Prayer with Rev. C.L. Franklin (Aretha's father) and the New Bethel Baptist Church Choir is absolutely electrifying.

Dorothy Love Coates & the Original Gospel Harmonettes

8 99½ *from* The Best Of
"Ninety-nine and a half won't do" – with her ragged voice, cracking and shaking with an emotion that carried the stamp of absolute conviction and commitment, Civil Rights campaigner Coates never gave less than a hundred percent, as she demonstrated here in 1956.

The Sensational Nightingales

9 Burying Ground *from* Global Roots: Gospel
The lead vocals on this frighteningly intense 1957 performance – by Wilson Pickett's idol Julius Cheeks – are as raw as they come.

The Staple Singers

10 Too Close *from* The Ultimate Staple Singers
There are other terrific versions of this song, by composer Alex Bradford and Bessie Griffin (also live), but this 1960 Vee Jay recording can't be beat for dynamics and atmosphere. Pops, Mavis and the rest of the family at their peak.

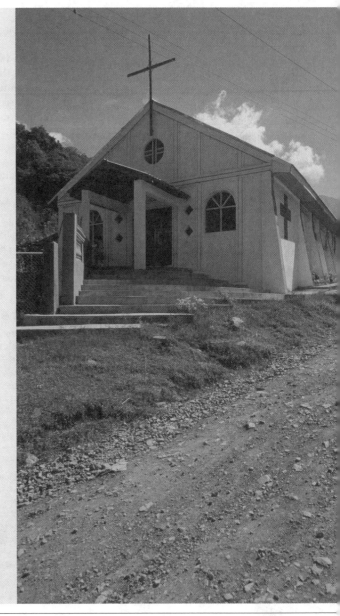

Laura Nyro

When Laura Nyro was recording her album *Gonna Take a Miracle* in Philadelphia, her producer, Leon Huff, made her a bet: $500 that she couldn't complete her vocal track in under three hours. Three hours later, Huff was $500 down and Nyro had recorded one of the finest white soul albums ever. Tracks such as her cover of Marvin Gaye's little-heard classic "The Bells" showcased one of the strongest and, at times, strangest voices in popular music. But it was as a songwriter that Nyro first made her name.

During the late 1960s and early 70s her songs were hardly off the radio. "Wedding Bell Blues" was one of several Nyro compositions taken to the charts by the Fifth Dimension. Then there was "Eli's Comin'" by Three Dog Night, "And When I Die" for Peter, Paul and Mary, and Barbra Streisand's showbiz cover of Nyro's "Stoney End". Laura drew inspiration from blues, jazz, gospel and classical music. Her songs reflected the girl groups she listened to at high school, the protest singers she heard coming out of Greenwich Village and the doo-wop she sang on Bronx street corners back in the 1950s, when her fingers snapped to every new R&B record she could lay her hands on.

Born in New York in 1947, Nyro first came to public notice during an ill-advised appearance at the Monterey Pop Festival in 1967, when her band, struggling to keep up with her intricate music, cut her set short to avoid embarrassment. In 1968 she recorded the first of her classic trilogy for Columbia, *Eli and the Thirteenth Confession*. It was followed by the album she called her "heart and soul", *New York Tenderberry*, and *Christmas and the Beads of Sweat*. Tracks such as "Poverty Train", "Emmie" and "Captain Saint Lucifer" articulated the complexities of her songwriting: tunes arise within tunes, tempos twist and turn, and there is always Nyro's swooping, soaring vocal, wringing emotion out of every line. Then came that stoned soul classic, *Gonna Take a Miracle*, cut with the band who would become LaBelle.

Her marriage dissolved in the mid-1970s, and she eventually found a life partnership with the painter Maria Desiderio, who owned a women's bookstore, in the early 1980s. By the early 1990s, Nyro had added just four more albums to her catalogue, with an increasing gap between them, and had spent the better part of two decades touring, playing clubs and concert halls around the world. Her final project, before being diagnosed with ovarian cancer in 1996, was a CD retrospective of her career. She died the following year.

Laura Nyro's work ranks alongside such American institutions as George Gershwin, the Motown label, Duke Ellington and Tin Pan Alley in its heyday. With songwriting so inventive, and lyrics so waywardly poetic, her cult status was always assured.

RW

playlist:

1 Stoned Soul Picnic *from* Eli and the Thirteenth Confession
Taken to the charts by the Fifth Dimension, the original is classic Nyro. An astounding arrangement of shifting time signatures, wailing horns and complex harmonies.

2 Captain for Dark Mornings *from* New York Tenderberry
Produced by Roy Hallee, on his way to "Bridge Over Troubled Water", according to instructions from Nyro expressed metaphorically: she apparently described the musical arrangements she wanted in terms of colours.

3 Desiree *from* Gonna Take a Miracle
Nyro and Patti LaBelle swoon through a Gamble and Huff-produced cover of a 1957 doo-wop hit by The Charts (originally titled "Deserie"). A near-perfect piano and vocal miniature.

4 Upstairs By a Chinese Lamp *from* Christmas and the Beads of Sweat
Fearing seasonal sales only, Columbia tried in vain to persuade Nyro to change the title of her fourth album. "Spring has swept the scarlet side streets," she coos, in one of her most intimate songs.

5 To a Child *from* Walk the Dog and Light the Light
"Now I can die", said Nyro, when asked how she felt when she had written this moving track from her final album. "I'm finished hassling with this world. I'm finished having children. This is my final statement." And what a sign-off it was.

Esther Phillips

She could've been... Aretha Franklin?

Ahmet Ertegun described the late Esther Phillips as simply one of the best singers he ever heard. As his Atlantic Records was home to some of the greatest black voices of all time, from Ray Charles to Aretha Franklin, it was some compliment. In 1973, Franklin gave her Grammy for best performance by a female R&B performer to Phillips on the grounds that she deserved it more.

With an astringent nasal voice that evokes comparisons with Nina Simone and Dinah Washington, she could sing anything from jazz and blues via soul and pop standards to disco and even country, injecting them all with the same fierce emotion. Yet despite a recording career that lasted for more than thirty years, today she seems an all but forgotten figure, except by a small band of hardcore soul and R&B aficionados.

Born Esther Mae Jones in Texas in 1935, she began singing as a thirteen-year-old with Johnny Otis's band. Billed as Little Esther, her "Double Crossing Blues" gave her an R&B number one a year later. She recorded for various labels in the 1950s in different styles, but by the end of the decade had been largely forgotten. Rediscovered singing in a nightclub in 1962 by country singer Kenny Rogers, she dropped the diminutive tag from her name and enjoyed a huge hit with a version of Ray Price's country weepie "Release Me", her intense, piercing soul vocal creating a fascinating juxtaposition with the rather corny arrangement. Signed by Ahmet Ertegun to Atlantic two years later, she recorded some great sides including an answer record to Percy Sledge's "When a Man Loves a Woman". Moving to the Kudu label, she recorded her finest album *From a Whisper to a Scream*, which caused Aretha to hand over her Grammy, and carried on making great records until her death from liver failure in 1984.

The reasons why she never achieved greater recognition are various. She was compromised by a heroin addiction from an early age. Her various record companies didn't always know how to handle her and the material she was given wasn't always well chosen. "Esther thrilled you no matter what she sang," Ertegun said before his death. "But finding a song that would have the magic that would get the teenagers to go out and buy was difficult. She was a mature singer who wasn't up for doing the kiddie shit. We had a tough time coming up with material that would let her release that emotion she had."

NW

Rotary Connection

Rotary Connection's story is one of bad judgement and an absurdly long wait for recognition as one of the most innovative acts of the late 1960s. The wrong turns started in 1969, when their manager declined an offer for the Chicago-based octet to play Woodstock, in favour of a better-paid festival in Toronto. They were also very difficult to categorize: their mixed-gender, multiracial line-up and unique brand of baroque-choral, psychedelic soul got them lumped in with MOR vocal acts such as Fifth Dimension, as well as the more streetwise Sly and the Family Stone, leaving them rather stuck in the middle.

Put together by Marshall Chess, of Chess Records, in 1966, Rotary Connection boasted a talented front-woman in the shape of Minnie Riperton who, with her enviable five-octave range, gave the sprawling outfit an almost operatic feel. Then there were the dramatic, Sergio Mendes-style rhythms, the spacious, trippy grooves and deep-soul beats – all of which would endear them to a new generation of club-goers and record buffs in later decades. In 1967 they were shunted onto Cadet Concept, the boutique imprint launched by Chess for their more adventurous acts, and were joined by session guitarist Phil Upchurch. But it was the recruitment of arranger and principal songwriter Charles Stepney that would define the band's sound.

Stepney's work on their eponymous debut established them as sophisticated purveyors of cool and the record even made the Billboard Top 40. It would be downhill from here. On the follow-ups – *Aladdin*, *Peace* and *Dinner Music* – Stepney's layered, jump-cut arrangements and hippy sheen were beginning to look overwrought and rather naff, and if listeners wanted naff they already had *Hair*. By 1971 Rotary Connection were on to their sixth and last album, *Hey Love*, which featured the soprano Kitty Heywood, contralto Shirley Wahls and tenor Dave Scott. There was still some compelling material here, but listeners had gone elsewhere.

The band went their separate ways – Riperton, in particular, to stardom as a solo act, until her untimely death in 1979. Rotary Connection were swiftly forgotten and languished in pop obscurity, attracting cult status. Then, in 1996, one track, "I Am the Black Gold of the Sun", was rejigged by Nuyorican Soul, on the Talkin' Loud label, with a treatment by the hip-house-jazz remix team "Little Louie" Vega and Kenny "Dope" Gonzalez. Tirelessly promoted in the UK by DJ Gilles Petersen, the remix became a club anthem and suddenly Rotary Connection were being hailed as forerunners of the new dance-floor sound.

RW

playlist:

1 I Am the Black Gold of the Sun *from* Hey Love
The track which resurrected the largely forgotten Rotary Connection, it was remixed in the 1990s for New York club-goers. Choral voices chime in a baroque arrangement from Rotary's eminence grise, Charles Stepney.

2 Loving You *from* Perfect Angel
Minnie Riperton's solo career took off straight after the Rotaries disconnected. This global hit from 1975, replete with the sound of twittering birds, showcased her extraordinary flageolet singing, the highest register of the human voice.

3 Sunshine of Your Love *from* Songs
Hard to believe before hearing it, but this orchestrated soul arrangement of Cream's mega-riffed classic actually works. Brooding – eerie, even – it made good use of the band's diverse talent.

4 Didn't Want to Have to Do It *from* Rotary Connection
A Tribe Called Quest nicked the quirky, distorted guitar line from "Memory Band" for their 1990 hit "Bonita Applebum". A much better track from the same album, however, is this smoky cover of a Lovin' Spoonful number.

The Spirit of Memphis Quartet

Modelling their name on the *Spirit of St Louis*, the aircraft in which Charles Lindbergh made the first transatlantic flight in 1927, the first incarnation of the Spirit of Memphis – a unit that was rarely, in fact, a quartet – was formed in the late 1920s. It was not until 1949, however, that the group settled down to its classic line-up, blessed by three outstanding lead singers. The thundering baritone of Silas Steele was bolstered by the contrasting tenors – warm and pure respectively – of Jethro "Jet" Bledsoe and Willmer "Little Axe" Broadnax.

Influenced by the impassioned intonation of the black preaching tradition, the appropriately named Steele (formerly of the Famous Blue Jay Singers) was perhaps the first quartet lead singer to sing in the "hard" gospel style. Little Axe, whose voice has been aptly compared to a ringing bell, went on to record briefly with two other great quartets, the Fairfield Four and the Five Blind Boys of Mississippi. Little Axe, it transpired, was in fact a woman living as a man, something only discovered by the world at large after Axe was murdered by his/her girlfriend in 1992. (The guitarist Skip McDonald later named his dub-blues project Little Axe.)

Bledsoe, meanwhile, adopted a seductively soulful approach, while other members – baritone James Darling, tenor Robert Reed and especially bass Earl Malone – filled out the group's incredibly rich, complex and powerful sound.

The Spirit's earliest recordings, made just before and after Broadnax joined the group, consisted of a couple of one-off singles and a fifteen-minute radio transcription from the WDIA station in Memphis (finally released by the

Gone). The latter featured versions of popular spirituals, interspersed with sung advertisements for Carnation Milk that concluded with Malone's deep bass intoning "Man, I'm really contented".

With their classic 1949–52 King recordings, however, the Spirit of Memphis reached the peak of gospel perfection, creating a body of work unparalleled for its absolute vocal mastery and profound emotional impact. It's impossible not to reach for superlatives when talking about these performances, all the more astonishing for being – with a couple of regrettable exceptions – entirely unaccompanied.

This is music that is the absolute antithesis of easy listening: its depth, intensity and seriousness are such that – as titles like "Blessed Are the Dead" suggest – it defies casual enjoyment. You may not find yourself listening to the Spirit of Memphis very often, but to hear them is one of the greatest experiences music can offer.

NF

playlist:

1 If Jesus Had to Pray *from* Happy in the Service of the Lord
Following Steele's fearsome bellowing, Little Axe's clarion, piercing, soaring entry at around the one-and-a-half-minute mark will raise the hairs on the back of your neck.

2 Lord Jesus *from* Happy in the Service of the Lord
Frustratingly cut short, and interrupted by a captivating chuckle, this stunning live two-parter – recorded in a Memphis church in 1952 – is a superb showcase for the supremely soulful Bledsoe's ability to work an audience. A live album would have been simply out of this world.

3 The Day Is Passed and Gone *from* Happy in the Service of the Lord
Gospel expert Anthony Heilbut describes this traditional song as "the most terrifying evocation of death in American folklore". Against the background of the most mournful moaning imaginable, and counterpointed by Bledsoe's keening, Steele

The Swan Silvertones

"**I** can't rip your heart out/Like the Swan Silvertones", sang Boo Hewerdine on "Swan Silvertone", from his 1992 album *Ignorance*, paying a rare tribute to one of the very greatest gospel quartets. Formed in 1938 by a bunch of miners in Coalwood, West Virginia, as the Four Harmony Kings, the group changed their name to the Silvertone Singers to avoid confusion with another gospel quartet and then to Swan's Silvertone Singers after their regular weekday performances on radio station WDIB in Knoxville, Tennessee, gained the sponsorship of the local Swan Bakery company.

The Swans were a peerless close harmony group, but what made them special was the counterpoint between the rough and smooth vocal styles of their lead singers. "Father of falsetto" Claude Jeter modelled his singing on the high tenor of Billy Williams of jubilee quartet the Charioteers, and in turn he influenced every soul man who ever ventured into the higher register, most notably Al Green. Jeter's cut-glass crooning was set against the rasping intensity of a succession of hard leads – from Solomon Womack (Bobby's uncle), through the Revs. Percell Perkins and Robert Crenshaw to Louis Johnson – with the ensemble benefiting from the brilliant arrangements of Paul Owens, previously of the Dixie Hummingbirds and the (Sensational) Nightingales, who joined the group in the 1950s.

Their later recordings, featuring classic material they recorded for Vee Jay records from the mid-1950s to mid-60s, show them at their stylistic peak. Indeed, top record producer Joe Boyd, who produced albums for Nick Drake and The Incredible String Band among others, once described the group's *Saviour Pass Me Not* as his favourite album of all time. The leading popular music archivist Michael Ochs was so stunned by his own belated discovery of the Swans that he started his own label to issue a one-off compilation LP of their Vee Jay titles.

The Swan Silvertones were also responsible for inspiring a song that has itself been an inspiration and succour to many. The lyrics for Paul Simon's "Bridge over Troubled Water" were inspired by a line – "I'll be a bridge over deep water if you trust in my name" – from the Swans' frequently anthologized version of "Mary Don't You Weep". Simon later returned the favour in a sense, bringing in Claude Jeter to sing on "Take Me to the Mardi Gras" on his album *There Goes Rhymin' Simon*.

NF

playlist:

1 I've Tried *from* The Swan Silvertones 1946–1951
This unaccompanied 1947 performance provides a superb showcase for Jeter's sublime, gliding, ethereal falsetto.

2 Trouble in My Way *from* Love Lifted Me/My Rock
With a raving Rev. Robert Crenshaw on lead and a basic drum-beat, the Swans take the listener to hard gospel heaven in two and a half minutes.

3 The Lord's Prayer *from* Move Up
This 1956 recording provides a complete contrast. Rather than trying to out-scream the competition in live performance, the Swans used to bring the house down with their beautifully delicate close-harmony arrangement of the Lord's Prayer. Magic.

Lewis Taylor

Perhaps only Todd Rundgren had made successful bedmates out of soul and prog rock – until Lewis Taylor came along, that is. The London-born musician is just as happy vamping Sam Cooke or the Isley Brothers as he is covering the prog-stomp "Frankenstein" or dropping in sly references to Deep Purple and Yes. Like Rundgren, Taylor was largely a one-man studio band, writing and playing everything himself. His recordings, mostly done at home, barely ventured beyond analogue technology: at one point he denied even owning a computer.

Taylor began learning the guitar and piano at the age of eight, whilst recovering from a serious road accident. He became proficient at almost every instrument he turned his hand to and was soon digesting the music of the day: prog rock, Motown, glam and funk. The young prodigy had a stint playing guitar with a 1980s incarnation of those progressive freak-beats The Edgar Broughton Band, and by 1986 the precocious Taylor, trading under the name Sheriff Jack, put out an album of psychedelic-tinged rock, *Laugh Yourself Awake*, now long-forgotten. Ten years on, and in his early thirties, Taylor was signed to Island on the strength of a demo. His self-titled album, entirely recorded at home, was released in 1996. It immediately gathered plaudits from all quarters. Elton John declared him "an undiscovered genius" and David Bowie championed Taylor's sweet soul music. "Major new artist alert" trumpeted *The Guardian*.

During the making of the album, Taylor was on a varied musical diet of Miles Davis, Tim Buckley, Tangerine Dream and Scott Walker, as well as soul heroes Sam Cooke and Marvin Gaye. Everything was thrown into the pot. *Lewis II*, issued four years later, continued in the same groove – circuitous melodies, four-on-the-floor dance numbers and densely layered harmonies pitched against feral guitar breaks and effects pedals. Taylor's sound was fresh and revealed a genuine soul, rare at the time amongst white British artists. There was only one problem. The albums didn't sell, perhaps considered too blue-eyed by hardcore R&B fans and too urban by the rock crowd. It wasn't unduly surprising when Taylor was dropped by Island after the underwhelming reception of his second album.

Rather than casting around for another deal, Taylor welcomed the liberation and control it offered him. He spent the next two years working on *Stoned Part I*, which appeared on his own Slow Reality label in 2002. The breakthrough hit he needed stubbornly refused to happen. There were a couple more overlooked albums, notably the even better *Stoned Part II*, but no evidence of impending commercial success. One of several below-the-radar non-releases with which Taylor entertained himself was a remake of Captain Beefheart's *Trout Mask Replica* album – not exactly something anyone could have anticipated. Playing everything himself, and making no attempt to emulate the Captain's feral growl, he acquitted himself surprisingly well.

Taylor's website announced his retirement from the music business in 2006. But it's hard to believe the soulboy of prog won't eventually resurface in some shape or form.

RW

playlist:

1 Lucky *from* Lewis Taylor
The opener for Taylor's debut album, this was his calling card and, in demo form, the track that got him signed to Island.

2 Eighteen with a Bullet single release only
Taylor transforms Pete Wingfield's mid-1970s doo-wop pop classic into an exuberant, Isley Brothers soul-groove with the help of Carleen Anderson, who shares vocal duties. A stand-alone single, it flopped in 1998, but it's well worth seeking out.

3 Lovelight *from* Stoned Part I
Given a "Kraftwerk vibe", as he put it, this track is emblematic of Taylor's diverse influences.

4 Positively Beautiful 2 *from* Stoned Part II
Quite why *Stoned Part I* failed to break through commercially was a mystery, especially with an enthusiastic endorsement from Elton John. It may have been a mistake to revisit the songs with new mixes, but the follow-up was arguably even more deserving of chart recognition.

5 Lost *from* The Lost Album
Taylor developed the songs gathered on *The Lost Album* in response to the critical triumph of his debut release, but issued the album only as he was preparing to bow out of the record business.

Bobby Womack

He could've been... Stevie Wonder?

I n the mid-1970s, Stevie Wonder released a series of records that broke ground by selling soul to a contemporary rock audience and oversaw the transition of black dance music from the singles charts to the album market. Yet he was not alone in making a new kind of mature soul music with an appeal beyond its traditional audience. After playing guitar on Sly & The Family Stone's epochal *There's A Riot Goin' On* at the start of the 1970s, Bobby Womack for the first time gained full artistic control of his own records and proceeded to make a trio of classic self-produced albums in *Communication* (1971), *Understanding* (1972) and *Facts of Life* (1973).

In the middle of this run, he also produced the superb soundtrack to the blaxploitation flick *Across 110th Street*. Tracks such as the tortured "That's the Way I Feel About Cha", "I Can Understand It", "Woman's Gotta Have It" and "Harry Hippie" did well on the R&B singles and albums charts. Yet unlike Wonder's similar output from the same period, they were ignored by rock radio and went unheard by the crossover audience that deserved to hear them.

It was typical of a career persistently scarred by underachievement. Born in Cleveland, Ohio, in 1944, he began singing gospel in a group with his brothers, who went on to become the Valentinos and enjoy secular R&B hits with "Looking For Love", "I'll Make It Alright" and "It's All Over Now" (swiftly covered by the Rolling Stones). He also became the guitarist in Sam Cooke's live band, but alienated the R&B audience in 1965 when, three months after the sainted Cooke's death, Womack married his widow. In the scandal that ensued, the Valentinos disappeared from the charts and Womack's first solo single, the great "I Found a True Love" was completely ignored. It was 1968 before the quality of his records forced a begrudging forgiveness and he scored his first solo R&B hit.

After his golden run in the early 1970s, Womack lost focus in a haze of drugs and other personal problems, but re-emerged strongly in 1981 with *The Poet*, on the Beverley Glen label, run by black entrepreneur Otis Smith. The record briefly rejuvenated his career but he fell out with Smith over money, which meant that the follow-up, *The Poet II*, was delayed until 1984. By then, Bobby Womack was already in his forties and it was all getting a bit late.

NW

PROG AND PROUD
keyboard solos and concept albums

Aphrodite's Child

Beverley, the braying seductress from Mike Leigh's TV comedy of manners, *Abigail's Party*, loved Demis Roussos. "For Ever and Ever", the balladeer's cheesy chart-topper from 1976, was her favourite. But the portly Greek with the fragile warble had a past largely unknown to his housewife audience in the late 1970s. Before those Europop hits, Roussos was one corner of the rock band Aphrodite's Child. And it's a fair bet that Aphrodite's Child never got a look-in on Beverley's music centre.

Formed in Athens in 1967, the four-piece featured the operatic Roussos, who also played bass, and another musician who would go on to chart stardom – the organist Vangelis Papathanassiou. They came together initially as Vangelis and his Orchestra, for an album of live and studio recordings made with the Greek recording star George Romanos. But Vangelis had ambitions beyond pop. The band relocated to London, via Paris, and signed to Mercury Records.

Inspired, perhaps, by the way in which Procol Harum had plundered Bach airs for "A Whiter Shade of Pale", their first release was a similar take on Pachelbel's *Canon in D Major*, which

the band retitled "Rain and Tears". Roussos had already taken the necessary step of singing in English and put some lyrics to the familiar melody. Good airplay and a novelty approach to the classic nudged it into the top thirty in November 1968.

Subsequent singles, with lacklustre titles such as "Spring, Summer, Winter, Fall", failed to repeat their initial UK success. But by the end of 1970 Vangelis had heard *Tommy* and hatched an ambitious plan for his own concept album. Like the Who's rock opera, *666* sprawled over two discs and told a story. Unlike *Tommy*, however, the theme was the ultimate in progressive rock – a musical interpretation of the Revelation of St John, complete with all of its apocalyptic imagery.

Accompanied by a "libretto" from Vangelis's friend Costas Ferris, the music was far more experimental than anything they had attempted before. It was long and bombastic, but it sold well. There was just one problem: with the success of *666*, Aphrodite's Child had turned into the Vangelis show. Roussos harboured aspirations of chart stardom for himself and he quit the band, uneasy with their new status as masters of prog. Before long, the Roussos phenomenon was the soundtrack to suburban soirees and Vangelis's scores for movies such as *Chariots of Fire* and *Blade Runner* made him, too, a household name.

RW

playlist:

1 Rain and Tears *from* End of the World
A period-piece hit from the era that made lacy-sleeved pop hits out of classical compositions. It was largely forgotten by the time Demis Roussos had become the housewife's choice.

2 Don't Try to Catch a River *from* End of the World
Sound advice from the Greek trio. Roussos's falsetto threatens to damage glass. Vangelis's organ throbs. Together, they reach a crescendo of paisley-clad proto-prog.

3 Altamont *from* 666
In 1970, when *666* was being written, the Altamont Free Festival of December 1969 represented a countercultural hell on earth. Fitting, then, that Vangelis should include a track about it in his vision of the apocalypse.

4 The Four Horsemen *from* 666
Anticipatory chimes tinkle the opening to one of the band's best-loved songs and Roussos warbles through the Book of Revelation like a man possessed.

5 Ritual *from* Earth
Compared to his leviathan keyboard work of the later 1970s and beyond, Vangelis's first solo outing, 1973's *Earth*, was a small-scale affair. It was supposedly inspired by ancient Greek music, which is especially evident on this percussion-led track.

The weirdest instruments ever played?

It seems bizarre that, after over fifty years of rock'n'roll, the same extensively tried and interminably tested combination of guitar, bass and drums is still the default setup for any group. You rarely see adverts in the windows of music shops asking for a bassoon player and a *bodhrán* player to complete a seven-piece avant-disco outfit. It's "bassist needed" or "guitarist wanted". And while some of that is undoubtedly down to the fact that guitars lend themselves particularly well to rock posturing (in the way that an oboe or a sousaphone certainly doesn't), it's also because developments in technology have made it a cinch for a band to sound superficially impressive. For the price of a couple of Marshall stacks and Gibson guitars, you can instantly sound like a classic rock artist without trying particularly hard.

That's not the case for those intrepid musicians who choose to go off-piste and play with alternative sound sources. They have to work a lot harder. Of course, today's computing technology means that there are an infinite number of noises that can be coaxed from a box measuring a few inches across – a process that would have had musicians of the eighteenth century squealing in terror and shouting "witchcrafte!". But it's not deft programming of synthesizers that we're interested in here. It's the obstinate, unwieldy, occasionally clanking mechanical instruments that never caught on and that kids never clamoured to learn, but which nevertheless created a sound that always stamped its identity on any track it was deployed on.

Some instruments fall just outside this category. The theremin, for example, was once an eyebrow-raising noise on "Good Vibrations" but a cheap model can now be bought in any high street music shop. Other instruments make incredibly familiar sounds, regardless of whether we know what's making it, such as the Mellotron used on "Strawberry Fields Forever", the Musitron on Del Shannon's 1960s hit, "Runaway", or even the *ondes martenot*, a keyboard instrument that crops up on every other Radiohead album. (Before Johnny Greenwood, it seemed that only French classical composers of the 1920s were interested in it.) No, these sounds are rare, precious, almost endangered – and a painstakingly synthesized recreation just wouldn't be the same.

This Heat

Cenotaph *from* Deceit
The Maestrovox was a valve synthesizer that first went on sale in 1952 at the British Industries Fair at Olympia, London, where it was hailed as the "Success of the Year". Today, fewer than a dozen remain in existence, but its idiosyncratic tuning and unpredictable vibrato found a champion in drummer Charles Hayward, who used one on stage and in the studio with his uncompromising and wonderful band This Heat during the late 1970s.

Momus

Lady of Shalott *from* Folktronic
Medieval instruments seem to have shed all semblance of street cred over the centuries. And the none-more-hippy Circulus, champions of all things early 1970s, aren't exactly helping. But cerebral Scottish minstrel Momus delved back in time on his *Folktronic* album and hauled the viol, krummhorn, sackbutt and regal into the twenty-first century. Combining the sounds with analog synths led to a memorable collision of lo-fi home demos and grand Deutsche Grammophon-esque productions.

Kev Hopper

Lamalou Les Bains *from* Whispering Foils
The eerie wailing of the theremin became a recognizable twentieth century pop sound, but it has a nineteenth-century Appalachian equivalent. The scraping of a violin bow across the blunt edge of a saw can, in expert hands, create the most beautiful tone. On this track Kev Hopper, of former John Peel favourites Stump, plays a lilting tune backed by Sean O'Hagan of High Llamas and Stereolab fame.

Optiganally Yours

Mr Wilson *from* Spotlight on Optiganally Yours
The kitsch value of Mattel's Optigan is far greater than its musical value – indeed, it's probably best remembered for its unerring ability to break down. But several artists – including Elvis Costello, Blur and Kraftwerk – have used one, while the band Optiganally Yours have based their entire sound around its scratchy, pre-recorded auto-accompaniments.

Television

The Fire *from* Adventure
After seeing the word Ondioline in the credits of a *Twilight Zone* soundtrack record, Tom Verlaine tracked one down to use on Television's second album. Another forerunner of the synthesizer, it was invented by a Frenchman in the early 1940s, has 24 keys, is powered by a vacuum tube, and is entirely responsible for the weird, reedy oboe sound you can hear throughout this track.

They Might Be Giants

Am I Awake *from* The Indestructible Object EP
Sometimes referred to using the less catchy moniker of "mandolin-guitar-zither", the Marxophone combined the three into one supposedly easy-to-play instrument that was hawked around by door-to-door salesmen in post-war America. John Linnell of They Might Be Giants claims, with some justification, that this track is probably the first ever recorded to feature a backwards Marxophone.

RM

Kevin Ayers

"**I** lost it years ago. A long, long time ago. But, in a way, I don't think I've ever had it," Kevin Ayers said on the release of his "comeback" album in 2007. He was talking about the ego and ambition that are an essential part of the make-up of your regulation, self-absorbed, avaricious, rock'n'roll celebrity. It is that very lack of the rock-star gene, of course, that has allowed Ayers to operate blithely outside the fads and fashions of the music industry and conferred such an engaging, freewheeling charm on his music over the years. It was once said that he only ever wrote three kinds of songs: drunk songs, drinking songs and hangover songs. It's a statement he's never protested.

His status as a nearly man who preferred the life of a bon viveur to the dedicated pursuit of fame and fortune was established early on. In 1968 he walked away from Soft Machine when they were Pink Floyd's main rivals as the most important act on Britain's burgeoning underground scene. After an American tour supporting Jimi Hendrix, he sold his bass to Noel Redding and split for Ibiza, with no greater ambitions than to get stoned and drink wine in the sun.

When he returned and launched a solo career he hired as sidemen the likes of Mike Oldfield and Andy Summers before anyone had heard of them, but his one tilt at mainstream success was disastrous. After signing with Elton John's manager John Reid in 1974, he shifted from the prog-rock label Harvest to Island, who attempted to give him a rock-star makeover in silver suit and platform boots. He went along with it but with considerable unease. Island put him on stage at London's Rainbow Theatre with John Cale, Nico and Brian Eno and heavily hyped the conglomerate as the ultimate alternative supergroup. Ayers slept with Cale's wife the night before. The atmosphere at the gig was terrible and the live album which was released afterwards completely flopped. Cale later wrote the magnificently vitriolic diatribe "Guts" about Ayers' behaviour on his 1975 album *Slow Dazzle,* featuring the immortal line "The bugger in the short sleeves fucked my wife".

The best of Kevin Ayers's work is almost all found on the four maverick albums he made for Harvest between 1969 and 1973. *Joy of a Toy* was a sumptuous affair, full of great melodic, witty songs sung in a lazy, sensuous baritone and it has endured far better than the jazz-prog sound that Soft Machine pursued after Ayers' departure. *Shooting at the Moon* was sonically more experimental, thanks to the wild brilliance of Ayers' short-lived band Whole World, which featured the free-jazz sax playing of Lol Coxhill, a youthful Mike Oldfield and classical composer David Bedford. The more languid *Whatevershebringwesing* was every bit as good and should have given Ayers a hit single with "Stranger in Blue Suede Shoes", while *Bananamour*, with backing from such Canterbury scene stalwarts as Robert Wyatt and Steve Hillage, is rated by many as his most consistent collection of songs.

During his tenure on Island, Elton John turned up as a guest on Ayers' 1975 album *Sweet Deceiver*. Tellingly, its more mainstream sound was not as well received as the collection released at the same time of odds and sods and outtakes rounded up from his Harvest sessions. By 1977, Ayers had had enough of hanging out with Elton and trying to be a rock star, and he returned to Spain in search of further sybaritic distractions from the fame game. He stayed there for the next twenty years, making periodic and pleasing but often half-hearted forays back into the limelight. He was hit hard in 1992 by the death from a drugs overdose of the guitarist Ollie Halsall, with whom he had worked closely for almost two decades. It was fifteen years before he made another album. By then a new generation had discovered the charm of his early albums, and his influence can be clearly discerned on the likes of Gorky's Zygotic Mynci and Super Furry Animals.

It's tempting to see Ayers as Soft Machine's equivalent of Syd Barrett. The two worked together briefly after they had left their respective bands but, although both were songwriting mavericks, they were very different people. Syd Barrett was suffering from a mental illness; he was seriously unwell. Ayers was simply rather decadent and a little injudicious. But he has proved to be a surprisingly tenacious, if louche, survivor: a collection of his early recordings for BBC Radio 1 released in 1998 was brilliantly titled *Too Old to Die Young*.

NW

It probably doesn't need pointing out, but Kevin Ayers is the one wearing the scarf.

playlist:

1 Stranger in Blue Suede Shoes *from* Whatevershebringwesing
"I'm tired of cheating and wasting my head/And filling the boss's bags with bread" – this song is Ayers' paean to tuning in, turning on and dropping out.

2 Lunatic's Lament *from* Shooting at the Moon
Canterbury-scene Kevin in edgy, free-form mode, with his soon-to-be-a-millionaire sideman Mike Oldfield on freak-out guitar.

3 Whatevershebringwesing *from* Whatevershebringwesing
Eight minutes of mellifluous magic: you have to work hard to sound so lazily casual.

4 Oh Wot a Dream *from* Bananamour
A whimsical, wonderful tribute to Syd from his maverick soulmate.

5 Lady Rachel *from* Joy of a Toy
Ayers at his most languidly swoonsome.

Gong

No other band is so immediately "hippie" as Gong. This was a group who appeared on stage in "pothead pixie" hats, who provided a space-metal soundtrack for getting stoned to, with songs informed by a breezy eroticism and Tolkienesque imagery. The genesis of Planet Gong began with Daevid Allen, a visionary Australian who fell in with the Canterbury scene in England in the late 1960s, playing guitar for the embryonic Soft Machine. After just one single, Allen left the band, having been refused re-entry into England after a French tour. He settled in Paris, where he set up a proto-version of Gong – "a large number of musicians and singers improvising around nothing for hours on end, completely stoned".

From this Allen drew up the Gong blueprint with his partner, poet Gilli Smyth. An early influence was minimalist composer Terry Riley, who inspired Allen's technique of "glissando guitar" and the tape textures that gave a base to Gong's pioneering self-styled "stratified" rock. This was in evidence right from the band's first recording, a film soundtrack entitled *Continental Circus* released in 1970, which Allen and Smyth had worked on around the time of the Paris 1968 uprising. Branded cultural agitators by the authorities, they had left France in a hurry. Allen and Smyth managed to release two further albums on the French Byg label, however: *Magick Brother, Mystic Sister* and *Banana Moon*. The music recalled Soft Machine, but lyrically all the Gong ingredients were in place – whimsical surrealism, sexual fantasy and, of course, drugs.

When Allen and Smyth returned to France in 1971, Gong's first stable line-up convened in a rural farmhouse commune to record *Camembert Electrique* "during the full moon phases" of the summer. Thus began both Allen's wacky wordplay with the names of his musicians, and the idea of Gong as a planet. Gilli Smyth became Shakti Yoni; Didier Malherbe

(sax/flute) transmuted into Bloomdido Bad De Grasse; and one Venux De-Luxe emerged as switch doctor and mixmaster; the line-up was completed by Pip Pyle (drums and breakages). The album itself was a wayward piece of space-funkery, but zesty enough to attract the attentions of the embryonic Virgin Records, who, echoing their promotional trick with *The Faust Tapes*, re-released the album as a 69p ($1) bargain buy.

The band launched themselves into a shamelessly psychotropic triptych of albums between 1973 and 74: *Flying Teapot*, *Angel's Egg* and *You*. These wonderfully trippy albums offered a sequence of songs and proto-ambient layers of electronics well ahead of their time. Steve Hillage's guitar and Tim Blake's synth provided a serene, mantric backdrop for Malherbe's eclectic sax patterns, while tight rhythms from Mike Howlett (bass) and Pierre Moerlen (drums) gave Allen and Smyth's ethereal poetry a solid structure. Live, the band were even better, an astonishing spectacle utilizing lasers, and dressed and lit like a mummer's play. Allen described the band live as like a "more feminine version of Hawkwind".

Unfortunately for this extended family of Utopian dreamers and deviants (which now included Hillage's partner, keyboard player Miquette Giraudy), the times were about to change. As the decade progressed, punk would tar Gong with the same prog-rock brush as Genesis, Mike Oldfield and co. Allen and Smyth pre-empted Gong's end by jumping ship for Spain in 1975 – Allen maintaining he had been prevented from appearing on stage one night by a "force field" of unspecified origin – and an ersatz Gong soldiered on without them. Hillage and Giraudy fronted the album *Shamal* in 1975, which was produced by Pink Floyd's Nick Mason, before finally docking into dry jazz-rock terrain as Pierre Moerlen's Gong, with Moerlen and Malherbe alone remaining from previous Gong incarnations. Their

"I was a psychedelic usher at the cinema of the French mind."

Daevid Allen

albums, *Gazeuse/Expresso* and *Expresso II,* of 1977 and 78, were Gong in name alone.

The spirit was kept alive more by Steve Hillage, whose spaced-out solo albums were marketed successfully by Virgin alongside the Sex Pistols. Oddly, Allen and Smyth returned to England much more in key with the times, re-forming as Planet Gong and enlisting musicians from punk-hippie hybrid Here & Now. The Live Floating Anarchy tour, conducted alongside the punk band Alternative TV, followed. The music (immortalized on a live disc) was a howl of psychedelic, urban squat polemic.

Allen moved to New York around 1978, made a few solo albums, and instigated a New York Gong project with Bill Laswell, before returning to Australia, where he wound up driving taxis. (A compilation of his post-NY Gong work, *Divided Alien Clockwork Band*, was released on Blueprint in 1997.) Gilli Smyth, meanwhile, recorded and toured as Mother Gong, producing a trilogy of cosmic feminist tracts, often accompanied by Malherbe. Tim Blake briefly joined Hawkwind, before basing himself in France and recording and performing as Crystal Machine. Hillage and Howlett became Virgin's in-house producers, manning the boards for Simple Minds and Martha & The Muffins, among others, before the former returned to the limelight with The Orb and his own System 7.

In 1988 Allen returned to England, settling in Glastonbury. He was a largely forgotten figure, but Gong material was beginning to be noticed by the techno crowd, and he reclaimed sufficient momentum to get a band together again, touring in 1992 as Gongmaison. Malherbe was back on reeds, and the accompanying tabla and techno-esque electronics suddenly sounded bang up-to-date, a measure of how many of the original musical tenets of golden-age Gong had come back into rock music. Allen went on to record with Kramer, mainman of Bongwater and Shimmy Disc, for 1993's *Who's Afraid* album.

In October 1994, Allen hosted a 25th birthday party for Gong at London's Forum, headlining a bill featuring some of the many spin-offs that had continued through the years. It was a testament also to the Gong Appreciation Society (GAS), which had been assiduously reissuing much of the extended Gong catalogue. A 1997 release, *Shapeshifter,* brought a lot of graduates from Allen's university back to the alma mater to show what they'd learned along the way.

To this day the group's catalogue continues to swell, with more and more recordings being unearthed: 2002's *Glastonbury 1971* is essential, as is much of Allen's newer solo material. In 2008, a terrific DVD of the "Gong Unconvention" – a three-day Gong festival held in Amsterdam – was released. And the music of Allen and Gong has since been discovered by like-minded freaks, from acid house producers to Acid Mothers Temple. Only the extraordinarily unobservant would fail to notice a certain common thread there. To this day Daevid Allen, Gong, and the Gong family of musicians and bands continue to record new and inventive music.

CB/GC

playlist:

1 You Can't Kill Me *from* Camembert Electrique
The song that has become Gong's anthem across the years – and which is still, more often than not, the song that opens a Gong concert.

2 Pot Head Pixies *from* Flying Teapot
I am, you are, we are... crazy! And somehow you just know that there's something really delightful about it all.

3 Tropical Fish/Selene *from* Camembert Electrique
Another staple from the Gong catalogue, this early psychedelic opus has stood the test of time admirably.

4 Radio Gnome Invisible *from* Flying Teapot
The Planet Gong, with its resident Pot Head Pixies, communicating by Radio Gnome Invisible, are introduced here, in the opening song to Gong's famous trilogy of albums.

5 Master Builder *from* You
Never has there been a better usage of an "om" mantra in psychedelic music. Hillage turns in a blistering solo as the band reaches an amazing crescendo. This is Gong at its musical peak.

6 You Never Blow Yr Trip Forever *from* You
The closing song from the trilogy puts forth one of the key philosophies of Gong amidst one of the headiest pieces of music you're likely to hear. "You are I and I am You".

7 I Never Glid Before *from* Angel's Egg
The influence of Steve Hillage within the band is fully realized in this funky classic.

8 Stone Innocent Frankenstein *from* Banana Moon
From Daevid Allen's first solo album, which also featured Gary Wright (Spooky Tooth) and Robert Wyatt (Soft Machine). The song, which became a huge cult favourite among Gong fans, will completely turn you on your ear.

10 Shapeshifter *from* Shapeshifter
From the most overlooked of Gong's albums, "Shapeshifter" showcases a more mature sounding Gong. The band has never stopped innovating across the years and this shows Gong experimenting with new sounds and instrumentation.

Henry Cow

Among the first batch of releases on Richard Branson's Virgin Records was not only Mike Oldfield's *Tubular Bells* but also *Leg End* (aka *Legend*), a strange and demanding set of arty noise by a militant tendency of avant-garde experimentalists called Henry Cow. One sold millions. The other proved to be the least commercial signing in Virgin's history. Yet it was the abstruse, uneasy listening of Henry Cow that over the past 35 years has proved to be the more influential, feeding an immense European genealogy of genre-defying music at the radical margins where the distinctions between rock, jazz, classical and free improvisation blur.

The first incarnation of Henry Cow was put together at Cambridge University in 1968 by guitarist Fred Frith and multi-instrumentalist Tim Hodgkinson. Describing their music variously as "dada blues" and "neo-Hiroshima", their name is widely held to have come from the twentieth century American composer Henry Cowell, although this has been strenuously denied. According to Hodgkinson, the name was simply "in the air" and had no concrete references.

They made their first performance supporting Pink Floyd at a college ball in May 1968, playing a semi-formed art-rock that drew on a mess of influences including Soft Machine, Captain Beefheart, Frank Zappa, Bela Bartok, Olivier Messiaen and the local composer and Cambridge lecturer Roger Smalley, who had studied under Stockhausen. Smalley's contribution was to suggest that they challenge themselves by writing music they could not play, and then teach themselves to master it. Various musicians came and went before a settled line-up emerged in 1970 with the addition of John Greaves (bass) and Chris Cutler (drums), followed soon after by Geoff Leigh (sax), later replaced by Lindsay Cooper (woodwind).

After John Peel had invited them to play a radio session, they moved to London in 1970, working on various theatre projects, staging their own "Cabaret Voltaire" concerts at Kensington Town Hall and mixing their serious, largely instrumental avant-garde music with left-wing politics. "Others experimented with drugs. We did it with radical politics," Cutler later recalled. Yet they had to wait until 1973 to make their recording debut, when they signed to the newly hatched Virgin label. Their first two albums, *Leg End* (1973) and *Unrest* (1974), were defiantly anti-commercial, full of weird time signatures and discordance but shot through with moments of odd beauty. Robert Wyatt pronounced them "me favourite band", finding common cause not only with their music but their Communist politics. But his was a minority view in every sense.

Virgin seemed untroubled. Mike Oldfield was selling albums by the barrow-load and the label's A&R policy at the time seemed to be based on proving its "alternative" credentials by spending the *Tubular Bells* windfall on signing the most eccentric acts from as far outside the rock mainstream as they could find. Among them was the trio of Peter Blegvad (guitar), Anthony Moore (piano) and Dagmar Krause (vocals). Formed in Hamburg in 1972 as Slapp Happy, their self-titled Virgin debut (the band had already released two LPs on Polydor) was an enchanting collection of tuneful but oddball songs that was widely ignored by just about everyone except Wyatt and Henry Cow.

Indeed, the Cow thought Slapp Happy were so wonderful that they promptly proposed marriage. The intention was that each party to the union should take the lead on alternate discs. Credited to Slapp Happy/Henry Cow, their first fusion, 1974's *Desperate Straights*, was written mainly by Blegvad and Moore. A dark and cerebral set of compositions loosely about the decline of the West (or the Occident, as they called it), with Krause in compelling voice, it was welded together by Henry Cow's trademark discordance. Critically well-received, again it sold zilch. Within less than a year, the marriage had been dissolved and the intended Happy Cow follow-up, *In Praise of Learning* (1975), was credited merely to Henry Cow. Moore had left before its release and Blegvad was sacked for being "too whimsical". Only Dagmar remained, joining Frith and Cutler as the core of the reconstituted Henry Cow. Despite these problems, *In Praise of Learning* remains perhaps the band's definitive statement, the radical freeform music and Krause's extraordinary voice matching the radical politics (the sleeve included John Grierson's call to class action: "Art is not a mirror – it is a hammer").

The group spent much of the next three years working in Italy and Spain, playing gigs for left-wing causes before split-

ting in 1978. Frith, Cutler and Dagmar formed the Art Bears, who were Henry Cow in all but name. After two albums that were somewhat more song-friendly than the Cow's erudite noise, they too split, in 1981. Since then, virtually all those who passed through Henry Cow have continued to work at the cutting-edge of musical experimentation. Cutler played with Pere Ubu for a while; Frith became a professor of composition and has collaborated with the likes of Brian Eno and radical saxophonist John Zorn; Blegvad has continued to record and tour sporadically, as well as launching a second career as a cartoonist. They have all remained in touch; wherever avant-rockers have come together to launch a new project, more often than not someone from the Henry Cow axis has been involved. In 1998, they reformed for *Ça Va*, their first album in 23 years. Needless to say, the record sank without trace. It wouldn't really have been Henry Cow otherwise.

NW

playlist:

1 Upon Entering the Hotel Adlon *from* Unrest
A furious explosion of sound that dispenses with conventional notions of tone and rhythm: Henry Cow at their most avant-garde.

2 Living in the Heart of the Beast *from* In Praise of Learning
Dense, moody arrangement, blood-curdling singing from Krause meets guitar pyrotechnics from Frith.

3 Nice Funerals of the Citizen King *from* Leg End
The track that acted as the band's musical and political manifesto on their debut album.

4 Some Questions about Hats *from* Desperate Straights
One of the highlights from the Happy Cow merger.

5 Nirvana for Mice *from* Concerts
A brilliant live version of Frith's guitar tour de force from their first album.

Robert Wyatt

A sk the world's songwriters whom they would most like to perform one of their compositions, and those primarily interested in the royalties might opt for Madonna or Robbie Williams. But it's a fair bet that among the less mercenary, many would nominate Robert Wyatt. He himself describes his faltering falsetto as sounding like "Jimmy Somerville on Valium". But Wyatt's reinterpretations of songs such as Elvis Costello's "Shipbuilding", the Monkees' "I'm A Believer" and Peter Gabriel's "Biko" are transformed by his conversational cadences so that they are hardly cover versions at all but entirely new creations. And he's no slouch as a songwriter either, with a proud body of compositional work to his name stretching back almost forty years.

Wyatt's career has its roots in the much-vaunted "Canterbury scene" of the early 1970s, an era of prog-rock that produced bands such as Caravan – and Soft Machine, of which he was a founder member. His early party trick involved singing note-perfect versions of Charlie Parker solos, a voice-as-instrument technique that was to shape the way he sang for the rest of his career.

Wyatt spent five years as Soft Machine's drummer, also composing and vocalizing in idiosyncratic fashion, before he was kicked out in 1971. He was glad to go, for he had grown out of sympathy with the group's overly muso jazz-rock fusions. After recording his first solo album, *End of An Ear*, he formed Matching Mole (a pun on "Soft Machine" in French), who recorded two prog-ish albums which also gave Wyatt room to develop his unique vocal style. The band also attained some notoriety for posing as Maoist revolutionaries on the cover of the second album, Matching Mole's *Little Red Record*. Yet this was not merely the glib posing of a fashionista – it was a genuine affirmation of Wyatt's Communist sympathies.

Matching Mole disbanded soon after its release and Wyatt began composing the material that would appear on his second solo album, *Rock Bottom* (1974). The album's preparation, however, was interrupted by a horrendous accident that was to alter Wyatt's life – and arguably his music – forever. Drunk at a party in June 1973, he fell to the ground from a fourth-floor window. He broke his back and was confined permanently to a wheelchair. He later called the event the beginning of his maturity and in hospital he continued to work on the songs that would appear on *Rock Bottom* "in a trance". Within six months he was back at work in the recording studio and appeared on stage at London's Rainbow Theatre with Pink Floyd and Soft Machine, who lent financial support by playing a benefit concert for him.

With Pink Floyd's Nick Mason in the producer's chair, *Rock Bottom* has come to be recognized as Wyatt's first great masterpiece. Intense yet also oddly mellow and soothing, the record's abstract sketches of pain, loss and suffering are shot through with vivid flashes of love and renewal, inspired as it was by his relationship with Alfreda Benge, whom he married on the day of *Rock Bottom*'s release. They went to live in Lincolnshire where they've stayed ever since, with Benge providing the artwork for all his album covers and considerable lyrical assistance.

The album was critically well-received and Wyatt even appeared on the cover of *NME* (with Ivor Cutler and Mike Oldfield alongside him in wheelchairs in solidarity). Sales were poor but there was an unlikely commercial success with a playful cover of "I'm A Believer", which made the singles chart and propelled him on to *Top of the Pops*.

After 1975's *Ruth Is Stranger Than Richard*, a kind of coda to *Rock Bottom*, a long period of reassessment followed during which time Wyatt and Benge immersed themselves in politics. Wyatt was struggling to write any new songs but he had a light-bulb moment in which he remembered that "Elvis and Sinatra never wrote a song in their lives". It led to a superbly imaginative series of covers, many of them collected together on the album *Nothing Can Stop Us* (1982). Among them was the anti-Falklands War lament "Shipbuilding", which found him bothering the charts for the second time in his career. It also helped to unblock his own songwriting and led to a new album of his own material, *Old Rottenhat* (1985).

Since then there have been just four albums of new material, every one of them an event. His most recent, 2007's *Comicopera* was another fine collection full of possibility, passion, warmth, humanity and a ripe maturity.

NW

playlist:

1 Moon in June *from* Third
His Soft Machine swansong: a side-long tour de force of improvised drumming and singing.

2 Oh Caroline *from* Matching Mole
The most affecting love song he ever wrote – and Alfie (Alfreda) inspired more than a few.

3 Rock Bottom
The entire album: if ever there was an LP that demands to be heard in its entirety, this is it.

4 Shipbuilding *from* Nothing Can Stop Us
A great song achingly and perfectly delivered...

5 Strange Fruit *from* Nothing Can Stop Us
A fearless version of one of the hardest songs in the world to sing.

As played by John Peel

You can blame the DJ John Peel for the obscurity of much of the music in this book. After 37 years of playing records on national radio that nobody else would spin, his death in 2004 left a void that can never be filled. Here are a select few of his favourites.

Medicine Head

Formed in Stafford in 1968, Medicine Head was a duo of John Fiddler and the Jew's harp player Peter Hope-Evans. Peel so loved their sparse original songs and their crude-but-glorious home-made R&B that he made them one of the first signings to his Dandelion label. The third of their six albums, released in 1972, was called *Dark Side of the Moon*. Had it not, like most Dandelion releases, completely bombed, Pink Floyd would have had to find a different title for their masterpiece the following year.

Half Man Half Biscuit

Essentially a vehicle for the idiosyncratic vision of Nigel Blackwell, Birkenhead's HMHB played a dozen Peel sessions between 1984 and 2004. Their early post-punk sound owed something to The Fall but after their second single, "Dickie Davies Eyes", made the top forty, Blackwell announced his "retirement". Success, he said, was causing him to miss too much daytime TV. He also missed a chance to appear on Channel 4's *The Tube* because he went to see Tranmere Rovers play instead. He reformed the band in 1990 – making the announcement on Peel's show, naturally.

Truman's Water

Formed in San Diego in 1991, the noisy improvisations of Trumans Water owed something to Captain Beefheart which, of course, was always going to give them an advantage in getting played on Peel's show. Even the band were taken aback, however, when John played their debut album, *Of Thick Tum* (1992), uninterrupted from beginning to end one night on Radio 1. The band's Glen Galloway later left to form an "experimental Christian hip-hop outfit", which proved an absurdity too far even for Peel.

I'm Being Good

The guitar psychoses of Brighton's I'm Being Good came to Peel's attention in 1991 when they released a single on their own Infinite Chug label, titled *Hate Sturdy Buildings*. They tried to release their first radio session for him on what was going to be their first CD but licensing problems intervened and their full-length debut, *Poisonous Life*, was delayed until 1998. By then they had also released another single featuring themselves on one side and fellow Peel protégés Truman's Water on the other. On Peel's death, they recorded the track "He Has Unborn Eyes On Long Tinsel Stalks" in his honour. He surely would have appreciated the gesture.

Wawali Bonané

In 1997, *The Guardian* newspaper asked Peel to compile a list of his all-time favourite twenty albums and, to the joy of world music fans and Andy Kershaw, he listed not one but two African acts. At number ten – one place above Pink Floyd's debut – he nominated the 1992 album *Enzenzé* by the Congolese singer Wawali Bonané, backed by Tabu Ley Rochereau's band. Nobody had sent him the album: he had bought a copy in Stern's specialist African music shop off London's Euston Road. Peel played the track "Bayanaya" on the radio on the birth of Kershaw's son in 1997, announcing it was "the best start in life" that the boy could have.

The Four Brothers

The second African album on Peel's fave albums list was *Makorokoto* by Zimbabwe's Four Brothers, an uplifting set of irresistible dance rhythms characterized by sweet, soaring vocals and rippling guitars, in similar style to the Bhundu Boys. Peel dubbed them "the best live band in the world" – and, after they had recorded a radio session, he booked them to perform in his back garden.

Wild Willy Barrett and John Otway

One of the oddest by-products of the punk rock explosion, Otway and Wild Willy weren't really punks at all, just crazed hippies with a DIY ethos. In 1977 Peel helped propel their bonkers debut single, "Cor Baby, That's Really Free", into the charts and onto *Top of the Pops*, where they gave what was probably the most riotously and wilfully incompetent performance in the show's history. Polydor then offered them a five-album deal and paid Pete Townshend a small fortune to produce their first album. It sold disastrously. Otway later called his autobiography *Rock and Roll's Greatest Failure*. Peel remained ineffably proud of his part in their non-success.

The Misunderstood

Those old enough to have heard Peel's original *Perfumed Garden* radio shows will fondly recall his endless playing of "I Can Take You to the Sun", a glorious psychedelic rush of acid-rock guitars by The Misunderstood. Peel had discovered the band in Riverside, California, when working as a DJ in the US and in 1966 helped them relocate to London. Despite his avid support, the brilliant guitar playing of Glenn Ross Campbell and a couple of great singles, they were doomed to become non-combatant casualties of the Vietnam War when their lead singer and main songwriter Rick Brown was drafted, leaving them to go down in rock history as one of the great lost bands of the era.

NW

BLUESMEN AND BAWLERS
the Delta and elsewhere

Elizabeth Cotten

Most people known the tune "Freight Train". It's long been one of the first tricks that any aspiring finger-picking guitarist attempts to master. Far fewer know it was written by Elizabeth "Libba" Cotten way back around 1907 – or that she herself didn't record it for half a century and only began her performing career when she was well past retirement age.

Born in North Carolina in the final decade of the nineteenth century (the exact year is the subject of some debate, although 1895 is most widely accepted), Cotten was essentially a folk musician but, as with many African-Americans who played folk, her music was rooted in the blues.

Her parents couldn't agree on a name, so she was called "Little Sis," "Babe" or "Shug" until her first day of school, when she announced that her name was now Elizabeth. She began playing her brother's banjo around the age of eight but when he left home, taking the instrument with him, she transferred to the guitar, buying a Stella with the money she saved after going into domestic service at the age of twelve. "From that day on, nobody had no peace in that house," she was fond of recalling in later years. With no teacher, she was forced to develop her own playing method, picking out the chords with her left hand using just two fingers with the instrument laid upside-down on her lap. Cotten developed an extensive repertoire of standards, dance tunes, rags and original compositions, one of which was the timeless "Freight Train".

Yet if she had any thoughts of pursuing a musical career (and there is no evidence that she did), they were shelved when she married Frank Cotten and had her first child, Lillie, at the age of fifteen. With her family she moved between Washington DC and New York, seeking domestic work. She concentrated on family life and the church, putting her guitar skills on hold for 25 years. After a divorce in 1940, she went to live with Lillie and five grandchildren in Washington DC, where she worked in a department store. It was there that an extraordinary turn of events took place. One day, she found a lost little girl wandering the store and returned her to her mother – one Ruth Crawford Seeger. The girl was

Peggy Seeger, the younger sister of Pete Seeger, and Cotten went to work for the family, which was already prominent in folk music circles. When Peggy began learning the guitar, it revived Cotten's interest and she began playing again, rediscovering an incredibly dextrous finger-picking style with a soft, flowing and almost classical touch. Inevitably, the style became known as "Cotten-picking".

"Freight Train" became famous before she did; Peggy Seeger moved to Britain in the 1950s and began performing Cotten's song. It was picked up and recorded by Nancy Whiskey and found its way back to America, where it was a hit for Rusty Draper. The first Cotten allegedly knew of it was when she heard Draper's version on the radio.

Cotten herself did not record until 1957, when another member of the family, Peggy's brother Mike Seeger, produced her first album for Folkways, the somewhat austerely titled *Folk Songs and Instrumentals with Guitar*. Needless to say, it included her definitive version of the now well-known "Freight Train". Three years later, Cotten and Seeger performed their first concert together and her performing career was launched at the age of 68. She went on to become a great favourite at folk festivals, mingling her songs with stories about her long life, and offering an unparalleled first-person documentation of music that went back almost unmediated to the early years of the twentieth century. She also toured with Taj Mahal, among others, although she did not leave domestic service until 1970.

Two further albums for Folkways followed with *Shake Sugaree* and *When I Am Gone* (both 1965) before 1985's *Elizabeth Cotten, Live!* won her a Grammy award at the age of 89. She gave her last concert at the 1986 Philadelphia Folk Festival and died the following year at the age of 92. Her recordings remain rare and exquisite examples of music that can be traced back to an era before the advent of recording. Those who have recorded her songs range from Peter, Paul and Mary ("Freight Train") to the Grateful Dead ("Oh Babe, It Ain't No Lie" and "Going Down the Road Feeling Bad") via Taj Mahal ("Georgia Buck"). Bob Dylan, who first met Elizabeth in the early 1960s, performed her "Oh Babe It Ain't No Lie" on numerous occasions live in the 1990s, often as a show opener.

NW

playlist:

1 Freight Train *from* Folk Songs and Instrumentals with Guitar
One of the most bathetic songs ever performed, with Cotten's vulnerable, barely in tune voice entirely hand in glove with the ruminations on mortality and escape in the lyrics.

2 Ain't Got No Honey Baby Now *from* Folk Songs and Instrumentals with Guitar
Fancy fingerpicking that's like down-home, countrified flamenco.

3 Going Down the Road Feeling Bad *from* Folk Songs and Instrumentals with Guitar
A universal folk complaint that any human being can relate to.

4 Oh Babe It Ain't No Lie *from* Folk Songs and Instrumentals with Guitar
The vengefulness of the self-righteous never sounded so quaint and charming.

5 Washington Blues *from* Shake Sugaree
A careful ragtime blues instrumental that cuts straight to the limpid core of the artform Scott Joplin took to the conservatoires.

6 Shake Sugaree *from* Shake Sugaree
Libba's voice was simultaneously carefree and world-weary – a tension summed up perfectly by this breezy tune about having all your worldly possessions stacked up at the pawn shop.

7 Fox Chase *from* Shake Sugaree
Almost Eastern European sounding at times, this minor-chord instrumental has speeding-up and slowing-down passages that possess all the drama of klezmer.

Sugar Pie DeSanto

Of all the great artists to record for Chicago's legendary Chess Records, perhaps the most unfairly overlooked is Sugar Pie DeSanto. She stood no more than five feet tall but, as she shouted in one of her better-known songs, "if you know how to use what you got it don't matter about your size". With her razor-sharp, don't-mess-with-me delivery she was every inch a match for similar red-hot mamas such as Koko Taylor and Etta James. She was a far superior singer to Tina Turner, with whom she toured – and a better dancer, too, with a famous stage routine that included acrobatic back-flips. And she was every bit as tough as her voice. According to Maurice White, who played drums on her Chess recordings and went on to found Earth, Wind & Fire, she could turn the air blue in the studio, using "cuss words that hadn't even been invented yet".

In the early 1960s James Brown was so impressed that he asked her to be his support act and kept her on the road with him for two years. She knocked out European audiences on an early tour, when she often upstaged Chess's better-known stars. She was also a hot songwriter, whose work was covered by the likes of Fontella Bass, Billy Stewart, Little Milton and the Dells.

Yet Chess were oddly reticent in making the most of her obvious talent. In seven years on the label she recorded thirty singles and released just one solitary LP. One story holds that the label feared she might cut into the success of Chess's other female stars, such as her cousin Etta James, with whom she recorded some fantastic duets. Or possibly Chess genuinely didn't realize just how good she was. Chess's judgement was often faulty: they were, for example, deeply unimpressed by Buddy Guy, whose guitar playing was famously dismissed by label boss Leonard Chess as "a motherfucking noise".

Yet how they could not appreciate the worth of such knock-out tracks as "Soulful Dress", "Slip In Mules", "Jump in My Chest", "There's Gonna Be Trouble", "Do I Make Myself Clear", "Use What You Got" and "Can't Let You Go" is hard to credit. The retrospective collection of the best of her 1960s Chess recordings, which belatedly appeared some thirty years on, is as good as anything the label recorded during that decade.

Sugar Pie, of course, was not her real name. She was born Umpeylia Marsema Balinton in San Francisco in 1935 and was dubbed "Little Miss Sugar Pie", on account of her diminutive size, by band leader Johnny Otis, who discovered her in a talent contest in the early 1950s. The name "DeSanto" was added some years later by Oakland disc jockey Don Barksdale. She made her recording debut with Otis in 1955 and recorded for Aladdin with Pee Wee Kingsley as Pee Wee and Sugar Pie before cutting "I Want to Know" for Veltone on 1960. Licensed to Chess, it made number four on the American R&B chart.

By then she was performing regularly at R&B venues such as the Regal in Chicago and the Apollo in Harlem, where she made such an impression on James Brown that she became his opening act for two years. Her live show was, by all accounts, almost as spectacular as that of the Godfather of Soul himself. "I tore it up, that's all there is to it. They dubbed me Lady James Brown," she later recalled proudly.

In 1964, she was the only female performer on the American Folk Blues Festival tour of Europe, on a bill that included Willie Dixon, Lightnin' Hopkins and Sonny Boy Williamson, while her R&B hits for Chess included "Slip in Mules" and the sassy "Soulful Dress" (1964) as well as duets with Etta James on "In the Basement" (1965) and "Do I Make Myself Clear" (1966).

After parting company with Chess in 1968 she moved back to San Francisco where she has been a stalwart of the local blues circuit ever since. She has continued to record, releasing albums such as *Sugar Is Salty*, *Classic Sugar Pie*, *A Slice of Pie* and *Sugar Refined*, all on the Jasman label. Also worth seeking out is *Hello San Francisco*, a mid-1980s compilation of her post-Chess material, recorded between 1968 and 1983.

"A lot of people dub me the Blues Queen," she said in a 1999 interview. "But I sing more than blues. I can sing anything. You know what I mean?" Believe it.

NW

playlist:

1 I Want to Know *from* Down in the Basement (The Chess Years)
"Please don't start no stuff 'cause I don't want to get rough."

2 Use What You Got *from* Down in the Basement (The Chess Years)
"Yes I got everything I know I need to keep my man satisfied, cause if you know how to use what you got it don't matter about your size."

3 Soulful Dress *from* Down in the Basement (The Chess Years)
"Don't you girls go getting jealous when I round up all your fella, cause I'll be at my best when I put on my soulful dress."

4 Slip In Mules *from* Down in the Basement (The Chess Years)
Her witty answer to Tommy Tucker's "Hi-Heel Sneakers".

5 Jump In My Chest *from* Down in the Basement (The Chess Years)
"Shut up when I'm talking to you... If you don't believe what I say, then jump in my chest!"

6 Down in the Basement *from* Down in the Basement (The Chess Years)
A double dose of blues power, as she trades lines with Etta James.

Jo Ann Kelly

The queen of British blues singers, Jo Ann Kelly could surely have been a major blues-rock star if she'd been so inclined. Instead, she turned down gilt-edged invitations to join Canned Heat and Johnny Winter's band in order to stick to the pure acoustic country-blues she loved best.

Born in south London in 1944, she discovered the blues via the skiffle craze, like many of her generation. She started playing guitar at the age of thirteen, and in 1962 formed an acoustic duo with blues pianist Bob Hall. Her recording debut came on a limited edition EP cut with Groundhogs guitarist Tony McPhee in 1964. As the blues explosion took off, she stepped up from the clubs to the college circuit, with a repertoire that included songs by Bessie Smith and Sister Rosetta Tharpe as well as Charley Patton and Robert Johnson. Singing in a voice of convincing authenticity, she accompanied herself with expert acoustic blues guitar, playing both six- and twelve-string instruments.

After singing on the debut album by the John Dummer Band, whose number also included her younger brother Dave, Kelly released her first full-length solo album on Columbia in 1969. On the cover she looked like a spinster librarian in her fringe and spectacles, yet inside lurked one of the world's feistiest blues mamas. That same year, she duetted with Mississippi Fred MacDowell on "When I Lay My Burden Down", and turned down an opportunity to join Canned Heat, with whom she had jammed on their British tour. She later refused a similar invitation to play in Johnny Winter's band: she preferred the acoustic blues, even if it offered little chance of riches and fame.

For a short while in the early 1970s she fronted a band with the politically correct name Spare Rib, and she also guested on various albums by British blues alumni, often credited as "Memphis Lil". She continued to tour and record throughout the 1980s, most notably in a show called "Ladies and the Blues", in which she paid tribute to her female role models. In 1988, she began suffering from painful headaches, and was diagnosed with a brain tumour. She returned to the stage after an apparently successful operation, but collapsed and died in 1990 at the age of 46.

She was a bona fide belter of a blues singer. There are precious few female guitarists – let alone from outside the US – to have performed on iconic 1960s albums by Mississippi Fred MacDowell, Stefan Grossman or John Fahey. The power and authenticity of her art was summed up neatly in an off-the-cuff remark made by Bonnie Raitt, while discussing her own approach to singing the blues. "It was hard to do 'Walking Blues' for instance," she explained to her interviewer. "But I was not born with a voice like Mavis Staples or Jo Ann Kelly."

NW

> "In those days, audiences were used to female singers being Joan Baez clones, and this small blonde girl in spectacles didn't look awfully like a blues person. She unpacked her frightfully cheap-looking guitar from a soft case, sat down, and immediately became an unholy mating between Memphis Minnie and Charley Patton."
>
> **Ian Anderson on Jo Ann Kelly**

Peter Green

He could've been... Eric Clapton?

For a brief period, Peter Green was effectively Eric Clapton's understudy. When the guitarist known as "God" left John Mayall's Bluesbreakers for the first time, Green stepped into the breach. A few months later, Clapton asked Mayall for his old job back and Green was sidelined again. When, a short while later, Clapton quit once again – this time for good – Green once more took his place, staying around long enough to record the album *The Hard Road* with Mayall. Green proved himself to be the guitar-playing equal of his come-and-go predecessor, before leaving to form Fleetwood Mac in 1967.

A working-class Jewish boy from London's East End, Green delivered sinuous licks with a haunting, sweet-yet-melancholy tone that helped to make Fleetwood Mac arguably the finest act to emerge from the British blues boom of the late 1960s. His combination of fluency, speed and technique was almost unrivalled. B.B. King described Green as "the only man to ever make me sweat".

Green pushed the blues idiom to its limits on three albums, all released in little more than twelve months between 1968 and 1969: *Mr. Wonderful*, *English Rose* and *Then Play On*. He also wrote a series of memorable hit singles for the band, including "Albatross", "Black Magic Woman" (later covered by Santana), the doom-laden "Oh Well", the autobiographical "Man of the World" and "Green Manalishi". All were testament to his seemingly unstoppable creativity. However, "Green Manalishi" also seemed to document Green's doomed struggle to halt his spiralling descent into madness. That all was not well had first become evident on an American tour in 1969. At the time he was taking LSD.

After one particularly vivid trip in which he claimed to have been visited by an angel holding a starving African child in her arms, he demanded that the band should give all its money away. Needless to say, he didn't receive any assent from his colleagues. The following year, during a tour of Germany, he announced after a three-day acid binge that he couldn't go on. "It was a freedom thing," he explained many years later. "I wanted to go and live in a commune. In the end I didn't. I had to get away from the group. Acid had a lot to do with it."

Diagnosed as schizophrenic, Green was eventually admitted to a psychiatric hospital in 1973. When he came out, he worked as a grave digger and a hospital porter. On one occasion, when Fleetwood Mac's accountant attempted to deliver him a royalty cheque, he chased him off with an air rifle. He was sectioned and given ECT treatment. "I was throwing things around and smashing things up," he recalls. "I smashed a car windscreen and the police came and took me to the station. They asked me if I wanted to go to hospital and I said yes, because I didn't feel safe going back anywhere else."

He did not return to music until 1996, when he reported that he had literally had to "relearn" how to play and had decided from now on to "keep it simple". There followed a prolific series of albums with the Splinter Group, including a 1998 collection of Robert Johnson covers – a good half a dozen years before Clapton's similar outing. It was good to have him back. He never completely regained his former virtuosity, which would have been a tall order, but his confidence and touch slowly returned.

NW

Charley Patton

But for the hiss and crackle and the generally poor sound quality which, prior to the wonders of digital restoration, always made his recordings notoriously hard to listen to, Charley Patton rather than Robert Johnson might have been crowned "the king of the Delta blues singers".

Born in southern Mississippi, estimates of his date of birth range between 1881 and 1891, although the latter is now generally accepted. There's not much agreement about the spelling of his first name, however. What we do know with some certainty is that towards the end of the 1890s, his sharecropping parents moved to the Will Dockery Plantation where the young Patton fell under the spell of the guitarist Henry Sloan, whom he copied and learned from. By his late teens he was by all accounts already a precociously fine performer and songwriter. Around 1910 he hooked up with the guitarist Willie Brown, who later accompanied him on many of his recordings.

Patton and Brown wandered all around the Delta, travelling north to Memphis and as far west as Arkansas and Louisiana, playing plantation picnics and dances. By 1926, a young Robert Johnson was following them around, eagerly picking up all the guitar tips he could.

Patton made his first recording in 1929, when Paramount invited him to travel 750 miles north to Richmond, Indiana, and he recorded fourteen sides in a single day, earning $700 dollars at $50 a song. He was invited to record again three months later, this time at Paramount's new studio in Grafton, Wisconsin, where he cut 22 more sides, some with accompaniment from fiddler Henry Sims. The tracks from both sessions bristle with an intensity that is unforgettable and which belies the fact that he was only five foot five inches tall and weighed 135 pounds. It was said that his voice could carry 500 yards without amplification and his gritty singing was an influence on Howlin' Wolf – just one of the many bluesmen he influenced.

The 1929 recordings, most of which were released as 78rpm singles, made him the biggest-selling blues singer of his time, but his showmanship had already made him a Delta celebrity before he even entered a studio. "Charley Patton was a clowning man with a guitar," fellow bluesman Sam Chatmon recalled. "He be in there putting his guitar all between his legs, carry it behind his head, lay down on the floor and never stopped picking" – and all this almost half a century before Jimi Hendrix. Other accounts recall a dapper, raffish figure who enjoyed his fame and was a noted womanizer and drinker. "He was a nice guy but he

just loved the bottle," Howlin' Wolf recalled. Honeyboy Edwards reckoned: "Charley always had a lot of women. Men didn't like him much because all the women was fools over him."

After his two 1929 sessions, he recorded again for Paramount the next year with Willie Brown and Son House accompanying him, but the onset of the Depression meant that he didn't cut his fourth and final session until a couple of months before his death in 1934, when he travelled to New York and recorded around 25 sides for the American Record Company, although only ten of them were ever released, the rest lost or destroyed. By then, his voice was a lesser instrument, after an assailant had attempted to cut his throat the previous year and damaged his vocal cords. When Paramount went out of business, the masters of his 1929 and 1930 recordings were sold off as scrap metal and allegedly ended up lining a chicken coop. Hence the greatest work in Patton's canon has only survived on scratchy 78s. Modern digital noise-reduction processes have helped, but have still not restored the sound to the kind of quality of Johnson's recordings, made only a few years later.

Yet he left an extraordinary body of work. His songs describe a narrowly defined landscape of Delta cotton towns, plantations and boll weevils that is almost parochial, yet there's still a universality about the passions and emotions he conjures that resonates to this day.

His vocal asides and phrasing and his hoarse, ravaged voice influenced a generation of Delta bluesmen. The propulsive beat and richly accented rhythmic sense of his guitar playing were equally widely copied, as was his slide technique, either played across his lap and fretted with a pocket knife, or upright with a bottleneck. Almost every bluesman who followed him would have sounded very different without his influence.

He died from a chronic heart condition in 1934 and his death certificate listed his occupation as "farmer". The tombstone erected many years later offers a more accurate measure of his importance with the inscription: "The voice of the Delta – the foremost performer of early Mississippi blues, whose songs became cornerstones of American music."

NW

playlist:

1 Mississippi Boweavil Blues *from* The Definitive Charley Patton
Patton's one-bar blues and bullish bellow fight off the driving rain of century-old tape hiss with deathless panache.

2 Pony Blues *from* The Definitive Charley Patton
Blues connoisseurs familiar with cockney rhyming slang will strenuously beg to differ with the title of this song.

3 A Spoonful Blues *from* The Definitive Charley Patton
Does a spoonful of blues help the medicine go down? You sense Mary Poppins and Charley Patton probably wouldn't have gotten along all that famously. Particularly if he was playing such inventive, off-the-twelve-bar-track chord changes, and singing such homicidal lyrics.

4 High Water Everywhere *from* The Definitive Charley Patton
Hear how Charley kept the dances going with all that guitar-body percussion that mirrors the song's subject matter: his tub-thumping sounds like the paddling of a canoe. Human beatboxers simply weren't needed back then.

5 Pea Vine Blues *from* The Definitive Charley Patton
One of the most drunk-sounding hollers a blues musician has ever committed to tape. Tom Waits, eat your heart out.

Professor Longhair

"**F**es" – as he was known to those who played with him – was one of that rare breed of singular artists who create their own musical style way outside the mainstream but come to define a new standard by which all others have to be judged. So it was with Professor Longhair and New Orleans piano-playing.

Born Henry Roeland Byrd as World War I was drawing to a close, the Prof grew up in a house with no piano. He learned his chops on the street – quite literally – on an old piano with broken keys and several hammers missing, which had been abandoned at the end of an alley. He later claimed that the entire instrument had only eight or perhaps ten fully functioning keys – and even those were hopelessly out of tune. Yet from such unpromising beginnings he fashioned a uniquely joyous style of playing, equally notable for its clarity and precision of tone as for its unbelievably funky syncopation. That other Crescent City legend Allen Toussaint called him "the Bach of New Orleans" and Fats Domino, Dr John, James Booker and Huey Smith were all deeply influenced by him.

After spells as a boxer, cook and professional gambler, and service in World War II, he was in his thirties before he made his recording debut under the name Professor Longhair and the Shuffling Hungarians with 1949's "Mardi Gras in New Orleans". It became his signature tune and defined his sound, with an extraordinary mix of influences from blues, jazz and ragtime to mambo, calypso and zydeco. Over the next few years he recorded most of his best-known tunes – "Tipitina", "Bald Head", "Big Chief", "Ball The Wall in the Night" and "Go to the Mardi Gras". Apart from "Bald Head", none was a hit outside the New Orleans area and by the 1960s he was languishing back in obscurity, making a living by hustling as a card sharp and working – with almost tragic irony – as a janitor in a record store. It was like Picasso turning house decorator.

Lionized by a new generation of disciples such as Dr John, an appearance at the New Orleans Jazz & Heritage Festival heralded a famous comeback. He headlined the 1973 Montreux Jazz Festival and two years later was flown by Paul McCartney to play at a private party for his wife Linda on board the *Queen Mary*. He was finally enjoying the acclaim due to a true original.

NW

Allen Toussaint

If you've ever enjoyed a record from New Orleans, the chances are that Allen Toussaint had something to do with it – whether as a singer, songwriter, pianist, producer, arranger, label owner or mover and shaker. Virtually every hit record to come out of the Crescent City since the 1960s has had the "Toussaint touch" either directly or via his all-pervasive influence.

His signature sound and the New Orleans sound have become practically synonymous. "Working in the Coalmine", "Ride Your Pony", "Brickyard Blues", "Get Out My Life Woman", "Southern Nights", "Freedom to the Stallion", "What Do You Want the Girl to Do", "Yes We Can Can" and "Everything I Do Gonna Be Funky" – which might have served as his motto – were all his compositions. Artists he's worked with from the city include Ernie K-Doe, Irma Thomas, Art and Aaron Neville, Lee Dorsey, The Meters and Dr John. Those from outside New Orleans who have sought his services include the Poynter Sisters, Robert Palmer, Willy DeVille, Solomon Burke, Frankie Miller, The Band and Boz Scaggs. The legions of others who have recorded his songs – sometimes written under the pseudonym Naomi Neville – range from the Rolling Stones to Otis Redding.

Born in 1938, Toussaint grew up in a New Orleans shotgun house – a narrow one-storey dwelling without halls – that was always full of musicians. By the time he was thirteen, he himself was playing in groups with them and before he was out of his teens he was already one of the most in-demand pianists and arrangers on the city's studio scene, playing on records by Fats Domino among others. In 1960 he went to work for Minit Records where, over the next three years, he shaped the New Orleans R&B sound, writing and producing most of the records on the label before going on to found his own production company. For which he employed the mighty Meters as his house band. By the 1970s their sound had got funkier, and white rock artists began making the pilgrimage to his home city to record at the Sea-Saint studio he opened in 1973. The process continues to this day – Elvis Costello recorded the 2006 album *River in Reverse* with him.

Toussaint has also maintained a solo career, releasing a number of albums at sporadic intervals, the best of which is probably 1975's *Southern Nights*, a psychedelic-funk-gumbo concept album about Dixie.

He sat out Hurricane Katrina in the city, behaviour typical of his consistent, dignified resolve. He was, however, forced to leave his beloved New Orleans briefly, moving temporarily to New York while his home was rebuilt.

NW

> "I must say that it wasn't a deliberate effort to make the sound different or anything. I was just going at what I wanted to hear, and it happened to come out like that…"
>
> **Allen Toussaint**

Cinderellas of the blues: eventually they got to have themselves a ball

Jack White of The White Stripes may have the fiery fingerwork and some pretty snazzy trousers, but until he actually experiences genuine suffering to a back-breaking degree for at least a decade or two, there will always be a little something missing from his blues sound. Matthew Johnson, who has been running his Fat Possum record label on the cusp of bankruptcy since 1992, had the right idea. Scouring the backwoods of Mississippi, he uncovered some of the last true bluesmen and recorded their twilight years, not as a historian, but because they sounded great.

"I was never in this as an archivist or a folklorist, recording these guys for posterity. It was the energy and intensity that attracted me," he said. They don't come much more intense than R.L. Burnside, Fat Possum's biggest seller. A convicted murderer, his sparse, hypnotic blues sound ended up earning him an appearance on the soundtrack to *The Sopranos* and gigs with young admirers the Beastie Boys and Jon Spencer Blues Explosion, with whom he recorded an album for Matador records, the fantastically titled *A Ass Pocket Full of Whisky*.

Learning his bare bones technique from neighbour Mississippi Fred MacDowell and cousin-in-law Muddy Waters, Burnside spent his life working as a tractor-driving sharecropper, playing guitar at parties. An attempt at a new life in Chicago in the 1950s was abandoned when, as detailed in his song "RL's Story", his father, his uncle and two bothers were all murdered there.

Back in Mississippi he spent six months in Parchman prison for a murder of his own, after killing a man who was trying to run him off his land. "It was between him and the Lord, him dyin'," he has said. "I just shot him in the head."

Fat Possum successfully marketed this elderly rogue to indie rock fans rather than blues purists, authorizing modern remixes of his music several years before Moby mixed traditional sounds with electronica on his hit album *Play* – and with much more interesting musical results. Burnside apparently hated it, however, but that's somehow very appropriate.

The label did similarly well with acts such as Junior Kimbrough, whose juke joint in Chulahoma, Mississippi was visited by U2 and the Rolling Stones, and T-Model Ford, another murderer who Johnson described as "a cheerful psychopath".

But when your cash cows are the last surviving Delta bluesmen, sooner or later a major problem is inevitable. Burnside and Kimbrough are both dead now, and T-Model Ford is well into his 80s. One Fat Possum artist who is slightly younger – approaching 70 – and still gigging is Robert Belfour. The most elemental-sounding of the Fat Possum roster, he has a voice like an oak tree and an impossibly deep guitar sound.

Fans of dirty blues now look to the relatively youthful Seasick Steve (not a Fat Possum artist) for their kicks. A sixtysomething white one-time hobo who performs using guitars with one, three and occasionally six strings, stamping on a box he calls his "Mississippi Drum Machine", his real name is Steve Wold. His album, *Dog House Music*, became an unlikely UK hit after an appearance on Jools Holland's New Year's Eve music TV show in 2006. Like his aged predecessors he simply seems bemused at such belated success that has seen him playing a headline slot at the Royal Albert Hall. None of these men has ever sought stardom; perhaps that's why their unpolished music seems so much more real and authentic.

DS

Robert Belfour, an oak-throated Fat Possum.

LET THERE BE ROCK
the amps that went up to 11

Blue Cheer

When Eric Clapton was asked in an interview in 2005 if Cream had invented heavy metal, without hesitation he answered "No, that was Blue Cheer". When the Cheer – named after a particularly potent strain of LSD – came roaring out of San Francisco in 1968, their fuzzed-up, full-tilt stoner rock scaled new heights of distortion and volume. They were so heavy that, in comparison, other Marshall-stacked power trios such as Cream and the Jimi Hendrix Experience sounded like radio-friendly pop bands. Led Zeppelin were later called "the hammer of the Gods" but one reviewer in the late 1960s reckoned Blue Cheer were "louder than God" – and he wasn't thinking of the hyperbole of Clapton-worshippers. In their wake, MC5 and the Stooges made plenty of noise but neither quite matched the riff-boiling, cacophonous heaviosity of early Blue Cheer albums.

Formed in 1967 by Dickie Peterson (bass/vocals), Leigh Stephens (guitar) and Paul Whaley (drums) after seeing Hendrix's performance at the Monterey Pop Festival, the trio decided the only way to go was to make the sonic boom patented by bands such as Cream and the Experience even louder, heavier and grungier. "We were second-generation punks with attitude and no skills," Stephens admitted in 2007. "Other bands tolerated us because it was San Francisco and nobody was into violence. Otherwise they would have kicked our asses."

One thing the Cheer did share with the other San Francisco groups, however, was a love of LSD, and their debut album, *Vincebus Eruptum*, appeared in a trippy-looking, embossed cover. "We were stoned on acid and thought 'wouldn't it be great if you could feel the album cover?'," Peterson says. The music had a gut-wrenching sound, driven by Whaley's walloping drums and Stephens' blues-drenched guitar noise. They even made the singles chart with their sledgehammer version of Eddie Cochran's "Summertime Blues". Other covers such as B.B. King's "Rock Me Baby" and Mose Allison's "Parchman Farm" betrayed a blues influence, but once again they had gone for the sound of the heaviest bluesman around, Howlin' Wolf – and then decided to amplify his roar tenfold.

On stage they were reputedly even heavier and louder. "Our goal was to make music a physical experience as well as an audio one," according to Peterson. "We wanted to bring the sound of music into the physical realm, so as you heard the bass, you didn't just hear the sound, it punched you in the gut."

A second album, *Outsideinside*, swiftly followed and, according to legend, recording had to be completed in the open air after the trio's high volume had destroyed the studio monitors. Stephens, however, was unhappy with the noise they were making, believing it was too primitive. When he heard a track from *Vincebus Eruptum* on the radio, he claims to have burst into tears at its Neanderthal noise. "We were too loud. We though it was cool, but it wasn't," he later insisted. He was also at odds with the band's chemical appetites and left around the time of the release of *Outsideinside*, another album of brain-crunching metal freak-out, although the less frenetic and more psychedelic "Feathers From You Tree" and "Gypsy Ball" are an indication of the direction Stephens probably would have preferred to pursue.

playlist:

1 Summertime Blues *from* Vincebus Eruptum
Eddie Cochran, as filtered through Hendrix's "Purple Haze".

2 Parchment Farm *from* Vincebus Eruptum
Did they deliberately misspell the name of Mose Allison's classic – and amid the cacophony did anyone really care?

3 Out of Focus *from* Vincebus Eruptum
Not just out of focus but completely off the dial…

4 Rock Me Baby *from* Vincebus Eruptum
B.B. King's sweet Lucille never made a racket quite like this…

5 Come and Get It *from* Insideoutside
The first speed-metal freak-out – whoever said it sounds like Lemmy with flu was spot on.

6 Magnolia Caboose Babyfinger *from* Insideoutside
A monstrously riffed-up instrumental later covered by Mudhoney.

7 Peace of Mind *from* New! Improved!
Randy Holden's finest hour, even if the title hardly describes a condition much associated with Blue Cheer.

8 Babaji (Twilight Raga) *from* The Original Human Being
The Cheer try something different, in large part thanks to the presence of former Kak guitarist Gary Yoder.

In his place Blue Cheer recruited guitarist Randy Holden from local garage band The Other Half. The new line-up launched with the album *New! Improved!*, a title that was not entirely accurate. The album found the band pulling in two different directions. The first side was the same high-octane, blues-rock racket, but side two allowed the formidable skills of Holden free rein, and he came up with translucent, prismatic beauties such as "Peace of Mind" and "Fruit and Icebergs". Like his predecessor, however, Holden found himself out of step with the band's drug use and left following a European tour to pursue a solo career.

By the band's fourth, self-titled album in 1970, Peterson was the only original member remaining. Blue Cheer made three more albums between 1970 and 71 and even tried to expand their heavy metal style into the more adventurous pastures of "raga-rock" with "Babaji (Twilight Raga)" on 1970's *The Original Human Being*. But the tide had turned against them. They were "headbangers", which in rock circles had by then become a term of abuse and, in any case, Grand Funk Railroad had arrived to steal their tumult. The band split in 1971, although there have been various reunions – the most recent being in 2007, when they released the nicely titled but underwhelming *What Doesn't Kill You*. Along the way, they influenced everyone from Black Sabbath and Mötorhead to Nirvana and Mudhoney. Those first three albums still contain some of the heaviest, crudest, most gratuitously excessive and joyously simple-minded rock'n'roll ever made.

NW

Great lost albums:
Guns N' Roses'
Chinese Democracy

If the saga of *Chinese Democracy* had been written into the *Spinal Tap* movie's script, the storyline would have been rejected as too preposterous even for rock'n'roll. At the time of writing, the world has been waiting 17 years for Guns N' Roses to follow up 1991's *Use Your Illusion I & II*.

Recording for *Chinese Democracy* began in 1994 in fraught circumstances, due to the volatile relationship between singer Axl Rose and guitarist Slash, who quit in 1996, claiming that Rose wanted "control to the point that the rest of us were strangled". The singer brought in new members more amenable to his bidding from Nine Inch Nails, the Replacements and the Vandals, and in 1998 sessions resumed again, with Geffen Records paying Rose $1 million up front to finish the album. A further $1 million was handed over the following year.

Queen's guitarist, Brian May, was drafted in to record the guitar parts on a track called "Catcher in the Rye", whilst another track apparently intended for the album, a piece of industrial metal called "Oh My God", appeared on the *End of Days* soundtrack in 1999. But instead of finishing the album, Rose shuffled the pack again, hiring, firing and rehiring band members in short order.

By 2001, there was still no album but it seemed like progress of sorts when Guns N' Roses played their first live shows in seven years. After an American tour in 2002, all went quiet again until 2004, when a high-profile festival appearance was announced and then cancelled due to the departure of Buckethead, Slash's replacement as guitarist, who is infamous for his headgear fashioned from a cardboard KFC takeaway bucket. The time saved would allow the band "the opportunity to take recording that one extra step further", an official statement declared.

By 2005, the *New York Times* reported that $13 million had been spent on recording the unreleased album. Presumably the figure has climbed even higher since. Demos of tracks have been leaking regularly onto the Internet since 2003, among them "Better", "Chinese Democracy", "I.R.S.", "Madagascar", "The Blues" and "There Was a Time". And on several occasions Rose has discussed the album's sound. "Some people are going to say, 'It doesn't sound like Axl Rose, it doesn't sound like Guns N' Roses.' But you'll like at least a few songs on there," he claimed in 2006 when the band played several live shows – including one in Stockholm, after which he was arrested for allegedly biting a hotel security guard's leg.

Back in America, further shows were cancelled. According to Rose this was to allow "valuable time needed by the band and record company for the proper set-up and release of the album", which he claimed would appear on 6 March 2007. A year later his manager claimed that both band and label were still "in negotiations". It's just possible that by the time you are reading this, Guns N' Roses' first new album in seventeen years will be sitting on top of the charts. But the odds must be stupendously high against it.

NW

George Brigman

In 2005, a CD called *Jungle Rot* by an eighteen-year-old guitarist from Baltimore called George Brigman was released to rave reviews. Some critics likened the combination of primitive heavy metal, ferocious acid-rock guitar soloing and general belligerence to The White Stripes. Others cited the Jesus and Mary Chain. One critic noted that *Jungle Rot* sounded like the missing link between 1970s punk and 1960s blues-rock. Yet it transpired that the album had actually been recorded in 1975 – the year that Jack White was born. Brigman may have recorded a classic album at a tender age, but he had to wait until he was 48 before it was properly released.

At the time he recorded *Jungle Rot*, Brigman had been playing guitar for just a year, inspired by his favourite band, the Groundhogs. He was such a fan of the British blues/prog-rock outfit that he named his first two bands Hogwash and Split, after the titles of Groundhogs albums, and the song "T.S." on *Jungle Rot* was a homage to the band's leader, T.S. (Tony) McPhee.

Brigman's second album, *I Can Hear the Ants Dancin'*, recorded with his band Split, was released in 1982. The primitive but crudely effective sludge of his debut was replaced by a sharper wail created by a bunch of guitar effects pedals, although the same unusual mix of blues-rock intensity and uncouth DIY punk aggression remained at the music's core. At the time it was only released on a privately manufactured cassette in a limited edition of 300 copies. After that, the trail went cold. It emerged thirty years later that Brigman had never stopped playing guitar but his "career" – barely existent in the first place – had ground to a shocked halt when his best friend, Split bassist Mitchell Myers, was murdered in the 1980s.

By the time of *Jungle Rot*'s reissue, Brigman was a middle-aged family man making his living as a software designer, although still with the same shoulder-length hair sported on his debut album cover. On its reissue, a small but devoted legion of fans started crawling out of the woodwork. It transpired that Brigman had an unknown underground following among cognoscenti of the obscure and arcane, particularly in Europe, where his material had been bootlegged.

Finally, in 2007, came the release of *Rags in Skull*, his first new album in 25 years. Inevitably it didn't have quite the raw abrasiveness or zest of his youthful recordings. But it was still a heart-warming coda to one of the oddest and most obscure careers to be excavated by recent musical archaeology.

NW

Earth

When it was first recorded in 1990, Earth's song "Divine and Bright" was not deemed good enough to make the leap from scratchy demo status to inclusion on any of the Seattle band's albums. They didn't know it at the time, but the song was going to be their one brush with big-league musical celebrity, featuring as it did a promising young vocalist called Kurt Cobain on lead vocals.

Earth mainstay Dylan Carlson would soon have a far darker connection to his friend from Nirvana. On 30 March 1994 he bought the shotgun that Cobain later used to commit suicide. The police statement noted the following: "Kurt provided the cash and Carlson made the actual purchase. Carlson states that Kurt did not want to buy the weapon in his name as police had recently confiscated four of his weapons and Kurt was afraid if the gun was bought in his name it would also be confiscated." It went on to say that he tried to persuade Cobain to buy a smaller gun, to wait a month before making the purchase or to leave the weapon with him, but none of these things happened. Less than a week later, Cobain was dead.

If it hadn't been for this connection, Earth would probably have chugged along in even deeper obscurity, with Carlson shepherding numerous different line-ups. Their sound was far less appealing to the mainstream than that of their Seattle contemporaries who would earn global fame as the giants of grunge. Earth took their name from that of an early version of Black Sabbath, and their take on the metal sound was to slow it right down and vary it as little as possible. Their first EP, 1991's *Extra-Capsular Extraction*, featured three tracks that were six, seven and eighteen minutes long respectively. Their debut album went still further, boasting what could be described as musical movements rather than songs – they clocked in at 15, 27 and 30 minutes each. Crawling along at a tectonic pace, they created a sound that was hypnotic and savagely beautiful. Many of today's post-rockers were influenced by their sound, but Earth's chief legacy lies with an even smaller sub-category that tends to be called drone rock.

After many personnel changes, the band are still going, releasing a sixth studio album, *The Bees Made Honey in the Lion's Skull*, in 2008. While track lengths have come down a touch, any commercial breakthrough remains extremely unlikely, especially when they insist on giving songs such horror movie titles as "Omens and Portents II: Carrion Crow". Today Earth are best known as a key influence on another much larger cult band, the deafening experimental duo that go by the typographically inventive name of Sun O))).

DS

where to start:

1 Divine and Bright *from* Sunn Amps and Smashed Guitars Live EP
It's a demo and sounds like it, but there is a familiar gloomy voice there in the dense murk. Whether it's Cobain's influence or not, this is also one of Earth's more memorable tunes.

2 Tallahassee *from* Pentastar: In the Style of Demons
Thick, rumbling guitar and a practically inaudible vocal generate a bleak, hypnotic backdrop, with only a brief closing snatch of lead guitar adding sharpness of focus to this highlight from Earth's most accessible album.

Kyuss

Before there was Queens of the Stone Age there was Kyuss. Playing their stoner-rock jams at impromptu free parties in the deserts of southern California, they were powered by their own generator, with only a small truckload of pharmaceuticals to refresh them.

High school friends Josh Homme (guitar), John Garcia (vocals), Brant Bjork (drums) and Chris Cockrell (bass) got together in the late 1980s under the name Katzenjammer (German for "hangover"). By 1990 they had become the Sons of Kyuss, taking their name from a Dungeons & Dragons role-playing game. Borrowing from the legacy of such bands as Blue Cheer and Black Sabbath, they set about creating a jam-heavy mix of punk, hardcore, metal and thrash, encasing their riffs in several layers of stoned euphoria, through which there still somehow throbbed a subtle, sexual groove. In 1990 their first recording, an ultra-rare EP called *Sons of Kyuss*, emerged out of their ferocious jam sessions. It was the only band recording to feature Cockrell, who in 1991 was replaced by Nick Oliveri.

The revamped line-up truncated the name to Kyuss and signed to the independent label Dali Records, while continuing to hone – if that's the right word for such a gut-wrenching onslaught – their sound at free "generator parties" in the desert around Palm Springs, attended by a cult following of fellow stoners. Their full-length debut *Wretch* appeared in the autumn of 1991 and included re-recordings of the songs on *Sons of Kyuss*, but poor production rendered the already sludgy sound virtually unlistenable. Nevertheless, there was enough there to excite the trained ear of kindred spirit Chris Goss, the singer and guitarist with Masters of Reality, who offered to help produce a follow-up that would make the sound more accessible without diluting its thunderous power. The result was 1992's *Blues for the Red Sun*, a mixture of distortion and psych-doom that defined stoner rock and was actually far heavier and more thunderous than the grunge that was attracting so much more attention up the coast in Seattle. The album didn't sell particularly well. But it marked them out as leaders of the underground pack, earned a deal with Elektra Records that led to an opening slot on tour with Metallica, and created the template for dozens of other American bands who took up the stoner mantle.

The following year Nick Oliveri left to be replaced by Scott Reeder, but whoever played bass, the sound was the same. *Welcome to Sky Valley*, released in 1994 and again produced by Goss, was if anything even heavier, albeit with a greater psychedelic eclecticism. Another line-up change, with drummer Alfredo Hernández replacing Brant Bjork, suggested all was not well in the Kyuss camp and their fourth album, 1995's aptly titled *And the Circus Leaves Town*, proved to be their swansong.

Yet in a way, their break-up in October 1995 was only the beginning of the Kyuss legend. Bjork turned up in Fu Manchu, Garcia went on to form Unida, and Homme initially headed to Seattle, toured with the Screaming Trees and briefly recorded as Gamma Ray. In 1998, he summoned Alfredo Hernández and a bunch of other stoner mates to form the Queens of the Stone Age. Before long another Kyuss alumnus, Nick Oliveri, joined and the rest, as they say, is history. QOTSA went on to become one of the biggest-selling American rock bands of the new millennium, bringing a tighter, more melodic and disciplined songwriting rigour to Kyuss's raw riffing. Many hardcore fans, however, still believe that the true heart of stoner rock lies in the sludgy, all-enveloping, sprawling jams of Kyuss. Sadly, a reunion seems unlikely. "I like that nobody saw Kyuss, and that it was largely misunderstood," Homme said when asked about the chances of putting the band back together. "That sounds like a legend forming to me."

NW

playlist:

1 Space Cadet *from* Welcome to Sky Valley
Spare, neo-acoustic psychedelia that builds and builds into seven minutes plus of neolithic jamming.

2 Supa Scoopa and Mighty Scoop *from* Welcome to Sky Valley

Galloping drums, monster guitars, thundering bass and the unstoppable momentum of a runaway train crashing through the barriers.

3 Green Machine *from* Blues for the Red Sun
Speed metal, desert stoner style.

4 One Inch Man *from* And the Circus Leaves Town

A slow, driving rhythm that builds through Homme's guitar until it resembles a motorway pile-up.

5 Hurricane *from* And the Circus Leaves Town
A thick, swirling slab of sound in which you can barely distinguish one instrument from another. But don't blame the producer – it's meant to sound that way.

Nuggets: the best garage comps you'll ever hear

As one of the earliest people to use the term "punk rock", in the liner notes he wrote for the first of his *Nuggets* compilations, Lenny Kaye gave the next generation of headbangers their blueprint for noisy abandon in one handy double album.

It contained 27 tracks by US bands from the late 1960s who sounded similar to stars such as The Beatles, The Who and the Rolling Stones but recorded on a far lower budget. The result was garage rock, freakbeat, pop/ psych and all sorts of hybrids in between. Raw sounds bursting with energy was the order of the day for the *Nuggets* comps: intense rock'n'roll in its most exhilaratingly primal form.

A few bands in the collection became marginally better known than the others – the Electric Prunes and the 13th Floor Elevators, for example, who are covered elsewhere in this book. But most wouldn't even qualify as one-hit wonders. *Nuggets* preceded the CD era's vogue for resurrecting forgotten sounds across endless compilations, and remains one of the greatest series of compilations

The Sonics – the garage band's garage band.

ever released.

When the 1960s hippies' wallets had become satisfactorily fat, *Nuggets* was reborn in 1998 as a luxurious four-disc box-set with an extra 91 tracks. It now included material from early incarnations of Creedence Clearwater Revival and Lynyrd Skynyrd, but still mostly featured previously unheralded songs so good that it was impossible to believe they hadn't been hits.

There was more to come. *Nuggets II* expanded the remit to include bands

from Britain, Holland, Brazil and Japan. *Nuggets III: Children of Nuggets* unearthed psychedelia from 1976 to 1995, and the fourth in the series zoomed in on the epicentre of the 1960s counterculture – San Francisco. To own this wealth of fine music, you now need to be wealthy yourself. But it will be worth every penny.

DS

The Jon Spencer Blues Explosion

They could've been... The White Stripes?

Perhaps it was the visual shock of their coordinated outfits, but when The White Stripes erupted onto the rock scene at the start of the millennium, it was easy to forget that they weren't the only bass-free blues-rock band doing the rounds. The Jon Spencer Blues Explosion, who these days appear to have deleted their leader's name from their moniker, have been churning out their own twisted modern take on the blues in New York since 1990, and with two guitars in the band rather than Jack White's one, the trio were often even louder.

"I don't think they're that influenced by us," said Spencer in 2002. "It's much more about pop music than about rock'n'roll. That, I think, is the big difference between the two bands." He had a point about the pop thing – Blues Explosion rarely came up with the tunes to give them wider appeal. They were more about channelling the spirit of rock'n'roll in all its messy, noisy glory.

Spencer didn't always come off all that brilliantly in the old debate about whether white men can play the blues. His irreverent, often humorous take on the sound – howling and jabbering like a deep South evangelist, continually falling to his knees like James Brown – led to accusations that he was a merchant of pastiche. Unlike earlier musicians who played the blues without having lived them, such as Eric Clapton and John Mayall, he seemed much less awestruck by the real thing. However, the band did have a close relationship with a genuine bluesman, R.L. Burnside, backing him up on Burnside's 1996 album *A Ass Pocket Of Whiskey* (sic), on which they modernized his sound rather than him tak-ing them back to the source. Nevertheless, music veterans seemed to embrace them, and the band would also go on to play with Ike Turner, Solomon Burke and Dr John.

Spencer's family background confirmed he wasn't the real thing. He grew up in comfy New Hampshire with a chemistry professor father, and studied semiotics at the Ivy League Brown University. After dropping out he formed Pussy Galore, an avant-garde punk band who delighted in confrontational titles such as "Groovy Hate Fuck", "Dial M For Motherfucker" and "Corpse Love". One of their con-ceptual pranks was to record a cover version of the Rolling Stones album *Exile On Main Street* in its entirety – a fore-shadowing of the Blues Explosion's fondness for Stones-style hard-edged blues and soul.

The Blues Explosion had arguably more scope than the Stripes, incorporating hip-hop and funk influences and working with Moby and the Beastie Boys on remixes, but they never wrote a big hit. Being one of the most intense live experiences around was more than enough.

DS

where to start:

1 Bellbottoms *from* Orange
The lead track from what is widely regarded as the band's most coherent album, this is a thrilling piece of punk blues mania that starts off loud and out of control, and then gets wilder.

2 Talk About the Blues *from* Acme
Produced by hip-hop man Dan "The Automator" Nakamura, this loping groove features distorted bass, funky drums, a squealing guitar riff and a typically holler-ing vocal from Spencer.

Melvins

Long before Nirvana sniffed teenage spirit and years after grunge had faded to an indelible stain, the Melvins have been flying the flag for sludge metal with an experimental twist. A huge influence on Nirvana, Soundgarden and the other bands that emerged from Seattle in the early 1990s, the Melvins in turn drew their influence from the likes of Black Flag and Black Sabbath, but the idiosyncratic qualities they have always added to their hardcore riffing means they have defied categorization – and has probably denied them more mainstream success. Formed in Washington State in the early 1980s by singer/guitarist Buzz Osborne (aka "King Buzzo") and drummer Dale Crover, the band took its name from a despised manager at the Thriftway store in Montesano, Washington, where Osborne worked.

Their beginnings as a hardcore punk band playing speeded-up covers of The Who and Jimi Hendrix were unpromising and failed to distinguish them from thousands of other bands taking their formative steps in garages all over America. They soon hit upon their own style, however, slowing down their riffs to a drone and playing them heavier than anyone else around.

Operating as a trio, over the years Osborne and Crover have recruited a number of different bassists, one of whom was almost – but not quite – the youthful Kurt Cobain. After acting as an unpaid roadie at several shows, he auditioned to join the band on bass but failed to get the gig – allegedly because he was so nervous that he forgot all the songs. The job instead went to Matt Lukin, who later formed Mudhoney. In 1988 Osborne and Crover relocated to San Francisco, which meant they weren't around the Seattle area

for the emergence of grunge, but their presence was still felt. Osborne recommended Nirvana bassist Krist Novoselic to the band and Cobain was highly vocal in crediting the Melvins as a major influence on the sound of grunge.

Following the spectacular success of *Nevermind*, his support helped to land the Melvins a major-label deal, with Atlantic, in 1993. That year's *Houdini* was their first album to dent the American album charts, at number 29, but it was the high tide of their commercial success. The deal with Atlantic turned sour when the label refused to release the experimental, dissonant *Prick* (it appeared instead on Amphetamine Reptile Records) and in 1997 they were unceremoniously dropped.

It was probably a blessing in disguise and the band has continued touring and recording ever since, often in an experimental vein that would have caused ructions if they were still on a major label. *Colossus of Destiny* (2001), for example, was a live set of synthesizer and sampling experiments containing just two tracks, one of which was an hour long and the other a five-second fragment.

NW

The Monks

When Elvis Presley stepped off a troop ship at Bremerhaven in September 1958, for a two-year posting as Sergeant Presley of the US Army, the most famous G.I. in the world brought rock'n'roll to West Germany in person. Five years later, after The Beatles and other British bands had passed through Hamburg's nightclubs and strip joints, the baton was taken up by a new band of disillusioned American soldiers.

The Torquays were five G.I.s stationed at Frankfurt, a regular beat group dishing out a diet of surfing covers, Chuck Berry standards and British Invasion staples. The name change to The Monks came with their discharge from the army in 1965 and an image transformation: heads were shaved in a tonsure and they took to wearing black habits and rope ties on stage. There was also a radical rethink of the music. Melody was stripped back to a minimalist conclusion, often driven down to an over-amplified, repetitive drone. Gary Burger fuzzed-up his Gretsch Black Widow guitar, Dave Day's electric, cat-gut banjo snapped to the beat, tom-toms were pummelled furiously and feedback wailed. "We concentrated on over-beat", as the bassist Eddie Shaw put it.

The covers set was junked in favour of self-penned songs that better expressed their boredom and anger at pretty much everything, from American involvement in Vietnam to disenfranchised teens and relationship breakdown. The song titles said it all: "Shut Up", "I Hate You", "Complication". This was punk rock ten years ahead of its time. After initial confusion, and not a little hostility, The Monks acquired a growing fanbase amongst German youth. The band signed to Polydor in 1965 and entered a Cologne studio to make an album that would change music in Germany and beyond in the decades to come.

Black Monk Time was a raw blast of moody garage-pop and blunt, minimalist proto-punk. It became cult listening amongst German record buyers and has since been hailed as one of the most important rock albums, despite its non-release outside Germany until the 1990s. The Monks have been name-checked by many, from Mark E. Smith to the Beastie Boys, and their idiosyncratic "über-beat" helped spawn Krautrock in the late 1960s and 70s. The band split in 1967 but, with a revival of interest in The Monks' legend, reformed in the 1990s for the occasional nostalgia gig. An album of early demos, *Five Upstart Americans*, was issued in 2000.

RW

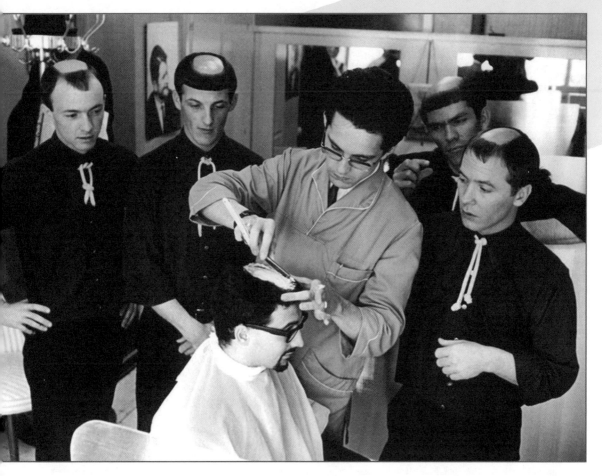

playlist:

1 Shut Up *from* Black Monk Time
Bam-bam, bam-bam-bam. The martial beat leaves
you feeling bruised and battered on this punch-drunk
proto-punk salvo from The Monks' classic 1965
album. A maniacal Hammond organ eddies and
whirls, as the band yell "Shut up! Don't cry!" – not
very Christian of you, boys!

2 I Hate You *from* Black Monk Time
"Just imagine the sound of the Titanic scraping along
an iceberg," said bassist Eddie Shaw, describing
their joyous discovery of monumentally noisy guitar
feedback. Burger's clearly hopping mad here, as he
splutters the lyric "I hate you with a passion, baby!"

3 Down to the Sea *from* Black Monk Time
A 1967 single-only release, added to the album
when it was reissued on CD. Notable for a curious
mariachi trumpet solo, it also lacks their trademark

"over-beat". The lyrics seem to suggest a reference
to transsexuality: "And then he went down to the sea,
and thought of the girl I used to be".

4 Complication *from* Black Monk Time
Few songwriters would think to rhyme "complication" with "constipation", especially to a backing of
"people kill". Burger searches and destroys: in just
two minutes, the song prefigures everything in rock's
loud, fast future, from Detroit punk to heavy metal.

Pretty Things

They could've been... the Rolling Stones?

Back in the mid-1960s when all good parents locked up their teenage daughters whenever Mick Jagger and his group of long-haired libertines hit town, only one band was regarded as shaggier, dirtier, lewder, wilder and more degenerate than the Rolling Stones. That band was the Pretty Things and they made a raw R&B noise as fearsome as their image.

Emerging from the same grey suburbs of Dartford as Jagger and Richards, founder member Dick Taylor played in the first incarnation of the Stones but left to take up a place at the Royal College of Art, where in late 1963 he teamed up with fellow Dartfordian and R&B enthusiast Phil May to form the Pretty Things.

Taking their name from a Bo Diddley song, they added Brian Pendleton on rhythm guitar, John Stax on bass and Pete Kitley (later replaced by Viv Prince) on drums. A television appearance on *Ready Steady Go!* before they had even released a record generated instant press coverage along the lines of "If you thought the Stones were a bunch of scruffy yobs, wait until you see this lot". May rivalled Jagger as a lascivious, hip-wiggling front man widely dubbed "the longest-haired man in Britain".

For a while, the carefully promoted sense of outrage worked well. Signed to Fontana they kicked off sensationally with a trio of high octane singles that remain as potent as anything created during the British beat boom. Their 1964 debut "Rosalyn" only charted at number 41 but the follow-up, "Don't Bring Me Down", made the top ten before the year was out, while the self-penned "Honey I Need" reached number thirteen in early 1965. They certainly had a major impact on the teenage David Bowie, who at the time was far more impressed with Phil May than Mick Jagger: when Bowie released his covers album *Pin-Ups* in 1973, paying homage to the music that had influenced him, it contained versions of both "Rosalyn" and "Don't Bring Me Down", and nothing from the Stones songbook. Other major fans were Led Zeppelin, who in the 1970s signed them to their Swansong label.

By the middle of 1965, however, British music was turning away from R&B and although the Stones effortlessly survived the transition of the public's taste to pop with "Satisfaction" and "Get Off Of My Cloud", the Pretty Things simply didn't have the songs to match. Their decline was dramatic: in March, their debut album made number six in the British charts. The follow-up, *Get the Picture,* released in December, failed to make the top fifty.

Bad luck continued to dog them ever after. In 1967 they reinvented themselves as a psychedelic band with the brilliant single "Defecting Grey", only for it to be rather overshadowed by Pink Floyd's "See Emily Play", which had a similar vibe and had used the same producer, Norman Smith. The following year Smith produced the album *SF Sorrow* for them. It bombed. Such lack of commercial success was wholly undeserved: the album was a psychedelic classic, and was widely hailed as the first "rock opera". One suspects that a grateful Pete Townshend was probably listening enthusiastically.

NW

Screaming Trees

The Seattle grunge scene's perennial nearly men, Screaming Trees blew every chance they had to become as big as their neighbours Alice In Chains, Soundgarden, Pearl Jam and, of course, Nirvana over the course of their long career. Hindrances came from all corners, starting with the sometimes violent relationship between founder members Van and Gary Lee Conner.

"We didn't have a damn thing in common except insanity. So we fought a lot. And we had two brothers who fought like brothers. Only they were huge," said singer Mark Lanegan, whose addiction to heroin during part of the Trees's lifespan was another major barrier to success. As a teenage petty thief and drug dealer, he only escaped prison by agreeing to a year of rehab. Schoolfriend Van Conner's parents gave Lanegan a fresh start by employing him to repossess hired electrical goods. Soon he was asked to join the Conner brothers' fledgling rock band, initially on drums, and then on lead vocals.

Established well before Nirvana, Screaming Trees had already released four albums before they were offered a major label deal, putting out their debut, *Uncle Anesthesia*, eight months before Nirvana's *Nevermind*. Their songs had a hard, unpolished rock sound similar to those of their grunge peers, and Lanegan had a gruff, sandpaper voice to match anyone in terms of primal power. But they had also widened their musical palette to incorporate blues, folk and psychedelic elements.

After *Nevermind*'s explosive success, all eyes were on Seattle. Screaming Trees did the right things, appearing on the soundtrack to Cameron Crowe's 1992 grunge romance movie *Singles* alongside other major local bands, and releasing an album, *Sweet Oblivion*, that sharpened their style. But they also did the wrong things, fighting relentlessly while Lanegan wrestled with his drug habit and recorded a solo album, *Whiskey for the Holy Ghost*. By the time the band were together enough to follow up *Sweet Oblivion* with *Dust*, four years had passed and all momentum was lost.

In many ways, it's arguable that the path of Kurt Cobain might have looked a little similar to Lanegan's, had he never become a superstar and taken his own life. The latter has spent his post-Trees career as a rasp for hire, performing with Queens of the Stone Age, P.J. Harvey and in several partnerships with fellow alt.rock survivor Greg Dulli of the Afghan Whigs, in The Twilight Singers and The Gutter Twins. Lanegan has also released two surprising albums with Scotland's Isobel Campbell, formerly of Belle and Sebastian, which are at times startlingly gentle, though always intense. It's a varied role that suits him far better than the grunge celebrity that might have been.

DS

where to start:

1 Nearly Lost You *from* Sweet Oblivion
The band's contribution to the *Singles* soundtrack was also their biggest hit, a strong melodic chorus augmented by a blazing guitar solo from Gary Lee Conner.

2 Bed of Roses *from* Uncle Anesthesia
Lanegan tries more of a rich croon on this tuneful highlight from the band's major label debut, a breezier number than the more intense rockers they favoured previously.

Vanilla Fudge

They could've been... Led Zeppelin?

On their first tour of the US, Led Zeppelin often found themselves supporting Vanilla Fudge. Indeed, on their first American date in Denver in December 1968, not only was the Fudge's name the one in big letters on the posters, Zep didn't even merit a mention. Six months later the two bands were appearing as co-headliners. Another six months after that, Zep were well on their way to being the biggest band in the world and Vanilla Fudge had broken up. The rock'n'roll carousel turned with giddying speed in the 1960s.

Yet the links between the two bands are closer than sharing a stage while one was on the way up and the other on the way down. Off-stage Vanilla Fudge rivalled Zeppelin in insalubrious rock'n'roll behaviour and were heavily implicated in the infamous "shark incident", the most notorious episode in the British band's pillaging of America. It happened in July 1969 when both bands were staying at the Edgewater Inn, Seattle, and involved a naked young woman from Oregon and a sexual adventure with a live (or maybe dead, according to some accounts) mud shark (or red snapper), a length of rope and various members of the Zeppelin entourage, including drummer John Bonham. A Fudge band member has since been reported as having admitted to "recruiting" the girl, and organist Mark Stein allegedly filmed what took place on his 8mm camera – a story reported but not denied on the Fudge's official website. The sordid events were later chronicled by Frank Zappa in the song "The Mud Shark", which named and shamed Vanilla Fudge.

Happily there was a less unsavoury and more musical connection between the two bands. Formed in New York by Martell, Stein, drummer Carmine Appice and bassist Tim Bogart in 1967, out of the ashes of Young Rascals' copyists the Pigeons, The Fudge's speciality was long, melodramatic, psyched-up and slowed-down covers of well-known songs such as "You Keep Me Hanging On", and "The Season of the Witch" characterized by the dynamic contrast between loud, headbanging passages and quieter, softer moments. It wasn't that far from the blueprint outlined by Jimmy Page to Robert Plant when they first got together of a "new kind of heavy music" driven by a dynamic drummer with dramatic contrasts of light and shade in which the singer and guitarist played off each other. Zeppelin utilized the blueprint to brilliant effect on "Babe I'm Gonna Leave You" on their debut album and further evidence that Zep were listening to and were influenced by the Fudge's modus operandi came when drummer John Bonham told Appice that he had copied the drum licks on the album's opener "Good Times Bad Times" from the Fudge's cover of The Beatles' "Ticket to Ride" on their first album.

After Vanilla Fudge broke up in 1970, Bogart and Appice joined forces with Jimmy Page's old Yardbirds colleague Jeff Beck in the ill-fated power trio BBA.

FORGOTTEN FOLK
taking the finger out the ear

Anne Briggs

Sandy Denny wrote a song about her. So did Richard Thompson. Jimmy Page and Bert Jansch revered her. She has influenced virtually every female folk revivalist who followed, from Shirley Collins to Kate Rusby, and is the wellspring for many now popular folk songs. So why isn't Anne Briggs better known?

Born in Nottinghamshire in 1944, Briggs is an English folk legend with a voice as fine and delicate as Nottingham lace. Back in the mid-1960s, as the folk music of the British Isles was shaking loose from the curators of the tradition to rub shoulders with the burgeoning beat boom, Briggs was a crucial link between the old and the new. Although she had little time for the electrification of folk, her devotion to the oral tradition brought many forgotten songs to the notice of many revivalists of the genre, including the Watersons, Thompson and Jansch, with whom she was especially close.

In 1962, Ewan MacColl came across the eighteen-year-old Briggs singing the traditional numbers "Let No Man Steal Your Thyme" and "She Moves Through the Fair". The purity of her voice so impressed him, he invited her up to the stage with him that night. She toured with MacColl, as part of a Communist arts organization and began to establish a name for herself. After recording

a handful of songs in the 1960s, she made just two full-length albums in the early 70s and gave up on a third.

When she wasn't in a studio, which was as good as never, Briggs travelled the country and beyond, pitching up at folk clubs and small venues. It made her difficult to pin down, but when she could be caught in performance, it was, by most accounts, a transcendental experience. Others close to Briggs remembered how she would stumble drunk on stage and, if she grew bored of singing a song, how she would simply switch to another. Richard Thompson recalled that he only ever met Briggs twice, and on both occasions she was paralytic.

But, above all, there was the voice and her stunning good looks. She was like a radiant Julie Christie, lifted from *Billy Liar* and dropped, in floppy woollens, to the dusty floors of London's folk basements. From the early 1960s, Briggs and Jansch formed an on/off partnership, both musical and personal, which would last the years. They wrote together – "for pleasure, when there was nothing else to do", as she told *Mojo* magazine in 1998 – and occasionally lived together. From Briggs, Jansch learned "Black Water Side", the song which would eventually find its way into Jimmy Page's hands and onto Led Zeppelin's first album (as "Black Mountain Side").

At times she had no permanent base: for several years her postal address was Collet's bookshop in Charing Cross Road. Briggs would disappear for months on end, at one time turning up in Scotland, where she formed a close bond with a local hero of the political folk scene, Hamish Henderson. Via Henderson, Briggs met other Scottish musicians, including the future Fairport fiddler Dave Swarbrick, and spent a brief sojourn in Edinburgh. When the folk collector Bert Lloyd invited her to contribute to an album of erotic folk songs, *The Bird in the Bush*, in 1966, Briggs moved back to England, before moving again to Ireland, where she teamed up with Johnny Moynihan and Andy Irvine of the band Sweeney's Men.

Five years of restless isolation followed, sometimes spent in a Suffolk caravan. With Moynihan, she hit the road whenever the fancy took her. If she was booked to play a club, the chances were she wouldn't show. As the decade wound down, she began writing material which she would gather, with some traditional songs, on her self-titled 1971 album for Topic. *Anne Briggs* was mostly Briggs singing unaccompanied, with Moynihan appearing on one track. 1971 proved to be Briggs' most active year in the studio. *The Time Has Come* followed within months, on CBS, featuring more self-penned numbers and Briggs accompanying herself on acoustic guitar. If she was ever a star, it was then. Sandy Denny wrote "The Pond and the Stream" in 1970, which mythologized Briggs' wanderlust, and the two 1971 albums were generally well received. But Briggs hated being boxed in with the folk-rockers, considering herself a purist, despite concessions to a slightly more commercial sound on her second release.

A third album was recorded in 1973, but Briggs was never really happy with it (or, indeed, the recording process itself). *Sing a Song for You* remained unreleased until the 1990s. After a stint as a market gardener, she retired with her family to the Scottish Hebrides and hardly sang a note for the best part of two decades, appearing only briefly to pay tribute to Bert Lloyd at a memorial concert for her friend in 1990, and then again in an awkward, short club tour in the early 1990s. Since then, the hatches have been firmly battened once more. It seems that Anne Briggs is content for others to keep her songs alive.

RW

playlist:

1 Go Your Way My Love from Acoustic Routes
In 1993, the BBC screened a documentary about Bert Jansch. In the programme, and on the accompanying soundtrack album, Jansch dueted with Briggs for a touching rendition of her signature tune.

2 Let No Man Steal Your Thyme from Edinburgh Folk Festival Vol 2
Later made famous by Pentangle, this is the traditional ballad Ewan MacColl heard Briggs singing at Nottingham in 1962. The young singer repeated her rendition at Edinburgh later that year.

3 The Recruited Collier from Anne Briggs: A Collection
Her most influential work was her earliest. The songs that appeared on Briggs's four EPs recorded for the Topic label between 1963 and 1971 still shimmer in their purity, recorded when she was just eighteen.

4 Black Water Side from Anne Briggs: A Collection
The song that Jimmy Page borrowed, by way of Bert Jansch, for Led Zeppelin's debut. Later covered by Sandy Denny, amongst others. Briggs, in turn, learned the tale of the "Irish lad" from Bert Lloyd.

5 The Whirly Whorl from The Bird in the Bush
Taken from Lloyd's collection of traditional songs about love and lust, tracks like this provided the blueprint for the later vocal stylings of singers such as June Tabor and Maddy Prior.

Vashti Bunyan

Most people have heard at least one song by Vashti Bunyan, even though they probably don't realize it. She's the owner of the fragile, winsome voice singing "Diamond Day" on the T-Mobile advert that was beamed into homes several times an hour on commercial TV stations throughout 2007. It's an astonishing turnaround in her music's exposure, given that according to producer Joe Boyd, the *Just Another Diamond Day* album, from which the song comes, sold less than a thousand copies on its original release in 1970. Discouraged, Bunyan left the music industry and spent the next three decades raising her children and tending her animals on a Scottish island, unaware that *Just Another Diamond Day* was slowly becoming a cult record. By the 1990s, rare vinyl copies were changing hands on eBay for $2000 and by the end of the decade she had become an inspiration to an entire new generation of performers. Devendra Banhart, Joanna Newsom and Adem weren't even born when she wrote and recorded "Diamond Day" and the other overlooked, ethereal gems that have since resulted in an improbable comeback and her elevation to the status of godmother of freak folk.

On her rediscovery an extraordinary story emerged. Born in London in 1945, Vashti had a family lineage that could be traced back to John Bunyan, author of *The Pilgrim's Progress*. After reading fine art at Oxford University for a year, she travelled to New York aged eighteen and heard Bob Dylan. Returning to London "with a heart full of musical ambition" she recorded some demos in 1964 and the following year was discovered by Rolling Stones manager Andrew Loog Oldham, who decided to turn her into the next Marianne Faithfull. Oldham pressed Mick Jagger and Keith Richards into service to write her debut single "Some Things Just Stick in Your Mind", added an orchestra and released it under the name Vashti, backed with her own song "I Want to be Alone". Despite being a fine piece of effortlessly groovy 1960s Europop it failed to sell, as did the 1966 follow-up "Train Song" and a third single, "The Coldest Night of the Year", credited to Twice As Much and Vashti.

"I have heard it said that Andrew Loog Oldham took this fragile little folk singer and made her a pop singer against her will," she wrote in 2007. "No, he didn't. I was never a folk singer. I was always a lover of pop music and my greatest dream was to break into the charts as a girl-with-guitar and a sad little love song." However, when in 1967 she decided to travel in a wagon drawn by a horse called Bess to the Isle of Skye, to join a commune on some land owned by Donovan, her under-achieving career as a pop singer appeared to be over.

But she was still writing songs and, following an introduction to Joe Boyd, she returned to London in 1969 to record her debut album. Boyd assembled a supporting cast from among his other acts – Simon Nicol and Dave Swarbrick of Fairport Convention, Robin Williamson of The Incredible String Band and Nick Drake's string arranger Robert Kirby – and the album appeared as *Just Another Diamond Day* on Phillips Records in late 1970.

Despite her protestations that she was never a folk singer, the style was quite different from the baroque pop records she had made with Oldham and the instrumentation was essentially folk-based. The cover depicted her as a modern-day raggle-taggle Gypsy, and the music inside matched, in a way. Enchanting, magical, gossamer-light and as bucolic as a green meadow, it hardly sounded like it belonged in the modern world at all. The modern world agreed, and only a couple of hundred people bought the record. "Nobody seemed to give it a second thought when it was released," she recalled years later. "In fact it was not really released, it just edged its way out, blushed and shuffled off into oblivion." She abandoned it, and music, going off "to travel more with horses and wagons, with children and more dogs and chickens."

The album eventually made its debut on CD thirty years later, in 2000. She returned to live music, taking the stage at London's Festival Hall that year. In 2005, on the occasion of her sixtieth birthday, she released *Lookaftering*, an extraordinarily belated follow-up to her 1970 debut. Featuring contributions from Devendra Banhart and Joanna Newsom, Vashti sounded little changed, simply the older, wiser sister of the romantic young woman who had made *Just Another Diamond Day* all those years earlier.

NW

playlist:

1 Some Things Just Stick in Your Mind *from* Some Things Just Stick in Your Mind
This breezy, pop cousin to Dylan's "Blowing in the Wind" from the pens of Jagger and Richards, has a vibe like Françoise Hardy flirting with The Zombies.

2 Diamond Day *from* Just Another Diamond Day
"Just another diamond day, just a blade of grass, just another bale of hay and the horses pass" – a measure of the album's simple, childlike charm.

3 Glow Worms *from* Just Another Diamond Day
"Whisper fairy stories till they're real" suggests Vashti, on a song that would have made the perfect soundtrack for campfires at 3am at the Glastonbury Festival in 1970.

4 Jog Along Bess *from* Just Another Diamond Day
The naïve but charming story of that extraordinary horse-drawn journey from London to the Scottish islands.

5 Against the Sky *from* Lookaftering
This jewel from Diamond's follow-up features elegant, filigree harp embellishments from the ingenious Ms Newsom.

6 Same but Different *from* Lookaftering
Arranger Robert Kirby reprises the high-class strings he contributed to *Just Another Diamond Day* 35 years earlier.

Karen Dalton

In recent years, Karen Dalton has collected almost as many posthumous celebrity endorsements as Nick Drake. Most of those now singing her praises never saw her perform, but one who did was Bob Dylan, who shared a stage with her at the Café Wha? in Greenwich Village in 1961. "My favourite singer in the place was Karen Dalton," he wrote in his autobiography, *Chronicles Vol. One*. "She was a tall white blues singer and guitar player, funky, lanky and sultry," he explained. "Karen had a voice like Billie Holiday's and played the guitar like Jimmy Reed." Others to have come to a late admiration of her records include Lucinda Williams, Joanna Newsom, Devendra Banhart, and Nick Cave, who wrote "When I First Came to Town" about her. It was the second song she had inspired, following The Band's "Katie's Been Gone".

In short, Dalton has come to be recognized as the great lost voice of the vibrant Greenwich Village folk scene of the early 1960s. While others, including Dylan, Tom Paxton, Tom Rush, Judy Collins and Richie Havens, went on to become household names, Dalton died in 1993 in total obscurity. It wasn't until a decade later that her two albums, *It's So Hard to Tell Who's Going to Love You the Best* from 1969, and 1971's *In My Own Time*, were reissued and she began to garner some of the acclaim that eluded her during her lifetime.

Born to a Cherokee mother in 1938, Dalton arrived in Greenwich Village sometime around 1960, having abandoned a husband in Oklahoma, and with her twelve-string guitar, a banjo and at least one of her two children, in tow. She began to sing at pass-the-hat folk venues in the Village, such as the Café Wha?, where there is a famous picture of her on stage in February 1962 with Dylan and Fred Neil, looking every bit as "funky, lanky and sultry" as Dylan described. She was in the right place at the right time, knew all the right people and was blessed with a rare talent – and yet for various reasons it never happened for her.

That she only played covers and didn't write her own material need not have mattered – after all, it didn't hinder Judy Collins. But Dalton had a self-destructive streak and was a junkie for the best part of twenty years. In addition, she was a reluctant performer who was uncomfortable playing live and loathed the studio even more. Her debut album was recorded by stealth when producer Nick Venet asked her to drop in on a Fred Neil session and then tricked her into singing when she didn't know the tape was rolling.

Her ambivalent attitude to performing meant that she remained unsigned throughout the "folk boom" when record companies were indiscriminately offering contracts to far less talented Village folk. By the time she eventually got to record *It's So Hard to Tell Who's Going to Love You the Best* in 1969, the world had decided that her covers of songs by fellow junkies Fred Neil and Tim Hardin, and of Leadbelly and Otis Redding numbers, sounded old-fashioned. Today her off-the-cuff, first-takes sound timeless; but on its release the album sank without trace.

Two years later she was somehow persuaded to record a follow-up at Bearsville in Woodstock, but allegedly insisted on returning home to Oklahoma first to fetch her two teenage children, dog and even her horse in order to make her feel more comfortable with the process. *In My Own Time* was more fully realized than her debut, with a crack session band and a distinct folk-pop sensibility, courtesy of producer Harvey Brooks, although he recalls that the sessions were somewhat fraught. "It was a lot of work, because her emotional personality had to be dealt with every step of the way," he has said.

Dalton sings with a welling heartache that, particularly on the eerie "Katie Cruel", is almost overpowering. Yet once again sales were dismal. After the album's failure she slowly drifted away from music and further into junkiedom. By the early 1990s she had pawned her guitars and was living on the streets of New York, where she died in 1993, reportedly of a drug overdose although friends say she just ran out of steam.

It was long a source of regret that no recordings existed of her from the early 1960s, when she had so impressed Dylan. However, in 2007, tapes from a brace of 1962 performances turned up and were released as the double CD, *Cotton Eyed Joe*. The recording quality is poor but it's still possible to hear how much more intense her part-hillbilly and part-Billie Holiday voice sounded before the heroin gave her the haunted, world-weary patina that characterizes the later studio recordings.

NW

playlist:

1 I Love You More Than Words Can Say *from* It's So Hard to Tell...
Otis Redding gets the unique KD treatment.

2 Ribbon Bow *from* It's So Hard to Tell...
The lament of a poor country girl...

3 It Hurts Me Too *from* It's So Hard to Tell....
"She sure could sing the shit out of the blues" – Fred Neil

4 How Did the Feeling Feel to You *from* It's So Hard to Tell...
And she sure liked songs by fellow junkies – this one by Tim Hardin.

5 Blues on the Ceiling *from* It's So Hard to Tell...
She sang this Fred Neil song with such feeling that he said he thought she'd written it.

6 Something On Your Mind *from* In My Own Time
Written by another old Greenwich Village friend, Dino Valenti.

7 Katie Cruel *from* In My Own Time
Darkly chilling version of a song that can also be found on the 1962 live tapes.

8 In a Station *from* In My Own Time
A beautiful reinvention of The Band's song.

9 Take Me *from* In My Own Time
A pining version of the George and Tammy weepie.

10 How Sweet It Is *from* In My Own Time
She really could sing anything – including the Motown songbook.

Nu folk:
altered roots

Everything becomes cool again sooner or later, even folk music, long tarnished with an image that was a big-bearded cliché involving yards of ale and chunky jumpers. In recent years folk revivals have taken place in both the UK and the US, led by musicians who take traditional music as a jumping-off point into much wider pastures.

The pixie at the head of the parade in America is Devendra Banhart, a barefoot, bearded mystic from San Francisco via Caracas. He has lived rough on the streets of Paris, he has written a song about plastic surgery for dogs, and his music has appeared on an advert for cheddar cheese. His snappily titled 2002 debut, *Oh Me Oh My ... The Way the Day Goes By the Sun Is Setting Dogs Are Dreaming Lovesongs of the Christmas Spirit*, contained 22 scratchy, hissy acoustic tracks all sung in his spooky, reedy, quivering voice. By 2005's *Cripple Crow*, his arrangements had evolved to include jazzy flutes, honky-tonk piano and droning sitar, and he was singing some of his songs in Spanish.

Banhart has said, "I get a psychedelic experience just hanging out in a garden, or looking at a tree, or eating an orange." His restless creativity, which extends to him drawing his own album artwork, clearly makes him inspirational company. *Cripple Crow*'s *Sgt. Pepper*-style cover featured friends and collaborators including Joanna Newsom, Vashti Bunyan and CocoRosie, the working name of two American siblings whose take on folk includes found sounds, the feel of gospel spirituals and black-as-pitch lyrics.

Estranged as teenagers, Bianca and Sierra Casady reunited in Sierra's Montmartre home to record their debut album, 2004's *La maison de mon rêve*. It is hard to believe that Sierra is a trained opera singer, for the bird-like voice she employs

Devendra Banhart: nu folk, old cardigan.

most resembles the vintage jazz of Billie Holiday. She plucks guitar while Bianca provides percussion, a job that extends to making noises with a squeaky gate, cranking up old machinery or popping popcorn. Their follow-up, *Noah's Ark* (2005), featured vocal contributions from both Antony Hegarty of Antony and the Johnsons and, surprise surprise, Devendra Banhart.

In the UK there are a couple of fast-growing annual festivals for this kind of thing. The Green Man festival is a back-to-basics affair in the Brecon Beacons, Wales, while Homefires is an indoor, weekend event in London. Both feature numerous young hipsters who have found a warm, welcoming home in folk, as well as resurgent musicians from the last time folk was cool, such as Bert Jansch.

At the more daring end of the folk music spectrum is the "folktronica" produced by Tunng and Four Tet, the alias of Kieran Hebden. Folktronica is a clunky name for music that samples snippets of old acoustic instruments and feeds them through a computer to create a sound that is simultaneously cutting-edge and soothing and familiar. It is a human sound made by machines, and Hebden's albums *Pause* (2001) and *Rounds* (2003) are two of its finest examples.

The songs of Hebden's schoolfriend and former bandmate Adem Ilhan, who organizes the Homefires festival, are less experimental but nonetheless very beautiful. His albums as Adem, *Homesongs* (2004) and *Love and Other Planets* (2006), consist mainly of strummed acoustic guitar, a touch of glockenspiel and Ilhan's yearning, cracked vocals, but some electronic tidying up has been done, editing the reverb of the guitar and rearranging creaking noises so they become percussion.

Then there are localized collectives of musicians who play gigs together and collaborate constantly, such as the Drift Collective on England's south coast, a label whose roster includes Birdengine, R.G. Morrison and Mary Hampton. At the other end of the country is the Fence Collective in Fife, Scotland, whose most famous alumnus is the pop rocker KT Tunstall, but who also spawned the gorgeous and more traditional sounds of King Creosote and James Yorkston. Creosote, aka Kenny Anderson, is the most prolific of the bunch, having produced some two dozen home-recorded albums before taking a tentative peck at the mainstream with major-label recordings including *KC Rules OK* (2005) and *Bombshell* (2007).

Another Scottish singer of note is Alasdair Roberts, who has recorded several albums released on the American indie

Caroline Weeks preparing to do battle.

label Drag City. It's a measure of folk's resurgence that a young man playing the hurdy-gurdy, singing songs such as "You Need Not Braid Your Hair For Me: I Have Not Come A-Wooing" can not only be appreciated for the great music that he is making, but can also be considered cool.

Most recently, British nu folk has thrown up the scene's best chance of a genuine star in the glamorous shape of Brighton's Natasha Khan, aka Bat For Lashes. A Brit Award and Mercury Prize nominee, and scion of a family of world-class Pakistani squash players, Khan put out her debut album, *Fur and Gold,* in 2006. It featured traditional instruments such as harp and harpsichord and had a dramatic, ethereal feel all of its own. While Khan's second album remains hotly anticipated, also worthy of note is the solo output of Lashes bandmate Caroline Weeks, whose 2008 debut, *Songs for Edna*, was a haunting collision of the old and new.

Without a cable-knit jumper in sight – well, maybe just a few – exponents of this new sound are proving to be a major factor in giving folk a wider appeal than it has enjoyed in decades.

DS

Dr Strangely Strange

Like their Scottish soulmates in The Incredible String Band, Ireland's Dr Strangely Strange could only have existed in the brave new dawn of late 1960s psychedelia – a time when not only was anything possible, but kaleidoscopic revelations on a cosmic plane were highly probable.

The mysticism of the new-age "Celtic-interest" fringe and the acid reveries of acoustic hippie music were tailor-made for each other. Dr Strangely Strange adapted traditional instruments such as penny whistle, fiddle, harmonium and mandolin to create a swirling tapestry of childlike whimsy, unfettered imagination and ancient, half-remembered folk tales of myth and magic.

Like many others at the time, the band's aesthetics were fired in the crucible of communal living. The core of the group consisted of a trio: Tim Booth, an Irish musician, met Ivan Pawle, an English musician, while studying at Trinity College in Dublin; they were joined by Tim Goulding, whose grounding in Irish traditional music jostled for space with his full-time occupation as a painter. They lived and rehearsed in a Dublin house owned by Goulding's girlfriend, who sang backing vocals under the name Orphan Annie. Their communal base became known as the Orphanage and became the camp for a whole generation of alternative Irish musicians, including Thin Lizzy's Phil Lynott and Gary Moore.

The Incredible String Band's Robin Williamson recommended them to Joe Boyd, their producer, manager and guru of psych-folk. Boyd travelled to Ireland in late 1968 to see the band perform as opening act for Gary Moore's Skid Row. Despite a few misgivings about their similarity to the ISB, he signed them to his Witchseason production company and a couple of months later the band travelled to London to record their debut album *Kip of the Serenes* under Boyd's direction. Its simple acoustic melodies, whimsically meandering vocals and acid-addled hippie philosophizing make it a charming period piece. Yet despite the inclusion of the characteristically quirky "Strangely Strange But Oddly Normal" on the big-selling cut-price Island sampler *Nice Enough to Eat*, alongside tracks by the likes of Free, Traffic and Jethro Tull, sales of the album were minimal.

As the 1960s expired, the Strange toughened up their fey sound and switched to the Vertigo label for their second album *Heavy Petting*, a more mainstream folk-rock affair buttressed by the contributions of Fairport Convention drummer Dave Mattacks and featuring Gary Moore on electric guitar. Shortly after, in true hippie style, Goulding retreated to a Buddhist monastery and the band folded. There have been periodic reunions and a third album, *Alternative Medicine*, appeared in 1997, setting what could well have been a world record gap (27 years) between albums. If it was, it was one broken in the new millennium by Vashti Bunyan, another of Joe Boyd's discoveries. (Boyd was a man with a keen eye for musicians destined for cult obscurity.) A fourth album, *Halcyon Days*, appeared out of the blue in 2007.

An odd coda to their story is that, when their debut album was reissued on CD in the 1990s, it sounded markedly different. Somehow, on the original vinyl release, the tapes had been speeded up, and it had taken more than twenty years to spot the mistake and rectify it. It was an error that was entirely in keeping with the physics of Dr Strangely Strange's world – one in which time was never really of the essence.

NW

Heron

The folk-music technique of recording "in the field" was taken literally by the acoustic soft-rockers Heron. The guitarist and singer Roy Apps formed the quartet in the folk clubs of Maidenhead in 1967, with vocalist Tony Pook, and guitarists Gerald "G.T." Moore and Martin Hayward. They were taken under the avuncular wing of producer Gus Dudgeon and were in good company alongside his other prodigies Elton John and David Bowie. Their style was accurately described by Dudgeon as "English pastoral, with a sunny summer's day feel".

Clinging to the underbelly of the British folk-rock boom, Heron signed to Dawn, Pye's "countercultural" imprint, and entered the studio. They hated it. In the confines of a sound-proofed room, they just couldn't get the right feel. Before the tape had finished spooling, Heron were in the Pye mobile recording unit and heading down the A40 to get it together in the country. They wound up in leafy Appleford in Berkshire. In the grassy acres behind a farmhouse there, guitars were strummed, accordions squeezed, mandolins picked and the tape rolled. Behind them larks ascended and insects floated on a pollen-buffeting breeze.

The music nodded towards contemporary pop acts such as Marmalade and Badfinger and the sun-dappled harmonies of Crosby, Stills & Nash. Between the songs, sparrows chattered and the band discussed nature. It was all very charming.

Issued in November 1970, the album *Heron* attracted good reviews but failed to sell. Not even the obligatory session on John Peel's Radio 1 show could help. A single also suffered from a vinyl shortage and a delivery-van drivers' strike.

Unabashed, Heron pressed on. In June 1971 they supported Bowie at a Radio 1 concert and plotted their second album. This time, the location was a pair of gamekeeper's cottages in the village of Black Dog, Devon. Settled in the back garden, the songs just kept coming – enough, in fact, to fill a double album. This was the early 1970s and so, despite their poor return so far, Dawn were more than happy to put everything out as *Twice as Nice and Half the Price*. There was some strong material and some delightful guitar picking, but not enough to rescue the sprawling gatefold LP from the bargain bins. Within a year, Heron had flown – into cult obscurity. The only mainstream legacy of their bucolic but brief recording career may have been an unwitting influence on Ronnie Lane – the former Faces guitarist followed suit in recording some of his own albums in a field.

There is a coda to their story, however. In 1997, the band returned to Black Dog with a new member, Gerry Power, a batch of fresh songs, and plenty of happy memories of the early 1970s. they cut a couple of enjoyable reunion albums and shot a video documetary.

RW

playlist:

1 Yellow Roses *from* Heron
Gorgeous, honeysuckle harmonies from the band's debut album, recalling the melodic end of post-Beatles chart pop. Mandolins, guitars and piano mulch in a garden-wall of sound.

2 Upon Reflection *from* Heron
"Sitting in your mother's garden, smoking Lebanese beneath the privet hedge", sings Roy Apps, summing up the British middle-class counterculture in one line.

3 Take Me Back Home *from* Twice as Nice and Half the Price
A McCartneyesque singalong from the second album. It flopped as a single and was lost amongst the rambling double set, but has an unabashed charm.

4 Move it on Up *from* G.T. Moore and the Reggae Guitars
After Heron flew the nest, guitarist G.T. Moore hit the pub circuit with G.T. Moore and the Reggae Guitars, issuing two albums: a self-titled debut and *Reggae Blue*.

5 Fields of Eden *from* Black Dog
Arguably the strongest track from their 1990s reunion, and a lot more successful than such experiments often are.

The Incredible String Band

"Some of the greatest times I've had were at Incredible String Band shows, just being carried away by the whole experience ... they were an inspiration and a sign. They were a big influence and some of that came out in the acoustic stuff that Led Zeppelin did."

Robert Plant on the ISB's influence on Zep

Many of the bands in this book sold virtually no records at the time of their release, yet their albums have gone on to achieve cult classic status. The Incredible String Band went the opposite way: in the late 1960s their albums regularly charted and their fans ranged from Robert Plant to the future Archbishop of Canterbury, Rowan Williams. Yet few listen to them today and they don't even have that required artefact of any self-respecting cult act: the comprehensive, outtakes-and-all box set. As their producer Joe Boyd puts it, the Incredibles have suffered "one of the highest fame-to-obscurity ratios it is possible to imagine".

Yet in its own weird and wonderful way, their second album, *5000 Spirits or the Layers of the Onion*, was as significant a summer-of-love landmark as *Sgt. Pepper* or *Forever Changes* – in 1967, Paul McCartney nominated it his favourite album of the year. The ISB opened ears to a greater array of strange new sounds and esoteric influences than anyone until the world music "boom" some two decades later. "The Incredibles were the first world music group, combining William Blake-style mysticism with exotic instruments and rich, inventive harmonies," Boyd put it. "There was a freedom and a joyful spirit that made every day an adventure." For a brief time before a dalliance with Scientology seemed to curb their collective imagination, the Incredibles' records exuded a thrilling sense that anything was possible.

The ISB emerged out of the Scottish folk scene in the mid-1960s as a trio comprising Robin Williamson, Mike Heron and Clive Palmer. After making their debut with a self-titled folk album in 1966 – a perfectly decent record but one which gave little indication of what was to come – Williamson took off for Morocco and Palmer for India. By the time Williamson returned to Britain, he'd acquired a collection of strange and exotic instruments and an eclectic musical vision to match.

"I had an interest in finding the threads that would link the music of the world," he says. "I was listening to Indian, African and Chinese music and you couldn't recreate those sounds on a synthesizer in those days, so it was a question of having a go at a lot of different instruments. It was that stoned 1960s notion of playing things that one couldn't really play. It was rags and patches but it was new and exciting."

With Palmer still in India, Williamson and Heron regrouped as a duo and threw all conventional notions of music making out of the window while they recorded *5000 Spirits*. "We started playing around and putting on layers of stuff," Boyd recalled. "We just had a ball discovering this brave new world, putting down vocal and guitar, then adding sitar and *guimbri* and flute and jew's harp and harmony singing and organ and harpsichord and you name it. We were in uncharted territory."

By now the group was moving away, at the speed of light, from the traditional folk orbit and playing underground clubs such as UFO and Middle Earth with the likes of Pink Floyd. The spirit of those heady times was wonderfully captured on *The Hangman's Beautiful Daughter*, an album which showcased the Incredibles as the ultimate musical magpies, tinkers of global sound skimming off everything they heard. The colours and textures they wove were dazzling and if today some of it sounds a little naïve, their sheer boldness remains striking. They lived and worked communally, too, in a row of nineteenth-century cottages in the Scottish borders. But Williamson and Heron had very different musical styles. Williamson's best compositions were full of mystical invocations and riddles with meandering melodies, in which East and West effortlessly merged. Heron's style was more earthy, although he too was capable of inspired flights of fancy.

At their height they were so overflowing with ideas that, six months after *Hangman's*, they released the double album *Wee Tam and The Big Huge* (1968). After that, things were never quite the same. Their playfulness and sense of experimentation declined as they became involved in Scientology and their intimacy was lost as they moved on to play larger stadium venues (including a disastrous Woodstock appearance). Nevertheless, they struggled on until 1974, when Williamson and Heron decided to go their separate ways.

"On the first four albums there was a pressure always to be different, but it came from within ourselves," Williamson recalls. "It was almost a game. We were just having fun. Then the music business got serious – 'hey, there's big bucks to be made here' – and it got corrupted by marketing. Today one might hesitate even to try what we did."

NW

playlist:

1 Way Back in the 1960s *from* 5000 Spirits or the Layers of the Onion
An old hippie looks back at his youth from sometime in the future millennium – written by Williamson in 1967 at the age of 23.

2 First Girl I Loved *from* 5000 Spirits or the Layers of the Onion
A song of childhood innocence, albeit one with a liberally 1960s attitude towards casual sex outdoors. Later covered ("First Boy I Loved") by Judy Collins.

3 Waltz of the New Moon *from* The Hangman's Beautiful Daughter
Ethereal, mystical and like nothing else in popular music before or since.

4 Koeeoaddi There *from* The Hangman's Beautiful Daughter
"The ice was nice/Hallo the invisible brethren" – endearingly nonsensical acid-fried nursery rhymes in the form of – supposedly – a riddle.

5 Witches Hat *from* The Hangman's Beautiful Daughter
"If I was a witch's hat, sitting on her head like a paraffin stove/I'd fly away and be a bat, across the air I would rove…" Thanks for sharing, Robin.

6 Mercy I Cry City *from* The Hangman's Beautiful Daughter
Heron's delightful protest against the hustle and bustle of the big smoke.

"There was no one quite like them ... it was a discovery of the holy: not the solemn, not the saintly but the holy, which makes you silent and sometimes makes you laugh and which above all makes the landscape different once and for all."
Rowan Williams, Archbishop of Canterbury

Joanna Newsom

She plays the classical harp. She has seventeen-minute songs. Her squeaking, cooing, wavering singing voice is the very definition of an acquired taste. And her lyrics are marked by a dense vocabulary that spills over with bewildering imagery. The precocious Joanna Newsom doesn't exactly make things easy for the listener – almost every aspect of her art is disorientatingly foreign. While her extraordinary, five-song masterpiece of 2006, *Ys* (named after a mythical Breton city pronounced "ees"), has been compared to Van Morrison's classic *Astral Weeks*, it frequently floats off to an utterly mysterious musical world – one altogether free of obvious reference points.

Newsom, who still lives in the northern California mountain town where she grew up, claims she first began begging her parents to buy her a harp when she was three or four. Years of childhood training ended in her dropping out of liberal arts college Mills in order to record her own songs. Her break came when respected singer-songwriter Will Oldham, better known as Bonnie "Prince" Billy, heard her demo tape and invited her to join him on tour. She has cited Bill Callahan, who has made scores of bleak, lo-fi albums as Smog and who duets on her song "Only Skin", as an inspiration, and the pair were rumoured to be dating.

Newsom's debut album, *The Milk-Eyed Mender*, was self-consciously quirky and, while there was little astonishing about it beyond her voice, pricked up a good few ears. Critics and listeners duly lumped her in with the San Francisco "freak folk" scene, led by hippy supremo Devendra Banhart. It was the follow-up's gigantic leap forward that put her in a class of her own. Forging the unlikely union of producer Steve Albini, famed for the savage rawness of his work on Nirvana's *In Utero*, and orchestral arranger Van Dyke Parks, co-creator of the Beach Boys' famed abandoned *Smile* album, its five epic tracks saw Newsom singing cryptically over meandering harp and rich strings that stab and swoop around the melodies, abandoning verse-chorus-verse structure to produce pure musical poetry. Like the music within, the album's cover presents a beguiling amalgam of mythical imagery and seemingly mystical signs and symbols. After critical raptures, Newsom's cult became large enough for her to tour prestigious arts venues and a select festival circuit accompanied by full orchestras.

Her songs, so she has said, are heavily coded explorations of personal experience, and her lyrics are beautifully incomprehensible. "Emily", for instance, is addressed to her astrophysicist sister, and includes a passage explaining the difference between meteors, meteoroids and meteorites. Newsom is unique among songwriters; *Ys* is surely the only album in existence to feature the words "hydrocephalitic", "sassafras" and "spelunking".

DS

playlist:

1 Cosmia *from* Ys
This majestic seven-minute tumble of harp, strings and extraordinary vocals closes Newsom's second album. (For those puzzling over the album cover's symbols, the framed insect in Newsom's right hand is in fact the Cosmia moth.)

2 Sprout and the Bean *from* The Milk-Eyed Mender
This whimsical waltz is undoubtedly the high point of her debut album, displaying both her unique ear for arrangement and her quirky approach to songwriting.

3 Clam crab cowrie cockle *from* The Milk-Eyed Mender
"The sky looks like a road" is one of Newsom's pithier observations; understated vocals and spare, judicious harp strums keep things beautifully simple here.

Phil Ochs

He could've been... Bob Dylan?

The search for "the new Dylan" has been going on for over forty years and with the exception of Bruce Springsteen most of those who have been saddled with the tag have found it to be more of a curse than a blessing. Phil Ochs was the first in a long line and arguably wanted to be the new Dylan from the moment the original arrived on the block.

Six months older than Bob, Ochs arrived in Greenwich Village around the same time at the beginning of the 1960s. Having studied journalism at Ohio State University, he described himself as a "singing journalist" and began writing topical songs about civil rights and the draft, often in the talking blues style that both he and Dylan had copied from Woody Guthrie.

They also often wrote about the same subjects. At the 1963 Newport Folk Festival, both unveiled songs about the death of black activist Medgar Evers at the hands of a white American racist. "I just can't keep up with Phil," wrote Dylan in a letter to *Broadside* magazine in 1964. "And he's getting better and better and better."

The latter half of the statement may well have been true. The former was certainly not, for by the time Ochs' debut album *All the News That's Fit to Sing* was released in 1964, Dylan was already moving on from protest and preparing to go electric. Ochs continued ploughing the fields Dylan had vacated on the albums *I Ain't Marching Anymore* and *Phil Ochs in Concert*, but he was also one of the few in the folk community who praised Dylan's new role as the electric messiah. At least he did until one day in 1965, when they were driving together through New York and he had the temerity to say he didn't think Dylan's new single "Won't You Please Crawl Out Your Window" would be a hit. Dylan stopped his limo and threw Ochs out of the car, allegedly yelling after him, "You're not a folksinger, Ochs. You're a journalist!"

Ochs was, however, proved right and the song only scraped the US charts at number 58. But it didn't do the pair's relationship any good. There was a brief reconciliation between the two "rivals" when Ochs persuaded Dylan to sing at a 1974 benefit concert at Madison Square Garden, which he had organized to protest at the coup in Chile that had overthrown Salvador Allende. But, after suffering severe bouts of schizophrenia, Ochs hanged himself two years later, while Dylan was on the Rolling Thunder Revue tour. Ochs had been invited along, and hoped to join him, but in the event was too ill.

In reality, anyone looking for a "new Dylan" is on a hiding to nothing of course. Bob was, and remains, *sui generis*. The tag does Ochs a disservice: he was an articulate, earnest and talented songwriter, equally as committed to speaking out against the injustices of the world as he was to the art of song.

NW

Linda Perhacs

Not many people keep an ear out for new musical talent while visiting the dentist. Film composer Leonard Rosenman was lucky enough to find a real treasure when he opened wide in 1970. Linda Perhacs mentioned to her patient that she wrote the occasional song, and Rosenman was polite enough to request a demo tape (not easy to do when you have metal implements in your mouth). When he got it, he called Perhacs at 8am the next morning and offered to produce an album for her.

What he had discovered was a folk singer who was out-there even by Californian standards. She may well have had the condition synaesthesia, a phenomenon found in many creative people, in which certain parts of the brain are unusually close together. It produces a commingling of the senses in which sounds are "seen" as colours, or "felt" as tastes. "I always saw light and colour in music and thought patterns," she said. "I have always seen them as one, like Japanese paintings – all in balance, but moving like a sound sculpture." In order to explain how her song "Parallelograms" should sound, she drew Rosenman a picture of green circles, blue waves and pink lines, requesting "sound moving from speaker to speaker to form shapes".

Whether he understood her or not, the end result was stunning, a cyclical acoustic melody with Perhacs' soft voice fluttering back and forth, and a freeform, psychedelic breakdown in the middle. Other songs, such as "Chimacum Rain", were almost as eerie, filled with nature imagery and with layered versions of her gentle tones sounding like a whole team of ghostly voices.

That, unfortunately, was that. Her record label, MCA, barely promoted or distributed the album. She never even played live. She returned disillusioned to the world of dentistry, little knowing that in a few decades' time she would join Vashti Bunyan as another one-album folk wonder ripe for rediscovery.

At the turn of the millennium, Brooklyn producer Michael Piper reissued *Parallelograms* on his The Wild Places label. As he couldn't track down Perhacs (not even at her old label, where her details had mistakenly been filed under "Linda Perhaps") he had to make a recording from a mint copy of the vinyl. When he finally met her in 2003, Perhacs gave him her copies of the original master tapes and a better version appeared with extra, previously unreleased tracks.

Now Perhacs is recording again as an idol of the new breed of left-field folkies led by Devendra Banhart, who features her on his forthcoming album. She brought "an otherworldly light to a tune, with her still-divine voice," he enthused. You would expect nothing less.

DS

where to start:

1 Parallelograms *from* Parallelograms
Her finest moment is a looping, multilayered masterpiece, with interweaving vocals singing "Quadrahedral, tetrahedral, mono-cycla-cyber-cilia" over echoing acoustic guitar. Maths never sounded so beautiful.

2 If You Were My Man *from* Parallelograms
Unreleased in 1970, this love song was added to the album's reissue and showed a more conventional side to Perhacs. Its mournful piano is less alien sounding, but still extremely beautiful. (And it was clearly outré enough for Daft Punk to include it in the soundtrack for their bizarre 2006 film *Electroma*.)

Judee Sill

Until a recent spate of re-releases, the music of Judee Sill had been all but forgotten. Her recordings appeared on David Geffen's Asylum Records in the early 1970s alongside such sun-dappled children of the Californian revolution as The Eagles, Jackson Browne, Joni Mitchell and Linda Ronstadt. Her music was soulful and moving as anything made by Laurel Canyon's beautiful people and she's even been called a "female Brian Wilson". Yet Sill's career spluttered, faltered and then fizzled out altogether. Her tragic story is the antithesis of the Californian dream – or perhaps its dark, hidden underbelly.

Judee was born on 7 October, 1944 in Studio City, California. Her father worked as an importer of exotic animals, was briefly a cameraman in Hollywood and owned a bar. When she was eight, her father died, her mother remarried and life was never the same again. Her stepfather abused her. Her mother became addicted to downers and alcohol. Feeling rejected and betrayed, Sill became a teenage wild child. At fifteen, she fell into a relationship with an older man, and the pair committed a series of armed robberies. After a string of Bonnie and Clyde-style hold-ups of gas stations and liquor stores (she claimed that during one robbery she was so nervous that her words came out as "This is a fuck-up, mothersticker"), she ended up in reform school, where she learned to play the church organ. On her release in 1963, she played piano with a college orchestra but soon dropped out. After her mother's death from cancer in 1965 she was left alone in the world and took up with keyboard player Bob Harris, whom she married. The pair soon developed his-and-hers heroin habits.

She supported their addiction by dealing, thieving and turning tricks on the street. She was soon back in jail for narcotics offences and passing forged cheques. "All I really cared about was getting that needle in my vein," she later told *Rolling Stone*. While in jail, she began writing songs, influenced by the likes of Joan Baez and Buffy Sainte-Marie. One of them, "Dead Time Bummer Blues", was later recorded by LA garage band The Leaves. After they split, the band's bass player Jim Pons graduated to The Turtles and persuaded the group to record her gorgeous song "Lady-O". Released as the group's final single in 1969, it wasn't a smash hit but it brought Sill to the attention of David Geffen.

Her debut, *Judee Sill* (1972), revealed a voice of bewitching purity on a set of intense and lyrical songs, many of which had an almost hymn-like quality, driven by the same inner pain that had led her to heroin. Among them was the wonderful "Jesus Was A Cross Maker", rich in bizarre religious imagery and bold, ambiguous depictions of Christ – although the role model for the song is said to be the singer-songwriter J.D. Souther, with whom she had an affair. Produced by Graham Nash, it was released as a single but, despite decent radio play, it failed to chart.

The album got lost as it was swiftly followed on the label by the debut releases by Jackson Browne and The Eagles. Perhaps Sill's spiky persona didn't help. Souther recalled one appearance when someone in the crowd asked her to sing a Judy Collins number. "I don't know that fuckin' song," she responded. "And if I did I wouldn't play it."

Her second album, *Heart Food* (1973), had the same lyrical intensity as her debut but was musically more sumptuous, particularly on such shimmering beauties as "The Kiss" and "The Donor", an extraordinary song that sounds like a choral requiem, complete with a repeated "Kyrie Eleison". The album failed to sell and she fell out with David Geffen.

Little is known about how she lived her final years. She abandoned sessions for a third album (although eight tracks intended for it surfaced with other material on 2005's *Dreams Come True*). She lived on a small private income from some oil shares left by her mother. She also had a string of female lovers and was fascinated by various forms of mysticism and occultism. A car accident which resulted in a serious back injury fuelled her return to drug addiction and she was found dead at her North Hollywood home on 23 November, 1979. The cause of death was given as "acute cocaine and codeine intoxication".

Sill aimed to make the listener "open up his heart". If you're not moved by her breathtaking music, you might just want to check your pulse.

NW

playlist:

1 Jesus Was a Cross Maker *from* Abracadabra: The Asylum Years
"One time I trusted a stranger 'cause I heard his sweet song/And it was gently enticing me, though there was something wrong".

2 Enchanted Sky Machines *from* Abracadabra: The Asylum Years
They're coming to take us away. And just in the nick of time, before the apocalypse, too. Circa 1972, this was a common belief in certain Californian communities.

3 Lopin' Along Through the Cosmos *from* Abracadabra: The Asylum Years
A heart-wrenching ballad in which she longs for a kiss from God.

4 Ridge Rider *from* Abracadabra: The Asylum Years
"He comes from under the cryptosphere where the great sadness begins" – we told you her songs weren't quite like anyone else's.

5 Lady-O *from* Abracadabra: The Asylum Years
The definitive version of a song that was a minor hit for The Turtles, re-recorded for her own debut album.

6 Soldier of the Heart *from* Abracadabra: The Asylum Years
A rare electric guitar outing among the piano-heavy ballads, this is the nearest she ever got to the soft-rock sound of her Laurel Canyon-dwelling contemporaries.

XTC's Andy Partridge on the strange spell of Judee Sill

"I must have been about nineteen when I first heard Judee Sill, around 1972. Initially I thought it was soppy girls' music because I wanted to be dead noisy at the time. Between her two albums coming out, I think the New York Dolls had hit me, but she must have got under my skin because I found myself playing it when my girlfriend wasn't around.

I came to love both albums immensely. Later people would assume the Beach Boys' albums were a big influence on XTC, but I hadn't heard a Beach Boys album until 1986, only singles. The mood and sound on our later albums comes from hearing Judee Sill, the layered vocals and beautiful arrangements. My music would have been very different but for her. If you're a fan of the more soulful, hymnal side of Brian Wilson then she is the female equivalent.

She sits somewhere near the very controlled icing-sugar world of The Carpenters – the timbre of her voice is not dissimilar to Karen Carpenter but her melodies are J.S. Bach with a twelve-string guitar. They are some of the most achingly beautiful melodies and chord structures I have ever heard and I'd even say that "The Kiss" is the most beautiful song ever recorded. I think she had a lot of things working against her and she had about every problem going. She was very gawky looking, she had a Pippi Longstocking sort of a face and, let's be honest, a lot of boys only got into Melanie or Carly Simon because they wanted to get into their drawers.

Her musicality struck me first, but I did pick up on the lyrics and found them oddly sexual in a religious way and oddly religious in a sexual way. They stir sexuality with a hymnal feel. I'm sure people heard this stuff and thought she was a Jehovah's Witness or in some obscure religious sect and so would have nothing to do with it. She was strangely obsessed with the idea of Jesus as a stud, so in "Ridge Rider" you get Jesus portrayed as a Clint Eastwood-type vigilante cowboy, or you get Jesus portrayed as a bridegroom coming to do you over on your wedding night.

You wonder how on earth someone that could make such beautiful and soulful music could have had such a screwed-up life. It's sickening that she wasn't recognized while she was alive – she must have just closed down. It's very easy to retreat into yourself when you feel no one gets what you are doing. Judee Sill is a million light years away from all those other denim-clad singer-songwriters; her music leaves the rest of that quasi-country crowd in the dirt."

Trees

Two bands towered over the English folk-rock scene of the late 1960s and early 1970s – the Pentangle and Fairport Convention. The length of their shadow was so long that no one saw the Trees for the wood, as it were. By the time the band issued its masterpiece, *On the Shore*, in late 1970, the taste-makers and trend-setters had already decreed that folk-rock had reached its high watermark with the Fairport's *Liege & Lief* and there was little more to be said. It wasn't until more than 35 years later, when Gnarls Barkley sampled "Geordie" from the long-forgotten album, that *On the Shore* received its "push back into the sunlight", as the liner notes of the record's first appearance on CD in 2007 aptly put it.

Trees were formed in 1969 by the guitarists David Costa and Barry Clarke, both of whom had misspent their youth hanging around London folk clubs listening to the likes of Martin Carthy and Davy Graham. Bass player and songwriter Bias Boshell lived in the same house as Clarke and was swiftly added to the band. He brought with him drummer and old school friend Unwin Brown. Searching for a singer, a workmate of Costa's suggested his sister Celia Humphris, who auditioned and was duly hired.

Only Costa knew much about folk music. "I certainly wasn't a folk fan," Humphris admitted when interviewed for the reissue of *On the Shore*. "I'd trained as an opera singer. I'd have loved to have sung blues or jazz but I had too light a voice. Folk suited my vocal limitations." Boshell, too, confessed that folk music was new to him but found that the traditional folk songs that Costa played him were "...so extraordinarily brilliant and moving that anyone would kill to put their name to them". Like Fairport's Richard Thompson, he swiftly learned to cast his own songs in the idiom of the great narrative folk tradition, while remaining innovative and contemporary at the same time.

Trees' debut album, *The Garden of Jane Trelawney*, appeared in early 1970. It's a record of naïve charm, combining classic folk-rock tropes with the kind of whimsical hippie pastoralism peddled by the likes of The Incredible String Band. According to Costa, a big influence on the album was listening to Buffalo Springfield: "That was when I realized you could have an acoustic and electric lead guitar working together." Interestingly, Fairport Convention had also arrived at their very specifically English sound via an infatuation with American music – for them it was the acoustic-electric mix of another West Coast band, Jefferson Airplane, that was the big epiphany.

Melody Maker's reviewer enthusiastically noted of *The Garden of Jane Trelawney* that "the long-awaited reconciliation between the folk and pop movements is actually beginning to happen". Standout tracks include extended versions of the traditional songs "Lady Margaret" and "She Moves Through the Fair", but *On the Shore*, recorded only a few months later, represented a quantum leap in both style and execution. It was evident they had been learning fast from Fairport Convention and the album opened with a stirring arrangement of the traditional "Soldiers Three", which they had learned from Fairport's fiddler Dave Swarbrick. It was followed by Boshell's composition, "Murdoch", characterized by Clarke's stingingly melodic Richard Thompson-like lead guitar lines and a rhythm section built very much in the style Mattacks and Pegg had forged with the Fairports.

Boshell's ability to absorb the argot and imagery of traditional song was impressively displayed on songs such as "Murdoch" and "Fool", while "Polly on the Shore", "Geordie" and "The Streets of Derry" were trad tunes reclothed in imaginative new arrangements and modal, psychedelic textures. The album's highlight, however, was a stunning version of "Sally Free and Easy", a song many musicians had discovered via the folk singer Cyril Tawney's version. Trees transform the song into a ten-minute epic that builds with thrilling tension and ranks alongside the Fairport's "A Sailor's Life" as a pinnacle in English folk-rock.

When the album failed to sell, the band underwent a couple of personnel changes and attempted to soldier on, but within eighteen months Trees had broken up for good. Humphris became the disembodied voice announcing the next station on the London Underground. Costa became Elton John's art director. Boshell wrote hits for Kiki Dee and played with the Moody Blues. Brown became a teacher and Clarke an antiques dealer. There the story might have ended – but for that Gnarls Barkley sample. Costa is sanguine about

the belated recognition that has allowed Trees to grow tall again. "It's the archeological nature of the Internet and the effect of Amazon that finally enabled people to beat a path to our door," he notes. "But part of what people love about Trees is that we were in and out, and then gone."

NW

playlist:

1 Lady Margaret *from* The Garden of Jane Delawney
Terrific arrangement of an old ballad collected by Francis Child, which Dave Costa probably learned from Martin Carthy.

2 She Moves Through the Fair *from* The Garden of Jane Delawney
A traditional Irish song recorded by the Fairports two years earlier but here given a new arrangement.

3 The Garden of Jane Delawney *from* The Garden of Jane Delawney
"I cannot explain anything about it," says Boshell. "I don't know who Jane Delawney is, what it means or what influenced me in writing it. It appeared as if from nowhere."

4 Murdoch *from* On the Shore
Written by Boshell, it sounds like it could be 200 years old with its elemental lyric full of "black-beaked crows" and "mountain shrouds".

5 Soldiers Three *from* On the Shore
Learned from Dave Swarbrick, it has a baroque and courtly guitar interlude that recalls Fairport's "Fotheringay".

6 Streets of Derry *from* On the Shore
Another inspired and semi-improvised reimagining of a trad song, this one learned from Shirley Collins.

7 Sally Free And Easy *from* On the Shore
Trees' finest moment.

8 Geordie *from* On the Shore
The one you know from the Gnarls Barkley sample.

9 Polly on the Shore *from* On the Shore
Another trad song turned into a folk-rock landmark by Clarke's exquisite lead guitar.

10 Fool *from* On the Shore
The most contemporary sounding track on the album, co-written by Boshell and Costa.

BLIPS, BEATS AND GLITCHES
techno-heads, MCs and electro-geeks

Boards Of

I t might not be quite in the same league as the mystery of Jack and Meg White's relationship, but for years the world understood Michael Sandison and Marcus Eoin – the inscrutable duo at the heart of electronic pioneers Boards Of Canada – to have been childhood friends. It wasn't until 2005 that they admitted they were brothers and that Marcus's name was Sandison, too. They had concealed their relationship to avoid comparisons with the electronic duo of brothers Phil and Paul Hartnoll in Orbital, they explained.

The admission was a rare personal insight into their weird and wonderful and highly private world. Boards Of Canada have seldom given interviews or offered any insights into their signature sound, a mix of dreamy electronics and hip-hop rhythms delivered with a nostalgic, Sesame Street-style oddness. Their music conjures up a distorted, Super-8 memory of a 1970s childhood and has a universal charm that appeals equally to fans of indie, techno and beyond.

As children, Michael and Marcus built up their musical skills while moving between Scotland, the south of England and Alberta, Canada. By 1980, Michael had put together a band on the northeast coast of Scotland, though Marcus wasn't a member. By 1986 Marcus had joined the troop playing bass; they gigged around their local area playing hard abstract electronic sets in support of an unlikely selection of glam-rock covers bands.

Taking their name, and a certain aesthetic, from the documentaries of the National Film Board of Canada, the fluid collective broadened its remit to include photography and filmmaking. The works were cryptic and wistful, featuring experimental soundtracks of found sound and sampled TV excerpts. Though many had been involved over the years, by 1989 Boards Of Canada had slimmed down to a three-piece: Mike, Marcus and Chris Horne. They built their own studio, initiated various happenings and other audiovisual projects, and were the driving force of a loose gathering called the Hexagon Sun collective, hosting so-called "Redmoon" nights in a ruin close to their studio.

Though several self-financed EPs and albums had already emerged on the band's own Music70 imprint, the first to reach the outside world was a lo-fi selection of haunting melodies underpinned by stark rhythms entitled *Twoism* (reissued by Warp in 2002). In 1996 a copy of *Twoism* found its way to SKam records in Manchester; within a matter of hours Autechre's Sean Booth had made contact with Boards Of Canada, by then the two-piece of Mike and Marcus. December 1996 witnessed the pair's first release for SKam: the *Hi Scores* EP, a stunning six-track collection of effervescent beats nestling in vast clouds of serene melody, with a typically retro reference of a title bringing to mind halcyon boyhood days of playing *Space Invaders*.

The following year more tunes surfaced on two limited-release compilations jointly put out by SKam and Musik Aus Strom, a label based in Munich. The first of these *Mask* collections featured a new Boards Of Canada cut, while the second included a selection credited to a Boards Of Canada alter ego, Hell Interface. As interest grew in the band and their genuinely original take on electronica's increasingly

Canada

formulaic blueprint, the scene witnessed more Boards Of Canada live appearances complete with Super-8 projections and remixes. But it wasn't until early in 1998 that it was announced that the duo had signed to Sheffield's Warp Records and an album release was imminent.

Music Has the Right to Children, jointly released by Warp and SKam in April 1998, was a masterpiece. The collection received rave reviews, drifted to the upper reaches of many end-of-year critics' polls, and eventually peaked at number seven in the UK Independent Chart the following February. The praise continued to pour in, Warp released the band's Peel session of the previous year as an EP and in May 1999 the *NME* cited *Music Has the Right to Children* in a list of the top psychedelic records of all time, alongside classics by the likes of The Beatles, Pink Floyd and Spiritualized.

A considerable period of silence followed, with only one EP being released in 2000: *In a Beautiful Place Out in the Country*. A second album didn't appear until 2002. *Geogaddi* was another fine collection, though its grooves lacked the immediacy of the duo's previous set, favouring instead sonic abstraction and richly layered amalgams of found sounds, lush synth chords and stark beats.

Their third album for Warp, *The Campfire Headphase*, appeared in 2005 and confirmed them as a unique force in reviving a genre that has tended to lazily follow the path of mediocrity. Their music is the sonic equivalent of simultaneous equations spelled out in Fuzzy Felt: at the same time studious and cuddly.

NW

playlist:

1 Peter Standing Alone *from* Music Has the Right to Children
The whole of BOC's *Music Has the Right to Children* album warrants inclusion in this playlist, but if there is one track that stands out, it is this. Though it relies less on novelty found sounds and samples than much of the rest of the album, its snap, crackle and pop break (yes, it really does sound like Rice Krispies) and slow oozing chord sweeps eloquently sum up the group's sound of that period.

2 Aquarius *from* Music Has the Right to Children
The meaning behind the constant repetition of the word "orange" remains elusive, though the fact that children laughing in the background seem so happy about it suggests that there is nothing sinister at work here. This, coupled with *Sesame Street*-style counting lessons and a distinctly funky, retro beat make for a track that is sure to delight anyone born in the orbit of 1970.

3 Sixtyniner *from* Twoism
The opening track from *Twoism* boasts all the hallmarks of the BOC sound, though with a certain level of detail and sheen stripped away. Not to say that this is a bad thing: the cleaner edge of this cut (and the others on the EP) illustrates both the band's evolution and their influences (such as early Kraftwerk and Neu!, among others).

4 In a Beautiful Place Out in the Country *from* A Beautiful Place EP
Haunting and beautiful, this track finds echoing beats and more laughter dancing like fireflies over a compelling vocal sample expounding the virtues of life in a rural religious community. It's very strange, and after several listens you will feel almost hypnotized to a point where you want to pack your bag, pack in your job, and go.

5 Music Is Math *from* Geogaddi
When *Geogaddi* was released, expectations were high, and there was always the worry that BOC would not deliver. The set was, thankfully, a triumph and took everything that had come before in some very new, brave directions. "Music Is Math" is a stew of operatic swell and churning hiss that opens the collection. Listened to loud it'll take your breath away.

6 Satellite Anthem Icarus *from* The Campfire Headphase
The heavier breaks of earlier recordings are here dispensed with, in favour of a far more pastoral sound — you might even be forgiven for labelling it as folksy. The electronic crimp that appeared elsewhere in the Boards Of Canada canon is now replaced by more acoustic instruments and great washes of seemingly analogue hiss and crackle — it's outer-space folk music like nothing else.

Doseone

Adam Drucker is quite an anomaly. The hardest-working surrealist in hip-hop, he has made music that doesn't really have any precedents. Doseone (Drucker's stage name) was one of the founders of the anticon collective, a record label that arose out of a loose conglomerate of rappers, DJs and producers who convened in San Francisco in 1997 with a shared interest in pushing hip-hop into uncharted territory. It nurtured such inventive rappers and musicians as Aesop Rock, Sole, Odd Nosdam and Why?, who have gone on to make some of the most interesting hip-hop of the last decade. But none of them has quite such a singular musical vision as Dose. The prolific slew of albums, EPs and collaborations he has unleashed since the late 1990s has gone much further than even the most adventurous of his fellow travellers in hip-hop's arty wing.

Nominally a rapper, his music has moved a long way from hip-hop: a Doseone album is as likely to feature dense, psychedelic songs of epic detail that are a twentieth-century update of prog-rock as to feature a block-rocking beat. But even his early rapping didn't have too many precedents. Only Freestyle Fellowship – an LA-based, jazz-influenced hip-hop crew who were celebrated for their impenetrably fast raps and general bohemian demeanour – are the real point of comparison. And even then, Dose's estranging, nasal, sing-song voice effectively removes his delivery from any mainstream points of reference: it's closer to the acerbic squeak of Perry Farrell (the singer with Jane's Addiction) or a more menacing variation on the dopey effeminacy of comedian Emo Philips than to the voice of any rapper you could think of. By turns wheedling, cajoling, waspish and soothing, Dose's voice is a cartoonish and stylized instrument, about as macho and burly as a yellow butterfly.

The *Hemispheres* album was the first the world heard of Doseone. It's probably his most conventional release, but it's also a very satisfying one. Aged 21, the Philadelphia-raised rapper put out a debut album that was recognizably hip-hop, with clear influences from the laid-back jazzy rap of A Tribe Called Quest. The overall vibe was very 1990s New York – all murky jazz samples and grainy drums. Dose's vocals

didn't quite have the camp, self-conscious tone he is now known for, and his lines even rhymed. He also displayed an idiosyncratic take on the boasts and put-downs that are the hip-hop MC's stock-in-trade – albeit with a rather esoteric bent. This was music in keeping with the cerebral, bohemian turn that the underground was taking in the coffee shops of New York and San Francisco at the time. Around the same period, Dose collaborated with fellow anticon rappers Alias, Sole and Slug under the name Deep Puddle Dynamics, and with Jel under the name Themselves. Both of these groups released albums of quirky, playful hip-hop, taking liberties with the conventions of their chosen form but remaining happily within them.

However, the album *Slow Death*, which Dose put out himself in 2000, gave an indication of the sort of limb he would soon be going out on. An unapologetically lo-fi recording, its morose electronic drones and enervated drum loops made no concessions to any recognizable genre. They accompanied stream-of-consciousness lyrics that were connected by the most tenuous of associative leaps. There was a general feeling of portentousness, with plenty of nostalgic references to early childhood and a fair few angst-ridden grumblings about having to grow up. But you could forgive him this, because he was a hip-hop MC who delighted in words for their own sake, with lyrics that suggested he had carefully chewed and thoroughly digested James Joyce's *Finnegans Wake*.

Circle (2002) saw Dose hooking up with producer Boom Bip. It was as if the Doseone of *Slow Death* had dyed his hair and gone out to a party: the lyrics had an effete, sardonic streak to them, while the music really stretched its legs. It was an album by two equal partners who trusted each other implicitly – music made for the hell of it, in the confidence that one or other of the pair would know what to do. While the music was based on samples and found sounds, there was a molten core of 1960s experimentation at its heart, with ideas from Brazilian psychedelia and baroque acid rock filtered through hip-hop and electro. Samples from old classical music and easy listening records were juxtaposed with lazy bongos and wandering synthesizers. The imagistic lyrics were as skittish as the music, with references to history, pop culture, religion and whatever else happened to be fizzing away in Doseone's head at the time. The CD's sleeve featured sepia photographs of Dose in fancy dress, wearing a tricorne hat and feathers, looking like a cross between an Elizabethan pirate and Big Bird from *Sesame Street*.

The strangely named album *cLOUDDEAD* proved to be a breakthrough of sorts. Dose had recorded a series of 10" EPs with fellow anticon rapper Why? and producer Odd Nosdam (aka Dave Madson), which were eventually collected together into an album. It was picked up in the UK by the adventurous hip-hop label Big Dada, and was released to rave reviews. An astonishing album, it contained some of the murkiest, grainiest music ever recorded: drums that sounded like lead pipes being hit with twigs, and basslines like twanged strings of chewing gum. Why? was a more than capable foil for Doseone's bravura non-sequiturs, and the pair's raps had an impressionistic poetry to them. Tricky and Boards of Canada were about the only other acts in the same orbit; cLOUDDEAD made dense, enveloping music that was wistful and comforting yet melancholic. Their album had more in common with the whimsical harmonium meanderings of Ivor Cutler, or the anything-goes jamming of The Fugs.

John Peel was a fan, and cLOUDDEAD recorded a session for him. A follow-up album, *Ten*, surfaced in 2004, which had a brighter sound and upped the psychedelic influences. Both Why? and Dose had more input into the songs, and the sound was even harder to categorize: perhaps if Brian Wilson had had samplers and synthesizers to play with while he was making the *Smile* album in the late 1960s, he might have come up with something like *Ten*.

A six-man live band, the pompously named Subtle, featuring keyboard player Dax Pierson and anticon rapper Jel, appeared to become Doseone's main focus for a while. The band released a string of albums and EPs, gigging and touring extensively. The music veered into post-rock territory: the detailed, layered songs were immense, and seemed to be attempting to compress every idea that the likes of Mum, Animal Collective and Tortoise had ever had. Dose had always multi-tracked his vocals – it accounts for the intimacy and menace in his work – but his stacked-up choruses were becoming hydra-headed monsters reminiscent of Prince. Indeed, albums such as *Ha* and *For Hero For Fool*

had a distinctly 1980s funk sheen to them, with a more-is-more attitude to the arrangements. They had a grandiose epic scale to them that recalled prog-rock – Peter Gabriel would surely have approved. Following them, *Softskulls* – an unadorned album of poetry that Doseone released in 2007 – was a refreshing listen. It made it clear to anyone who hadn't been paying attention that Dose was part of a tradition of American experimental writing informed by William Burroughs, Allen Ginsberg and Clark Coolidge.

Doseone's musical trajectory has repositioned him as an American male equivalent of Björk: an immediately recognizable voice that thrives on collaborations, making music with unexpected twists that somehow always sounds *sui generis*.

MM

playlist:

1 Dead Men's Teal *from* Circle
Slowed-down Brazilian percussion propels a looped fragment of muffled 1960s psychedelia: the whole thing is like a hip-hop cover version of "Dear Prudence".

2 Art Saved My Life *from* Circle
Taking a beautiful pinch from Prokofiev's *Peter and the Wolf*, this lopes along wistfully, sounding simultaneously nostalgic and menacing. "There's some serious music inside of me," he confesses – as if it needed pointing out.

3 Self Explanitory *from* Hemispheres
Probably the closest Doseone will ever come to toeing a line: wordy, arty hip-hop that actually boasts and disses like a "proper" rapper should.

4 Ha *from* Ha
Cyborg accordions and tin-pot percussion create a soundworld oddly reminiscent of English post-punk: it's like Prince jamming with The The in 1981.

5 Axejaw *from* Ha
A surprisingly straightforward old-school electro track: you could imagine one of the more imaginative software developers licensing it for a violent computer game soundtrack.

6 The Keen Teen Slip *from* Ten
Has there ever been another song that required a group of young men to harmonize the repeated word "Pants" over a single piano note produced by the jumping stylus of a scratched children's record?

7 Apt. A (2) *from* cLOUDDEAD
A melancholy tune is whistled by a chorus of what sounds like detuned blown bottles: a soiled comfort-blanket for Doseone and Why?'s sour but wistful rapping.

Kool Keith

"The Chicken Song" was a deliberately irritating comedy hit single in 1986 from *Spitting Image*, the satirical TV series that used latex puppets to caricature celebrities and politicians. The song was a parody of the inane Mediterranean-summer-holiday disco hits of the time, its lyrics issuing a string of increasingly surreal instructions to the dance floor, such as "climb inside a dog" and "behead an eskimo". One of its supposedly absurd injunctions was to "pretend your name is Keith". Clearly, the name Keith was not something any sensible person could ever think of as cool. In 1980s hip-hop, rappers routinely rechristened themselves with such self-aggrandizing monikers as Big Daddy Kane and Ice Dog – a rapper calling himself Kool Keith stood out like a sore thumb. The stage name of Keith Matthew Thornton is just one of the many things that are not quite right about his art.

The world first heard of him for the part he played in the Ultramagnetic MCs, a hip-hop crew that formed in the Bronx, New York, in 1984. The team of Keith, Ced Gee, TR Love and Moe Love had a sound that was the hardest and most inventive in hip-hop at the time, thanks to the pioneering and inventive beat-making of Ced Gee's production, heard to great effect on their startling debut album *Critical Beatdown*. It was a hell of a racket and extremely funky. Whereas most hip-hop was still reliant on drum machines, *Critical Beatdown* used samples of other records throughout, and in a meticulously detailed and layered fashion. Highly influential, its sound directly informed the clattering drums and shrieking sirens that were Public Enemy's modus operandi and gave plenty of pointers to the UK's drum'n'bass scene. Hip-hop beats were suddenly a whole lot louder.

Keith's lyrics were equally striking. He paid lip service to the MC's stock-in-trade of braggadocio, but his boasts were unusually abstruse and metaphysical. He threatened to graffiti his name on the inside of our skulls. He promised to take our brains to another dimension. Like Sun Ra, a fellow visionary of black American music, he was obsessed with science fiction and space. "The world's my area ... a fresh interior", he asserted on "Ain't it Good to You", intent on collapsing notions of inside and outside, and challenging the places a black human was allowed to be.

Keith didn't exactly shout either. His strangely clipped, insistent bark sounded not hard but slightly robotic. And weirdly... cool.

The Ultras' belated follow-up, *Funk Your Head Up*, emerged in 1992, and was a disappointment to many. Hip-hop by numbers, it had suffered from having outside production and remixes imposed upon it by an unhappy record label. Part of the crew's appeal was its oddness, and Keith has always sounded like a fish out of water when playing by the rules. But the album produced one success. The remixed single, "Poppa Large", could well be a contender for hip-hop's best ever use of a fat double-bass, and it became quite a New York anthem. An impatient-sounding Keith spat out a freewheeling, syncopated rap in a voice that suggested he couldn't give a toss whether anyone wanted to hear it or not. The video showed Keith strapped to a chair in a straitjacket, his shaven-head locked in a bird-cage, being routinely sedated by men in white coats. A beefy, jazz-infused third album, *The Four Horsemen,* appeared the following year. Its dark, smoky sounds complemented a sleazier side of Keith that was starting to emerge.

Things went quiet for a while. Keith recorded a few songs with Godfather Don, a rapper who had appeared on the *Four Hoursemen* and produced some of its songs. Then came something nobody could have predicted: a hip-hop concept album rapped in the fictional persona of a time-travelling, sex-obsessed, animal-fetishizing obstetric gynaecologist. *Dr Octagonecologyst* was an album positively overflowing with the pop-culture references it had chopped up and juiced. Its name punned on Dr Octopus, the eight-armed mad scientist from the *Spider Man* comics, while the music, produced by Dan the Automator, appeared to take its cue from 1970s sci-fi and horror movies. As the titular Dr Octagon, Keith was unnervingly deadpan but often laugh-out-loud funny, as he recounted obscene confessions from the operating theatre. It's like an episode of *The Muppet Show* directed by David Cronenberg; an assault on the bastion of scientific jargon by a bestiary of the imagination.

It was a hard act to follow. *First Come First Served* saw Keith killing off his alter-ego and replacing it with a different one: Dr Dooom (so badass he needed an extra "o"). The album set the template for a persona that seems to have resurfaced through all Keith's subsequent releases: part self-deprecating geek, part ladies' man and part serial killer. The album cover used all the plug-ins at PhotoShop's disposal to create a monstrous collage of Keith foregrounded against a rotting tenement building, proffering potential listeners a humungous rat burger in his giant outstretched hand. Tracks such as "You Live at Home with Your Mom" and "Welfare Love" had a certain charm, with Keith's shlocky surrealism tempered by a few personal reminiscences about growing up in the slums. The album also featured some appropriately strange music, courtesy of Kutmasta Kurt. Rarely have synthesizers sounded so cheap, and rarely have cheap synthesizers sounded so queasily disquieting, as on the albums Kurt produced for Keith: *First Come First Served, Black Elvis, Diesel Truckers* and *Masters of Reality*.

Kool Keith has now released a body of work that's as swollen and amorphous as the freakish creatures that populate it. Albums such as *Pimp to Eat* (a collaboration with Ice-T), *Sex Style, Matthew, Project Polaroid* and *Mr Nogatco* are often utterly distasteful, and often lazily throwaway, but there is always something worth listening to. It is hard to fathom quite what is going on inside Keith's head. Some of Keith's early lyrics made references to having been institutionalized in New York's Bellevue psychiatric hospital for depression. Keith has later distanced himself from this, stating that he was joking. The person that emerges from his chaotically prolific career is certainly a mass of contradictions. Is he for real? His lyrics make it hard to tell. You get the impression he probably doesn't know the answer either, and probably wouldn't even see the point of the question.

MM

playlist:

Ultramagnetic MCs

1 Make You Shake *from* The Basement Tapes 1984–1990
An outer-space echo effect and an antique drum machine are the only backing on this early rap from the Ultras. Sounding as if it were recorded in a damp puddle in Quatermass's pit, this is possibly the most low-fidelity hip-hop ever recorded.

2 Biscuits and Eggs *from* New York What Is Funky
Kool Keith never sounds creepier than when he is supposedly being romantic. Backed by discordant soul music samples, Keith appears to be proposing marriage to someone while protesting at being offered breakfast.

3 Funky *from* Critical Beatdown
Having sampled a piano riff from Joe Cocker and booted it unceremoniously on top of a beat that doesn't quite fit, it's a happy accident that the resulting funky beast is so speaker-bludgeoningly uplifting.

4 Travelling at the Speed of Thought *from* Critical Beatdown
Keith's transcendental boasts sound almost votive, as if he really could gain the power of flight through time and space were he to brag about it enough.

Kool Keith

1 Blue Flowers *from* Dr Octagonecologyst
A bunch of sickly violins vibrate hysterically somewhere in between Mantovani and Bernard Herrmann as the good Dr Octagon dazedly walks the hospital grounds. It's the album's very own "Strawberry Fields Forever".

2 Neighbors Next Door *from* Dr Dooom
"Rotten skulls on my waterbed", grumbles Keith, in serial killer mode. The mordant Moog and horror synths from a misplaced Dario Argento movie probably aren't helping Keith's headaches.

Joe Meek

Joe Meek was an inspiration to many of rock's most idiosyncratic performers. "He conjured the sound of another world," sang Wreckless Eric, "That Tin Pan Alley thought was too absurd". Eric's tribute to the late producer rejoiced under the admirably no-nonsense song title of "Joe Meek". But it's not only Wreckless Eric who has paid tribute. Matmos, Pluto Monkey, Graham Parker, Sheryl Crow and, er, Jonathan King have all recorded homages to Joe Meek. Pop music's first space cadet, Meek was an eccentric English equivalent of Phil Spector, who used the recording studio brilliantly, as an expressive instrument in itself. Yet he was also a troubled young man who, in 1967, at the age of 37, used a borrowed shotgun to murder his landlady, before turning the weapon on himself.

Meek's most famous hit was The Tornados' "Telstar", which in 1962 became the first record by a British group to hit number one in the American charts. He also produced hits for John Leyton, Heinz and the Honeycombs but his greatness lay in a raft of other weird records that didn't chart, by obscure artists such as The Blue Rondos, Glenda Collins, David John and the Mood, The Cryin' Shames and The Buzz, full of tapes played backwards and sci-fi effects – often recorded with his guitarist in the bathroom and the singer on the stairs of Meek's home-studio at 304 Holloway Road. Also central to his posthumous cult reputation is his concept album *I Hear a New World – An Outer Space Musical Fantasy*, a landmark in its innovative use of electronic sounds that was recorded in 1960, but not released in full until 1991.

Born in 1929 in the Forest of Dean, Meek developed an obsession with gadgets working for the Midlands Electricity Board. By 1956 he was working as an engineer on Lonnie Donegan records.

In 1960 he founded his own independent label, Triumph Records, and his own production company, but his commercial success was short-lived – perhaps because he was always more interested in "sounds" than in tunes. He was also paranoid, although as a gay man at a time when homosexuality was still illegal it is perhaps unsurprising. (It has been rumoured that he was blackmailed about his sexuality.) Meek was convinced Decca Records had hidden microphones behind his wallpaper in order to steal his ideas and also accused Spector of artistic theft. He was also obsessed with Buddy Holly, claiming he had communicated with him beyond the grave, and on the eighth anniversary of Holly's death, he ended his own life. A blue plaque at the location of his former studio in north London today commemorates his life and work.

NW

M.I.A.

"**A**s the first Sri Lankan artist in the West, what am I supposed to sound like? There's no rules for me," said Mathangi "Maya" Arulpragasam, explaining how she managed to create one of the most original sounds in modern pop: the sound of London and Jamaica and Sri Lanka and India and Africa and Brazil.

Fêted by the likes of Gwen Stefani, Missy Elliott and even Ricky Martin, she preferred to work with little-known acts including Nigerian rapper Afrikan Boy and aboriginal child hip-hop crew The Wilcannia Mob. Working under the name "Missing In Action", her songs featured didgeridoos, clattering dancehall beats, Brazilian baile funk, Bollywood strings, tribal beats and buzzing synthesizers. Neither a rapper nor a singer, her vocal chants added yet another alien quality to music that straddled every corner of the globe while sounding out of this world.

She was always going to sound like a one-off, given an upbringing unlike that of any other musician. Born in Hounslow, west London, as a baby she was moved to Sri Lanka, where her father grew more involved in the civil war between Tamil separatists and the Sri Lankan government. He was a co-founder of the revolutionary group EROS, a wanted man who spent most of M.I.A.'s childhood in hiding. In the West, his political name Arular is best known as the title of his daughter's debut album. "My dad's been a myth in my life," she said. "He used to come round once a year for twenty minutes at three in the morning."

M.I.A. also spent some of her early years living in India, before returning to a south London housing estate as an eleven-year-old refugee with her mother, older sister and younger brother. She embraced London's dance music scene as a fan, but first attempted a career in filmmaking after attending prestigious Central Saint Martin's College of Art and Design. Her dayglo, cut-and-paste artwork, full of images of guns, petrol bombs and tigers, now graces her album sleeves.

A job filming a tour documentary for Britpop band Elastica enabled a friendship with confrontational electro support act Peaches, who showed M.I.A. the way around her music sequencing machine. Soon M.I.A. had made some demos and was snapped up by indie label XL, the home of Dizzee Rascal and The White Stripes that has a well developed eye for the unique.

Her sound has proved too strange for the charts, but her influence, particularly on US hip-hop, is extensive. Always astonishingly ahead of her time, her magpie sensibilities will perhaps finally snatch her a shiny celebrity status in another few decades, when everyone else finally catches up.

DS

where to start:

1 Galang *from* Arular
The early track that first brought her to the attention of dance floors, it features gibberish chanting, distorted dancehall drums, siren synths and, a rare thing for M.I.A., a catchy tune.

2 Bird Flu *from* Kala
Children yell, birds squawk and M.I.A. shouts loudest of all as the beats clatter with overwhelming intensity. Yet although the title may have suggested a timely subject matter, lyrics about "making bombs with rubber bands" proved to be typically aggressive soundbites that roamed far off topic.

New Kingdom

Rap and heavy metal have plenty in common, but they have rarely made beautiful music together. Granted, there have been good Schoolly D tracks that have successfully spliced the best of both genres into an irresistibly primitive whole, and a few fantastic albums by Run DMC and the Beastie Boys managed the same trick. But that's about it. There is a long roll of dishonour, featuring names such as Rage Against the Machine, Limp Bizkit and Urban Dance Squad, of acts whose painfully earnest vocals and martial rhythms were the last word in rebellious cool for fourteen-year-old boys, but who seemed just a tad silly to everybody else.

Perhaps that's one of the reasons why New Kingdom were ignored. But it's probably more likely that they just didn't fit into any kind of template. When New Kingdom first surfaced, there was an existing constituency for rap-rock crossover music. And New Kingdom, like many others, had recognized that the juddering pomp of heavy metal power-chords and the involuntary head-nodding that all solid hip-hop provides spring from a similarly elemental source. However, unlike others who fused rock and rap, they didn't just shove some guitars on top of hip-hop beats. For one thing, their sound was so sludgy, it was impossible to tell quite what instruments were making those noises. They made a messy racket, a noise that was neanderthal but highly evolved.

Jason "Nosaj" Furlow and Sebastian Laws started making music together as New Kingdom after meeting at Canal Jeans in New York City. Judging by their lyrics, this was destiny: New Kingdom songs contain an unlikely amount of blue-collar boasts as to the cheapness of their jeans, which is symptomatic of their overall attitude to life. They were scuzzy and proud – card-carrying adherents of 1970s stoner fashion, lifestyle and music. Sebastian was arguably more of a rocker, having played in a few punk bands, while Nosaj was more into psychedelic soul and funk. Both were huge hip-hop fans.

Their sound began to take shape after they hooked up with producer Scotty Hard in 1990. Scott Harding was a Canadian sound engineer who had moved to New York where, working at Calliope Studios, he had engineered tracks for the cream of the NYC hip-hop scene: Prince Paul, De La Soul, the Jungle Brothers, Ultramagnetic MCs, Stetsasonic and Black Sheep had all benefited from his expertise. He produced Nosaj and Sebastian's first demo, and helped them to hustle it around the record labels for a deal.

They signed with Gee Street Records in 1992, and released their first single, "Good Times", the following year. Its vibe was undeniable, with thunderous, pummelling drums of the John Bonham school and a wheezing, ramshackle funk groove that was like an unsteadier version of Cypress Hill's trademark lope. Nosaj and Seb rapped in strained, gnarled voices that channelled the spirits of Captain Beefheart and Tom Waits, growling out assertions about how cheap their trainers were and how cheap their car was, while shouting out dedications to Greenpeace. They had a look to match too, with giant afros, wayward sideburns and clothes that appeared to have been raided from the wardrobe of a lumberjack: two black John McCriricks in big shades.

The album *Heavy Load* came out in 1993 and confirmed Kingdom as anti-materialist eco-friendly beatniks – who revelled in escapist wordplay celebrating the joys of the open road and a potent brew or too. The titles of their songs spoke volumes: "Cheap Thrills", "Are You Alive?" and "Mother Nature". New Kingdom looked like the Fabulous Furry Freak Brothers and they referenced Big Brother and the Holding Company albums: De La Soul had been described as hip-hop hippies, but they had nothing on this pair.

Heavy Load had some undisputedly mighty peaks. But it was hard not to compare and contrast with the Beastie Boys and Cypress Hill and find the Kingdom a little wanting. While they all sounded good, the songs were a little too much like unfinished sketches: once they'd hit upon a good groove, they were content to rasp their charismatic, skew-whiff vocals over it, but that wasn't quite enough to make any of their songs wholly satisfying. The title of the last song, "Lazy Smoke", gave an indication of what might have been hindering the album – a lack of clarity and a certain laid-back approach. It was, however, a novel approach to the "shout-out track", a venerable tradition on hip-hop albums that now seems to have died out, whereby the closing track would effectively do all the thank-yous and dedications that rock albums would leave for the liner notes. The New Kingdom way of doing this was to namecheck all their buddies that Nosaj claimed to have seen in the midst of a particularly observant trip.

The critics loved them. They shot some promotional videos, toured internationally and gave a suitably shambolic and anarchic performance in front of a cowed and bewildered audience on *The Word*, a nadir of post-pub Friday night television that aired in the UK throughout the 1990s.

Three years later, in 1996, New Kingdom gave the world their most valuable legacy: *Paradise Don't Come Cheap* was their masterpiece. Kicking off with "Mexico or Bust", the two rappers sounded like proselytizing cult leaders shepherding a flock of stoned disciples across the Southern border over music that was like a 1960s R&B revue band performing underwater. The book set the tone for the whole album: innumerable references to ancient civilizations, advancing hordes and journeys both mental and physical were complemented by music that moved at a sluggish but irresistible creep.

Perhaps it was the input of the musicians, but the songs had a bit more structure and were more dynamic. Scotty Hard added guitar, and brought in jazz musician John Medeski, who contributed some stupendously uplifting organ to "Unicorns Were Horses". But New Kingdom had not lost their knack for a psychedelic song title or their love of grimey noise: tracks such as "Valhalla Soothsayer" and "Journey to the Sun" featured a wall of undifferentiated sonic tissue, with punishingly loud drums being the only conventional instrument you could wholly identify.

"This is *my* Mount Olympus" warned Seb in the lyrics to "Terror Mad Visionary", as if he were an irate god from the Greek deistic pantheon warning a trespasser to get off his land. "It's in the tradition of experimental black music," said Nosaj of their music at the time. "In the same tradition as our jazz brothers and sisters, Ornette Coleman and Sun Ra." Listening to *Paradise Don't Come Cheap*, with its music fashioned from collected scraps of dirt, you have to concede he had a point.

It's unlikely New Kingdom were expecting a hit album that would make them rich, but *Paradise* didn't garner half the acclaim it deserved. It was the last album the pair have made together. They have, however, made music individually. Nosaj continues to make music under the *nom de plume* of Nature Boy Jim Kelly. As hip-hop goes, it's quirky and inventive, although it's a few colours short of the hell-raising kaleidoscope of New Kingdom's visions. Sebastian cropped up on two tracks on Scotty Hard's superb *The Return of Kill Dog E*, an album that demonstrated how much Scotty had contributed to the New Kingdom sound. Seb also played with Scotty in the short-lived band Truck Stop, who released two EPs that pushed the New Kingdom template further into rock music territory. The small amount of music Truck Stop recorded was great stuff – garage rock of the dirtiest cloth – but it was released in such minuscule quantities that even the Internet file-sharing revolution has passed it by.

MM

playlist:

1 Cheap Thrills from Heavy Load
"Done smoked the moon and the stars/Can you dig it when I'm out this far?". While you probably wouldn't accept a lift from them if you were hitchhiking, if you can't dig it when they're out this far, there's something wrong with you.

2 Mars from Heavy Load
With its confusing, abrupt changes of speed, and a high intensity of messiness and chaos, this is *Heavy Load*'s strongest hint at the grandiose madness to come on their follow-up.

3 Unicorns were Horses from Paradise Don't Come Cheap
The title's hippie-ish riff on Jimi Hendrix's "If sixes were nines" is by no means the only poetry here: if Buddhists ever intoned war chants, they would sound like this song's chorus – one of the most uplifting in music.

4 Kickin' Like Bruce Lee from Paradise Don't Come Cheap
Completely unintelligible rapping meets drums and scratching that were evidently recorded through the gummed filter of several burned-out mattresses in an attempt to knock several rungs out of hip-hop's evolutionary ladder.

5 Shining Armor from Paradise Don't Come Cheap
The pair's fetishization of all things ancient and south of the US border (Mexican road trips and marching conquistadores) reveals itself again here, summoned by music that is the closest a hip-hop track could get to being a Black Sabbath song without actually being one.

Silver Apples

Their first two records were never big sellers in the 1960s, when they were issued, but Silver Apples anticipated much experimental rock that followed, from Eno's knob-twiddling ambience and the pulsating melodies of Air, to German Krautrock and much electro dance music of the 1980s and 90s. Silver Apples began in 1967 as the five-piece Overland Stage Electric Band. When the band's vocalist and keyboard player, Simeon (otherwise known as Simeon Coxe III), flicked the switch on a homemade synthesizer fashioned from an old oscillator, the guitarists walked, leaving just the drummer, Danny Taylor. Simeon didn't seem to mind: with three guitarists there had been a lot of solo breaks during which he had nothing to do. Guitars, he figured, weren't necessary: there was a lot you could do with a synthesizer and drums.

Taylor, a former backing musician for Jimi Hendrix, soon picked up the beat, filling in around Simeon's oscil-

lations. Inspired by their new-found direction, the duo rebranded themselves, taking their name from Morton Subotnik's composition for the Buchla synthesizer, "Silver Apples of the Moon", by way of a W.B. Yeats poem of the same name. They began putting poems to music, accruing a cumbersome collection of oscillators as they wrote. The equipment was routed through telegraph keys, as they explained it, and used to make "rhythmic beeps and boops" with a lead oscillator swooping through each "song". When they took their minimalist show on the road and played to a thirty thousand-strong crowd in Central Park – appearing alongside Sha Na Na and the Mothers of Invention – they made the following day's headlines.

Their first, self-titled, album appeared in 1968, on New York's KAPP records, the band billed as "an organic mechanism composed of Simeon and the Taylor Drums". *Contact*, the second – and, for 25 years, the last – Silver Apples album appeared the following year. This was recorded while the band were on tour in Los Angeles, and was mixed back in

New York. When KAPP folded as the decade turned, Simeon and Taylor pulled the plug on the Silver Apples and slid into digital obscurity until 1994, when the albums were reissued, amid growing recognition of their work as electro pioneers. Simeon toured again, with a new Silver Apples line-up. Taylor unearthed tapes of an unreleased third album, *The Garden*, and in 1998 the original band were oscillating once more, releasing more new material, before Taylor's death in 2005.

In some ways Silver Apples were very much a product of their time – their 1960s albums are much more trippy than any of the celebrated psychedelic bands of the era. Yet they were also totally apart from it, filling in the gaps between James Brown and Steve Reich, and putting the funk into futuristic space noises.

RW

playlist:

1 I Have Known Love *from* Silver Apples
A love song, of sorts, from the duo's debut offering. Discordant sighs and space-age noodling take us to the rim of the known 1960s pop world. Features lyrics provided by the band's unseen backroom boy, Stanley Warren.

2 I Don't Care What the People Say *from* The Garden
The opening track from the third album, released in 1998, almost thirty years after the second introduced the new Silver Apple, multi-instrumentalist Xian Hawkins. But it was like they'd never been away.

3 You and I *from* Contact
A jet plane roars overhead and Simeon's by-now-familiar bleeping oscillators kick in. There is a tone of quiet desperation in the lyrics, which muse on how life's "important things" get in the way of everyday living.

4 Lovefingers *from* Silver Apples
It builds from a droning drum-and-bass figure into a minimalist soundscape that might have been built from a home electronics kit. Pop rarely got this weird in 1968.

Ripe for rediscovery: Clipse's Hell Hath No Fury

Terrence and Gene Thornton, two brothers from Virginia otherwise known as Pusha T and Malice, have had a snakes-and-ladders of a career. Which is perhaps surprising, when you consider that the two rappers have long been friends with Pharrell Williams – one half of prolific production duo The Neptunes and one of the most powerful men in hip-hop – since before he was famous, in fact. Then there were the guest appearances they made with the likes of Justin Timberlake and R&B firebrand Kelis.

The duo's first album as Clipse was never released, after an early single of theirs flopped in 1999 and the duo lost their record deal with Elektra. A second album, *Lord Willin'*, appeared on The Neptunes' own Star Trak label and became a minor hit in 2002, but once again record company problems meant a loss of momentum. The merger between parent label BMG and Sony somehow left Clipse abandoned on the Jive subsidiary, home to Britney Spears and the Backstreet Boys. Jive's lack of enthusiasm for their third album, *Hell Hath No Fury*, led to the duo embarking on the lengthy process of suing the label in order to release it themselves.

This meant that an album that was written in late 2003 didn't appear in the UK until early 2007, by which time it was only the music bloggers, rather than any of the mainstream music-buying public, that remained excited about the pair's

grim yet thrilling cocaine-dealing horror stories. Ironically, at a time when producer Williams's latest solo album was considered underwhelming, *Hell Hath No Fury* was a reminder of the chillingly sparse, alien noises he had been coming up with several years previously. The woozy, minimal sound of *Hell* was as flab-free as hip-hop gets. Which only makes it more of a shame that the leanness of its sound was matched by such meagre sales.

DS

Slick Rick

A pioneer of hip-hop who has spent more time in court than in the recording studio, Rick Walters had many of the qualities of a gangsta rapper before the genre had been invented. His eyepatch made him intimidating, even though it was the result of a childhood accident with glass rather than anything criminal. As his star rose it was complemented by enough gold accessories to start a mobile jeweller's. Then his gun collection started to grow.

Lyrically he was also ahead of his time, surpassing the boasting of most 1980s hip-hop (though he certainly did a fair bit of it) with detailed storytelling. There did seem to be a moral element to his dark tales – the criminals depicted in his early tracks "The Moment I Feared" and "Children's Story" end up in jail or dead – although it is much harder to defend his most notorious song, "Treat Her Like a Prostitute".

His distinctiveness was amplified by his unusual voice, a laid-back mid-Atlantic drawl that was the result of his spending the first ten years of his life in Wimbledon in the UK, before his Jamaican parents moved to the Bronx. There he became involved in the rap battles at the block parties where hip-hop culture began, and there he befriended beatboxer Doug E. Fresh. He provided an unorthodox backdrop for Rick's already unique vocals on the classic 1985 single "The Show"/"La Di Da Di" by Doug E. Fresh and the Get Fresh Crew. The hit earned Rick a deal with the illustrious label Def Jam and the solo album that followed, *The Great Adventures of Slick Rick*, would become one of the first rap records to go platinum. This is where his troubles began.

Increasing paranoia about being robbed led to him shooting his cousin and former bodyguard, Mark Plummer, as well as an innocent bystander in July 1990. There followed a police car chase, which ended in a crash in which both his pregnant girlfriend's legs were broken. He served time for the attempted murder of Plummer, although a work-release programme also allowed him to record another album in the meantime, *Behind Bars*.

Things only got worse, however. In 1993 the US Immigration and Naturalization Service set about doggedly trying to deport him to his British birthplace. Since then he has ping-ponged in and out of prison as complex legal appeals go back and forth. At one point it was even claimed he had deported himself by going on a short cruise. Sadly, music has taken a long-term back seat while this former rap great continues to live with an uncertain future.

DS

where to start:

1 Children's Story *from* The Great Adventures of Slick Rick
With its deep bass and rolling piano, this is an old school rap classic, with Rick putting on numerous different voices as he tells the gripping tale of a life of crime turned sour.

2 Street Talkin' *from* The Art of Storytelling
Rick's best album, aside from his unimpeachable debut, features numerous younger admirers such as Nas, Snoop Dogg and, on this mellow strut, Outkast.

Tunng

Folk, the musical field most typically allied to tradition, has been changing fast in recent years. This is thanks to a group of outsiders, mainly based in the far from pastoral surrounds of London, who have inadvertently committed the biggest crime of all in the eyes of the purists – making folk fashionable.

Not since Bob Dylan sauntered on stage with an electric guitar has folk been so awash with new sounds. Along with Four Tet and Adem, the six-strong experimental group Tunng are chief architects of the sub-genre clunkily known as folktronica. They use acoustic guitars and softly spoken male and female vocalists, but they also employ samples from films, horse-racing commentaries, skittering electronic beats and "a bloke who's got a bit of rope tied between two bits of metal with seashells and a bit of wood hanging off it which he plays with his feet while he plays the clarinet", in the words of founder member Mike Lindsay.

Lindsay was a heavy metal guitarist from Southampton, but when he met Tunng singer and co-founder Sam Genders he was making abstract electronic music under the name Dirtbox and running a Soho recording studio called Exploding Music. It was based underneath a lingerie boutique and had to be accessed via the ladies' changing rooms. There's something of a saucy common thread here, for Lindsay had also been a TV composer and written music for some of the soft-porn films on the Fantasy Channel.

Genders came to Exploding Music from his home in Matlock, Bath, in 2003, to record a demo of his singer-songwriter music. But once Lindsay had finished with him the pair had created something far more radical, a welding of the ancient to the futuristic that sounded fantastic in the present.

Fascinated by the more unsettling elements of English folk, Tunng have covered "The Maypole Song" from *The Wicker Man*, a movie that contains both ribald traditional songs and disturbing imagery of pagan rituals. In Tunng's own songs, a woman is turned into a hare ("Woodcat"), a murderer contemplates his crime inside a Little Chef restaurant ("Jenny Again") and another character is described watching angry TV host Jeremy Kyle with a feeling of mounting dread ("Secrets").

The electronica and found sounds that flutter around the guitars may horrify traditionalists, but they only amplify the haunting qualities of music that deserves to last well beyond its current hip status.

DS

Ripe for rediscovery: UNKLE's Psyence Fiction

In retrospect, James Lavelle was a victim of his own talent for self-promotion. Founder of the supercool Mo' Wax label and commander of the multiple talents behind the UNKLE moniker, in the mid-1990s London scene Lavelle was so cool he risked frostbite.

Clad in rare Japanese fashion wear, and a collector of the kind of overpriced toys you can't play with, he was a prototype for the Hoxton wannabe Nathan Barley in the 2005 TV satire of the same name. But he also had an acute DJ's ear for new sounds, releasing groundbreaking electronic music on his *Headz* compilations, and in 1996 putting out *Endtroducing...* by his greatest discovery, the monomaniacal sample-hound DJ Shadow. It regularly features in lists of the best albums ever.

However, UNKLE's debut album, *Psyence Fiction*, does not – despite the fact that it largely features music put together by Shadow. Lavelle was guilty of spending too much on promotional videos and hyping the album to such an extent that at one point he compared its construction to the making of *Apocalypse Now*. The trip-hop sound it featured – all hip-hop beats and moody strings – was one Lavelle had long championed, but it was a style that had been thoroughly assimilated by other acts and had rather drifted out of fashion by the time of the album's release.

It seems that Lavelle was due a critical mauling, and when *Psyence Fiction* turned out to be less than the greatest album of all time, he got it. Listening to it now, however, it's clear that DJ Shadow's dominant beats have not dated at all. Furthermore, Lavelle demonstrates a consistent prescience, featuring a then-unknown Badly Drawn Boy on "Nursery Rhyme" and giving Radiohead's Thom Yorke an electronic backdrop well before

his experiments with bleeps and glitches on *Kid A*. And the rappers who make guest appearances – the Beastie Boys and Kool G Rap – still sound as on-point as the man from UNKLE once was.

DS

White Noise

"**M**any sounds have never been heard – by humans: some sound waves you don't hear – but they reach you. 'Storm stereo' techniques combine singers, instrumentalists and complex electronic sound. The emotional intensity is at a maximum." Do not let this absurd piece of twaddle on the sleeve of the 1968 debut album by White Noise put you off. Inside lies one of the most audacious explorations of inner space in the early history of electronic and psychedelic music.

White Noise was the brainchild of David Vorhaus, a classically trained American composer, and Delia Derbyshire, a pioneering sound sculptor from the BBC's Radiophonic Workshop (where she had realized the theme tune to *Dr Who*, among other things). Joined by Brian Hodgson, also from the BBC workshop, in 1968 they recorded the album *An Electric Storm* with a £3000 advance from Island Records' boss Chris Blackwell. Electronic music was still in its infancy but the trio were true artisans, making the most of their carefully constructed home-made gadgets, using various tape manipulation techniques and the first rudimentary British synthesizer, the EMS Synthi VCS3. Human sounds of orgasmic sexual frenzy were mixed in with the electronic noise, and the effect is, at times, unsettling and even sinister.

Divided into two parts, side one of the album was titled "Phase In", and contained five short songs; side two was called "Phase Out" and consisted of two long tracks that voyaged to the outer parameters of known sound. The first track – "The Visitation" – took three months to record. An eleven-minute intense cacophony of sound, its eerily panned voices create ghostly effects.

By contrast, the final track – "Black Mass: Electric Storm in Hell" was recorded live, as they had to deliver Island a finished record the following day. It begins with a Gregorian chant and ends in the screams of lost souls doomed forever to float in space, via the spookiest drum solo you've ever heard. "Storm stereo" indeed. For some reason, Island did not promote the album at all, but it has since become a cult classic. Hugely influential, its praises have been sung by the likes of The Orb and Julian Cope.

Vorhaus has continued to release albums at infrequent intervals under the White Noise name, but without Derbyshire and Hodgson. By 2000, he had reached *White Noise V*, but music technology had overtaken his vision long before. Yet the passage of time and the widespread use of digital mixing boards, computer music software and surround-sound in electronic music cannot detract from the startling impact of that first album: its genesis was literally experimental, unlike much music routinely tagged with the word.

NW

Yellow Magic Orchestra

It's debatable, but there's a strong case for saying that rock'n'roll was pretty much an Anglo-American monopoly until electronic music came along. It took decades for the idea of rock music being sung in anything other than US-accented English to take hold. However, once the rest of the world discovered the limitless possibilities of the synthesizer, the sequencer and the drum machine, it was a different story. In Germany, Kraftwerk's pioneering electro-pop on their 1974 album *Autobahn* changed the face of popular music forever. Three years later, Japan produced the equally trailblazing techno-pop of Yellow Magic Orchestra. They were, in fact, more of a Yellow Magic Chamber Group – just three men and their shiny machines.

Consisting of Haruomi Hosono, who already had a string of solo albums to his name, the keyboardist and composer Ryuichi Sakamoto, and Yukihiro Takahashi, formerly of art-rockers the Sadistic Mika Band, their first, self-titled album owed much to Kraftwerk and combined electronic innovation with instant snyth-pop accessibility on such singles as "Cosmic Surfing" and "Computer Game" (which would eventually give them a British top twenty hit) and an unlikely cover of "Bridge Over Troubled Water".

Originally conceived as a one-off, the album was so well received in Japan that the trio turned into a full-fledged touring band, sporting futuristic haircuts and adopting a whole robotic visual style and accompanying typography to match the sound. An international recording deal followed and for the next six years the trio subsumed their solo careers to the demands of YMO. The decision paid dividends on their second album, 1979's *Solid State Survivor*, a near-perfect union of man and machine in music, combining brilliant use of technology with strong songs with English lyrics by Chris Mosdell. Proof that these were songs that could stand on their own, without the electronic backdrop, came when Eric Clapton covered the album's "Behind the Mask" and had a rather middle-of-the-road worldwide hit with the song in 1986.

Xoo Multiplies, in 1980, was something of a mistake, featuring not one but two cover versions of "Tighten Up" and a series of misconceived comedy skits, but the brilliant synth-pop excursions of their two 1981 releases, *BGM* and *Technodelic*, were a return to form. In 1983 *Naughty Boys* was an ambitious swansong before they all returned to solo projects, with Sakamoto going on to enjoy the highest visibility of the three, as a film composer. By the 1990s, YMO's music was being widely sampled by dance and house producers, resulting in the 1993 remix album *Hi-Tech/No Crime* in which the likes of Orbital and 808 State respectfully tackled their work with results far more successful than most similar projects. The original trio reunited the same year for the album *Technodon*, which featured readings by William Burroughs. They got back together once more in 2007 for a performance at the Japanese leg of the "Live Earth" climate change event, demonstrating that, while the world may be slow in recognizing green technology, at least Japan endorses green techno.

NW

PSYCHEDELIC RELICS
the troubadours of tie-dye

The Electric Prunes

You're rehearsing in the garage one day when a passing real estate agent hears the racket and says she knows somebody in the music industry. That somebody turns out to be the Rolling Stones' LA-based engineer. He sends the band over to Leon Russell's place to record some demos and a record deal follows. Next thing you know, your band are releasing a rock opera concept album mixing Gregorian chant and psychedelic pop with vocals in Latin. It's a misunderstood acid-rock classic, and the band immediately breaks up. The record company carries on releasing records by a completely different band under the same name with the old group's picture on the cover. That, in a cosmic acid drop, is the story of the Electric Prunes. No wonder their first hit was called "I Had Too Much to Dream Last Night".

Like any other bunch of American high school hopefuls, guitarist James Lowe, bassist Mark Tulin, lead guitarist Ken Williams and drummer Michael Weakley decided the best way to pull girls was to form a band. They started out as The Sanctions and then became Jim and The Lords. The name of Barbara Harris is little known in rock'n'roll circles but she was the real estate agent and her friend was Dave Hassinger, the resident engineer at RCA studios, who had worked on many Stones records, including "(I Can't Get No) Satisfaction".

From the demos he sent them to record at Russell's Sky Hill Studios came a deal with Reprise and the first Electric Prunes single – a cover version of the Gypsy Trips' "Ain't It Hard". It flopped, heralding a line-up change which found Preston Ritter replacing Michael Weakley on drums and guitarist James Spagnola bolstering them to a quintet.

Hassinger also brought in songwriters Annette Tucker and Nancie Mantz, who came up with "I Had Too Much to Dream Last Night". The original was a slow piano ballad, but by the time the Prunes had finished with it, the song was an echo-drenched psychedelic fantasia of shimmering guitars, distorted fuzz tones and an eerie double-tracked vocal from Lowe. Released in November 1966, it made the US top twenty in early 1967. Today it's best known as the brilliant opening track of the acclaimed compilation box set, *Nuggets*.

The follow-up single "Get Me to the World On Time" continued their penchant for trippy bad puns, and was just as good. Their debut album of 1967, *The Electric Prunes (I Had Too Much to Dream Last Night)*, however, was a rushed job with Tucker contributing eight of the songs, none of which matched the excitement of their two hit singles.

During the recording of their second album, *Underground*, there were further personnel changes. But this time the band contributed more of their own material, with Tucker restricted to just three songs. It was a great improvement, with the psychedelia tempered by a harder-edged garage rock feel on such standout tracks as "The Great Banana Hoax", "Hideaway" and a terrific cover of Goffin-King's "I Happen to Love You".

Enter David Axelrod, an LA-based producer and an A&R man for Capitol Records. Brought in by Hassinger, Axelrod had come up with the ambitious – some might even say ridiculous – idea of recording a psychedelic setting of the Mass. Other than the vocals, the original Prunes seem to have had little to do with the recording, as Axelrod drafted in such top session players as Carol Kaye on bass and Earl Palmer on drums. Gloriously over the top, the album was both ludicrous and magnificent at the same time, its surreal quality encapsulated by the sight of the band miming "Kyrie Eleison" on the *Pat Boone Show*. The same track was also used to brilliant effect in the acid trip scene in the film *Easy Rider*.

You might think an acid-rock Mass was a stunt that could only be pulled off once, but Axelrod then went and did it all over again with the similarly styled *Release of an Oath* in 1968, this time combining Jewish and Christian liturgy. By then, the original band had fallen apart but Hassinger, who owned the Electric Prunes name,

assembled an entirely new line-up, whose first single, "Hey Mr President", was confusingly issued in a picture sleeve depicting the original band. After Axelrod's excesses, the only album these pseudo-Prunes released was most pointedly called *Just Good Old Rock and Roll*. This wasn't much of a USP. The album sank without trace.

That was the end of the Electric Prunes until a reunion in 2000, which reignited sufficient interest to spark the reissue of several lost recordings from the 1960s. As for Axelrod, he was still playing the same portentous game over a quarter of a century later, when he released *Requiem: Holocaust* in 1993. Then, when the original Prunes reformed, he responded by releasing *David Axelrod*, which added new arrangements to unreleased rhythm tracks originally recorded for a proposed follow-up to *Release of An Oath*.

NW

playlist:

1 I Had Too Much to Dream Last Night *from* The Electric Prunes (I Had Too Much to Dream Last Night)
The world's first taste of the Prunes – stoned and stewed.

2 Get Me to the World On Time *from* The Electric Prunes (I Had Too Much to Dream Last Night)
An outrageously thrilling mix of Bo Diddley/Rolling Stones garage rock and psychedelic experimentalism.

3 I Happen to Love You *from* Underground
Goffin and King never sounded quite like this before.

4 Kyrie Eleison *from* Mass in F Minor
If you can't face the full Mass, seek this out on the *Easy Rider* soundtrack.

5 Agnus Dei *from* Mass in F Minor
The closing over-the-top movement from the Prunes' finest excess.

Mighty Baby

Mighty Baby are arguably the great lost band of 1960s psychedelia – the closest Britain ever came to producing its own version of the Grateful Dead. Fired by the extraordinarily versatile guitar playing of Martin Stone, they produced two albums, both brilliant but very different in style, and a memorable live recording from the very first Glastonbury festival. It's a small legacy but one which, almost four decades on, deserves to be heard – Mighty Baby have yet to experience the kind of Internet-age rediscovery that in recent years has brought so much other great neglected music back into the light.

As psychedelic pioneers, Mighty Baby had unlikely roots, emerging from the ashes of mid-1960s mod band The Action, who put out a succession of singles produced by George Martin. Minus singer Reggie King, in 1968 they transformed into Mighty Baby, with a line-up of Alan "Bam" King and Martin Stone on guitars, keyboardist Ian Whiteman, Roger Powell on drums and Mike Evans on bass.

Their self-titled 1969 debut album appeared on the appropriately named Head Records (and found an unlikely home on the R&B label Chess in the US), sporting a superb gatefold sleeve by Martin Sharp (who was also responsible for the cover of Cream's *Disraeli Gears*). Inside was some of the finest British acid-rock ever produced, from the jazzy, West coast-style guitar interplay of "Egyptian Tombs" to the stoned, psychedelic vibe of "Same Way from the Sun", which would not have sounded out of place on *The Notorious Byrd Brothers*.

In between its release and the appearance of its follow-up, *A Jug of Love*, several members had become Sufi Muslims. The result was a mellower, more reflective sound, with tracks such as "Virgin Spring" and "Slipstreams", mirroring the journey of many of their American counterparts around the same time towards a folksier, more acoustic style. A review of the album in *Melody Maker* noted that it was "so laid-back that the band must have been floating a couple of feet above the studio floor when they recorded it", although it does also include the lengthy electric jam, "Keep on Jugging".

Martin Stone went on to play in the country-tinged Chilli Willi and the Red Hot Peppers (who rivalled Brinsley Schwartz as the best of the early 1970s pub-rockers) while Alan King found success with Ace.

Mighty Baby's finest moment on record is probably the long live jam based on John Coltrane's "India", which labours under the marvellously addled title "There's a Blanket in My Muesli". (There's a similar jam on "India" that was never released – a 44-minute epic from 1969 – which you might be able to find online if you're lucky.) It was recorded, appropriately enough, at the 1971 Glastonbury festival and was released on the ultra-rare triple-LP *Glastonbury Fayre* the following year. It captures them as the fluid acid-rock improvisers of wondrous psychedelic imagination that they were – the "British Grateful Dead" comparisons ring true.

NW

The Big Three

They could've been... the fab four?

There are still a few Merseybeat veterans around Liverpool who will tell you that the finest group that ever played the Cavern was not The Beatles but The Big Three. They will tell you that, with their repertoire of Chuck Berry and Ray Charles numbers, the Three were louder, more powerful and more aggressive than the early Fab Four. They will then add with a sorrowful shake of the head that when Brian Epstein took over their management, he ruined the group by trying to tame them, pressuring them to record bland and unsuitable material, changing their wild image by forcing them into suits and generally marketing them like they were Gerry and the Pacemakers instead of a full-on, raunchy R&B combo. While Epstein's other charges went on to conquer the world, by the end of 1963 The Big Three had already broken up in utter disillusionment.

Formed in Liverpool in 1961 out of a popular Merseyside group called Cass and the Cassanovas, the line-up of Adrian Barber (guitar), Johnny Hutchinson (drums) and Johnny Gustafson (bass) swiftly became Cavern Club favourites. They made what at the time was considered an earth-shattering noise, due in no small part to their giant amps, standing over five-feet high, hand-built by Barber and nicknamed "coffins". On stage the Three were wild and unruly and Liverpool loved them. Epstein swiftly added them to his management stable and, on 1 July 1962, he sent them off to a residency at Hamburg's Star Club in Germany, to follow in the footsteps of The Beatles. While there, they were joined by Brian Griffiths, another Liverpool guitarist, but when Barber – like Stu Sutcliffe of The Beatles – decided to stay on in Hamburg, as stage manager at the Star Club, the group returned to Britain as a trio once more.

On their first day back on British soil, Epstein whisked them off to an audition at Decca – the label that had famously turned down The Beatles. They recorded Ritchie Barrett's

R&B standard "Some Other Guy". It went well, but the band were furious when Epstein informed them that this test recording was going to be released as it was. The band felt that the demo failed to capture the aggression and energy of their live performances. They were even more dispirited when they were forced to record Mitch Murray's "By The Way" as a follow-up, and in July 1963 they terminated their partnership with Epstein.

In November the live EP *The Big Three at the Cavern* appeared, featuring club legend Bob Wooler introducing the tracks "What'd I Say?", "Don't Start Running Around", "Zip-A-Dee-Doo-Dah" and "Reelin' and a Rockin". The recording was fraught with difficulty – Decca engineers spent all day trying to get the microphones in the right position in the tiny club, and the end results only conveyed a hint of the band's raw edge. Upon its release, Griffiths and Gustafson announced they were leaving to return to the German club circuit. Proof that not everything Epstein touched turned to gold.

NW

Moby Grape

California was the place to be in 1967. In Haight-Ashbury, the Grateful Dead and Jefferson Airplane were spearheading the acid-rock revolution. Down the coast in the clubs along LA's Sunset Strip, The Doors and Love were lighting fires and presiding over a world that was forever changing. For a brief moment in that first summer of love, the name of San Francisco's Moby Grape was up there in psychedelic lights, too. Then it all fell apart.

What went wrong? Well it's hard to know where to begin. Try a high profile bust for corrupting the morals of underage girls, a manager who not only took off with the band's back catalogue but also claimed the rights to the band's name, and a schizophrenic guitarist who was institutionalized after trying to murder two of his fellow band members with an axe. The only wonder is that they still managed to make such great music. Yet it took another three decades before a slew of CD reissues finally rehabilitated Moby Grape as purveyors of some of the finest psychedelic rock ever to come out of America's West Coast.

Formed around the triple-guitar attack of Skip Spence, Jerry Miller and Peter Lewis, with Don Stevenson on drums and Bob Mosley on bass, Moby Grape signed to CBS in early 1967 and made an immediate impact when the label released ten of their debut album's thirteen tracks as five singles-plus-B-sides on the same day. The stunt helped the album into the top thirty but the hype ultimately backfired as such attention-grabbing marketing tricks obscured the fact that their debut album was a near-flawless collection of tight, melodic songs, bright harmonies, magically interweaving guitars, manic energy and experimental psychedelic touches. As a snapshot of a unique moment in time, it belongs alongside Love's *Forever Changes*. All five members contributed to the songwriting and several of the songs – "8:05", "Hey Grandma" and "Omaha" to name but three – might well have been hits had they not all been released on the same day.

The arrest of three band members for an incident involving dope and underaged girls attained the band a degree of notoriety, but although the case was eventually dropped, the protracted legal process took its toll. On its release, their second album *Wow* (1968) was panned. Hip reviewers hadn't forgiven them the pop singles hype and the more straight-laced pop critics weren't going to heap praise on a bunch of degenerates who were threatening the morals of the nation's youth. The band didn't help themselves by releasing *Wow* as a double LP with a second disc of largely indulgent, unfocused material called *Grape Jam*. But *Wow* had some fine tracks to match their stunning debut, particularly the storming "Murder in My Heart for the Judge", Lewis's baroque ballad "He" and Spence's biker anthem "Motorcycle Irene". In retrospect, even *Grape Jam* has its moments, including the bluesy "Never", the lyrics of which long-term fan Robert Plant borrowed for "Since I've Been Loving You" on *Led Zeppelin III*.

By the time of *Wow*'s release, Spence had been committed after chopping down a hotel door with the apparent intention of murdering Stevenson and Miller with a fire axe. Following six months in hospital, he was released and recorded his unhinged solo album, *Oar* (1969), a record which seemed to document his slide into paranoid schizophrenia but which at the same time is a compelling, disjointed, oddball masterpiece. The record has since achieved cult status, its legend only enhanced by the fact that Spence was never really heard from again and spent the rest of his life in and out of psychiatric institutions until his death in 1998.

Moby Grape soldiered on as a quartet and released *Moby Grape 69* (1969). It included the occasional dazzling reminder of how good they had been, such as Spence's Grape swansong, "Seeing", a piece of foreboding psychedelia with sizzling guitar leads, haunted harmonies, and crazed cries of "Save me!"

When Mosley quit to enlist in the Marine Corps, the band was reduced to a trio and travelled to Nashville to record the country-rock album *Truly Fine Citizen*. The group then fell apart but briefly re-formed for *20 Granite Creek* (1971), another country-rock-tinged collection on which Spence bizarrely reappeared playing a *koto* on the instrumental "Chinese Song".

Over the years there have been various reunions, none of which has recaptured their early glory. But among those who admit to having been influenced by them are Robert Plant, the Doobie Brothers, REM, Teenage Fanclub and Weezer, while Spence's *Oar* spawned an entire tribute album in its own right, with covers of the original songs by Plant, Beck, Tom Waits and Robyn Hitchcock, among others.

NW

playlist:

1 Omaha *from* Moby Grape
Perfectly phased 1967 dream psych-rock.

2 Hey Grandma *from* Moby Grape
Great riff, crazed lyric ("Hey grandma, you're so young/Your old man's just a boy") and later covered by The Move.

3 8:05 *from* Moby Grape
Poignant, diamond-chiselled loveliness.

4 Motorcycle Irene *from* Wow
Tough-edged "motorcycle mama" anthem written by Spence in a rare moment of lucidity.

5 He *from* Wow
Grape at their sweetest on a lovely baroque ballad by Lewis.

6 Murder in My Heart for the Judge *from* Wow
A great, soulful Mosley vocal over Lewis and Miller's wailing guitars.

7 Never *from* Grape Jam
Grape blues with a lyric later borrowed by Robert Plant.

8 Seeing *from* Moby Grape 69
A typically disturbing but compelling look into the abyss from Spence with all-too-real cries of "Save me!"

9 Cripple Creek *from* Oar
Deep, dark, haunted folk-rock from Spence's legendary solo album.

Nirvana

The London-based Nirvana, as opposed to the Seattle one, can chalk up an impressive list of "firsts". Not only did they use the band name some twenty years before Kurt Cobain, but they also recorded what can justifiably be claimed to have been rock music's first narrative concept album. And they made the first record to use the "phasing" effect – that wooshing, cosmic, sweeping sound – all the way through. Both of their albums are very much period pieces but it was a nice period to have a piece of: they have stood the test of time as charming reminders of a simpler, more innocent age when pop music was still young and full of wonder rather than cynicism. Nirvana also appeared on French TV with Salvador Dali, who splattered them with paint, a unique honour that in the annals of art-rock surely rivals the Velvet Underground's association with Andy Warhol.

The band was essentially the songwriting team of Patrick Campbell-Lyons and Alex Spyropoulos, who came together via Dublin and Athens respectively. In early 1967 they persuaded Island Records founder Chris Blackwell to give them a contract to record a concept album about a boy who yearns to fly and who eventually becomes a space traveller. Blackwell was at the time just beginning to build his label into a powerhouse of British prog-rock with bands such as Traffic and Spooky Tooth, and he saw the duo as a key component in cornering the emerging psychedelic market, about to explode in 1967's summer of love. They began with a pair of singles, "Tiny Goddess" and "Pentecost Hotel" – the latter extracted from their debut album. Neither charted but they established the Nirvana sound: all multi-layered art-pop with shimmeringly baroque arrangements, ethereal vocals and quasi-classical overtones.

Then came *The Story of Simon Simopath* in 1967, a 25-minute song cycle that pre-dated both the Pretty Things' *S.F. Sorrow* and The Who's *Tommy*. Its baroque, soft-core psychedelia and slightly saccharine sentiments are closer in spirit to Mark Wirtz and Keith West's pop hit "Grocer Jack (Excerpt from A Teenage Opera)", or perhaps the more florid elements of The Zombies' *Odyssey & Oracle*, than to the tougher rock edge of the Pretty Things or The Who. But its charm is undeniable.

It didn't sell and the 1968 follow-up, *All of Us,* was heavier, while retaining the harpsichords and symphonic elements. The album also included their acknowledged classic, "Rainbow Chaser": with its fabulous use of heavy phasing effects, it's their most overtly psychedelic track. Oddly, the British record-buying public remained resistant even to this. Blackwell was convinced he had a number one hit on his hands but it struggled to reach a lowly 34 in the British charts.

Disappointed by its failure, he declined to release their third album and sold the master tapes back to the duo. They remixed the record as *Nirvana – To Markos III* and it appeared on Pye in 1970, only to sink without trace. Nobody thought much about Nirvana again until Cobain and crew came roaring out of Seattle and the predictable legal action followed. They're a band whose music deserves more than a mere footnote about some squabble over a moniker.

NW

Ripe for rediscovery: the Rolling Stones' Their Satanic Majesties Request

Even the Stones seem embarrassed by *Their Satanic Majesties Request*. "I don't think any of the songs are very good," Mick Jagger states, while the ever-blunt Keith Richards describes their 1967 outing into the more phantasmagorical realms of psyche-delia as "real crap". Critics, too, have been unforgiving down the years, damning the record as a misguided attempt to jump on a bandwagon and out-psych The Beatles' *Sgt. Pepper's Lonely Heart's Club Band*.

It certainly doesn't sound very much like the Rolling Stones. Coming between "Let's Spend the Night Together" and "Jumpin' Jack Flash", it's an album unconnected to anything recorded by the band before or since, a weird and deviant blip on the radar that doesn't fit on some conveniently linear graph of the Stones' musical development.

Yet there is another school of thought that says *Their Satanic Majesties Request* is an all-time psychedelic classic, superior to *Sgt. Pepper* as a document of that first British summer of love, an acid-laced hippie manifesto of swirling sound, and a thrilling example of the brave new world of wide-eyed wonder and spaced-out experimentation that was suddenly possible in the recording studio. Marianne Faithfull attended many of the sessions, and her voice is buried somewhere in the druggy chat-tering and noises-off that punctuate several tracks. She had this to say about the album: "It's very much of its time, but it sums up an era. I think it's been unfairly maligned."

The album opens with "Sing This Song All Together", a 1960s campfire clap-along that's also a collage of free jazz, ex-otic eastern percussion, guitar noodlings worthy of the Grateful Dead, and tinkling bells, topped off with a hippie chorus led by Jagger singing "open our heads and let the pictures come". The record's hallucinatory haze continues in similarly chaotic fashion, but Jagger is wrong that there are no good songs.

Hidden inside the innovative use of tape loops, early synth experiments and the hallucinatory, slightly silly ambience (all of which make the record fascinating enough as it is), sit at least two classic pop tunes: "She's A Rainbow", a swirling piece of orchestral-pop with a typically 1967 baroque charm; and the spooky, futuristic visions of "2000 Light Years From Home", which influenced David Bowie's "Space Oddity" two year later.

Among the few to appreciate the unique place the album holds in the Stones canon is Noel Gallagher, who claimed in 2004 that he wanted Oasis to make a record that sounded like a cross between Dylan's *Highway 61 Revisited*, *Their Satanic Majesties Request* and The Stone Roses' debut. The Brian Jonestown Massacre are a band you might well expect to be fans of the album, and you'd be right: they recorded a whole album in homage entitled *Their Satanic Majesties' Second Request*.

It may be self-indulgent, sloppy and unstructured. But *Their Satanic Majesties Request* also happens to be one of the most gloriously spaced-out albums ever made.

NW

Soft Boys

Robyn Hitchcock tells a revealing story about an early Soft Boys show in Manchester during the late 1970s. "We played to the usual reaction of two people clapping and two people yelling 'Fuck off!'," he recalls. "Later, some bloke came up to me at the bar and said, 'I like your band, but we haven't had a harmony up here in six months'."

For those who found the nihilism of punk hard to take, the Soft Boys were manna from rock'n'roll heaven. Hitchcock and the Soft Boys arrived at the peak of the punk revolution with jangling Byrds guitars, glassy vocal harmonies, a love of 1960s psychedelia and crisply beautiful arrangements of genuinely great songs. With hindsight, we can trace their enduring legacy through the mid-1980s Paisley underground bands, via the world-conquering REM and on to the likes of Yo La Tengo. But at the time, for those who used punk just as an excuse to throw glasses at anyone on stage they didn't like, the Soft Boys were the enemy. They weren't just swimming against the tide – they were, as Hitchcock puts it, "the wrong ship on the wrong planet." Their voyage into obscu-

rity ultimately took them to 1980s *Underwater Moonlight*, their quintessential, sparkling neo-psychedelic masterpiece, which stands as one of the greatest albums of that difficult decade. It sold pitifully, of course, and the band broke up a year later.

Yet the ghosts of the Soft Boys refused to go away and they now look like heroes for keeping pop's joy and jangle alive. "People accused us of being hopeless revivalists: why weren't we looking to the future?" Hitchcock says today. "But people keep coming back to that form of music. They obviously can't leave it alone. Maybe we were the first people to look backwards. And people are still trying to do it, by the shovelful."

The prime mover behind the band, Hitchcock numbered Bob Dylan, John Lennon and Syd Barrett among his formative musical heroes. Moving from London to Cambridge as a 21-year-old in 1974, he played the local folk clubs and built a rapport with a group of local musicians who by 1976 had become the embryonic Soft Boys. Their first EP, *Wading Through a Ventilator*, appeared the following year on Raw

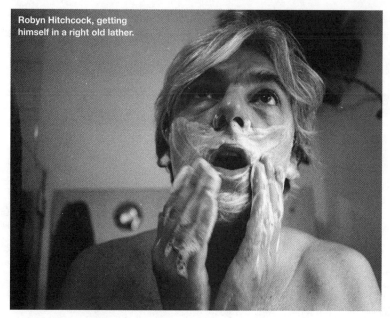
Robyn Hitchcock, getting himself in a right old lather.

Records and was still some way from the sound they would perfect on *Underwater Moonlight*, all grinding guitars and thrashing drums, with surreal lyrics delivered by Hitchcock in a post-Beefheart growl. The good Captain was a touchstone at the time and Hitchcock has spoken of his vision to cross *Abbey Road* with *Trout Mask Replica*. The results were "a kind of heavy metal/barbershop doo-wop/country and western/psychedelic/folk blues band".

The arrival soon after of guitarist Kimberley Rew from rival Cambridge group The Waves was critical, and helped to cement a richer mesh of harmonic guitars. But the Soft Boys were still a band in search of a sound. A 1978 single for Radar Records, "I Want to Be an Angle Poise Lamp", was praised by *Melody Maker* but bombed, and after scrapping an entire album's worth of tracks recorded at Rockfield in Wales, the band left the label and decided to go it alone.

Their debut album *A Can Of Bees*, released on their own Two Crabs label, still didn't quite get it right and another bunch of material recorded in 1979 was also scrapped, only to appear in 1983 as the posthumous album *Invisible Hits*.

Finally it all fell into place on *Underwater Moonlight*. Recorded on four- and eight-track tape for less than £600, it's one of those special records that once heard is never forgotten. In the liner notes of its expanded 2001 reissue, *Underwater Moonlight and How It Got There*, which included ten further tracks unreleased at the time, long-time fan David Fricke wrote: "We can listen to these songs now and wonder why the world did not freeze in astonishment."

Sadly, for the most part the world didn't even listen, let alone marvel. After their inevitable split, Hitchcock made some intriguing solo records before reuniting with the Soft Boys rhythm section as the Egyptians. Rew achieved brief success with Katrina & The Waves. By the 1990s, however, the Soft Boys had been posthumously transmogrified into one of rock'n'roll's great lost bands and given the full box set and reissues-with-bonus-tracks treatment. It led to a 1994 reunion tour and another in 2001, followed by an album of brand new material, *Nextdoorland* (2002), before the band broke up again, once more to sink back into influential obscurity. **NW**

The 13th Floor Elevators

The 13th Floor Elevators hailed from Texas, not San Francisco. But they rivalled any of the Haight-Ashbury's psychedelic warriors in their belief that the 1960s represented the dawning of a new enlightened age. "The new system involves a major evolutionary step for man," they proselytized in the sleeve notes for their 1966 debut album. "The new man views the old man in much the same way as the old man views the ape." Inside was a record that married driving garage rock to sturdy folk-rock tunes and hazy psychedelia, led by the band's classic hit single "You're Gonna Miss Me". As an early hippie manifesto, it's a better record – and more convincingly psychedelic – than the debuts by the Grateful Dead, Jefferson Airplane and Big Brother & The Holding Company, all of which were more blues- or folk-based. The Elevators' progress up the skyscraper of rock'n'roll fame, however, was rendered erratic due to the mental state of the band's yelping, semi-crazed singer Roky Erickson, whose self-destructive tendencies were exacerbated by his copious drug use. By the late 1960s he had been committed to a state mental institution. His subsequent solo career was similarly unhinged but fired with an intermittent brilliance that has helped him attain semi-mythic status, alongside the likes of Syd Barrett and Skip Spence, as one of rock's great inspired crazies.

Formed in Austin, Texas, in 1965 from two other local bands, The Lingsmen and The Spades, the initial line-up had Erickson joined by Stacey Sutherland (guitar), Ronnie Leatherman (bass), John Ike Walton (drums) and – most significantly – University of Texas graduate Tommy Hall, a key foil who provided most of the esoteric lyrics and much of the hallucinogenic indulgence by feeding the band daily doses of LSD, as well as helping to create their signature sound with his spooked electric guitar playing.

As the psychedelic movement grew, the Elevators sought wider exposure with visits to play in its epicentre of San Francisco, although unlike many other bands of the era they declined to move to California and concentrated on creating their own counter-cultural scene deep in the redneck heart of Texas. Unsurprisingly, they were soon attracting the attention of the forces of law and order and were busted for drugs.

A key figure in the Elevators' story was Lelan Rogers, who founded the International Artists label in Houston in 1965. Rogers himself was no hippie: in his forties, he was the elder brother of country singer Kenny Rogers. But he saw commercial potential in the emerging psychedelic scene and among those he signed to his label were not only the Elevators but fellow psych pioneers the Red Krayola. In later years it was his proud – if contestable – boast that the San Francisco sound first emerged not on the West Coast but on his label in Texas.

The drug busts and the departure of their rhythm section in early 1967 halted the Elevators just as they should have been emerging as one of the key groups in the psychedelic revolution. The core trio of Erickson, Hall and Sutherland eventually recruited Dan Galiano (bass) and Danny Thomas (drums) but the summer of love was over by the time they re-emerged at the end of 1967 with *Easter Everywhere*, a second fine collection of

playlist:

1 You're Gonna Miss Me *from* 13th Floor Elevators
Garage rock goes psychedelic, creating an all-time 1960s jukebox classic.

2 I Don't Ever Want to Come Down *from* Easter Everywhere
The song title that is the Elevators' philosophy in a nutshell.

3 She Lives (in a Time of Her Own) *from* Easter Everywhere
The gentler, more fragile and meditative side to their driving psych-rock.

4 Splash 1 *from* 13th Floor Elevators
Melodic folk-rock on one of Erickson's finest compositions.

5 I Have Always Been Here Before *from* Gremlins Have Pictures
Gorgeous, acoustic, solo Roky from the late 1970s.

"Like Buddy Holly on acid"

REM's Peter Buck on Roky Erickson

Roky Erickson

psych classics, including the great "I Don't Ever Want to Come Down".

By their third and final studio album, 1969's *Bull of the Woods*, Erickson was pretty much hors de combat. Hall subsequently became a born-again Christian, while Sutherland was imprisoned for drug possession and was later shot dead in a domestic dispute in 1978. After being busted for narcotics possession in 1969, Erickson told the court that he came from Mars and was sent to a mental institution where he spent three years receiving electro-convulsive shock therapy. On his release, he formed Bleib Alien ("bleib" being a corruption of bible), later renamed the Aliens. His stop-start solo work has been patchy but sporadically brilliant as his problems with schizophrenia continued.

The 1990s saw the release of a tribute album, *Where the Pyramid Meets the Eye*, featuring covers of Erickson songs by the Jesus and Mary Chain, REM, Julian Cope, Doug Sahm and Primal Scream among others. The album title came from the cryptic answer Erickson once gave when asked to define psychedelic music. In 2001 Erickson's youngest brother was granted legal custody of him and he set about helping his sibling to return to the live stage. In 2005 he gave his first full-length concert in twenty years, and he has since made his first tour of Europe. At the time of writing he was reportedly working on a new album with none other than Billy Gibbons, of those grey-bearded and dark-shaded boogie monsters ZZ Top.

NW

Dino Valenti

He only released one solo album and they spelled his name wrong on the cover. With no promotion, few ever got to hear it. Yet inside the unassuming sepia-tinted sleeve was a record of esoteric psych-folk beauty that visited places only Tim Buckley was accessing among other 1960s troubadours.

The ten meandering songs were virtually bereft of conventional verses, choruses, hooks and bridges. The lyrics consisted of stream-of-consciousness musings rooted in hippie philosophy. The voice and twelve-string guitar were swathed in layers of shimmering reverb and the chords were the weirdest you'd ever heard outside a jazz album.

The sleeve said "Dino Valente" although he called himself "Valenti". Neither was his real name, for he'd been born Chester Powers in 1937 to carny folk who worked a tent called the "Hootchie Cootch" – in effect, a stripshow. In a reversal of filial conventions, at seventeen he ran away from the carnival to join the US Air Force. On his discharge, he pitched up in Greenwich Village, where he played with Fred Neil and wrote "Get Together", which became a top-ten hit for the Youngbloods. By 1964, he was on the West Coast, playing around San Francisco with Quicksilver Messenger Service. But before the band signed a record deal, he got busted for marijuana possession and, while awaiting trial, was busted again. There are conflicting stories about how long he served. At some point it appears he was paroled and he was seen at San Francisco's First Human Be-In in 1967, "running through the crowd, playing a flute, skipping in and out of groups of people like a minstrel from the Middle Ages

thrown into modern America by a time-warp," as the flowery description of Ralph Gleason puts it.

At some point he was sent back to the can and while he was incarcerated, Quicksilver signed to Capitol and included his "Dino's Song" on their first album. He did eventually rejoin the band after he'd been freed again, but beforehand he managed to record his solitary solo album for the Epic label in LA in 1968. According to Quicksilver guitarist Gary Duncan, who played on the album, one version of the record was cut with producer Jack Nitzsche, who arranged the songs and edited them to make a "palatable, saleable product". Valenti immediately junked the record as too commercial. "It was too clean for him," Duncan says. "But it was a great record. It would've made him a fucking millionaire."

Epic were furious. Bob Dylan's producer Bob Johnston was brought in to get an album out of him but, the way Duncan tells it, a decision was taken not to promote it, and Dino's name was deliberately misspelled.

The Johnston-helmed sessions have since become the stuff of legend. When Dino didn't feel like singing, they spent two days making paper airplanes and throwing them around the studio. He wanted bagpipes so they got in two Scottish pipers, in full Highland regalia. (Dino then changed his mind.) He also had his personal harem in tow. "There was like anywhere from ten to thirty little girls popping up and out," Johnston recalls.

Bass player Carol Kaye, who was hired and then fired, counts it as the most hellish session she ever played. Valenti would start a song and still be playing the same number an

1 Let's Get Together *from* Love is the Song We Sing: San Francisco Nuggets
Dino's original 1964 demo for Autumn Records of his best-known song. He sold the copyright and so never enjoyed royalties from the hit versions.

2 Time *from* Dino Valenti
Shimmering, echoing twelve-string guitar magic from another time and place.

3 Something New *from* Dino Valenti
Seven minutes of Dino at his most Buckley-esque and the only song ever to mention unicorns and still sound cool...

4 My Friend *from* Dino Valenti
Fluttering flute and muted trumpet but the mood is still hippie-beatific with a lyric about barefoot girls wearing beads.

5 Me and My Uncle *from* Dino Valenti
A John Phillips song also covered by the Grateful Dead. Needless to say, Dino's version knocks spots off theirs.

6 Tomorrow *from* Dino Valenti
A change of mood from the rest of the album: a great symphonic-pop arrangement that sounds like it's the only track rescued from the earlier sessions with Jack Nitzsche.

7 Children of the Sun *from* Dino Valenti
Wonderful jazzy chords that, according to Gary Duncan who played on it, were nicked from "My Funny Valentine".

hour later. "It was a *lot* of drugs there, turning the lights totally off, lighting candles," she recalled. But for Valenti's elliptical acid-folk it was clearly perfect. The joke among his friends was that if the record was only bought by every teenage girl Dino knew, it would be a surefire number one. But the lack of promotion meant that most of them probably didn't even know the record was out. Although Valenti talked excitedly to *Rolling Stone* in 1969 about his next solo record, it never happened. There was a brief attempt to form a band with Gary Duncan called The Outlaws. Then in 1970, he rejoined Quicksilver, his songs appearing under the pseudonym Jesse Oris Farrow on the albums *Just For Love* and *What About Me*. After Quicksilver split there were no further recordings and Valenti died of emphysema in Santa Rosa, California, in 1994.

The one solo album he left is a record so of its time that it effectively defines that era. And yet, miraculously, it still sounds as alluring today as it did back then. "Time" opens the album, all shimmering acoustic twelve-string guitar, and Dino's echoing voice sings "Time slipping away, new dreams born every day". A tinkling harpsichord joins the dance and the spell is cast. *NW*

Quicksilver Messenger Service: Dino is second from the left.

Michael Yonkers

Back in 1968, a rock'n'roll-mad Minneapolis teenager called Michael Yonkers entered a local studio with his band to record a bunch of songs for their debut album. He had just signed a deal with the New York-based Sire Records and his future stretched out before him. He then had a difference of opinion with his manager, who told him to lose his beard and his band and move to New York to write Top 40 pop songs. Yonkers declined, the contract was revoked and the songs of his album remained unheard until 1997, when Minnesota-based collector and historian Jim Oldsberg started compiling a collection of unreleased tracks from the city's Dove studios, where Yonkers had recorded. The compilation, released on Pittsburgh's Get Hip label as *Free Flight: Unreleased Dove Recording Studio Cuts 1964–69*, garnered good reviews, particularly for two cuts by Yonkers called "Microminiature Love" and "Kill the Enemy."

Those tracks sent collector and De Stijl Records head Clint Simonson on a four-year hunt to find the reclusive Yonkers. He eventually tracked him down, asked if there was more and offered to put the original 1968 album out. The seven-track *Microminiature Love* eventually appeared in 2002, some 34 years after it was recorded, although even then it was issued as a vinyl-only release. That was the form in which it was originally intended to appear, and the conceit appealed to Yonkers' love of retro technology. A CD eventually appeared on Sub Pop a year later with six further previously unreleased tracks of 1968 vintage; Yonkers suddenly found he had become a cult hero.

playlist:

1 Microminiature Love *from* Microminiature Love
A great blues-rocker with distinct shades of Cream and Jimi.

2 Boy in the Sandbox *from* Microminiature Love
A classic anti-war song about a boy who plays with toy soldiers in his sandbox, who grows up to fight a real war and dies in a "tomb of sand".

3 Kill the Enemy *from* Microminiature Love
Another Vietnam song with a deep, gloomy vocal from Yonkers – sounding much older than the teenager he was.

4 Scat Jam *from* Microminiature Love
One of the additional tracks that bears a certain resemblance to early Led Zeppelin, or even Comets on Fire.

Even today the album sounds fresh and intense. What kind of impact it might have made at the time we can only guess. The droning guitar sound – discovered when Yonkers knocked his guitar off a stand and kept the unusual open tuning that resulted – anticipates Sonic Youth. The dissonant rhythms presage Pere Ubu, while the crude, raw production recalls the Stooges. The urgent, concerned lyrics have a hyper-real quality, many of them provoked by the Vietnam War. On "Boy in the Sandbox" a widow weeps over a letter pronouncing her GI husband dead, while holding a toy soldier in her hand. In "Kill the Enemy", God, wrapped in an American flag, declares: "If you make it home, then you'll be old enough to vote." Finally released on the eve of the Iraq war, such lyrics took on a brand new resonance. Timeless, did someone say? Well Yonkers does sing "1492 is now" on the opening track "Jasontown" and, without subsequent knowledge of rock history, the record sounds like nothing so much as the missing link between the dirty swagger of 1960s garage, psychedelic blues-rock and the angrier aesthetic of 1970s punk.

Following the belated release of *Microminiature Love*, the full Michael Yonkers story slowly began to emerge. After discovering rock'n'roll via watching Elvis on the Ed Sullivan show, Yonkers' first band, Michael and the Mumbles, played surf music, clad in matching vests and neat Beatles haircuts. Within a year, Yonkers had discovered dirty rock'n'roll via the Rolling Stones, and when psychedelia came along, Yonkers and his band (consisting of his brother Jim Yunker on drums and Tom Wallfred on bass) dressed in kaftans and love beads.

Yonkers also had a fascination with gadgetry. He made his own effects pedals, shredded his speakers with a razor to get a nastier, more distorted sound and customized his Fender Telecaster guitar, cutting down the body in a way that made his instrument look more like a weapon than ever.

After the debacle of the Sire recording contract, Yonkers' band fell apart. He took a job working in a local electronics warehouse and started building his own low-budget early synths. In a horrendous accident, a pile of equipment toppled over on top of him and destroyed his back. After surgery he developed a degenerative condition of the spinal cord and took up dancing as therapy. Somehow he managed to record several collections of gentle, off-kilter folk songs at home, releasing them himself. They were the stylistic opposite of his 1968 recordings with the band, and he later played local solo electric-guitar shows with backing tapes and special effects. " In my own mind, I'm already a success," he announced on his rediscovery. "Not financially, not in status, not anything like that. But I can't imagine living a more interesting life."

NW

NOT FOR EXPORT
world, reggae and more

Horace Andy

It must be frustrating when you have been making fine records under your own name for forty years and yet you are best-known to the world as "that reggae singer who guests with Massive Attack". When not singing with the Bristol-based trip-hoppers on albums such as *Blue Lines*, *Protection* and *Mezzanine*, Andy's haunting high tenor (often described as a falsetto, which he insists it is not) is ranked by hardcore aficionados of Jamaican music alongside the likes of Winston Rodney (Burning Spear), Joseph Hill (Culture) and Toots Hibbert. Like a Jamaican Al Green, he has the ability to shift effortlessly from a sultry croon to a full-throated wail. He's also a gifted songwriter and over a long career has managed to encompass reggae, dancehall and ragga styles.

Born Horace Hinds and widely known in Jamaica as "Sleepy", he was given the name Andy in tribute to the singer Bob Andy by Coxsone Dodd, for whom he made his first recordings in the late 1960s at Studio One. Part of the second generation of reggae vocalists following in the footsteps of the likes of Ken Boothe, John Holt and Delroy Wilson, by the age of 21 he was already a veteran hit-maker with the likes of "Something On My Mind", "The Love of a Woman", and "I Found Someone" to his credit, plus the thunderous, self-penned "Skylarking", which, with its looping, insistent bass line, has become a kind of signature tune. There were also love songs such as "Fever" and a cover of Al Wilson's "Show and Tell". But his most enduring early work provided razor-edged commentaries on the social conditions of the Jamaican ghetto, on songs such as "Illiteracy",

"Help the Children", "Conscious Dreadlocks", "Zion Gate", "Materialist", "Money Money (Is the Root of All Evil)" and "This Must Be Hell", most of them self-written. Like many Rastafarian singers, he also turned to his bible for inspiration on songs such as "Psalm 68", "John Saw Them Coming" and "God Is Displeased".

Many of his best 1970s sides were recorded with producer Bunny Lee, including the original spine-chilling version of "You Are My Angel", a reggae hit on Lee's Smash label in 1974. But his unique voice meant he was in constant demand and he worked with most of the great Jamaican producers, including Keith Hudson (with whom he recorded the menacing "Don't Think About Me (I'm Alright)"), Derrick Harriott, Winston "Niney the Observer" Holness, Errol Thompson and King Tubby.

In 1977 he went to New York to work with producer Everton DaSilva and recorded the superb album *In the Light*, his voice soaring gloriously over the rhythms of a crack band that included Augustus Pablo, Leroy Sibbles and Horsemouth Wallace. By the mid-1980s the hard-to-find recording was regarded as a kind of holy grail by reggae collectors. It was reissued on CD by the splendid Blood & Fire label in the 1990s, complete with King Jammy's dub versions of the ten tracks.

During the 1980s Andy worked in London with the producer Lloyd Barnes (aka Bullwackie) and when reggae's sound went digital around 1985 he was unfazed by the change of style. Yet despite his acclaim in reggae circles, he remained little known in the wider music world until 1990, when he appeared on Massive Attack's debut album *Blue Lines*. He embraced the opportunity to broaden his horizons and dramatically reworked some of his older material as "Spying Glass" (formerly "Spy Glass"), "Man Next Door" (formerly "I've Got To Get Away") and "Angel" (formerly "You Are My Angel"), even if most Massive Attack fans remained unaware of the original roots versions of the songs.

Massive Attack also gave him the opportunity to further his solo career, and he released *Living in the Flood* on their Melankolic label in 1999. Three years later came *Mek It Bun*, recorded with Sly and Robbie. In 2004 he recorded *Horace Andy Meets Mad Professor – From the Roots* and found himself blacklisted on the website Murder Inna Dancehall, which monitors homophobic lyrics in reggae music, and which took exception to the song "Runaway", which crassly linked "chi chi man and lesbian" with "wicked Babylon".

More recently, he contributed to the *1 Giant Leap* project, an ambitious but slightly bland album and DVD attempting to build bridges between different musics from around the world under the banner of chilled-out ambient dance. A far more interesting collaboration was Horace's contribution to the *Radiodread* album, a reggae version of Radiohead's *OK Computer*: he sang vocals on the opening track, a cover of the Oxfordshire band's "Airbag".

NW

playlist:

1 Spying Glass *from* Skylarking
The "best of" album released on Massive Attack's own label opens with Andy's solo version of this song and closes with the group's reworking. So take your pick...

2 You Are My Angel *from* The Prime of Horace Andy: 16 Massive Cuts from the 70s
The sublime original of the song he later reworked on Massive Attack's debut.

3 Every Tongue Shall Tell *from* Skylarking
Horn-driven roots reggae "reality".

4 Skylarking *from* Skylarking
Andy's signature tune is an all-time Jamaican classic.

5 Natty Dread A Weh She Want *from* Skylarking
A brilliant Tapper Zukie production from 1978.

The Congos

So what is the most righteous reggae album ever recorded? Some might vote for the epochal *Exodus* by Bob Marley and the Wailers. Others could reasonably plump for *Marcus Garvey* by Burning Spear. A few might even nominate *The Right Time* by the Mighty Diamonds. But many reggae connoisseurs will tell you that the philosopher's stone of Jamaican music is an obscure record by a vocal duo called the Congos.

The reason why so few people ever got to hear *Heart of the Congos* is mired in convoluted politics and bitter feuding – as so much in the Jamaican recording industry tends to be. At the time *Heart of the Congos* was recorded in 1977, producer Lee "Scratch" Perry was in dispute with Chris Blackwell's Island Records, which had successfully released a number of his previous productions for the likes of Max Romeo and Junior Murvin. But with Perry denouncing Blackwell as "Chris White-Hell", instead of getting an international release on the label that had made Marley the Third World's first superstar, *Heart of the Congos* appeared on Scratch's own hopelessly under-resourced Black Ark label. The Congos also pressed up copies themselves and distributed them in haphazard fashion as best they could.

Island would have promoted the record as a major international release and racked it up in every high street and shopping mall in Britain and America, at a time when mainstream interest in reggae was at a peak. Without its backing, *Heart of the Congos* trickled out of Jamaica dressed in a cardboard cover of such shoddy flimsiness and cheap design that it resembled a cereal packet rather than a record sleeve and on vinyl of such poor quality that it probably would have sounded better had it been pressed in cow dung.

To find a copy, you had to track down specialist shops and market stalls in the back streets of Brixton or Handsworth. When you did, through the hiss, crackle and pop could be heard the most sublime, spiritual music – by some way the most consistent, breathtaking and beautiful record that the great but erratic Perry ever produced. It took nearly two decades for *Heart of the Congos* to reappear, finally reissued with a clutch of choice bonus tracks by the Blood and Fire label in 1996. In remastered high fidelity, it sounded even more spectacular than on its original botched release.

In many ways the Congos were unlikely contenders. The group was a vocal duo, consisting of falsetto singer Cedric Myton and tenor singer Roydel "Ashanti" Johnson, who got together in 1976 and approached Perry about recording an album at his Black Ark Studio. Neither had much of a track record. Born in 1947, Myton had sung in rocksteady group the Tartans and then when reggae hit town, the Royal Rasses. Johnson, born in the same year, had been a bit player in Ras Michael and the Sons of Negus and then joined the totally unknown Brother Joe and the Rightful Brothers.

Their two voices had a unique sound – Curtis Mayfield is the only close equivalent to Myton's breathtaking falsetto. Gentle, high and mercurial, their harmonies were almost airborne. They also wrote potent songs. Rooted deep in Jamaican culture, mythology, ritual and biblical prophecy, with titles such as "Ark of The Covenant", "Sodom and Gomorrow" and "Solid Foundation", many of them sounded more like traditional Jamaican folk songs rather than the skanking dubwise reggae anthems of the 1970s.

The pair's sound was so airy, delicate and yet fervently spiritual that it might easily have collapsed under the deep, bottom-heavy production style of the Jamaican studios at the time. But Perry knew how to take care of that. He brought in the deeper bass voice of Watty "King" Burnett, then rounded up most of his favourite musicians. Further backing vocals were supplied by Gregory Isaacs, the Meditations and members of the Heptones. Perry turned to members of his usual crew, the Upsetters, and added Ernest Ranglin on guitar. Then he added his own swirling production genius, using an Echoplex reverb unit and a Mutron phaser to give the sound a sympathetic, gauzy dub haze. Everything is structured around the timbre of the vocals soaring above.

At every turn you meet an unexpected arrangement or a surprising rhythm as handmade beats knot through Perry's soundboard wizardry with an alchemical magic. Never has reggae music before or since sounded so "dread" or so divine. Yet the album remains a glorious one-off. Myton made three further LPs as the Congos without ever again reaching the same heights, while Johnson laboured as Congo Ashanti Roy with similarly nondescript results.

NW

If only they'd sung in English:
a brief history of non-Anglophone pop

More than fifty years of rock and pop history have conditioned listeners in English-speaking countries to be suspicious of material that's sung in any other language. While you could explain away our unwillingness to embrace the popular music forms of, say, Asia or Africa as perhaps a "musicultural" thing, it would seem that our distaste for home-grown German pop music is merely based on the fact that it's sung in German. But hey, the Germans love it! Surely 82 million people can't be wrong? These countries lap up the music that we sling in their direction; it doesn't particularly matter to them if they can't decipher the meaning behind "U Can't Touch This" by MC Hammer. Actually, we don't have much of a clue what MC Hammer is on about either, but we sent him to number three in the charts in the UK, while the far more musically inventive MC Solaar never got so much as a sniff of success over here with his vastly superior Francophone rap.

The Eurovision Song Contest, sadly, must take its fair share of the blame. This annual event has thrown up so much dross in the name of musical entertainment that we've been conditioned to respond to pop music sung in Dutch, Danish or Serbo-Croat by sniggering contemptuously. The few foreign language tracks that do reach prominence in the UK are instantly viewed as "novelty" hits – regardless of any inherent musical quality they may have – and those artists inevitably turn out to be one-hit wonders. But if they had decided to sing in English, they may have been welcomed with open arms. Have you heard any Abba songs sung in Swedish? Unsurprisingly, they're just as catchy.

Our prejudices don't just extend to chart music; while we've happily lapped up the sounds of Sigur Rós, and before them the Cocteau Twins, and before them Magma – all of whom have sung using some kind of self-devised language – if they had dared to give it to us in Icelandic, Gaelic or French, we'd probably have turned our backs pronto. As a result, almost inconceivably, huge swathes of the world's rock and pop music have just passed us by. It's impossible to even begin to scratch the surface – but here are some choice selections of stuff we really should have been humming in the shower:

Ultra Bra
Minä Suojelen Sinua Kaikelta *from* Kroketti

It shouldn't have worked, really. A twelve-piece Finnish group (with four singers) playing expansive, orchestral songs about eyebrow-raising subjects such as the life of Nigerian activist Ken Saro-Wiwa. But the Finns immediately took them to their hearts, and the band ended up producing four albums of tip-top twenty-first-century pop music, as beautifully constructed as Abba while, surprisingly, still keeping a political conscience. Indeed, their lyricist is now a member of the Finnish parliament.

Asha Bhosle
O Saathi Re *from* Muqaddar Ka Sikandar

It's hard to conceive of any self-respecting Bollywood compilation that doesn't feature this breathtakingly beautiful tune. It's strangely reminiscent of Buddy Holly's "Raining in My Heart", but lovingly embellished with those typically sweeping Bollywood strings; a translation of the lyrics reveals the song to be like an Indian version of the Beach Boys' "God Only Knows": "Oh darling, what is living without you? Without you my life, without me your life, is not a life..."

Bob Hund
Förträngda Problem *from* Omslag: Martin Kann

If, in the mid-1990s, you saw Blur's Graham Coxon sporting his Bob Hund T-shirt, you may have imagined it was some cute German kids' cartoon. But no, Bob Hund were a Swedish indie band coupling way-above-average tunes with an uplifting, boisterous live show. Even the Swedes couldn't always understand the singer, Thomas Öberg (he sang in the local Skånska dialect), but they loved him, regardless – and the band went on to win two Swedish "Grammis".

Other worthy alternatives? If you're bored with Belle & Sebastian, maybe give Swedes Raymond & Maria a go. Mylene Farmer, the French answer to Madonna, has produced some great work over the last 25 years, from bubblegum pop to overblown gothic disco – or, if you prefer your Gallic pop to have a little more street cred, there's Sparks' favourites Les Rita Mitsouko, who've been going even longer. Hungarian band Kampec Dolores produced some stunning guitar-driven albums in the 1990s that would have embarrassed their British shoegazing contemporaries (had they ever actually heard them) while German band Wir Sind Helden thankfully continue to avoid the histrionic stereotypes associated with most Teutonic rock bands.

RM

Count Ossie

As with most developments in popular music, it's hard to credit a particular individual with the invention of reggae. The guitarist Ernest Ranglin is one claimant who was in there at the start, and became an early mentor to Bob Marley. Another is the mysterious Count Ossie, who introduced African drumming into Jamaican music and whose backing on the original recording of "Oh Carolina" in 1960 is regarded by some as the first page of the opening chapter in the reggae story.

Whatever the precise order of events, there is no doubt that Count Ossie and the Mystic Revelation of Rastafari were one of the most uniquely original of all Jamaican groups, with a sound built on a rock-solid foundation of drumming and chanting, the pulse of which was often slowed to a heartbeat. Known in Jamaica as Nyabinghi, the style was captured gloriously on *Grounation: The Indomitable Spirit of Rastafari*, a three-LP set first released in 1973 that included an updated version of "Oh Carolina" as well as the mesmerizing groove of the title track, which lasts in excess of thirty minutes.

Born Oswald Williams in the rural Jamaican parish of St Thomas in 1926, in his twenties Ossie joined a Rastafarian community where he learned the techniques of vocal chanting and hand-drumming associated with Nyabinghi. The word has a complicated history. Originally associated with an uprising against European colonial rule in southwestern Uganda during the late nineteenth and early twentieth centuries, the movement was led by a charismatic healer who was believed to be possessed by the spirit of a legendary Amazon Queen, Nyabinghi. The movement was condemned by the British as witchcraft and eventually crushed, but the term entered Rastafarian mythology because the Ethiopian government of Emperor Haile Selassie I – regarded by Rastas as a god – was also known as the House of Nyabinghi.

In Jamaica the term came to be applied to island-wide religious gatherings of Rasta brethren who would "chant down Babylon" to a three-part drum ensemble; the chants and drumming have been memorably described by one commentator as "Rasta hootenanny music, with herb taking the place of sourmash". The music came to form the basis of the annual Grounation celebration on 21 April, an important Rastafari holy day commemorating Haile Selassie's 1966 visit to Jamaica.

Ossie had formed his first drum ensemble in the late 1950s, long before Selassie's visit. He was living in Camp David, a Rastafarian hideout in the hills above Kingston, and spending time in the Back-A-Wall squatter camp in West Kingston, where he was taught to play the African *funde* drum by a Rastafarian called Brother Joe. His first venture into a recording studio came in 1960 when Prince Buster produced a version of "Oh Carolina" by the vocal trio the Folkes Brothers and invited Ossie and his drummers to back them. One of the first Jamaican records to look to Africa as well as America for its inspiration, Ossie's Nyabinghi rhythms helped to make the record an instant hit.

Independence was on the horizon and the sound played a significant part in giving Jamaican culture its own identity. On Independence Day itself, 4 August 1962, "Count Ossie and his Afro Drums" were listed in the *Jamaican Times* as backing both Jimmy Cliff and Derrick Morgan at celebration parties that night in Kingston.

As the Rastafarian influence grew within the Jamaican record industry, Count Ossie and his drummers were increasingly in demand on productions by Harry Mudie, Clement Dodd and others. Among the records on which they can be heard are Winston & Roy's "Babylon Gone", Lascelles Perkins' "Destiny" and the Mellow Cats' "Rock A Man Soul". In 1973, he formed Count Ossie and the Mystic Revelation of Rastafari to record *Grounation*, a marvellous, sprawling hybrid combining trance-like drumming and chanting with a great horn section (led by Cedric Im Brooks), organ, acoustic bass and guitar.

The results were a unique kind of improvised, open-ended African reggae-jazz, with covers of Charles Lloyd's "Passin' Thru" and the Jazz Crusaders' "Way Back Home"

nestling alongside classic reggae tunes like "Oh Carolina" and "So Long Rastafari". *Tales of Mozambique* followed in 1975 in similar if less meandering and more structured style. Ossie died the following year, aged fifty, leaving behind a unique legacy as the man who put pre-slavery African roots back into Jamaican music.

NW

playlist:

1 Oh Carolina *from* Grounation
This is the hypnotic, drum-laden 1973 version of a song he first recorded in 1960 – and with which Shaggy later had an international hit.

2 So Long Rastafari *from* Grounation
Dennis Brown's hit gets Ossie-fied.

3 Grounation *from* Grounation
Thirty minutes of chants, deep rhythms and mumbled prayers – more like a field recording of a Rasta celebration in the hills than a studio performance.

4 No Night in Zion *from* Tales of Mozambique
A tighter, more focussed Ossie, with surreal organ and some wonderfully spirited singing.

5 Run One Mile *from* Tales of Mozambique
Fabulous drumming that seems to evoke the rush and tumble of slaves escaping to freedom.

Francis Falceto's Ethiopiques

When most people hear some music they like at a party, they may scribble a name on a piece of paper and possibly buy an album weeks later, if they remember. When French concert promoter Francis Falceto heard Mahmoud Ahmed's voice for the first time, at a gathering in Poitiers in 1984, he jumped on a flight to Ethiopia a month later and set about organizing a European tour for the Addis Ababa singer.

It was the beginning of Falceto's long love affair with the sounds of a nation that has not enjoyed even a fraction of the crossover success of music from Mali, Senegal or South Africa. Falceto has now released 23 volumes of his *Ethiopiques* CD series and, with the 2007 collection, *The Very Best of Ethiopiques*, the Western world finally has the perfect jumping-off point into a remarkably varied, startlingly evolved soundworld – one which may well have all but disappeared again.

The roots of modern Ethiopian music can be traced to 1924, when Ras Tafari (later better known as the Emperor Haile Selassie) met a marching band of Armenian orphans in Jerusalem, and arranged to bring them to Addis Ababa as the imperial band, introducing horns and military music to the traditional sounds of the Ethiopian lyre and harp. Decades later, the country's finest musicians would be employed by other institutional groups: Ahmed sang in the Imperial Bodyguard Band, while Alèmayèhu Eshètè, whose grunts and yelps were inspired by James Brown, sang with the Police Orchestra.

This was not as restrictive a set-up as it might sound. In fact, Ethiopia had an eruption of creativity that mirrored that of

Britain and America during the 1960s and 70s, when Selassie was relaxing his rule and US Army base radio stations were broadcasting soul, funk and jazz. The members of the official bands were free to play wilder music after hours in Addis nightclubs, a scene that compiler Falceto compares to swinging London. The sound the band produced was alien and hypnotic, Gétatchèw Mekurya's snake charmer saxophone dancing wildly over a tense organ groove, and Tèwèldè Rèdda's intricate jazz guitar weaving around tribal beats. The melodies feel mournful, but the rhythms are irresistible.

Sadly the Derg military dictatorship put a stop to all the fun in 1974, overthrowing Selassie, closing the clubs and enforcing a nightly curfew that stayed in place for seventeen years. Falceto himself believes that was the end of truly great Ethiopian music, despite having released some astonishing albums of traditional Ethiopian music recorded during the 1990s. Even if he is right, his unearthing and repackaging of the lost treasures from the period he adores clearly isn't over yet.

DS

where to start:

1 Sèw *from* The Very Best of Ethiopiques
Mulatu Astatqé Yekermo is probably the best-known Ethiopian musician in the West, thanks to the extensive use of darkly groovy instrumentals such as this one on the soundtrack to Jim Jarmusch's 2005 film *Broken Flowers*.

2 Tchero Adari Nègn *from* The Very Best of Ethiopiques
Alèmayèhu Eshètè is the Ethiopian James Brown. Here, his primal barks hustle along a wavering, Eastern-sounding wail on a fast-paced funk workout.

Nusrat Fateh Ali Khan

In the hundred or so years of recorded music, there have been very few singers who could summon the same yearning, emotional power or convey the myriad shadings of agony and ecstasy that characterized the voice of Nusrat Fateh Ali Khan. Billie Holiday, perhaps. Maria Callas, certainly. Egypt's Oum Kalthoum would also have a strong claim, as would Aretha Franklin at her soul-gospel peak.

All women, of course, which arguably leaves Nusrat as the greatest male vocalist of the twentieth century. That's a bold statement, but then Nusrat was the boldest of singers, venturing where other voices dared not go. His live performances, which tended to last for hours, left listeners dazed and ecstatic as his voice soared ever higher in search, and in praise, of his God. He died in 1997 at the tragically young age of 48, when he was at the very height of his powers. As the British newspaper *The Independent* observed on his death in 1997, "The immense narrative propulsion of his music was enough to raise even the most secular listeners to a state of bewildered grace."

In the West, Peter Gabriel is often credited with the "discovery" of Nusrat. But that's like saying Columbus "discovered" America. Nusrat had been a musical legend in his home country of Pakistan long before European adventurers became aware of his existence. Gabriel's role was crucial: he invited Nusrat to perform for a Western audience for the first time at the WOMAD festival in 1985, he employed his voice on the soundtrack of Martin Scorsese's 1988 film *The Last Temptation of Christ* and recorded him for his Real World label.

Gabriel's patronage also led to a remix by Massive Attack; to Jeff Buckley calling him "a God" and incorporating elements of his style into his own vocal improvisations; and to the Red Hot Chili Peppers writing a tribute song to him called "Circle of the Noose". Nusrat's voice was used at climactic moments in Oliver Stone's film *Natural Born Killers* (1994) and Tim Robbins' *Dead Man Walking* (1995) – the former against his wishes and the latter as part of a thrilling duet with Pearl Jam's Eddie Vedder.

Yet none of that had much impact in the Islamic world, where he had long been revered as *shahen-shah-e-qawwali* – the emperor of *qawwali*. The word literally translates as "utterance"; it's an ecstatic style of Sufi devotional singing of which Nusrat was the brightest star.

Born in Pakistan in 1948, Nusrat came from a line of qawwals stretching back over six hundred years to the late thirteenth century when the music arrived from Persia in the Indian subcontinent and established itself in something like its present form. He trained with his father Ustad Fateh Ali Khan and uncle Mubarik Ali Khan, but by the 1970s both were dead and Nusrat was ready to take up the mantle of qawwali master.

His greatest hits on the Oriental Star label, recorded for his domestic audience without ambient, dance and trip-hop remixes or guest vocals by big-name rock stars, run to more than fifty volumes. Many of them are concert recordings, and many of his fans believe the live setting shows him at his inspirational best, as he created endless, elaborate variations on a phrase in surging, hypnotic repetitions, eventually peaking in rapturous crescendos. But the most accessible introduction for first-time listeners are the more glossily produced albums on Gabriel's label.

These include more traditional recordings such as *Shkaken-shah* (1989), *Shahbaaz* (1991) and *The Last Prophet* (1994), as well as a brace of more experimental but sensitive albums produced by the Canadian electronic music maverick Michael Brook in *Musst Musst* (1990) and *Night Song* (1996). His crossover albums inevitably attracted some criticism from more conservative fans in Pakistan that the devotional character of the music was being debased.

Nusrat himself had no such problem; his open-mindedness was based on a belief that his East-meets-West crossover recordings provided a bridge to his more traditional work. Whether you hear in his sublime, ecstatic voice a spiritual devotion being offered to the Sufi saints and prophets, or the expression of a more secular and sensual love, the choice is really yours.

NW

playlist:

1 Jewleh-lal *from* Shahbaaz
A 25-minute chant down to ecstasy.

2 Musst Musst *from* Musst Musst
From Baluchistan to Bristol, Massive Attack remix qawwali in a trip-hop style.

3 Passion *from* Passion: Music for the Last Temptation of Christ
Gabriel offsets Nusrat's anguished tones with the purity of a boy soprano.

4 The Long Road *from* Dead Man Walking OST
A stunning duet from Nusrat and Eddie Vedder. With Ry Cooder along for the ride too.

5 Ghazal *from* En Concert A Paris Vol 2
A taste of the live experience recorded in 1985, Nusrat's magnificent voice is backed by harmonium, tabla and chorus on a setting of words by the greatest of all Sufi poets, Rumi.

Los De Abajo

Mexico's location makes it the perfect breeding-ground for exhilarating musical fusions, though few achieve a blend as striking as Mexico City's Los De Abajo. They call their breakneck sound "Tropipunk", while David Byrne, the Talking Heads singer who signed the group to his Luaka Bop record label, calls it "punk salsa". But these are simplistic ways of describing songs overloaded with cross-continental influences.

They intersperse dub reggae with Latin rock, samba, ska and horn-heavy hip-hop. Their track "Anda Levanta" is that all too rare thing: 100-miles-per-hour Mexican polka music with a human beatbox interlude. Those who don't speak Spanish needn't miss out, for Byrne helpfully had their lyrics translated in their album liner notes. The band are fiercely political. Their name translates as "Those From Below" and is taken from Mariano Azuela's 1915 novel about the Mexican Revolution. Strong supporters of Mexico's radical Zapatista movement, they have played numerous concerts to aid the cause, and a Zapatista leader, Comandante Esther, pops up on their most recent album.

However, Los De Abajo are not a po-faced bunch of politicos. The music comes first. Lead singer Liber Teran said that he wanted their sound to be "100 percent danceable", stating that they "always had an itch to mix the local with the global". They are at their most effective in concert, where every band member dances like a maniac, recalling Madness or the Specials in their flamboyant stage moves, and mass pogoing is a frequent occurrence. Having formed in 1992 as a quartet of school friends, the expansion in their number brought about a widening of their sound and an escalation in entertainment levels.

If they have suffered from any barriers to success it has been a struggle to capture their flamboyant live experience on record. Their debut album, *Latin Ska Force*, had to be released on their own label after lack of record company interest, although it has since gone on to sell some twenty thousand copies in Mexico City alone. Byrne was the champion who enabled their crossover success, his endorsement instantly pricking up the ears of world music fans globally.

In 2002 the band won a BBC Radio 3 World Music Award for their third album, *Cybertropic Chilango Power*. But it is 2006's *LDA vs The Lunatics* that is their most coherent – and fun – work. By recording mostly live, with the help of British producers Temple of Sound, an accurate snapshot of their wide-ranging thrills has finally been captured.

DS

where to start:

1 Sr. Judas *from* Cybertropic Chilango Power
The lyrics are a bitter rant against politicians who "feed on treason and lies". The music, in contrast, shifts irresistibly from reggae to shimmying salsa via bouncy hip-hop.

2 The Lunatics (Have Taken Over the Asylum) *from* LDA v The Lunatics
The band's most explicit tribute to their influences – a Latinized cover of a Fun Boy Three hit from 1981 – features original Fun Boy Neville Staples as guest.

Jimmy Cliff

He could've been... Bob Marley?

I n 1971, Island Records boss Chris Blackwell branched out into film. He cast the Jamaican singer Jimmy Cliff in the starring role of the film *The Harder They Come*. Blackwell had been grooming Cliff for several years to be the first reggae singer to cross over to a white rock audience, teaming him with British musicians on covers of songs such as "Whiter Shade of Pale". In the film Cliff played the notorious Kingston outlaw Ivan Rhygin. Watching the rushes of *The Harder They Come*, Blackwell grew more and more convinced that he could achieve his ambition by marketing Cliff as an updated version of the character he played in the film – a modern-day Rasta rebel with a swaggering, romantic sex appeal and an outsider image that an international audience would find irresistible.

Before Blackwell could put his plan into action, however, Cliff left Island Records for EMI. Given Blackwell's plans, it's rather ironic that Cliff's complaint was that his former label boss spent too much of his time on his rock catalogue to look after the interests of his reggae acts. A week after Cliff walked out in early 1972, Bob Marley walked in to Blackwell's London office. Marley's group, the Wailers, were stranded and penniless, and Marley asked Blackwell for help funding their fares back to Jamaica. Blackwell struck a deal, giving him £4000 in return for the delivery of an album. "I didn't know what to do after Jimmy Cliff left, because I had a plan but nobody to carry it out," Blackwell later recalled. "I was dealing with rock music, which was really rebel music. I felt that would really be the way to break Jamaican music but you needed someone who could be that image. When Bob walked in, he *was* that character, the real one that Jimmy had created in the movie." Later that year, Marley and the Wailers delivered Island an album called *Catch a Fire*, and the rest, as they say, is history.

Had Jimmy Cliff not left Island, would he have become an iconic king of reggae – the Third World's first genuine superstar? It's a question the singer must have asked himself a thousand times. Cliff's subsequent career didn't manifest the prolific songwriting genius of Marley's, yet who's to say what might have happened had he been given the push that Bob received?

Even in his sixties, Jimmy Cliff remains one of the great Jamaican singers, and anyone who has seen *The Harder They Come* will not need reminding of his charismatic presence. After the film, he made some fine records and enjoyed moderate success. But it might all have been so very different.

NW

Os Mutantes

Arnaldo Baptista has an intriguing explanation of what makes Brazilian music so compelling. "It's the historical mix – Incas, Africans, Europeans and beings from outer space," he says. There was certainly something otherworldly about his band, Os Mutantes, the Brazilian psychedelic legends who were often called the "South American Beatles" but who arguably had more in common with Pink Floyd and the strange, surreal acid visions of Syd Barrett: one of their biggest hits in Brazil was tellingly titled "Ando Meio Desligado" ("I'm Feeling Spaced Out").

Back in the late 1960s, Os Mutantes (Portuguese for "the Mutants") were effectively the house band of the Tropicalia movement, launched by Gilberto Gil and Caetano Veloso. Fusing Brazilian rhythms (with or without extraterrestrial influences) and sounds drawn from the progressive end of British and American rock, they recorded half a dozen extraordinary albums. But by the mid-1970s the band had fallen apart, collapsing under the weight of their philosophy of free love and liberal drug use beneath the oppression of a military dictatorship. At the time, few outside Brazil ever got to hear them, and by the 1980s Os Mutantes had become little more than a footnote in Brazilian music's history.

Then an extraordinary thing happened. In the early 1990s, a number of leading American rock stars started dropping the Os Mutantes name in conversation. Kurt Cobain begged them to reform, Beck named his album Mutations after them and David Byrne brought their music to a new audience with a compilation titled *Everything Is Possible*, released on his Luaka Bop label. When they finally reformed in 2006 to play their first ever show outside Brazil at London's Barbican Centre, Devendra Banhart wrote to the band asking if he could be their roadie. They rewarded his eagerness by making him their opening act instead.

Formed in 1966 by two Beatles-loving teenage brothers from São Paulo, Arnaldo Baptista (bass and keyboards) and Sérgio Dias (guitar), with Arnaldo's girlfriend and lead singer Rita Lee, the rebellious daughter of Italian-American immigrants, Os Mutantes swiftly became the most inventive and irreverent rock'n'roll group in Brazil. They found natural comrades and allies in the Tropicalia movement, backing many of its leading artists including Veloso and Gil, prior to their arrest and subsequent exile.

Tropicalia was a melange of bossa nova, samba, African and Portuguese influences, and rock'n'roll, fired by socially and politically conscious lyrics and based on the aesthetic of *antropofagia*, a kind of musical cannibalism which swallowed wholesale influences from diverse genres and cultures without prejudice in order to concoct something new and unique. "In Brazil, we received information as if through a kaleidoscope," Sérgio recalled many years later. "We never got the full picture, which actually is a good thing. We collected bits and pieces and made our own quilt out of it – not just The Beatles, but black American music and the avant-garde music of the time."

With a lack of decent equipment, Mutantes were also forced to find inventive ways of recreating the psychedelic sound effects they heard on imported rock records. According to one story, they didn't know how to replicate the backwards tape sounds they heard on "Tomorrow Never Knows" but found an approximation of the effect by aiming a can of fly killer at the microphone. A similarly improvised contraption was used to create the sound of a guitar wah-wah pedal. It was all done not merely with ingenuity but with a subversively surreal sense of humour. They also developed an eccentric stage presence, with Lee taking charge of dressing them up. For one gig they would appear as conquistadors, for the next they might be dressed as witches and the week after that they'd be attired as aliens.

Their peak didn't last long. Arnaldo's heavy LSD intake put him in a mental asylum and by 1973 he was no longer in the band. The following year Lee left. Sérgio Dias soldiered on with a ragbag of other musicians until 1978. And that was it until the 2006 reunion (which did not include Lee). Truth told, as the live album *Mutantes Ao Vivo – Barbican Theatre, Londres 2006* illustrates, it was a reunion that was longer on sentiment than musical excellence. But those original albums still sound fresh and intoxicating to this day.

NW

playlist:

1 Le Premier Bonheur du Jour *from* Os Mutantes
Gloriously catchy psychedelic pop at its most infectious.

2 A Minha Menina *from* Os Mutantes
Samba scuzz-rock that would do Link Wray proud – as covered later by The Bees.

3 Baby *from* Everything Is Possible
A swooning version of a Caetano Veloso classic.

4 Bat Macumba *from* Os Mutantes
Gilberto Gil's Tropicalia anthem, psyched-up Mutantes-style.

5 Ando Meio Desligado *from* A Divina Comédia Ou Ando Meio Desligado
The Brazilian Pink Floyd indeed … and a much funkier one at that.

6 Ave, Lucifer *from* A Divina Comédia Ou Ando Meio Desligado
Slithering between rural Brazilian folk song and a very *Wicker Man* pagan trippiness, this song oddly anticipates the ugly-but-beautiful vertigo of The Pixies.

Ernest Ranglin

Ernest Ranglin's first instrument was the ukulele, and his first musical hero was the American jazz guitarist Charlie Christian. Yet it is the music of Jamaica – the birth of ska and then its mutation into reggae – that the guitarist was so influential upon. He is in many ways the godfather of modern Jamaican music. Besuited, bespectacled and benign of both manner and speech, he perhaps cut an unlikely figure as reggae's guru. He also had no time for Rastafarianism and regarded its adherents as deeply misguided. Yet without him the work of most of the island's greatest musicians, from Prince Buster to Bob Marley, might have sounded very different.

Born in rural Jamaica in 1932, Ranglin's family moved to Kingston when he was fourteen. He taught himself to play the guitar from tuition books and by watching the Jamaican dance bands of the day. By the age of sixteen he was playing in one of them. At the time Jamaican big bands were more or less straight copies of their American counterparts, with perhaps a touch more Cuban mambo to them. The event that was to change Ranglin's career – and the course of Jamaican music – came in 1958 when he was playing at the Half Moon Hotel in Montego Bay. He was heard by a youthful Chris Blackwell, who immediately offered him the chance to make a record. It was also Blackwell's first production and the first ever release for Island Records.

The following year, as the guitarist with Clue J & His Blues Blasters, Ranglin recorded the instrumental "Shuffling Bug", widely regarded as the first example of ska, emphasizing the shuffle rhythm of the New Orleans jump beat to create the sound that has been pretty much the bedrock of Jamaican music ever since. Ranglin's guitar was then heard on Prince Buster's groundbreaking early hits, and he teamed up again with Blackwell to record "My Boy Lollipop" in London with teenage singer Millie Small. The record made number two in the British charts in 1964, the first time ska or anything like it had infiltrated the vocabulary of Western pop music. Ranglin also became something of a mentor to Bob Marley and is widely credited with helping him slow down the ska rhythm to create the simmering variant that became known as reggae.

Almost forty years after their first association, Ranglin teamed up again with his first label boss for a series of fine reggae-jazz instrumental albums on Blackwell's new label, Palm Pictures. While they were as suave and cosmopolitan as any release on Blue Note, they always had that home thud of bass and clip-clop of guitar that is reggae's root – one Mr Ranglin always returned to.

NW

The weirdest voices you've ever heard?

Thanks to myriad cunning technologies in today's studios, modern recordings feature perfectly competent singing performances. These might not actually represent what emerged from the singers' mouths, but we end up hearing nicely compressed vocal performances, gently tweaked to the right pitch and banishing any human error. We've almost come to expect this. And, as a result, unusual idiosyncratic voices tend to be a lot thinner on the ground. Rather like the techniques of athletes, they've been standardized to conform to a generic norm.

So where can we dig up some off-kilter, expressive voices that show some genuine emotion? If you ask a cross-section of music fans what the greatest singing voices in the worlds of rock and pop are, the same names will keep cropping up: the almost operatic pizzazz of Rufus Wainwright; the gravelly, untutored tones of Johnny Cash; the occasionally primal wailings of Jeff Buckley, and before him his father Tim; or the effortless leaps and trills of Liz Fraser from the Cocteau Twins. There are other instantly recognizable voices – Morrissey or Roy Orbison for instance – whose familiarity has almost dampened our appreciation of their talent. Indeed, while the Bee Gees were once lampooned for their effeminate vocal style, today they're accepted as part of the musical backdrop, and while Björk has become an Olympic Games-opening global megastar, we forget quite the stir she made back in 1987 when The Sugarcubes' "Birthday" hit the airwaves for the first time.

But while these names are familiar to most of us, there are plenty of unsung heroes to rewind and discover, each with a fearsome pair of lungs. From the warbling counter tenor of the Tiger Lillies' Martin Jacques to the hoarse, almost desperate roar of Swans' Michael Gira; from the nervous squeak of MC Doseone to the preposterously expressive shriek of Diamanda Galas – they're all to be cherished for never needing or indeed wanting to be subjected to the oppressive regime of the studio's Auto-Tune function. Oh, and let's not forget the screams of black metal and speedcore bands. Even if you don't like what you hear, you've got to admit that they can sing.

Yma Sumac

Magenta Mountain *from* Miracles
The self-styled "Inca Princess", born in Peru back in the early 1920s, Yma Sumac has astonished audiences for decades with her ability to slide effortlessly up and down the musical scale – indeed, her range was claimed to be around five octaves when she was at her peak. This particular track opens with a remarkably high melody line that threatens to be audible only to dogs.

Fantomas

The Omen Ave Safari *from* The Director's Cut
If you're not that fond of Faith No More, why bother investigating any of the side projects of singer Mike Patton? Because he probably has the biggest range of styles of any rock singer you can think of. You can hear them quickly and easily in the chop/change music of Fantomas – caressing whispers and fully fledged screaming in the space of a few seconds. You won't accidentally fall asleep, that's for sure.

Laibach

Tanz Mit Laibach *from* Wat
Laibach's singer, Milan Fras, was making us tremble with his throaty bellow while the majority of the current wave of German and Scandinavian black-metallers were still in nappies. If you were feeling uncharitable, you could lay the blame at his door for spawning dozens of sub-standard imitations – but his voice has lost none of its power over the years, as demonstrated by this extraordinary track from 2003.

Huun-Huur-Tu

Mountain Voice *from* Spirits from Tuva
While most of our extraordinary singers were born with a larynx that produced something out of the ordinary, Tuvan throat singing (from the plains of Siberia) is a technique that takes decades to master. The overtones it generates give the effect of a voice singing in harmony with itself, and the singer of Huun-Huur-Tu – Albert Kuvezin – is acknowledged as one of the world's finest exponents.

Dead Can Dance

Sauvean *from* Toward the Within
The word "haunting" is bandied about far too often in music reviews, and usually used to describe things that are merely not very jolly. But Lisa Gerrard's contralto could genuinely be classified as such, from the earliest albums of her band, Dead Can Dance, to her more stately solo and soundtrack work.

David Thomas

Confuse Did *from* Sound of the Sand
Pere Ubu's David Thomas could never be described as having a great technique, but what he lacked in musicianship he made up for with sheer bravado. That eye-popping tenor voice emerging from his bulky frame always made for a disconcerting but fantastic spectacle, and recognition of his talent has taken him out of the world of rock and into theatres and concert halls across the world.

RM

Ali Farka Touré

If the dusty trance blues of Ali Farka Touré is not among the most mesmerizing music you've never heard, then you should probably trade this book for a new pair of ears. Jimmy Page once likened hearing him for the first time to discovering Robert Johnson, and it's not without reason that *Savane* is sub-titled "King of the Desert Blues Singers", in homage to the classic Johnson LP.

Born on the banks of the River Niger in northwest Mali in 1939, Ali lived for most of his life in the village of Niafunké, where he eventually became the local mayor. He was his mother's tenth son, but the only one to survive past infancy. According to a custom observed in such tragic circumstances, a surviving child is given an unusual nickname. In Ali's case, it was Farka, meaning donkey – an animal of strength and tenacity. A devout Muslim, Ali also had a profound belief in the power of the djinns, or spirits, believed to inhabit the river, and as a boy was captivated by the traditional music played at village ceremonies to summon them. The legend goes that Robert Johnson acquired his guitar skills by signing a pact with the devil, whom he met standing at a crossroads on the twelfth stroke of midnight. There's a similarly mythical tale concerning the musical epiphany of Ali Farka Touré. As a child he had an encounter with a strangely marked snake, which wrapped itself around his head before he brushed it off. He then suffered a series of dizzying "attacks", and spent a year at the village of Hombori being cured. Upon his return, he found he could communicate with the spirits very well, a gift that was quickly recognized by the village.

Ali had made his first instrument, a one-string guitar known as a *djerkel*, at the age of twelve, only graduating to a borrowed six-string instrument in 1956. His musical enthusiasms were not encouraged by his family, but in addition to his considerable guitar skills Ali also learned percussion and accordion skills – rumour has it that he even played some Charles Aznavour numbers at a couple of shows. After years spent absorbing a vast repertoire of traditional music from different ethnic sources, including Sonrai, Peul and Tamaschek, he first heard American music in 1968, when a friend in Bamako played him imported records by James Brown, Albert King and John Lee Hooker. He always insisted that his own music was not influenced by them; any similarities between what he played and American blues and funk was merely down to their common West African roots.

By the 1970s, he had moved to Bamako, Mali's capital, where he spent a decade working as an engineer for Radio Mali. He also recorded regular acoustic guitar recitals for the station and the best of these were later compiled on *Radio Mali* in 1996. Although the recordings are rudimentary in terms of audio fidelity, the tracks possess an undeniable power, and in 1975 he sent tapes of them to a specialist label in Paris. A few months later, his first Western release appeared on vinyl LP. Over the next few years, the French label released six more LPs, all recorded in Bamako. The original albums are now hard to find, but

playlist:

1 Monsieur le Maire de Niafunké *from* In the Heart of the Moon
A wonderfully stately duet between Ali and Toumani Diabaté, written by the *kora* player as a tribute to his collaborator.

2 Erdi *from* Savane
The deepest desert blues, with wailing harmonica from London's own Little George Suaref.

3 Lasidan *from* Talking Timbuktu
Magical guitar alchemy between Ali and Ry Cooder.

4 Mahini Me *from* The Source
With Taj Mahal on second guitar, recorded backstage at the Waterfront, Norwich.

5 Yulli *from* Ali Farka Touré
A song about camels – perhaps the best song ever written about camels – composed by Ali way back in 1963.

6 Kenouna *from* The River
A fishing song of the Bozo people of Mopti, with an added touch of the Irish courtesy of fiddle and bodhran from a couple of Chieftains.

7 Ali's Here *from* Niafunké
"This is a message to my people that honey does not taste good in one mouth. I'm here and I'm going to share it. Everything I have gained through my music goes back to the land for the people."

8 Yer Mali Gakoyoyo *from* Radio Mali
Acoustic wizardry recorded in the 1970s when, in Ali's own words, "I was an absolute fool for the guitar".

9 Devele Wague *from* Red & Green
Devil woman, Malian-style – needless to say the voodoo of Ali FT is significantly more potent than Cliff Richard's.

10 Tabara *from* Vieux Farka Touré
One of Ali's final recordings and one of his finest, recorded for his son's debut album.

two of them were later re-released on CD as *Red & Green* in 2004.

Disillusioned by his financial dealings with the Western music industry, Ali had effectively retired by the 1980s, returning to Niafunke to farm his land. Then in 1987 he was tracked down by the London-based World Circuit label and persuaded to play his first concerts in Western Europe. While in London, he cut his first album to be recorded outside Mali. Although it still sounded authentic and earthy, *Ali Farke Touré* (1988) benefited hugely from Western studio production. It was followed by *The River* in 1990, which found Ali rocking out on electric guitar. *The Source*, two years later, was another advance and included two duets with Taj Mahal, recorded backstage in a dressing room in Norwich, of all places.

The collaboration with Taj Mahal led to the idea of Ali travelling to America to record an album of gui-

tar duets with Ry Cooder. Ali hated Los Angeles but found a rare empathy with Cooder and the resulting album, *Talking Timbuktu* (1994), won a Grammy. After that, he became increasingly reluctant to leave his West African fields, insisting that he was a full-time farmer and a part-time musician. To make 1999's *Niafunké*, his label had to ship a mobile studio and generator to his village and record him by night, after the day's labour had been done. Another seven years lapsed before *Savane*, recorded in Bamako. At the same sessions he also recorded *In the Heart of the Moon*, a stunningly beautiful set of guitar and *kora* duets with the master of the African harp, Toumani Diabaté. These two virtuosi had never recorded together before but there was a feeling of destiny to their long-anticipated rendezvous. If the album's music lacked a little of the bluesy grit of Ali's vintage work, it had a majesty and stateliness all of its own. Ali died from bone cancer in 2006. The last recordings he made squared the circle – playing guitar for the debut album by his son, Vieux Farka Touré.

NW

Suppressed music:
the illegal, the persecuted and the obscene

Ever since Elvis first swivelled a hip in the direction of America's teenagers and opened unprecedented floodgates of hormonal hysteria, pop music has outraged just as many people as it has thrilled. The sound of rebellion, shocking the squares is part of its *raison d'être*. The US censorship lobby achieved a victory of sorts with the arrival of the "Parental Advisory: Explicit Content" sticker in 1985, although in reality it is hard to conceive of a warning that would appeal more to curious children.

Freedom of expression is a vital facet of any art form, so a musician really has to go the extra mile to be banned outright. And bans have often been blessings in disguise. The BBC's refusal to air "God Save the Queen" by the Sex Pistols, released during Her Majesty's Silver Jubilee year, resulted in enough publicity to guarantee the single a high chart placing in June 1977.

Today, the Internet allows even the most controversial recordings to be heard. Hip-hop producer Brian "Danger Mouse" Burton's 2004 recording, *The Grey Album*, gained overnight notoriety for reasons of copyright infringement, but that didn't stop it from becoming what the New York Times called "the most popular album in rock history that virtually no one paid for", and receiving rave reviews for its music. As a calling card to show off his skills to industry insiders, Danger Mouse had painstakingly put together an incredibly inventive mix of vocals from the rapper Jay-Z's *Black Album* with hip-hop beats derived from music on The Beatles' *White Album*.

After it leaked onto the Internet, The Beatles' record label,

EMI, ordered Danger Mouse and retailers carrying the album to cease distribution. On 24 February 2004, nearly 200 websites made the album available to download for 24 hours, a coordinated act of civil disobedience that participants dubbed "Grey Tuesday". The album is still available on peer-to-peer file-sharing sites, and made enough of a name for Danger Mouse that he went on to more respectable success with Gorillaz and Gnarls Barkley.

More unsavoury was the 1987 obscenity trial of Californian punk band the Dead Kennedys, whose band name was just the tip of the iceberg in terms of the controversy they generated. Inside the sleeve of their third album, *Frankenchrist*, they included a poster of H.R. Giger's Landscape #20, a photograph of three rows of penises penetrating anuses. Singer Jello Biafra and record label boss Michael Bonanno were put on trial for distributing harmful matter to minors. Although they were cleared after a hung jury, the legal costs and distraction of the case irreparably damaged the band. They split soon afterwards, although the acerbic, creative punk rock of *Frankenchrist* is still well worth a listen. Stuffed with jibes at the corpulence of America's pop culture and satirical protests at the injustices of the US economy, the album hears the DKs extending their musical range well beyond the hardcore thrash they're best known for. There are spaghetti-Western horn parts, Mexican surf-guitar riffs and grinding industrial keyboards backing up Biafra's camp and petulant sneers.

Yet the travails of Western cultural provocateurs are nothing compared to those endured by Czech rock band the Plastic People of the Universe. The band formed after the Soviets invaded Czechoslovakia in 1968, putting an end to the brief, hopeful period of political liberalization known as the Prague Spring.

The band's psychedelic rock'n'roll, inspired by the Velvet Underground and Frank Zappa, was banned after they were denied musician's licences in 1970.

They went underground, performing secret gigs and writing songs using lyrics by the banned Czech philosopher and surrealist Egon Bondy. Founder Mejla Hlavsa said they felt "more like a guerrilla group than a rock'n'roll band". In 1976 they were arrested and imprisoned for "organized disturbance of the peace", a significant event that partially inspired Václav Havel and his cohorts to write the Charter 77 manifesto, which eventually led to the Velvet Revolution and Havel's presidency. There aren't many musicians who can say the act of playing rock music has changed the history of their country.

DS

THE ART SCHOOL
conceptualists, bohemians and the too-clever-by-half

Amon Duul II

The northern borough of Schwabing was Munich's very own Greenwich Village – in the late 1960s, it was home to a bohemian band of artists, musicians and politicos. The English pop band Kippington Lodge landed at Schwabing in 1968, on a tour of Germany. Featuring a line-up that included a young Nick Lowe and bassist Dave Anderson, they settled into a two-week residency at the PN Hit House club, playing their brand of Home Counties psychedelia to Munich's acid heads and doped-up hippies.

They shared their Monday nights at the Hit House with an extraordinary local band who had an even odder name. Amon Duul were emblematic of the communally minded, creative spirits that had put cities like Munich on the post-war countercultural map. To begin with, the dozen or so members of the Amon Duul collective used music simply to promote their artistic and ideological pursuits – politicized by Germany's traumatic history, they fervently embraced the causes of the day. As factions arose within the commune, the group split into two distinct bands. It was soon clear that it was Amon Duul II who held all the musical cards.

Amon Duul's music was so weird that Anderson and Lowe kept going back to see them. As the fortnight drew to an end, Anderson was so enchanted by the German rock-

ers he auditioned to be the bass player, an experience which, he says, turned into a competition to see who could smoke the most joints. Lowe and company moved on to the next town and Anderson joined Amon Duul, alongside the nucleus of the band – guitarists Chris Karrer and John Weinzierl, drummer Peter Leopold and singer Renate Knaup.

Amon Duul's Teutonic, post-psychedelic ur-glam invited comparisons with early Pink Floyd, and one could perhaps tag them as a German Velvet Underground. Studios saw them as a liability, and probably not a little frightening, so the band recorded quickly and viewed rehearsals as a largely superfluous exercise. *Phallus Dei*, the first release, was done and dusted in 24 hours. *Yeti*, the bombastic double album that broke them in the UK and gave them a fearsome reputation, took just three days to make. After a couple of years in Munich, an exhausted Anderson returned to London and, in 1970, signed up with their British equivalent, Hawkwind – leaving Amon Duul to a further thirty-odd years of recording and playing.

RW

playlist:

1 Phallus Dei *from* Phallus Dei
A rumbling bass underlines the title track from the band's extraordinary debut album, pointing the way ahead for German rock at the dawn of the 1970s. The title didn't exactly help sales.

2 Archangel Thunderbird *from* Yeti
Renate's distinctive vocal is pitched somewhere between Yoko Ono and PiL-era John Lydon on this immense, riff-laden track from the band's breakthrough album.

3 Yeti *from* Yeti
Krautrock goes prog in a full-on, twenty-minute cosmic improvisation that stretches out into the future, yet leaves you with the feeling you're still light years behind.

4 All the Years Round *from* Carnival in Babylon
More conventional songs were beginning to fall to earth by the fourth album. This heavenly track became the closest thing the band had to a radio hit in the early 1970s: they even made a promo video for it.

5 Wie der Wind am Ende einer Strasse *from* Wolf City
It's not all doom and gloom on the fifth album: this early example of world fusion floats by in a deep trance, to an exotic (in 1972) pulse of tablas, tambura and sitar, complemented by Paul Heyda's expressive violin.

Can

The Beatles put the German avant-garde composer Karlheinz Stockhausen on the cover of *Sgt Pepper's Lonely Hearts Club Band* (fifth from left, back row, between W.C. Fields and Lenny Bruce). Can, on the other hand, had two members who had actually been students of Stockhausen. They also had a drummer schooled in improvisational free jazz. It's surely no accident that it took a group of German musicians from a culture that had no rock'n'roll tradition of its own to step outside the box and create a sound so revolutionary. It was music for the head, but you could dance to it too. "We were never a normal rock group," noted the band's keyboardist Irwin Schmidt. "Can was an anarchist community."

Formed in Cologne in 1968, the core members of Can all had backgrounds in avant-garde and improvisational music. Schmidt and bassist Holger Czukay, both of whom were born in pre-war Germany, had studied under Stockhausen and were involved in the contemporary classical repertoire. Drummer Jaki Liebezeit was of a similar age but was involved in free jazz. Guitarist Michael Karoli was a decade younger and a pupil of Czukay with an interest in art-rock, who turned teacher when he introduced his tutor to the music of Hendrix, Zappa and the Velvet Underground. Out of these diverse backgrounds they formed an improvisational group initially called Inner Space which soon became Can (an acronym for "communism, anarchism, nihilism").

Such a strange "geometry of people" as Karoli described it, required an equally unusual singer. Can were lucky enough to find two over their lifespan: first the black American Malcolm Mooney and then a backpacking Japanese busker called Damo Suzuki. Neither could be called a singer in any conventional sense. Both specialized in demented acid-visionary howling that was perfect for the kind of avant-funk that Can were refining.

Can's early works were raw and exploratory but by the end of 1970, when they moved their "anarchist community" into a castle outside Cologne and set up a studio called Inner Space, the building blocks were in place. Inspired by the writings of Aleister Crowley, *Tago Mago* (1971) was the result. The machine-like drumming and the throbbing bass lines created a locked-down groove that owed much to black dance rhythms. The distorted guitars and keyboards owed more to the sound-scapes of Pink Floyd – though free of the Floyd's tendency to portentousness. They were fused together via a jam-and-chop methodology that involved hours of collective improvising that was then edited into coherent tracks. Never had music sounded so abstract and yet so physical at the same time.

Ege Bamyasi (1972) was conceived in similar vein but *Future Days* (1973) found them advancing on all fronts, an aural vision that was blissful, sensual, melancholic, euphoric, glacial, ambient and undulating but flecked with violent squalls and moments of abrasion, and which on many levels still sounds futuristic today. Following its release, Suzuki left to become a Jehovah's Witness but Can had one more masterpiece to unleash from inside their castle walls with *Soon Over Babaluma* (1974). An iridescent, abstruse brain-funk collage, if you could hear an M.C. Escher drawing, one critic remarked, it would surely sound something like *Soon Over Babaluma*.

Can's growing cult following earned them a contract in 1975 with Virgin and although there is still some great music on their later albums, for whatever reason they never sounded quite so revolutionary again. By the time of *Saw Delight* (1977) they had added a couple of rock journeymen percussionists in Reebob Kwaku Bah and Rosko Gee and were sounding dangerously like a prog-rock band. By the end of the 1970s they had disbanded but they reformed briefly in the late 1980s for the surprisingly good *Rite Time* (1989). Even more surprising was the return on the record of a much calmer-sounding Mooney, apparently motivated to get back in touch when he found an air ticket to Europe down the back of an old sofa. *NW*

playlist:

1 Halleluwah *from* Tago Mago
Eighteen minutes of monster trance/funk beats – like James Brown jamming with the Velvet Underground.

2 Aumgn *from* Tago Mago
Dense and intense, it took rock music to places it had never been before.

3 Mushroom *from* Tago Mago
A sonic storm of polyrhythms, later covered by the Jesus and Mary Chain and "borrowed" by the Flaming Lips.

4 Bel Air *from* Future Days
Bucolic and beatific, complete with birdsong and animal sounds.

5 Quantum Physics *from* Soon Over Babaluma
Polydimensional funk mathematics.

Captain Beefheart

Don Van Vliet has long been accepted as a major figure in rock history, revered by critics and name-checked by countless other artists. But although just about everyone acknowledges him as a seminal figure, few have actually spent any serious time intimately getting to know *Trout Mask Replica*, *Shiny Beast (Bat Chain Puller)* or any of the other dozen albums he made in a fifteen-year spell of extraordinary creativity, before prematurely ending his recording career in 1982. His music is more often talked about than listened to.

He formed the first Magic Band in 1965, built around his own Howlin' Wolf-style vocals. Signed to A&M, their sound swiftly grew more experimental and the label was so appalled when Beefheart delivered the demos for the band's first album that they promptly dropped them. With the addition of Ry Cooder on slide guitar, the band reworked the material, which eventually appeared on the Buddah label as *Safe as Milk* in 1967. In comparison to some of what was to come later, *Safe as Milk* sounds like a relatively conventional blues-rock record, with some typical late-1960s touches. But at the time its mix of blues, rock and jazz time signatures, growled, unconventional lyrics and unusual instrumentation, such as the theremin, was groundbreaking and quite unlike anything else, even in the experimental pastures of the underground rock scene.

Cooder didn't hang around for the second album, *Strictly Personal* (1968), a more overtly acid-rock affair with the addition of phasing and backwards tape loops. The album was later reissued in 1992 as *I May Be Hungry But I Sure Ain't Weird*, without the psychedelic embellishments, and it's a fascinating exercise to compare the two.

Buddah was a pop label and an unlikely home for Beefheart's increasingly surreal visions. Enter

Frank Zappa. He formed his own Straight label in 1968 and immediately signed Beefheart, with a promise of total artistic freedom. With Zappa producing, everything about *Trout Mask Replica* (1969) shouted "weird", from its bizarre fish-head cover to the surreal song titles and the even odder appellations he gave the Magic Band, in which guitarist Bill Harkleroad became "Zoot Horn Rollo", bassist Mark Boston was "Rockette Morton", drummer John French became "Drumbo", and second guitarist Jeff Cotton was rechristened "Antennae Jimmy Semens".

The angular, distorted, iconoclastic music inside drew on Delta blues and free jazz. But Beefheart fashioned it into an entirely new sonic universe, with distended rhythms, frenzied slide guitar, and squalling saxophone and bass clarinet, topped off by his own unimaginably alien vocals. To many, Beefheart's lyrics were impenetrable nonsense. Yet buried in the weirdness was a rich seam of allusion, wordplay and metaphor, and *Trout Mask Replica* is one of the few records that genuinely did change the way rock music sounded. Few, if any, attempted to imitate: Beefheart was far too unique for direct mimicry. But almost every rock'n'roll surrealist who came after owed a debt to *Trout Mask Replica* for reimagining what was possible in popular music.

Lick My Decals Off, Baby (1970) was fashioned in similar vein and found Beefheart addressing ecological and environmental issues long before it was fashionable to do so.

Then came a series of albums that disappointed his hardcore followers – *The Spotlight Kid*, *Clear Spot*, *Unconditionally Guaranteed* and *Bluejeans and Moonbeams* (both 1974). Beefheart was accused of attempting to join the commercial mainstream. Such accusations were relative and his take on soft rock still sounded a world away from the Eagles, but it was undeniable that the feral unpredictability of *Trout Mask Replica* had been tamed.

Shiny Beast (Bat Chain Puller), long delayed due to legal wrangling, eventually appeared in 1978 and represented a return to his earlier, more challenging style and, in a prolific and creative coda to his strange career, he signed off with a brace of further Magic Band classics in the two early 1980s albums *Doc at the Radar Station* and *Ice Cream for Crow*. After that, he retired to the Mojave Desert, California, to concentrate on painting and sculpting and has never been tempted back to music.

A biography by Colin David Webb, *Captain Beefheart: The Man and His Music*, began with the words: "Genius, charlatan, freak show or egomaniac?" The probable answer is that he was all four. What is certain is that, while he's an avowed influence on everyone from Johnny Rotten to Mark E. Smith, Tom Waits, Nick Cave and P.J. Harvey – to name a few – nobody before or since has ever sounded quite like him.

NW

playlist:

1 Sure Nuff 'N Yes I Do *from* Safe as Milk
The opening track from the debut album is the first an astonished world heard of Don's magnificently mutant blues – and his psychedelically warped band.

2 Electricity *from* Safe as Milk
Buzzing theremin, the mighty Ry Cooder on slide guitar and the Captain's best feral bellow.

3 Ah Feel Like Ahcid *from* Strictly Personal
Psychedelic blues at its most unsettling... bad trips and bummers are guaranteed.

4 Ella Guru *from* Trout Mask Replica
Almost a pop tune. Then the guitars fracture, the sonic hurricane blows and Don delivers a bestial vocal in one of the best moments from his peerless masterpiece.

5 My Human Gets Me Blues *from* Trout Mask Replica
Discordant, abrasive guitars, crazed time signatures and a rollercoaster ride of surrealist abandon. An average day for the Captain, then.

6 Dachau Blues *from* Trout Mask Replica
Dark, convoluted visions of the atrocities of war, with a vocal so intense you barely notice the music – notwithstanding a blistering clarinet solo from "The Mascara Snake" (the Captain's cousin).

7 Neon Meate Dream of A Octafish *from* Trout Mask Replica
Neo-Beat poetry meets folk myth against a backing of mind-boggling musical complexity as the Captain gasps out the sexual lyric with asthmatic excitement.

8 I Love You, You Big Dummy *from* Lick My Decals Off, Baby
Romance the Van Vliet way – "Love has no body ... Nobody has love" – probably wouldn't shift many Valentine's cards.

9 Big Eyed Beans from Venus *from* Clear Spot
"Mr Zoot Horn Rollo, hit that long lunar note and let it float" – one hell of an insight into the Beefheartian school of musical direction.

10 The Past Sure is Tense *from* Ice Cream for Crow
And it's good night from Don.

Faust

F lush with the success of *Tubular Bells*, Virgin had a great idea to promote their newest signing. Faust came from the same stable as fellow West Germans Can and Amon Duul and were proving, if anything, even more difficult to sell in the UK. In 1973, two albums into their career, the band pressed up some informal home recordings, as a stop-gap release. Virgin's wheeze was to issue *The Faust Tapes* at the price of a single: 49 pence. Thousands of copies were sold in a matter of weeks – Virgin claimed sales peaked at 60,000. If "Revolution #9", from The Beatles' *White Album*, is the most widely circulated piece of avant-garde pop, then *The Faust Tapes* is probably in second place.

The cut-and-paste format of *The Faust Tapes* is still hard to get your head around, and was all the more so back in 1973. Heavy-duty organ improvisations segue into random sax honks and trance-like electronics. Amid ambient chit-chat, footsteps plod towards the sound of telephone dialling. Shunting drum-and-bass riffs dissolve into gorgeous piano ballads. It's "the sound of yourself listening", as Julian Cope so artily puts it in his book, *Krautrocksampler*. On the original sleeve, none of the 26 tracks was titled and the band themselves were a mystery. Just who the hell were Faust?

Hans Joachim Irmler, Jean Hervé Peron, Werner "Zappi" Diermaier, Rudolf Sosna, Gunther Wusthoff and Armulf Meifert first convened as Faust in Wumme, West Germany, in 1971, brought together by the producer Uwe Nettelbeck. With an advance from the go-ahead German division of Polydor, Nettelbeck converted a disused schoolhouse into a recording studio. In isolation, the band crafted a unique, minimalist deconstruction of rock music.

Even without hearing it, it was clear that their first album was going to be something rather unusual. *Faust* was pressed on clear vinyl and packaged in a transparent sleeve. It acquired a cult following but sold next to nothing. The second, *So Far*, caught the attention of Virgin, who signed them in 1972 but ditched them two years later, after the commercial failure of the slightly more accessible *Faust IV*. Virgin's big giveaway may not, as they claimed, have lost the label money (indeed, they repeated the gimmick with Gong's album *Camembert Electrique*). Even if many of the 60,000 copies did end up in the trash or the local charity shop, it established this hard-to-categorize band as one of the most intriguing and least compromising of the Krautrockers.

RW

playlist:

1 Chère chambre *from* The Faust Tapes
The exception that proves the rule. Sung in French and German, Jean-Hervé Peron's closing number for the anarchic *Faust Tapes* is an intimate ballad, revealing Faust to be a band full of surprises.

2 Krautrock *from* Faust IV
Nudge up the volume and this one-chord exercise in ear-bleeding noise will burst from your hi-fi like a speeding bullet, recorded in the comfy confines of Virgin's Manor studio.

3 It's a Rainy Day (Sunshine Girl) *from* So Far
The opening number of *So Far* builds from a stark tom-tom rhythm to a climax with an impressive sax solo, and was amongst the tracks that got them noticed at Virgin.

4 J'ai mal aux dents *from* The Faust Tapes
In 1994, when the band played this key *Faust Tapes* track live in Hamburg, an American approached them to thank them for playing his favourite song, which he'd misheard as "Shempal Buddha". Since then, the band has referred to it by this mondegreen.

5 Giggy Smile *from* Faust IV
"Psychotic and jumpy", in the words of Julian Cope, it owes something to John Cale's work with the Velvet Underground, with a little Spanish flamenco and space-rock thrown in.

The Justified Ancients of Mu Mu

Bill Drummond and Jimmy Cauty are a duo probably best remembered for creating a deliberately nauseating number one single in 1988. Under the name The Timelords, they combined elements of Gary Glitter's "Rock and Roll" with the theme from *Doctor Who*, then wrote a bestselling "manual" about how they did it. They ultimately burned a million pounds of the money they earned from the project – either as a profound artistic statement or an elaborate publicity stunt, depending on your point of view.

But long before that, the two music biz veterans had already courted controversy as one of the first acts to wake up the cosy world of music copyright to the nemesis that was sampling. In early 1987, 12" white labels of a hip-hop track entitled "All You Need Is Love", and credited to The Justified Ancients of Mu Mu, began circulating among British music journalists. It heavily sampled The Beatles – a practice which even today is a non-negotiable impossibility – along with MC5, Samantha Fox, and a government public information film warning of the dangers of AIDS. While distributors refused to handle the record, it created enough of a buzz for the Justified Ancients of Mu Mu (as they were then styling themselves) to do a re-cut, replacing enough of the sampled material to get the record into the shops. When it was eventually released in May 1987, this collage of found sounds was heralded as a triumph of the cut-up technique. While breakbeat had already established the practice of using existing tracks to build new ones, this wholesale ransacking of material proved something of a revelation, and combined with the chilling AIDS-related message it made for one of the most exhilarating records of that year. Emboldened by the success of the 12", the JAMMs recorded their debut album, *1987, What the Fuck is Going On*, and pushed the abuse of copyright to extremes: the track "The Queen and I", for example, is little more than Abba's *Dancing Queen* overlaid with a hip-hop beat. Indeed, it was Abba who put a substantial Swedish spanner in the works, with a legal showdown forcing the album to be withdrawn and all existing copies burned. The JAMMs did this, with typical flair, in a Swedish field with a photographer from the *NME* present. Artistically, the group would never equal *All You Need is Love* – not that they were particularly bothered. Less than a year later, their grotesquely Frankensteinian masterpiece "Doctorin' the Tardis" reached number one in the charts – a record that veteran DJ Richard Skinner described as "an aberration". Drummond and Cauty must have been delighted.

The pair never looked back, and had a string of hit singles under the name KLF that trod a fine line between exhilarating chart house music and irritating novelty song. They roped in such unlikely collaborators as the country singer Tammy Wynette and, for one infamous live performance, thrash metallers Extreme Noise Terror and a freshly slaughtered sheep.

It's their straightest material that seems to have stood the test of time the best. The original version of their endlessly revised and remixed signature tune "What Time Is Love?" has an intensity and economy that holds its own against the meanest of house music from 1988 – a vintage year. Bill Drummond's solo album *The Man*, recorded with Aussie rock band The Triffids, is a curious and charming country-rock set. And 1990's *Chill Out* is probably the only ambient album anyone will ever really need.

RM

3:00 AM

Pere Ubu

"**P**ere Ubu is not now, nor has it ever been a viable commercial venture," David Thomas once asserted. "We won't sleep on floors, we won't tour endlessly and we're embarrassed by self-promotion. Add to that a laissez-faire attitude to the mechanics of career advancement and a demanding artistic agenda and you've got a recipe for real failure. That has been our one significant success to this date: we are the longest-lasting, most disastrous commercial outfit to ever appear in rock'n'roll."

What's in a name? Sometimes an awful lot. You probably don't need to hear a single note by Pere Ubu to realize that a band taking their name from a play by the French absurdist Alfred Jarry is hardly going to be your standard meat-and-two-veg, Midwestern garage rock combo. Led by David Thomas, the band's only constant presence for more than thirty years, Pere Ubu early on perfected the raw punk aggression you'd expect from a band that came roaring out of the decaying industrial wasteland of the rust-bucket that was Cleveland, Ohio, in the 1970s. But from the outset, Thomas had a fascination with found sound, musique concrète, industrial noise and other more abstract, abstruse and avant-garde forms.

The son of a professor of American literature and a book illustrator, Thomas was an improbably bookish candidate as an iconoclastic punk rocker: his brother became a chemical engineer and his sister a US government geologist. After his first group, the Stooges-influenced Rocket From The Tombs, fragmented in 1975, several members coalesced as The Dead Boys while Thomas put together Pere Ubu with guitarist Peter Laughner. They set out their avant-garage manifesto with a brace of early singles, including "30 Seconds Over Tokyo" and "Final Solution", which created a sonic bombardment that mixed punk thrashing with arty dissonance, spooky analogue synths and Thomas's weird, atonal howling. This led to dates at Max's Kansas City in New York and eventually to a record deal with Polygram's short-lived new wave label, Blank. But by this time Peter Laughner had left the band, taking his

nihilistic aesthetic with him. He died of acute pancreatitis at the age of 24, brought on by drug and alcohol abuse.

The band's 1978 debut *The Modern Dance* was one of the defining albums of the era. This was punk rock informed by experimental influences such as Captain Beefheart and Eno-era Roxy Music, but with a strange frequency all its own. When Pere Ubu toured the UK in 1978, Thomas was not overly impressed with the British punk scene. His emotional intelligence and artistic curiosity had far more in common with such post-punk bands as Joy Division than with the two-chord nihilists.

Four more albums followed with an increasingly fractured and cryptic sensibility, with the arrival of Red Krayola's Mayo Thompson in 1980 only adding to the obtuse surrealism. None of the albums sold well and a disillusioned Thomas broke up the band in 1982 for a solo career. Five years later, he reassembled Pere Ubu with the band's original synth wizard Allen Ravenstine. The comeback album, 1988's *The Tenement Year*, was an unexpectedly vibrant pop delight, accessible and yet still off-kilter, credible and intelligent.

Subsequent albums mined the same rich vein of idiosyncratic pop, culminating with 1993's *Story of my Life*, arguably the most commercial release of the band's entire career, although it failed to find favour with the mainstream. Perhaps as a result, Pere Ubu's next album, 1995's *Ray Gun Suitcase*, returned to the staccato, industrial cacophony of their earlier style with added slide guitar and melancholic-sounding electronics. "We allowed ourselves to lose control, we were content to follow the herd. No more," they noted on the sleeve.

Thomas had intended the album to be Pere Ubu's swansong but the return of original member Tom Herman in 1995 after a twenty-year absence persuaded him otherwise. Although Herman departed again in 2005, Pere Ubu's album *Why I Hate Women* appeared the following year. Among its tracks were a few that continued a long-held Ubu tradition – David Thomas's habit of reappropriating, for no apparent reason, titles from pop songs. Such Pere Ubu songs, bearing no detectable relation to the predecessors they share a name with, include "Blue Velvet", "Sentimental Journey" and "Drinking Wine Spodyody".

NW

The Red Krayola

Few bands have broken up and reformed as many times as The Red Krayola. Over more than forty years they've come and gone and returned again with a bewildering series of line-up, label and stylistic changes, but the one constant has been the singer and guitarist Mayo Thompson, who the cognoscenti rank alongside the likes of Captain Beefheart and Lou Reed as an art-punk visionary; one whose abstruse musical journey has found him travelling from psychedelia to post-rock via new wave, free jazz, Dadaist humour, experimental noise and rustic Americana. If he has one, his closest European counterpart and soulmate might arguably be Robert Wyatt.

Formed in Houston, Texas, in late 1966 by art students Thompson, drummer Frederick Barthelme (brother of novelist Donald Barthelme) and bassist Steve Cunningham, the Krayola began its life playing straightforward mid-1960s American rock, covering songs such as "Hey Joe". Before long, however, they were filling their live shows with experimental, improvisational jamming of the kind that was starting to become all the rage at the Fillmore West and Avalon Ballroom in San Francisco. This, however, was not the West Coast but conservative, redneck Texas. Their free-form approach allegedly made them the least popular band in the state, although they did attract a hardcore following of nascent hippies and hallucinogenic dabblers who became known as the Familiar Ugly and would join the Krayola on stage for the mass freak-out with which they invariably ended their shows.

The Familiar Ugly followed the band into the studio, too, when in early 1967 they recorded their debut album, *The Parable of Arable Land*, in San Francisco. The Uglies – up to one hundred of 'em – provided the "Free-Form Freak-Out" intermissions between the five songs. Roky Erickson, of label-mates the 13th Floor Elevators, also appeared on two tracks, adding harmonica to "Transparent Radiation" and organ to "Hurricane Fighter Plane", while the album's title track was a tape loop of electronic sounds over which the band improvised wildly. Today it's regarded as an underground classic of the psychedelic era, although at the time the record-buying public took little notice.

Nor was their record company, International Artists, enamoured of the growing experimentalism which they had signposted on the album's title track. A concert in Berkeley found them attaching a contact microphone to a sheet of aluminium foil positioned under a block of melting ice. This apparently proved too much even for a hip Bay Area audience and they were reportedly paid to stop the performance. International Artists then rejected their second album *Coconut Hotel* for its lack of commercial potential. It included such self-descriptive tracks as "Organ Buildup" and "Free Guitar" plus a series of atonal "one-second pieces" for piano, trumpet and percussion. The album eventually saw the light of day on CD in 1995. Another recording from the time, with the experimental folk guitarist John Fahey, has never been heard and the tapes are presumed lost.

In the face of such discouragement, The Red Krayola broke up for the first time, although they reformed shortly after, with Thompson and Cunningham recruiting new drummer Tommy Smith to record the 1968 album *God Bless the Red Krayola and All Who Sail in Her*. With the spelling of their name changed for legal reasons, the record was quite different from the psychedelic cacophony of their debut, consisting of short, minimalist and melodic pieces, creating an album which was, as *Spin* magazine put it, "stuffed to the tits with small songs full of quiet terror and acoustic confusion."

When it failed to sell and The Red Krayola split up for the second time, Thompson went off to create a brilliant but ignored solo album in 1970, *Corky's Debt to his Father*, on which he eschewed the Krayola's avant-garde leanings for more conventional songs in a variety of styles, including blues-rock, Tex-Mex and Gram Parsons-style country-pop – albeit with some very odd lyrical twists.

After joining forces with the avant-garde conceptualist collective Art & Language for the album *Corrected Slogans* in 1976, Thompson relocated to London at the height of the punk explosion. He enjoyed the abrasive atmosphere and went on to record 1979's *Microchips & Fish*, the first Red Krayola album in eleven years. The even better *Soldier Talk* followed that same year and around the same time he joined up with Pere Ubu.

Kangaroo?, from 1981, credited to The Red Krayola Plus Arts & Language, boasted such quirky titles as "A Portrait of V.I.Lenin in the Style of Jackson Pollock" and "The Mistakes of Trotsky" and also featured Gina Birch of The Raincoats, Epic Soundtracks of Swell Maps and Lora Logic of X-Ray Spex. After 1983's *Black Snakes*, The Red Krayola were mothballed again while Thompson concentrated on production, working with a wide variety of rock acts, including The Fall, The Raincoats, Scritti Politti, Blue Orchids, Cabaret Voltaire, Stiff Little Fingers, Kleenex, The Chills and Primal Scream.

Another relocation – this time to Düsseldorf, Germany – produced the 1989 Red Krayola album *The Malefactor*. The 1990s found another reinvention as Thompson aligned himself with Chicago's post-rock scene and the Drag City label, releasing the albums *Red Krayola* (1994), *Hazel* (1996) and *Fingerpainting* (1999), working with the likes of Jim O'Rourke and Tortoise.

On the occasion of the Krayola's fortieth anniversary in 2006, Thompson released *Introduction*, although it wasn't, as the title suggested, a compilation of past work at all but an album of entirely new material. In his time outside of music, Thompson works as an art critic and teacher. But it seems unlikely we have heard the last of The Red Krayola.

NW

playlist:

1 Transparent Radiation *from* Parable of Arable Land
This slice of glorious psych-pop was later covered, perhaps unsurprisingly, by Spacemen 3.

2 Hurricane Fighter Plane *from* Parable of Arable Land
Listening to this, you can understand why he hooked up with Pere Ubu a dozen years later.

3 Ravi Shankar: Parachutist *from* God Bless The Red Krayola
Syd Barrett fans: start here.

4 The Sloths *from* Black Snakes
Quirkily brilliant musical rewrite of James Thurber's short story, *The Unicorn in the Garden*.

5 Good Brisk Blues *from* Corky's Debt to his Father
Thompson at his most Dylanesque.

Michael Rother

It might have been Kraftwerk who got Afrika Bambaataa's feet moving, as he pioneered hip-hop in the Bronx during the early 1980s, and it may well have been Can who got Johnny Rotten's juices flowing in his Finsbury Park bedroom ten years earlier. But there was another, all too often overlooked influence on popular music coming out of Germany between 1970 and 1975.

Directly or indirectly, the work of Michael Rother and his musical partner Klaus Dinger has helped shape the whole spectrum of twentieth-century rock. The Düsseldorf duo are there, in spirit, in David Bowie's mid-1970s recordings, from *Diamond Dogs* to *Lodger*, and in the lo-fi thrash of early punk. They can be heard in post-punk's angular drone and the synthesized electro-pop of the following decade, in 1990s ambient dance workouts, world music crossovers, and in Radiohead's more leftfield experimentation. Rother is credited with having a hand in the development of New Age music and has become a name to check. Devotee Julian Cope even wrote a song about him.

The story begins, as does so much modern Deutsche Musik, with Kraftwerk. Rother, born in Munich in 1950, and Dinger, born in 1946, were invited to join the granddaddies of German rock in 1971. The mainstays, Florian Schneider and Ralf Hutter, had already made a pair of groundbreaking, if rather austere, albums. Rother and Dinger were multi-instrumentalists and brought to the band an expressionism and warmth previously lacking. Although Schneider settled into the new line-up, Hutter felt the essence of the band was being compromised. The electro purist bailed out. And then there were three.

Within the year, Rother and Dinger were also straining at the leash. They left Schneider to resume work with the errant Hutter and bunked off to Windrose Studios in Hamburg. Out of the partnership emerged a new band – and what better name for them than Neu!, the German for "new". With Krautrock's chief sonic architect Conrad Plank at the controls, Rother and Dinger recorded their first album for a local label, Brain Records. Issued in the UK in 1972, alongside early releases from Amon Duul II and Can, *Neu!* was a cult hit.

Boosted by the success, the pair took to the road and on a round trip to Hamburg they cut a follow-up album in 1973. Midway through recording *Neu! 2*, however, they ran out of cash and resorted to speeded-up and slowed-down mixes of two non-album tracks, "Neuschnee" and "Super", as cheap fillers. Rother was unhappy and quit after the album was released.

Elsewhere on Brain Records, Cluster, another proto-electro duo, comprising Dieter Moebius and Hans-Joachim Roedelius, had two albums of Germanic experimentation behind them, *Cluster 71* and *Cluster II*. Now they were casting around for a new direction for their disorienting blend of improvisation, industrial thrash and musique concrète. Moebius and Roedelius welcomed Rother with open arms and the three set about a new project – Harmonia. In 1974, the Krautrock supergroup issued *Musik von Harmonia*, an elegantly pulsating, hypnotic masterpiece.

Rother was on a roll and, with Dinger back on board, had another swing at Neu!, cutting their comeback album, *Neu! 75*. Like the bleach bottle that towered on the cover of *Musik von Harmonia*, the new improved brand was bigger and better. The melodies were sweeter and the riffs harder. Tracks like "See Land" and "Hero" sounded like little else from the mid-1970s musical doldrums. *Neu! 75* was a vision of the future and is generally considered one of the essential albums of the genre. It was the epitome of Krautrock's trademark "motorik" rhythm – the repetitive, machine-like compulsion which staked out the link between Bo Diddley's syncopated rock'n'roll shuffle and disco's 4/4 stomp.

Brian Eno claimed Harmonia to be the "world's most important rock group" and the following year, the former Roxy Musician found himself in their studio in Forst, by the river Weser, recording the material that would eventually appear in the 1990s as *Tracks & Traces*, under the name Harmonia 76. Eno rushed excitedly back to tell Bowie, who promptly invited Rother to help out on the recording of his second Berlin album, *Heroes*. Sadly, the collaboration never happened – Rother blamed Bowie's management.

During the late 1970s and 80s, Rother issued an impressive run of solo albums – *Flammende Herzen*, *Sterntaler*, *Katzenmusik*, *Fernwaerme* – often with Connie Plank producing and featuring Can's drummer, Jaki Leibzeit. Since then he has been involved in various remix and video projects.

In the twenty-first century, Neu!'s albums have been reissued and the band has even made an impact in Hollywood, albeit only on the soundtrack to the 2003 Quentin Tarantino film *Kill Bill*. More recently, Rother has jammed with the Red Hot Chili Peppers, taken the stage at the All Tomorrow's Parties festival with The Mars Volta, and toured with a reformed Harmonia.

RW

playlist:

1 Seeland *from* Neu! 75
Taken from Neu!'s most satisfying album, this is a karmic and soulful soundtrack for a rainy day – and a blueprint for Bowie and Eno's sonic explorations on *Low* and *Heroes*.

2 Hallogallo *from* Neu!
Fresh from their sojourn in Kraftwerk, Rother and Dinger cut *Neu!*, featuring this paradigm of the famed "motorik" beat. Riff-free grooving around a bassless rhythm, accompanied by backwards guitars: in 1971 there were no maps for this sort of journey.

3 Dino *from* Musik von Harmonia
Stately yet sprightly, this is the kind of hypnotic groove that, in the mid-1970s, prompted Brian Eno to proclaim Harmonia as the best rock band ever.

4 Untitled #1 *from* Cluster 71
Krautrock without the rock, as organs, Hawaiian guitar, cello and audio generators are electronically "treated" by Conny Plank. This was the kind of state-of-the-art *kosmische musik* Moebius and Roedelius were making in 1971.

5 Flammende Herzen *from* Flammende Herzen
Rother's vibrato guitar and floating, dreamlike melodies on tracks such as this helped invent New Age music in the late 1970s.

Sudden Sway

If you'd tried to tune in to the John Peel show on one particular evening in late 1983, you may have been thrown off the scent by the bizarre sound of a guide to the process of evolution, interspersed with the fizz and crackle of a computer program and a recipe for spinach gnocchi. That would have been the sound of Sudden Sway, a pop group from Peterborough with an almost unparalleled creative streak. In the end, the sheer scale of their ambition proved to be their undoing; having done everything a band could possibly do, there was nothing left to do but stop being a band.

The aforementioned tracks recorded for Radio 1, "Let's Evolve" and "Relationships", remain their best-known, thanks to a vinyl release on the Strange Fruit label. But they were the tip of an extraordinary iceberg. The EP *To You With Regard*, for example, was a James Joyce-inspired take on the troubles of a London girl from a four-way historical perspective; today, our reverse snobbery might well send it packing, but back in 1982 it sold fifteen thousand copies. The follow-up was *Traffic Tax Scheme*: an EP, a wallchart, a computer program and a fairy story. Things were getting odd – and about to get a whole lot odder. The band signed to WEA and, suddenly, funds were at their disposal. They recorded a double-album's worth of mind-bending material, put it in a yellow cardboard box along with charts, quizzes and cut-out-and-keep mementos, and sold it as a personal development programme called *Spacemate*. The single from the album, "Sing Song", was released in eight different versions, all with identical sleeves; one producer described working on the project as like "knitting with fog". WEA were, apparently, "delighted" with Sudden Sway's unique approach to marketing themselves – not realizing that it was an ironic sideswipe at the band's major label paymasters.

All this might give the impression that the Suds were all concept and no tune. Not at all. Like many of their 1980s peers and near-contemporaries – Scritti Politti, Japan, Cabaret Voltaire and Orange Juice, for instance – they walked the line between artful musical experimentation and whistleable, sophisticated pop that you could imagine being played in trendy wine bars.

Almost inevitably, Sudden Sway started moving into other media: an exhibition at the ICA called "Home is Heavenly Springs" made triumphant visits to both the Edinburgh Festival and a BBC2 television studio; *76 Kids Forever*, a soap-opera musical whose plot was revealed over a series of ten-minute phone-in instalments; and ultimately 1990's *Klub Londinium*, a series of disorienting walks through central London with a Sudden Sway-produced cassette tape as your guide. And that was that. As a pop group, they were just so far ahead of the pack that they simply disappeared over the horizon. And they're probably still there.

RM

CONSERVATOIRES AND COCKTAIL BARS
classical misfits, jazz hepcats and the pioneers in between

Alkan

Of the many brilliant pianist-composers of the mid-nineteenth century, only a handful produced music that is widely listened to today. Chopin, Liszt, Schumann, Mendelssohn and Brahms are all up there with the greats of classical music, but the likes of Henselt, Thalberg, Hiller and Kalkbrenner have sunk into almost complete obscurity. For the most part this is deserved, but there is one figure – highly respected by his peers – who deserves to be more than the cultish figure he has become. His name is Charles-Valentin Alkan. Born in Paris in 1813, into a highly musical Jewish family, Alkan was a musical prodigy. Enrolled at the Conservatoire at six, he won the top piano prize at eleven and published his first work at fourteen. His playing put him in touch with the cream of Parisian society, including Victor Hugo, George Sand and Chopin, and he became one of the leading virtuoso pianists of the day. Then from around 1839 it all started to go wrong. After the birth of an illegitimate son he stopped playing – possibly for reasons of religious guilt.

When he did return to the concert platform in the 1840s, he suffered a double blow with his failure to win the top teaching post at the Paris Conservatoire and the death of his friend, and artistic hero, Chopin. For over twenty years he was a virtual recluse, spending his time composing and in serious study of the Bible and the Talmud. He still had pupils – notably his gifted son Elie-Miriam Delaborde – but he was becoming by his own admission "more and more misanthropic and misogynous". He finally re-emerged in 1873 and began giving regular weekly concerts at the showrooms of the piano manufacturers Pleyel and Erard. He died in 1888. Legend has it that his death was the result of a large bookshelf falling on top of him as he was reaching for a Jewish theological text, but there is no evidence to support this story.

A wonderfully mysterious photograph of Alkan (left), suggests a deeply enigmatic figure – a notion strongly reinforced by his music. Alkan composed almost exclusively for the piano (his "Funeral March on the Death of a Parrot" is a delightful exception to this rule), writing pieces to show off his own playing – both its sensitivity and technical brilliance. There are big grandiloquent works, such as the *Grande Sonate Les quatre âges*, that are incredibly difficult to play and seem orchestral in their ambition, but there are also smaller poetic miniatures, like his 48 *Esquisses*, which attempt to distil a mood, an image or an idea. What they all have in common is an acute awareness of the expressive possibilities of the piano, coupled with a personal – often quirky – vision that can switch between passion, morbidity and wit with astonishing rapidity. He may not be a great melodist like Chopin, and there's a strain of naïveté running through his musical ideas, but Alkan's brilliance is self-evident, his effects rarely predictable and his sincerity strangely compelling.

JS

playlist:

1 Barcarolle (opus 65 no 6) *from* Hamelin plays Alkan (Marc-André Hamelin)
This gently undulating evocation of water is one of Alkan's best-known works, played here by Marc-André Hamelin.

2 Les soupirs (opus 63 no 11) *from* Alkan – Esquisses (Steve Osborne)
Les soupirs (the sighs) are suggested by gentle washes of sound in one of Alkan's 48 *Esquisses*.

3 Les cloches (opus 63 no 4) *from* Alkan – Esquisses (Steve Osborne)
The shortest of atmospheric miniatures from *Les Esquisses*, in which a single repeated note represents the tolling bells of the title.

4 Scherzetto (opus 63 no 47) *from* Alkan – Esquisses (Steve Osborne)
Brilliantly animated and skittering fingerwork, which seems like a homage to Mendelssohn, another great Jewish composer.

5 Super flumina Babylonis (opus 52) *from* Symphony for Solo Piano (Marc-André Hamelin)
A mournfully poetic response to Psalm 137 ("by the waters of Babylon we sat down and wept").

6 Le festin d'Esope (opus 39 no 12) *from* Hamelin plays Alkan (Marc-André Hamelin)
A hugely witty set of variations in which the rather banal march tune theme is undermined, exploded and generally dissed. Alkan at his most thrillingly demented.

Duelling pianists

Going to a classical music concert hasn't always been the slightly precious experience it is today. Performers of the past – who almost exclusively performed their own music – were not averse to introducing a large dose of showmanship in order to boost their reputations. Gladiatorial contests, with one performer set against another, were commonplace. Even as serious a figure as J.S. Bach was prepared to take part in an improvisation contest at Dresden with the famous French organist Louis Marchand. The story relates that the contest never happened because Marchand heard Bach practising the evening before and decided to flee while the going was good. In 1790s Vienna, the young Beethoven made a point of competing with rival pianists, picking them off one by one through his superior ability as an improviser. In one trial of skill he humiliated the admired Daniel Steibelt (who had sat impassively through a Beethoven piano trio) by seizing the cello part of Steibelt's *Piano Quintet*, turning it upside down and, with the first eight notes as a theme, devising a set of twenty variations.

Competitive virtuosity reached its peak in the nineteenth century, spurred on by the extraordinary figure of Niccolò Paganini. With his gaunt figure, long hair and piercing gaze, this preternaturally gifted violinist was as concerned with his image as he was with his playing. His demonic presence and dazzling skill thrilled as many as it appalled and he became something of a role model for a number of solo performers – even those, such as Frédéric Chopin, who made their mark by a combination of technical brilliance and poetic sensitivity.

On his arrival in Paris in 1831, the twenty-one-year-old Chopin was simply one star pianist among many. His concert debut, early the next year, was on a bill which included the most celebrated pianist of the day, Friedrich Kalkbrenner, then at the height of his career. Kalkbrenner had just published his *Méthode* for playing the piano and had set up a training course which he proposed to Chopin that he join – for three years. Chopin was a great admirer. "I long to play like Kalkbrenner," he stated. "If Paganini is perfection itself, Kalkbrenner is his equal but in quite a different field." Wisely, however, he declined the invitation.

Despite the presence of Kalkbrenner, Chopin – who played his F minor piano concerto and *Mozart Variations* – proved a huge success. Liszt and Mendelssohn were present, and both were greatly impressed by him, despite their own utterly different styles as composer-pianists. Chopin's playing was particularly admired for the variety of his touch, and for the singing quality (or *cantabile*) of his right hand. He was also adept at using a highly distinctive interpretative device called *rubato* (literally "robbed"),

whereby rhythm, instead of being applied in strict time, was expressively distorted by shortening some notes and lengthening others, an effect likened by Liszt to the movement of a tree's leaves in the breeze.

But Chopin was neither physically nor temperamentally cut out for a career as a virtuoso, and he performed infrequently in public, preferring private recitals in the salons of the aristocracy – a milieu which better suited the poetic intimacy of his style. Kalkbrenner's true successor was Chopin's younger contemporary, Franz Liszt, who, having been mesmerized by the technical brilliance of Paganini, determined to extend the piano's range so that it was simultaneously capable of virtuosic display and expressive depth. Liszt's ascent was temporarily halted when, to avoid scandal, he fled to Switzerland in 1835 with his mistress Countess Marie d'Agoult, and Sigismund Thalberg arrived in Paris. A Kalkbrenner pupil, who had also studied with Hummel and Ignaz Moscheles, Thalberg was a crowd-pleaser and a brilliant technician who was portrayed by the cartoonist Dantan as having ten arms. Renowned for his extraordinary singing tone and his aristocratic froideur, his immediate and overwhelming success prompted Liszt to return to Paris the following spring.

There then followed a protracted critical debate, both in print and among the beau monde, on the relative merits of each pianist: the critic and composer Fétis championed Thalberg, while Liszt was supported by both Berlioz and Chopin. Liszt himself was not above stirring things up by attacking the superficiality of Thalberg's compositions in an article in the *Revue Musicale* – a slightly hypocritical charge when one considers the flashy brilliance of so many of Liszt's own piano pieces. Things came to a head when the Princess Cristina di Belgiojoso, a salon hostess, organized a concert for Italian refugees at which both men performed. Liszt played a fantasy on Pacini's *Niobe*, Thalberg a fantasy on Rossini's *Moses*. When no consensus emerged as to the victor, the princess organized an even more ambitious concert, this time inviting no fewer than six of the capital's top pianists – including Herz, the veterans Pixis and Czerny, and Chopin – to write and perform a variation on the march from Bellini's opera *I Puritani*, collectively entitled *Hexameron*. After each pianist had performed their variation at a separate piano, Liszt delivered the unexpected *coup de grâce* in the form of a further three variations parodying the styles of Pixis, Herz and Thalberg (but sparing his former teacher Czerny and his ally Chopin). While the immediate humiliation of Thalberg may have re-established Liszt's position as the supreme piano virtuoso of the age, it seems to have done little damage to Thalberg's own reputation or career.

RB

Laurie Anderson

I n 1981 the tiny New York label One Ten Records released the single "O Superman" by the 33-year-old sculpture graduate and performance artist Laurie Anderson in a limited edition of one thousand copies to be sold via mail order. A beguiling electronic minimalism, for Anderson it was just one of a number of avant-garde creations of hers that included a self-playing violin, a pillow which sang to the sleeper, a concerto for automobiles, a musical book and a strange human installation piece that involved her playing a violin while wearing ice skates embedded in a melting block of ice.

Then John Peel started playing "O Superman" on British radio, a distributor ordered forty thousand copies and it reached number two in the singles chart – only kept off the top spot by Dave Stewart and Barbara Gaskin's "It's My Party". Needless to say, the freak success was a one-off and Anderson never charted again. But it was the start of a uniquely innovative journey as a postmodern art-rock auteur with a consistently challenging and always fascinating vision.

Born in Illinois in 1948, Anderson moved to New York as a student in the late 1960s and threw herself into the avant-garde art scene, working as a teacher, critic and performer. Then came the improbable success of "O Superman" and a record deal with Warner Brothers, which released the extraordinary album *Big Science* in 1982. Mixing pop with minimalism and electronic instruments with violins, its ironic commentaries on post-industrial American life explored the junction of culture and technology in a way that was highly unusual, even for the time. The album included an extended version of "O Superman" and other pieces from the unreleased *United States* set, as well as new songs.

Anderson's idea of promoting the album was characteristically challenging. Instead of taking to the road and playing rock shows, she developed an eight-hour performance piece and staged it in New York, London and Zurich, an event commemorated in the five-LP (and 4-CD box set) *United States Live*.

Her next studio album, 1984's *Mister Heartbreak*, opened with the synclavier-led track "Sharkey's Day" and closed with a guest reading from William S. Burroughs on "Sharkey's Night". In between, Peter Gabriel provided backing vocals on "Excellent Birds" (an alternate version of which appeared on his album *So*) and "Gravity's Angel" maintained the erudite literary atmosphere by borrowing imagery from Thomas Pynchon's *Gravity's Rainbow*. Most of the songs on the album were later performed in her 1986 concert film, *Home of the Brave*.

Strange Angels followed in 1989, with a striking cover portrait shot by Robert Mapplethorpe. It was something of a departure, in that for the first time Anderson sang rather than talked her way through most of the songs. She had taken singing lessons and claimed to have discovered that she was a mezzo-soprano ("not necessarily a good thing", as critic Richard Fontenoy noted). There was certainly a greater musicality about the record, which also features guest vocals from Bobby McFerrin, but true Anderson fans regarded it as a retreat from the avant-garde aesthetic of her performance art.

Another five years elapsed before she returned to music. In the meantime she published a book, *Stories from the Nerve Bible*, and promoted it with a small-scale theatrical tour. It seemed that she wasn't quite sure where she wanted her musical career to go. However, 1994's *Bright Red* saw her back on track. Produced by Brian Eno, it also featured vocals from her partner Lou Reed, most prominently on the track "In Our Sleep".

Life on a String, her next album, relied heavily on her violin and included "Slip Away", concerning the recent death of her father, plus works from her multimedia staging of Herman Melville's *Moby-Dick*, in which she used a "talking stick", resembling a harpoon, to control a bank of computers.

In 2003, she became NASA's first and, so far, only artist-in-residence, which inspired the performance piece, "The End of the Moon". Then she was off on another series of genre-hopping artistic projects, staging an art exhibition about dreams, narrating a documentary about Andy Warhol and contributing to a Leonard Cohen tribute project, while still finding time to keep us up to date via a series of work-in-progress shows at which she performed material from her next album, *Homeland*.

NW

playlist:

1 O Superman *from* Big Science
Beguiling but accessible mantra-like
electronic minimalism.

2 Sharkey's Night *from* Mister
Heartbreak
Worth the price of entry just for Bur-
roughs' gumshoe noir narration.

3 Excellent Birds *from* Mister
Heartbreak
Imaginative, lyrical, melodic and yet still
unmistakeably avant-garde Anderson.

4 In Our Sleep *from* Bright Red
The first and arguably best of several
collaborations with Lou Reed, on both his
and her albums.

5 Slip Away *from* Life on a String
Written following the death of her father
and performed with just the right mix of
head and heart.

Albert Ayler

"If they don't get it now, they will," said Albert Ayler of the primal, unhinged howl of his saxophone, the wildest sound of the free-jazz movement. Broader acceptance of his music never came about during his brief lifespan. He drowned in Brooklyn's East River in November 1970, at the age of 34. Even now, when jazz is generally considered cosy, not radical, his music remains too fierce to find even the audiences so often morbidly attracted by tragic back-stories.

Mystery surrounds his disappearance and demise, despite the official verdict of death by drowning. In the weeks following his discovery, rumours circulated that he had been murdered either by the police or the mob, or that the incident was linked to Jimi Hendrix's death a few months previously in some kind of plot against black musicians. Others believed that he had killed himself due to his depression over the mental illness of his brother and bandmate Donald, or his failure to find a mainstream audience for his music, even after incorporating vocals and R&B sounds in his later work.

The wider world may not have been listening, but Ayler had respect in the right places, notably from huge fan and patron John Coltrane. The sax legend found the younger man's untamed work an inspiration to his own free-jazz explorations, helping Ayler to secure a record deal with his label, Impulse. Ayler performed at Coltrane's funeral in 1967, a request made by the dying musician.

What Coltrane appreciated so deeply was an astonishingly powerful tenor sax sound that the writer Amiri Baraka compared to "singing from a black hole" and the poet Ted Joans compared to "screaming the word 'fuck' in Saint Patrick's Cathedral on a crowded Easter Sunday". Fellow free-jazz pioneers Cecil Taylor and Don Cherry were part of his early band, all of them focusing on feeling above melody and rhythm, and Ayler received great acclaim for their recordings and performances. When his trumpeter brother Don joined as part of a new quintet, Albert added melodies from old hymns and marches to the mix, creating a link between the earliest forms of jazz and its free-form future.

Total musical freedom was, and still is, too difficult for most listeners to apprehend, and Ayler remains far less

well-appreciated than other jazz experimentalists such as Coltrane and Ornette Coleman. But, at his brief peak, Ayler generated an undeniable, overpowering sound that once heard, is never forgotten. The Hendrix of jazz may have died young, but he still sounds like the future.

DS

where to start:

1 Summertime *from* My Name Is Albert Ayler
An early session recorded for a Copenhagen radio station saw Ayler tackling standards while restricted by the musical limitations of a Danish backing band – yet he still brings an elevated beauty to the Gershwin classic with his soon-to-be-familiar wail.

2 Ghosts (first and second variations) *from* Spiritual Unity
Ayler's best-known tune, much covered by free-jazz disciples, sounds more like three musicians improvising simultaneously than a band playing together, and features some of the saxophonist's stormiest blowing.

W.F. Bach

Despite being one of the most prolific and over-worked composers of the eighteenth century, Johann Sebastian Bach found time to father twenty children by his two different wives. Of those who survived into adulthood, Wilhelm Friedmann, Carl Philipp Emanuel and Johann Christian all became outstanding musicians in their own right. The most naturally talented of this trio, Wilhelm Friedmann (W.F.) also had the most erratic and frustrating career, at least in part because of his spiky personality and fondness for drink. Although he held down several good jobs, and had an unrivalled reputation as an organist, his irascibility eventually made him unemployable and he died in poverty in Berlin in 1784 at the age of 74.

It all started well enough. After a surprisingly wide-ranging education – music studies with his father and a course in law, philosophy and mathematics at Leipzig University – he gained the position of organist at the church of St Sophia in Dresden in 1733. As the capital of the kingdom of Saxony, Dresden was a beautiful and culturally sophisticated city, and Wilhelm Friedmann had close contacts with the court and its musicians. His next appointment, as organist of the Market church at Halle, made a stark contrast. It may have been a more prestigious position but his duties were much more onerous. Halle was the centre of a particularly strict form of Lutheranism called Pietism, and Wilhelm Friedmann clashed regularly with his employers – about his pay, his responsibilities and his tendency to take unofficial leave.

In 1750, six years into his twenty-year stay there, his father died, thus removing the most stabilizing influence from Wilhelm Friedmann's life. Five years later, the start of the Seven Years War made life even harder, as did his employers' decision not to raise his salary. He now had a wife and daughter to support, and regularly sought out new positions but, when he was finally offered the role of music director at Darmstadt, his delay in accepting, or perhaps a change of heart, meant that it fell through. He finally walked out on the Market church in 1764 and from then on his career went steadily downhill. There were even suggestions of him passing off other people's music – including his father's – as his own.

Unlike his brother C.P.E. Bach, Wilhelm Friedmann was casual about his own manuscripts and those of his father that he had inherited. A lot of his music has disappeared. What survives, however, is of the highest quality. It includes work in all genres, but it's his keyboard music that is his main legacy. With his fame as an organist being largely based on his ability to improvise, it's unsurprising that his keyboard pieces are both individual and imaginative. Along with those of C.P.E., they form the stylistic missing link between the complex, multi-layered work of J.S. Bach and the more elegant, melody-based writing of Mozart and Haydn; between Baroque grandiosity and Classical refinement. There are also frequent flashes of drama and intense emotion which add a particularly intimate feel to the music. Both these qualities are in evidence in the twelve *Polonaises*: the best-known works of this little-known composer and a good place to start. The best recent recording is by Steve Barrell for the Dutch label Globe, while Christophe Rousset plays a fine selection of other keyboard pieces on the Harmonia Mundi label.

JS

Alice Coltrane

The wife of John Coltrane, a giant of the saxophone, Alice played piano and orchestral harp, but she chose spiritual questing over a conventional musical career. Replacing the piano great McCoy Tyner in her soon-to-be husband's band – one of the finest in jazz – left Alice Coltrane wide open to accusations of nepotism in 1965. They were unfair: she was an accomplished bebop pianist with a long history of musical achievement in her own right, having studied classical music as a child and having been taught by the celebrated pianist Bud Powell in Paris.

In 1963, Alice McLeod was playing in a quartet led by vibraphonist Terry Gibbs. John Coltrane's band were on a double-bill with them at the New York jazz club Birdland and it was there that she met the man who would become her bandmate and, all too briefly, her husband until his death in 1967. Coltrane's increasingly abstract musical explorations and desire to express "the truly religious life" in his music was increasingly alienating McCoy Tyner and drummer Elvin Jones, who left Coltrane's "classic" quartet. But Alice found herself inspired, and immersed herself fully in Coltrane's spiritual sounds, which drew on Indian and Middle Eastern music and philosophy much more than Western traditions.

Already marginalized by her gender – there are still relatively few female musicians in jazz – she took up the harp, an instrument unheard of in jazz. Its flourishes were the prime characteristic of much of her solo work, alongside Pharoah Sanders's saxophone. Flutes, Wurlitzer organ and north African *oud* also appeared on her records, as her sound became increasingly hypnotic and meditative.

"Everything I do is an offering to God," she said in 1968. She converted to Hinduism, and by 1975 her religious pursuits had become her main focus. She founded a spiritual study centre in California called the Vedantic Center, became the *swami* of the first Hindu temple in the San Fernando valley, and changed her name to Swami Turiyasangitananda, Sanskrit for "the highest song of God". From then on, jazz fans heard little from her, with the exception of the odd cassette-only devotional recording, although she did also manage the archive and estate of her late husband.

In 2004, after decades spent out of the spotlight, she rejoined the secular world briefly with a comeback album produced by her saxophonist son Ravi, entitled *Translinear Light*. It showed her sound to have changed little from the transcendental epics of the early 1970s. But the album, and three major US concerts with Ravi in late 2006, did not mark a permanent return to her performing roots. Rather, they were a final brief exploration of the music that was the early soundtrack to her lifelong spiritual search.

DS

where to start:

1 Ptah the El Douad *from* Ptah the El Douad
The title track of Alice Coltrane's third solo work, from 1970, keeps the horn-dominated sound of jazz thanks to saxophonists Joe Henderson and Pharoah Sanders, but more unusual instrumentation from around the world indicates the direction in which she is headed.

2 Hare Krishna *from* Universal Consciousness
Regarded as her classic album, *Universal Consciousness* used arrangements by Ornette Coleman for harp, organ, violin and tamboura to articulate Alice's religious devotion on songs of slow-moving, meditative beauty – of which this track is the most accessible highlight.

Anthony Holborne

When NASA launched the space probes *Voyager I* and *Voyager II* in 1977, each craft carried with it a golden phonograph containing representative samples of mankind's achievements. On the off-chance that it might one day fall into the hands of an alien space traveller, the record contained – among other things – a selection of different musics from across the globe. The choice of music was eclectic, not to say eccentric, ranging from J.S. Bach (who got three hits) to Blind Willie Johnson, by way of Navajo Indian chanting and a Pygmy female initiation song. The sole piece from the UK was a minute and a half of instrumental music: "The Fairie Round", by an Elizabethan composer of such obscurity that even early music buffs would be hard-pressed to name him.

Anthony Holborne was certainly a celebrated composer in his own lifetime, a period coinciding with a golden age for English music and English culture in general. Little is known about his life: he may have studied at Cambridge University before becoming a gentleman-musician at the court of Queen Elizabeth I. His friends in high places included the all-powerful Sir Robert Cecil, Elizabeth's leading minister and spymaster, who paid Holborne to carry letters to the United Provinces. Could Holborne have been a spy? It's a tantalizing thought but there's no other evidence for it.

Holborne's special skill as a performer was on plucked string instruments: the lute – as popular an instrument then as the guitar is today – the wire-strung cittern and bandora. In 1597 he published a book of 59 pieces for such instruments, *The Cittharn Schoole*, but his best music is found in his *Pavans, Galliards, Almains and other Short Aiers both Grave and Light in Five Parts* of 1599. These pieces are "for viols, violins, or other musicall winde instruments" and could be played in virtually any combination of instruments, such groups being known as consorts.

Pavans, galliards and almains were all dances, but only really nominally so – they were dances to listen to rather than for strutting your stuff. In any case, the music is mostly slow and stately, and sounds especially sombre when played by a consort of viols (a family of bowed stringed instruments played on or between the knees). This general gloominess reflects the contemporary cult of melancholy – think of Hamlet's studied gloom and the music of Holborne's more famous colleague John Dowland – which is reinforced by the names Holborne gave several of his pieces. These include the pavans "The image of Melancholly" and "The Funerals", and the galliards "The Sighes" and "The teares of the Muses". To hear these played by a viol consort is to enter a dark and velvety sound-world, in which introspection is mitigated by a rich sensuousness.

An exception is the sprightly, syncopated galliard "The Fairie Round" – when danced, the galliard involved much hopping and leaping. Which makes it even odder that some unknown enthusiast – the music was chosen by a committee chaired by astronomer Carl Sagan – should have argued for the inclusion of not just an unknown composer to accompany the *Voyager* mission, but one of his least typical works.

JS

playlist:

1 Bona Speranza *from* The Teares of the Muses (Hesperion XX/Jordi Savall)
The title means "good hope", but you wouldn't think so from this richly gloomy pavan played by a consort of viols. The essential Holborne.

2 Lullabie *from* My Selfe (The King's Noise/Paul O'Dette)
A gentle, lilting galliard that would certainly soothe, if not send you to sleep.

3 The Night Watch *from* My Selfe (The King's Noise/Paul O'Dette)
A jaunty almain that's not difficult to imagine being danced to.

4 Passion *from* My Selfe (The King's Noise/Paul O'Dette)
A charming lute solo with an abrupt ending.

5 The Fairie Round *from* Henry VIII and his Six Wives (The Early Music Consort of London/David Munrow)
The original sprightly galliard that is now wending its way across the universe. God knows what the Martians will think.

6 Decrevi *from* The Teares of the Muses (Hesperion XX/Jordi Savall)
Another slow and lugubrious pavan. "I have decreed" is the enigmatic meaning of the title.

Moondog

There's a wonderful photograph of Moondog taken on the streets of New York, where during the 1950s and 60s he became almost as famous a landmark as Times Square or the Empire State Building. There he stands dressed like the Norse god Thor, with headdress, horns, cape and spear. Walking past him and studiously trying to pretend that this vision of countercultural otherness does not exist at all is an all-American middle-aged couple – she in a floral hat, her husband in white shirt, neatly knotted neck-tie, dark suit and trilby. That they could not bring themselves to acknowledge the Viking on the corner was their loss, for Moondog was the most benign of eccentrics: articulate, friendly and a highly serious artist.

Had they stopped, he would have engaged them animatedly in intelligent debate about the Vietnam War, the New York art scene or American history. He would have probably read them a few of his verses and tried to sell them some sheet music or a record. They would also have discovered that, despite his bizarre attire, he was a respected musician, with connections to the New York Philharmonic, and a composer of orchestral music and madrigals which he wrote in Braille after being blinded at the age of sixteen when a dynamite cap exploded in his face.

Born in 1916 in Kansas, Louis Hardin was the son of an Episcopalian minister. His first musical interest was percussion, and he played Indian drums in a high school band. After he lost his sight, his older sister Ruth read aloud to him every day. She helped him to devour works of philosophy, history, mythology and science, and when she read him a book called *The First Violin* by Jessie Fothergill, it inspired him to want to become a composer.

Hardin taught himself to play several instruments to a proficient standard and then attended the Iowa School for the Blind, where he learned to write music in Braille. He married, in secret, a socially prominent older woman. The union was annulled by her family, but not before she had secured him a stipend from a wealthy patron to concentrate on his composing. Without his wife but with the stipend, he took off alone for New York, arriving in the city sometime in the early 1940s.

Hanging around the performers' entrance at Carnegie Hall, he was befriended by various members of the New York Philharmonic, including its conductor, Artur Rodzinski, who encouraged his composition of both music and poetry. They subsequently fell out over, among other things, his increasingly bizarre dress sense – he refused to wear anything other than his own home-made clothes, based on his interpretation of the Norse god Thor. The costume was his way of disassociating himself from Christian culture and it led to him becoming known as "The Viking of Sixth Avenue". His other adopted name arrived in 1947, in memory of his pet's penchant for howling at the moon, a sound captured on the 78rpm recording of his *Moondog Symphony*. He had various other releases in the 1950s, which spanned jazz and classical forms and even stretched to an LP of his arrangements of nursery rhymes featuring a young Julie Andrews.

After a decade's absence from recording, in 1969 Columbia staff producer James William Guercio (who made his name producing Chicago and Blood, Sweat & Tears) took him into the studio and recorded definitive versions of many of his signature pieces. The label promoted him as the psychedelic Viking warrior of Gotham City and included his track "Stamping Ground" on the sampler album *Fill Your Head with Rock* alongside Bob Dylan, Santana, The Byrds and Janis Joplin (who had already covered his madrigal "All Is Loneliness" and had urged Columbia to sign him). His own focus was elsewhere, however, and his greatest

playlist:

1 Invocation *from* The Viking of Sixth Avenue
A ten-minute, sixteen-part canon backed by symphony orchestra and recorded live when Elvis Costello invited him to perform at London's Meltdown Festival in 1995.

2 Paris *from* Sax Pax for a Sax
A joyous outburst with saxophone ensemble and male voice choir from one of Moondog's finest European-recorded albums.

3 Lament 1: Bird's Lament *from* Moondog
In memory of Charlie Parker, this one was later sampled by Mr Scruff as "Get a Move On".

4 Stamping Ground in D Minor *from* Moondog
Recorded with a full orchestra and used by the Coen Brothers in the film The Big Lebowski.

5 All Is Loneliness *from* Moondog II
Written by Moondog as a madrigal, later covered by Janis Joplin as a blues.

pleasure was not to share vinyl with rock royalty but that his self-titled album overtook Leonard Bernstein's *Greatest Hits* in the charts.

The follow-up, *Moondog II*, appeared in 1971 but was less well promoted and in 1974, after more than thirty years as a New York institution, he left the city for Europe. He lived in Germany until his death in 1999, although it hadn't been his intention to. Unable to afford the air fare home, for a year he lived on the streets of various German cities before he was taken in by a family. His new domestication gave him the space and security to write and record some of the best work of his life and he only returned to the country of his birth once, for a tribute concert organized by Philip Glass in 1989.

Hugely influential, his music has been a revelation to minimalist composers, jazz musicians, electronica producers and acoustic folkies alike. It is naïve yet intelligent; it is highly idiosyncratic yet instantly familiar. His tunes sound like something you might have heard once in a dream.

NW

Dory Previn

When it comes to conferring the crown on the queen of the 1970s confessional songwriters, the claims of Joni Mitchell and Carole King cannot be ignored. But Dory Previn was arguably the most revealing and emotionally troubled of them all, and both Tennessee Williams and John Lennon were big fans. Jarvis Cocker has described hearing Previn's "Lady with the Braid" on the radio as revelatory – "one of those moments where you have to stop what you're doing and pay full attention".The songs came pouring out of Dory following a breakdown and an ensuing spell in a mental institution, where she was subjected to electric shock therapy. The four extraordinary but modest-selling albums she recorded between 1970 and 1972 explored areas that, as she put it, younger writers wouldn't dare to.

For Previn was a generation older than the likes of Mitchell and King – she was even older than Leonard Cohen. By the time she made her classic albums in the early 1970s she was already a showbiz veteran well into her forties. Born in 1925, she had recorded her first album, *The Leprechauns Are Upon Me*, in 1958, with accompaniment from Kenny Burrell and André Previn, to whom she was married from 1959 to 1970. She went on to write dozens of songs for films – many with Previn – such as the themes to *Valley of the Dolls* and *Last Tango in Paris*. There was an Oscar on the mantelpiece for her music to *The Sterile Cuckoo* and Frank Sinatra, Tony Bennett, Judy Garland and Doris Day all recorded her songs.

There had been plenty of trauma in her life: her father, who had been left deeply disturbed by his experiences in World War I, boarded up the entire family in their home and held them at gunpoint for several months when she was in her teens. But it was the breakdown following the disintegration of her marriage to Previn when he left her for Mia Farrow that was the catalyst for her greatest body of work. While receiving electroconvulsive shock treatment, she concluded that writing songs about what had happened to her was better therapy than allowing the doctors to wire her up to the electric grid – and they were songs like she had never written before.

"Writing for Hollywood until that point, your work is compromised by the competing egos of directors, actors, pro- ducers and the studios. It meant that I'd been writing universal songs from an objective point of view," she recalled more than thirty years later. "It was only after my breakdown that I started to write subjectively. It was based on true experiences. The music I wrote for films was not. These songs were for me. I know myself better than anyone else, so it helped me. It was self-revelation. There's nothing I wouldn't say."

Her first confessional album, *On My Way to Where*, appeared in 1970 and was cast in acoustic, folkish arrangements. The subject matter included mental breakdown, child abuse, her Catholic upbringing and the end of her marriage. The follow-up, *Mythical Kings and Iguanas* (1971), was more lavishly orchestrated, while *Reflections in a Mud Puddle* the same year was jazzier, many of its songs dealing with her relationship with her father. It was followed by *Mary C. Brown and the Hollywood Sign* (1972), an ambitious song cycle intended as a Broadway stage production, although it never ran. Her final album, *We're Children of Coincidence and Harpo Marx*, appeared in 1976. After that there were no more recordings. The songwriting therapy had done its job and staked her claim to be the most honest and harrowingly self-confessional female troubadour of them all.

NW

playlist:

1 Mythical Kings and Iguanas *from* Mythical Kings and Iguanas
Tennessee Williams quoted its lyrics to her and declared: "That's so good, I think I must've written it."

2 Beware of Young Girls *from* On My Way to Where
Especially the ones "who come to the door, wistful and pale, aged 24" and who happened to be called Mia Farrow.

3 Lady With the Braid *from* Mythical Kings and Iguanas
"Would you care to stay till sunrise, it's completely your decision/It's just the night cuts through me like a knife/Would you care to stay awhile and save my life?" Surely the greatest female seduction song ever written.

4 With My Daddy in the Attic *from* On My Way to Where
Chilling nightmares of child abuse and fantasies of incest.

5 For Sylvia, Who Killed Herself in 1963 *from* On My Way to Where
Not a song, but a poem about Sylvia Plath: "I have been where Sylvia's been/She did not survive/I came back."

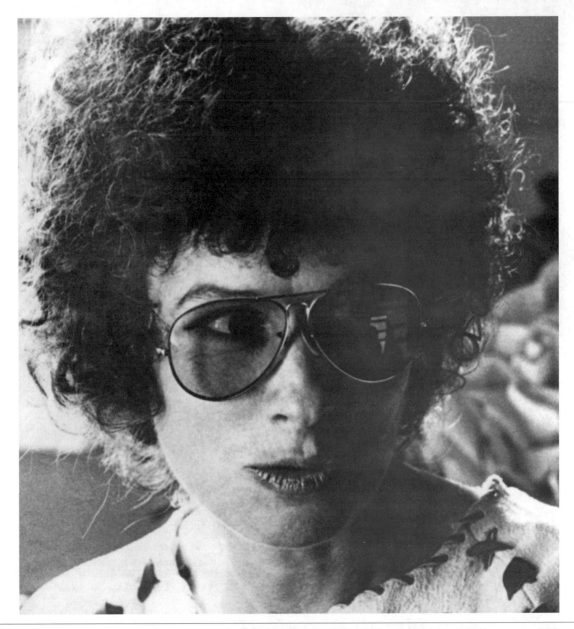

Jimmy Scott

"Little" Jimmy Scott had Kallmann's syndrome, a rare condition that left him with the tiny body of a pre-pubescent for his entire life and a high, vibrato singing voice that was neither male or female but more like the castrati of seventeenth- and eighteenth-century opera. One would think that it would be hard for the music biz to forget such an unusual talent – yet forgotten he was. He was invited to sing at the inaugurations of presidents Eisenhower and Clinton, but in between he spent his post-1960s career as a lift operator, hotel shipping clerk and a care worker in a retirement home. During the 1980s his wife phoned a radio station to request one of his songs and was informed that he was dead, which was news to her and her husband.

Scott's languid balladeering, hovering over each syllable at length and capable of sustaining endless high notes, had most in common with female stars of the day such as Judy Garland and Billie Holiday, who was a fan. An early hit as a vocalist with Lionel Hampton's band demonstrated his great promise and kept him in work through the 1950s, but it wasn't until 1962 when what appeared to be his real break arrived – a contract with Ray Charles's Tangerine label and the recording of an album, *Falling in Love Is Wonderful*, on which Charles played piano throughout.

However, after just a month on the shelves the album was withdrawn from sale, when a previous record company boss, Herman Lubinsky of Savoy, insisted Scott still belonged to him. Lubinsky did the same thing when Scott recorded another career highlight, *The Source*, in 1969, and neither album was available to buy again until the early twenty-first century.

It was 1991 before he resurfaced as a musician, singing at the funeral of his songwriter friend Doc Pomus. Seymour Stein, head of Sire Records, was in attendance and signed the singer the following day. Since then, people have fallen over themselves to praise the diminutive star. His 1992 comeback album, *All the Way*, featuring Ron Carter and Kenny Barron, was nominated for a Grammy. Madonna said he was the only singer who could make her cry. Nick Cave asked him to perform at his wedding, and Lou Reed persuaded him to sing backing vocals on his *Magic and Loss* album. But he is still best remembered by younger generations for his appearance in the finale of David Lynch's TV series *Twin Peaks*, singing "Sycamore Trees" to a confused Kyle MacLachlan and a slow-dancing dwarf. It was an odd climax to a most unusual career.

DS

where to start:

1 Everybody's Somebody's Fool *from* Everybody's Somebody's Fool
Scott's biggest hit, not under his own name but as a singer with the Lionel Hampton big band. Finally issued with much of his early material on this 1999 collection, it's a typical slowie on which that voice is already dripping pathos.

2 Sometimes I Feel Like A Motherless Child *from* The Source
A signature tune for Scott, whose mother was killed in a road accident when he was thirteen. Over a bleak, minimal backdrop, his anguished vocal is absolutely devastating.

Alessandro Stradella

"Live fast, die young" is a rock'n'roll cliché. But it's one that the composer Alessandro Stradella did his best to live up to in the second half of the seventeenth century. Born in 1644 into the kind of upper-class Tuscan family that gave him access to the classiest circles, his musical career was interrupted by a series of scrapes, generally involving either money or women.

From the age of nine Stradella was in Rome, living in the grandiose Palazzo Lante, where he served as a pageboy. Culturally, this was one of the city's greatest periods, with aristocrats and rich Cardinals all vying to outdo each other as patrons of the arts. By the time he was in his twenties Stradella was getting plenty of commissions, writing operas, *oratorios* (a kind of religious opera), and one-off vocal pieces (*cantatas*) for special occasions.

It was a promising enough career, but Stradella still seemed unable to make ends meet – probably as a result of being paid late. A sideline as a marriage broker seemed to be the solution, until he and his business partner (a *castrato* named Vulpio) somehow arranged a match between an elderly, lowborn woman and a relative of a highly influential Cardinal. The resulting scandal precipitated a hasty move to Venice where – among other openings – he was hired by Alvarise Contarini to give music lessons to his young mistress, Agnese Van Uffele. These clearly proved a little too enjoyable for both parties, since a few months later he and Agnese eloped to Turin with Contarini in hot pursuit. On the brink of marrying her, Stradella was set upon by two thugs – presumably in the pay of Contarini – and left for dead. The record then goes quiet on what happened to Agnese.

On recovering, Stradella's next port of call was Genoa, where he was employed by a group of nobles as the musical director of the Teatro Falcone. A number of successful operas followed (including one entitled *The War of Heroic Love*) but – perhaps unfortunately – his private teaching continued, with Genoan high society providing its fair share of young female pupils. Nobody is certain what Stradella did or did not get up to with them, but we do know that one evening in 1682 he was on his way home when he was stabbed by an unknown assailant – this time fatally.

Because of his colourful life, Stradella was never entirely forgotten, even though his music was only known to very few. The recent interest in his work was partly kickstarted by a 1992 recording of his oratorio *San Giovanni Battista* (St John the Baptist), and this is the best place to start. Though nominally religious, it's incredibly dramatic, with fully rounded characters, a huge range of emotions and a remarkable immediacy – all conveyed by stunningly ornate and beautiful melodies. And while San Giovanni is the protagonist, ultimately it's the corrupt and incestuous court of Erode (Herod) that generates the piece's psychological power.

JS

Sun Ra

There are plenty of characters in this book that could be described as "out there", but only Sun Ra took the term literally. Throughout his long career the bandleader insisted he was from Saturn. It rather spoils the fun to cite the Earth birth date of 22 May 1914 for a boy from Alabama called Herman "Sonny" Blount. But that hasn't stopped numerous others, particularly the dozens who would make up his band over the years, from becoming true believers in this most mystical of musicians.

Alternately known as the Myth Science Arkestra, the Astro Infinity Arkestra, the Jet Set Omniverse Arkestra or plain old Arkestra, Ra's fellow musicians had all the qualities of a cult. They dressed in sparkling robes and outlandish headgear, abstained from drugs and sex and lived together in communal houses in New York and Philadelphia, rehearsing day and night and surviving on large pots of a vegetarian dish Ra called "moon stew".

This was not an instant transformation for Ra. As a young jazz pianist in the 1930s and 40s he played in various straight bands in his hometown and led the Sonny Blount Orchestra both there and in Chicago. In the early 1950s, he began claiming he had been abducted by aliens who told him to speak to the world through his music, and legally changed his name to Le Sony'r Ra. A fascination with Egyptology, numerology and, of course, outer space, would manifest itself in music that became ever more unorthodox once Ra relocated to New York in the 1960s. Though sometimes close to unlistenable, it was also pioneering and majorly influential. Ra was one of the first musicians to experiment with electronics and synthesizers, and also broke new ground in jazz, using electric bass, massed polyrhythms and ambitiously atonal music.

Even the way he released his music was unconventional, using his own Saturn label to put out endless studio and live recordings, often with hand-illustrated covers. A definitive discography has proved virtually impossible to compile, but estimates hover at around two hundred albums, many now long out of circulation. He was in many ways an eccentric figure of fun, but Ra had a healthy sense of humour himself – how could he not, wearing those outfits? Near the end

Sun Ra (far left) duels with "The Overseer" (Ray Johnson) for the fate of the black race in *Space Is the Place* (1972). Could this scene be a blaxploitation sci-fi homage to Ingmar Bergman?

of his career he filled his sets with Disney standards, and though he never backed down on his claims about his intergalactic heritage, he definitely saw the funny side. "Some call me Mr Ra, some call me Mr Re. You can call me Mr Mystery," he would tell audiences.

His incredible music lived on after his death in 1993 – 83-year-old saxophonist Marshall Allen still leads the Arkestra on tour. And it will, no doubt, continue to be heard on other planets long after this one has disappeared.

DS

playlist:

1 Kingdom of Not *from* Super-Sonic Jazz
Here the Arkestra has a more conventional bop sound, but there are early signs of the structural freedom that was to come. The easiest route into Ra's weird world.

2 Enlightenment *from* Jazz in Silhouette
Still in transition from the Chicago period, this horn-led track opens up playing it straight, floating casually over simple piano, before changing its pace and tone ever more rapidly and beginning to touch on dissonance.

3 The Magic City *from* The Magic City
The slogan of Ra's hometown, Birmingham, Alabama, came to mean something far more outré in the hands of its strangest son. Ra explores the limits of free jazz, experimenting with tape delay effects over battling horns, flute, piccolo and clavioline.

4 Otherness Blue *from* Brother the Wind Vol 2
An early and enthusiastic adopter of electronic keyboards, Ra received a prototype version of a minimoog from the inventor of the influential organ, Robert Moog. Electronics provide a calm backdrop while the horns really break free.

5 We'll Wait For You *from* Space Is the Place OST
John Coney's film starring Ra and his Arkestra is a kind of sci-fi blaxploitation flick, in which the bandleader resettles the black race on a new planet with the help of his fantastical music. A female voice yells about "Another world!" while keyboards shift from unsettling rumblings to full-blown freakout.

6 Whistle While You Work *from* Second Star to the Right (Salute to Walt Disney)
Massed vocals, handclaps and a truly unique take on a childhood standard.

Galina Ustvolskaya

Ustvolskaya's music is like nothing you've ever heard before. Raw, elemental, basic, it seems to be carved out of blocks of pure sound. Rhythms tend to be simple and passages are repeated relentlessly, but without the inexorable logic or momentum of Minimalism. The uncompromising starkness of her work has led the critic Arnold Whittall to question whether it qualifies as art at all: "If Cage's most radical achievement was to aestheticize non-music, Ustvolskaya ... manages the more difficult task of de-aestheticizing music itself." Although she uses conventional instruments, Ustvolskaya does so in startlingly original combinations. Her *Composition 1*, for instance, is scored for piccolo, tuba and piano; *Composition 2* for eight double-basses, percussion and piano; and *Composition 3* for four flutes, four bassoons and piano. Like several of her later works, these three (written in the early 1970s) were inspired by Christian texts, although her response to them does not suggest a religion of reassurance or redemption so much as an anguished ritual of pain and suffering.

What makes Ustvolskaya's work all the more remarkable is the fact that much of it was composed within the prescriptive and restricted cultural environment of the Soviet Union. Born in Petrograd (later Leningrad, now St Petersburg), she studied with Shostakovich at the Leningrad Conservatoire in 1940 and again at the end of World War II. Her relationship with him was complicated: she may have been fourteen years his junior and his student, but Shostakovich admired her greatly. "I am a talent..." he once told her "You are a phenom-

enon." For a time she was his muse and he twice asked her to marry him.

In later years she was begrudging about Shostakovich's influence, even though early works – such as the *Concerto for Piano, Timpani and Strings* of 1946 – suggest that it was strong. Her own voice emerged quickly, however, and demonstrated a fascination with simplicity and musical first principles that remain unchanged throughout her working life. But it would be wrong to think of her as some kind of avant-garde visionary who worked in total isolation. Her performed works include the spiky *Violin Sonata* of 1952 which, when played to a delegation of American musicians, was memorably described by one of them, Roy Harris, as "kind of ugly". Like all Soviet composers, she also produced music on demand, including propagandist cantatas, symphonic works and film scores.

Her "discovery" in the West occurred in the 1990s and she rapidly acquired something of a cult following, largely because the primitivism and directness of her sound world had no obvious counterpart among the European avant-garde. Her output is small, with hardly anything written during the 1960s, but all of it is worth hearing – at least once. The piano figures in nearly all of her music, essentially as a percussion instrument capable of extreme quietness and loudness (her *Piano Sonata No 6* features the marking "fffff" – a hyperbole of fortissimo beyond normal levels of loudness). But she is also capable of moments of delicacy, as in the twelve *Preludes for Piano*, concentrated miniature sound-poems that have all the spareness and clarity of an epigram.

JS

Silenced by the Nazis

When the Nazis came to power in Germany in 1933, they were quick to see the effectiveness of the arts in promoting their twisted values and ideology. Under the auspices of the Reichsmusikkammer (RMK), those composers regarded as essentially Germanic were celebrated, while those viewed as undermining or corrupting the German "ideal" were denigrated. Composers such as Beethoven, Bruckner and, above all, Wagner were extolled as examples to follow, whereas anybody writing avant-garde or jazz-inspired music was held up to ridicule and persecution. Then there was the question of ideology and ethnicity: to be left-wing was to be beyond the pale, while to be Jewish or black – "non-Aryan" – was to be regarded as less than human. By 1937, all music written by Jews – even by such universally admired figures as Mendelssohn and Mahler – was proscribed, and Jews were rapidly purged from all aspects of cultural life. Jazz itself fared marginally better: though disapproved of as "Americano, nigger, kike jungle music", its popularity meant that it never entirely disappeared.

The Nazi position was most clearly articulated at an exhibition mounted in Düsseldorf in May 1938 entitled "Entartete Musik" (Degenerate Music), advertised with a poster showing a crude caricature of a top-hatted black man playing the saxophone with a star of David on his lapel. Organized by Dr Heinz Ziegler, the exhibition displayed offending scores, photographs of "degenerate" composers, and booths where you could listen to and laugh at their work. Everything was presented as evidence of a Bolshevik/Jewish conspiracy to sully the purity and strength of Germany's musical heritage.

In the face of such repression, many composers (as well as performers) went into exile, some – such as Korngold and Kurt Weill – to enjoy further successes, others – like Berthold Goldschmidt – to struggle in obscurity. Still others, for instance Boris Blacher and Karl Amadeus Hartmann, chose "internal exile" – staying in Germany but remaining silent for the duration of Nazi rule. For those Jewish composers unfortunate enough not to escape, the future looked particularly bleak as the persecution of the Jews became more and more extreme. There were many composers who were either murdered in the death camps or simply hounded to death. The composer Franz Schreker died from a stroke in 1933, following dismissal from his teaching posts and anti-Semitic rioting at the premiere of his opera *Der Schmied von Gent*. Erwin Schulhoff died at Wülzburg concentration camp in 1941, Edwin Geist was shot by the SS in 1942 while Leo Smit was gassed at Sobibor in 1943.

In central Europe, many artists and musicians were interned at Terezín, a former garrison town about sixty kilometres northwest of Prague. Built by the Austrian emperor Josef II in the 1780s and given the German name Theresienstadt, it was used as a concentration camp from 1941 until the end of the war. Although conditions were horrendous and there were regular transports to Auschwitz, the town was largely run by the inmates themselves. The result was an extraordinarily active cultural life, despite the squalid privations of the camp itself, with lectures, art classes, theatre, concerts and opera performances. Among several professional musicians at the camp were four remarkable composers: Gideon Klein, Pavel Haas, Hans Krása and Viktor Ullmann. Klein was the youngest – just 22 when he arrived at Terezín – and a highly gifted pianist who not only performed at the camp but wrote a handful of chamber works including a string trio there, widely regarded as his masterpiece. Klein also encouraged Pavel Haas, a pupil of Janáček, to compose while at the camp. Only a few of his works survive, among them the haunting *Four Songs to Chinese Poetry* for voice and piano, and the *Study for Strings* – conducted at Terezín by leading Czech conductor Karel Ancerl.

Hans Krása and Viktor Ullmann were even more distinguished figures. Krása's *Symphony for Small Orchestra* (1921) had been performed by the Boston Symphony Orchestra and he had won a Czechoslovak State Prize for his opera *Verlobung in Traum* (1930). His children's opera, *Brundibár*, premiered at the Jewish orphanage in Prague in 1942, was performed repeatedly at Terezín (by virtually the same cast, who had been transferred there from Prague). Another opera, Ullmann's *Der Kaiser von Atlantis* (1943), became a *cause célèbre* in the camp's history. A thinly veiled allegorical satire on Hitler's destructive megalomania, mixing cabaret-style music, operetta and sumptuous late-Romanticism, performances were forbidden after SS officers attended the dress rehearsal. Arguably the greatest work to emerge from Terezín, *Der Kaiser von Atlantis* was finally premiered in Amsterdam in 1975.

In June 1944, prior to a visit from the Red Cross, the authorities "improved" the camp – solving the "problem of overcrowding" by sending many inmates to Auschwitz. They followed this up with a film, directed by Jewish inmate Kurt Gerron, which attempted to show how well the Jews were being treated: fake shops were erected, gardens planted and extracts from performances of *Brundibár* shown. The reality was very different. Of around 140,000 Jews at Terezín, about 30,000 died there while 90,000 were moved on to other camps and almost certain death. These included Klein, Haas, Krása and Ullmann. Much of the music written at Terezín has now been recorded: there is an outstanding Decca CD of *Der Kaiser von Atlantis*, albeit currently out of print, while Deutsche Grammophon have recently released a recording of songs composed at Terezín sung by Anne Sofie von Otter and Christian Gerhaler.

RB

OUTSIDERS
the musicians that never fitted in

Kevin Coyne

Few singer-songerwriters were ever as singular and uncompromising as Kevin Coyne. A qualified social worker and therapist, his experience working with drug addicts and the mentally ill provided the material for many of his uniquely striking songs, in which he gave voice to society's outcasts and misfits. It was hardly subject matter designed to appeal to the mainstream and nor was his voice, an abrasive instrument that perfectly matched the uncomfortable topics he often sang about.

Coyne jealously guarded his reputation as an anti-star and one of rock music's permanent outsiders, although in truth the stance came naturally. "My greatest fear is to walk into a room full of hit records," he once joked. In terms of his own output, there was little danger of that ever happening, but over a career lasting three decades and more, he maintained a prolific output, averaging almost an album a year. If the quality was sometimes variable, his best work was frequently stunning and always challenging.

Born in Derby in 1944, he studied at art college where he developed a passion for the early blues masters. In 1965 he became a therapist working with mental patients at a Lancashire hospital. Three years later he moved to London to work on a Soho-based drug counselling project. With Dave Clague he formed the group Siren, becoming firm favourites with John Peel, who invited them to record numerous radio sessions and made them one of the first signings to his Dandelion Records in 1970.

Siren's self-titled debut album was a blues-heavy affair but included an astonishing song called "Asylum", a disturbing, guttural monologue about a man losing his sanity, which created the template for Coyne's future style and subject matter. Like everyone else on Peel's label, Siren sold records in minuscule quantities, and they broke up in 1972 after the release of a second album, *Strange Locomotion*. Peel kept faith with Coyne and that same year Dandelion released his debut solo album *Case History*, which drew heavily on his work with mental patients. One track, "Sand All Yellow", was a strange, opaque song sung from the point of view of a doctor (and/or nurse) addressing a dying patient, with lyrics that chillingly juxtapose soothing words of comfort with lists of surgical implements.

When Dandelion folded, Coyne signed to Richard Branson's new Virgin imprint, having reportedly rejected an approach to join The Doors, following the death of Jim Morrison. (He didn't fancy wearing the leather trousers, he joked in later years.) He continued instead on his own unconventional solo course and in 1973 delivered perhaps his finest album, *Marjory Razorblade*, a sprawling collection of songs-as-character-studies oozing with a rage, anguish and alienation that ranked him up alongside other great English outré figures such as Syd Barrett, Kevin Ayers and Robert Wyatt.

Coyne stayed with Virgin for ten more albums. After 1974's *Blame It on the Night*, he recruited a heavyweight band including future Police guitarist Andy Summers and keyboard player Zoot Money to play on 1975's *Matching Head and Feet* and the following year's *Heartburn*. By then punk had arrived and Coyne was in his thirties. But his artistic credo of honesty over finesse matched the punk ethos and he was hailed by Johnny Rotten as an influence. He reciprocated, in a sense, on the 1978 album *Dynamite Daze*, the title track of which was a paean to the energy of groups such as the Sex Pistols.

After another strong set in 1979's *Millionaires and Teddy Bears*, he recorded the controversial song-cycle *Babble* with the German singer Dagmar Krause. The songs alluded to the relationship between the two Moors Murderers, Myra Hindley and Ian Brady, and protestors picketed the theatre when the work was turned into a stage production. Two more albums followed in 1980, the difficult *Bursting Bubbles* on which he howled like a man possessed, and *Sanity Stump*, which included contributions from Robert Wyatt. But the new decade brought a new commercial imperative to the record industry and when the accountants took a look at his sales chart, Virgin dropped him.

He was by now a serious alcoholic and the raging voice heard on *Bursting Bubbles* turned out to be an uncomfortably accurate reflection of his own mental state, when in 1981 he suffered a breakdown. Signing to Cherry Red Records, he made three troubled albums, *Pointing The Finger* (1981), *Politicz* (1982) and *Beautiful Extremes Etc* (1983), but after a painful divorce, in 1985 he emigrated to Germany in search of a fresh start. Claiming that he had swapped alcoholism for workaholism, he entered a prolific phase that continued unabated until his death. He exhibited his paintings around Europe – bold, childlike, cartoonish art in the naïve style that was often just as disturbing as his songs. He also wrote fiction and released a further dozen albums. These included 1993's *Tough and Sweet*, which featured his sons Robert and Eugene – both practising musicians – and 1995's *The Adventures of Crazy Frank*, which was also performed as a stage musical with Coyne playing the title role.

Coyne was diagnosed with lung fibrosis in 2002, but remained active until the end. He died in December 2004, just three weeks after attending the funeral of John Peel, the man who had first set him on his meandering, creative way.

NW

playlist:

1 Asylum *from* Siren
"And trees are talking, and the bushes, they got fleas" – the monologue of a man at the end of his tether.

2 Sand All Yellow *from* Case History
A true story about the medical staff scrapping over the body of a dying patient.

3 Uggys Song *from* Case History
When Coyne read about a black tramp who was bullied and then allegedly murdered by the police in Leeds, he immediately decided it was perfect material for a pop song.

4 Old Soldier *from* Marjory Razorblade
"One of yesterday's heroes".

5 Eastbourne Ladies *from* Marjory Razorblade
Acidic satire about the rich old biddies of the south coast with their "tea and lemon ice".

6 Marlene *from* Marjory Razorblade
Coyne's answer to the Rolling Stones' "Satisfaction"? A dysfunctional ode about trying to get some action from the beautiful but reluctant Marlene.

7 House on the Hill *from* Marjory Razorblade
A harrowing, highly personal description of his life working in a mental hospital.

8 Dynamite Daze *from* Dynamite Daze
Kev salutes the punks in a song dedicated to Sid Vicious.

9 Having A Party *from* Millionaires and Teddybears
A mutant blues about pop's wild party – from which honest Kev is kicked out for lacking the treachery required to become a star. Later covered by the Mekons.

10 Dead Dying Gone *from* Babble
Dark, murky and disturbed howlings, with each line contradicting its predecessor – it's like being inside the head of a schizophrenic with a death wish.

Ivor Cutler

Poet, singer, songwriter, storyteller, humorist, teacher and eccentric, Ivor Cutler was an offbeat Scottish national treasure whose recondite admirers – the word fans doesn't do Cutler's appeal justice – spanned several generations and ranged from Billy Connolly to the philosopher Bertrand Russell. Their number also included John Peel (who once noted that Cutler was the only performer whose work had been featured on all four BBC radio stations) and The Beatles, who invited him to appear in their film, *Magical Mystery Tour*. In case you're wondering, he played the bus conductor Buster Bloodvessel, who told his passengers, "I am concerned for you to enjoy yourselves within the limits of British decency" and then developed a passion for Ringo's aunt Jessie.

Accompanying himself on a harmonium, his poems, songs and monologues were delivered in a soft Scottish burr. Sometimes sinister, sometimes silly, they were almost always full of wit and wordplay and, more often than not, shot through with unexpected insights into the absurdity of the human condition. "Imperfection is an end; perfection is only an aim," was one of his aphorisms.

Born to Jewish parents in Glasgow in 1923, his childhood was the source for much of his later material and he invariably presented his upbringing as dour, spartan and even sadistic. He was convinced that he became a lesser being in his mother's eyes after his brother was born and at the age of three allegedly attempted to kill his younger sibling with a poker. He also suffered at school from anti-Semitic teachers but gave early notice of his later performing abilities when he won a prize at the age of six for his rendition of Robert Burns' "My Love Is Like a Red Red Rose".

Still in his teens, he joined the RAF and trained as a navigator during World War II. He later liked to claim that he had been dismissed for being too dreamy and absent-minded, apparently more interested in admiring the clouds from the cockpit window than mapping a flight path over Germany. He finished the war as a storeman and then trained to become a schoolteacher. He spent more than thirty years teaching and, inevitably, the experience produced further rich material for his songs and poems, particularly during a spell spent teaching arts and English at A.S. Neill's controversially libertarian Summerhill School, which he claimed unlocked his own dormant creativity.

A late starter, it was not until 1959 that he began broadcasting on BBC radio, under the patronage of the writer Ned Sherrin. This radio experience led to the recording of his first album, *Who Tore Your Trousers?*, and his second LP, *Ludo* (1967), was produced by George Martin. Recorded with a jazz trio, Cutler on piano and harmonium, it was the most musically conventional of his recordings, although conventional is a relative term when talking about Cutler. Martin was not amused by his eccentric behaviour in the studio. The Beatles, however, found him unsurpassably funny and at Paul McCartney's insistence a part was written into *Magical Mystery Tour* for him. The Martin-produced album sold next to nothing, which was a blessing in disguise for it ended Cutler's career as a jazz musician and returned him to his oddball harmonium explorations, perplexing epigrams and humorous monologues.

After being taken up by John Peel – by which time he was already in his late forties – he found a new, younger audience that led to him signing to Virgin Records, for whom he recorded three albums in the mid-1970s while still working as a teacher for the Inner London Education Authority. Sometimes confounding and not always in the best taste but full of humanity, intelligence, charm and wit, these albums represent the core of Cutler's best work. He made further albums for Rough Trade in the 1980s and in the 1990s for Alan McGee's Creation Records, making him unlikely labelmates with Oasis. He continued working into old age, only retiring from live performance following the onset of Alzheimer's disease, from which he died in 2006. He was frank and philosophical about death, ruminating publicly on his own demise: "I shall be glad to get away from loud pop music and motor cars but I shall miss the beautiful kindnesses of those people to whom courtesy comes naturally."

NW

playlist:

1 If Your Breasts *from* Velvet Donkey
"If your breasts are too big you will fall over, unless you wear a rucksack", cautions Ivor. All those years as a teacher, yet he never really got the hang of biology...

2 Life in a Scotch Sitting Room Vol 1 *from* Jammy Smears
This brief, eccentric observation on his childhood later led to Vol 2, an entire album of similar musings.

3 Bicarbonate of Chicken *from* Jammy Smears
On which he puts the harmonium away, tinkles some appealing boogie-woogie piano and sings like a Scottish Groucho Marx.

4 Go and Sit upon the Grass *from* Velvet Donkey
Later covered by Robert Wyatt, a man who also asked Cutler to play harmonium on his classic album *Rock Bottom* album.

5 Dad's Lapse *from* Dandruff
"My father once had intercourse with a polar bear in Canada. If you ask him, he will deny this. 'Canada?' he will shout, playing for time." Well, it would explain a lot...

Nick Drake

Although many now know and love his music, Nick Drake is in a sense the patron saint of this book. The first of rock music's Van Gogh figures, his talent was almost totally ignored in his lifetime and his greatness only recognized long after his death.

In the age of the Internet, long-forgotten classics are being rediscovered, reappraised and reissued on an almost weekly basis. But it was Drake, who died at the age of 26, who unknowingly created the template. Since his oeuvre was collected together posthumously in the four-CD box set *Fruit Tree* in 1986, his influence has continued to grow as new generations have been seduced by his intricate guitarwork, introspective songs and understated English voice.

Born in Burma in 1947, where his father worked as an engineer, Drake moved back to England with his family when he was a child and settled in leafy Tamworth-in-Arden, Warwickshire. While boarding at Marlborough public school, he bought his first acoustic guitar in 1965 and began to neglect his studies in favour of music, although he still managed to secure a place at Cambridge University reading English literature. By the time he arrived at university in October 1967, he was writing songs and performing. One of his early gigs was seen by Fairport Convention's Ashley Hutchings, who introduced him to Joe Boyd, the band's producer.

Boyd could scarcely believe how accomplished the songs were and signed Drake to his Witchseason Productions company. Drake skipped lectures to attend recording sessions in London, and released his first album in 1969 while still at university – the Boyd-produced *Five Leaves Left*, named after the message near the end of a packet of Rizla papers. In retrospect, it seems astonishing that the record so totally failed to make any impact. The intimate beauty of Nick's voice, the clarity of his guitar playing, the warmth of the string arrangements (by Nick's friend and fellow Cambridge student Robert Kirby) and the elegiac lyrics all have a classic sensibility and a stoned innocence that rank the album alongside such contemporary releases as Tim Buckley's *Happy Sad* and Van Morrison's *Astral Weeks*. Yet the album was both a critical failure – with *NME* pretty much voicing the general consensus when their reviewer concluded there was "not nearly enough variety to make it entertaining" – and a commercial flop, selling fewer than 5000 copies.

But Drake was sufficiently optimistic about his future to drop out of university to concentrate full-time on his music. He moved to London and played some live dates, but he couldn't conceal the awkwardness he always felt playing concerts – by most accounts, his shows were painful to watch – and he swiftly abandoned live performance to concentrate on writing and recording. His second album, *Bryter Later*, appeared in 1970 and if anything it was even better than his debut. The songs were more poetic and the arrangements more confident. But when the album was launched, the reaction was even more disappointing than the first time around. *Melody Maker* called the album "an awkward mix of folk and cocktail jazz" and it sold fewer than 3000 copies.

At least part of the problem was of Drake's own making, as he wouldn't tour and was deeply reluctant to do any promotion. But his life became a vicious circle. His failure made him even more introverted than he already was, and sent him into a deep depression, which in turn made him even less capable of engaging in any of the activities required to sustain a career. He was still writing songs, however, and in late 1971, he called sound engineer John Wood and announced that he wanted to make a third album.

Pink Moon (1972) was recorded in just two days, with Drake accompanying himself on guitar and adding a piano overdub to the title track. Only Drake and Wood were in the studio throughout, and the results were stark and bare – the eleven songs clocking in at just 28 minutes in total.

After completing the album, Drake delivered the tapes to Island Records, reportedly handing them to a receptionist and leaving without speaking to anyone. The tapes, so one story goes, sat there unnoticed for several days. When the album was eventually released, part of Island's publicity campaign read: "*Pink Moon* – Nick Drake's latest album. The first we heard of it was when it was finished." It sold even fewer copies than his first two albums and, cripplingly depressed, Nick went back to live with his parents.

During this period he had a breakdown and was hospitalized. Yet he was still writing songs, and in early 1974 he again contacted John Wood with a view to recording a fourth album. He managed just a single day in the studio, during which four tracks were attempted. Drake was in poor shape – unable to sing and play the guitar at the same time – and according to Boyd the sessions were chilling. Among the four tracks they did manage was "Black-Eyed Dog", which seemed to be a bleak premonition of his own death. On 25 November 1974 Drake died at his parents' home from an overdose of the antidepressants he was being prescribed. It has never been resolved whether he committed suicide or whether it was a tragic accident.

At the time, nobody would have imagined that Nick Drake's three albums would have the enduring, penetrating influence that they continue to hold over generations of listeners. His songs are melancholy yet welcoming, and they have communicated with people in a way that Nick Drake himself found impossible during his short and troubled life.

NW

playlist:

1 Time Has Told Me *from* Five Leaves Left
Country guitar and a leisurely swing brings shades of Townes Van Zandt to Nick's ruminating on "a troubled cure for a troubled mind".

2 River Man *from* Five Leaves Left
With its lush, expansive strings and leisurely folk-jazz guitar, "River Man" is like Dave Brubeck's "Take Five" slowed down and rewritten for English summer picnics.

3 All My Trials *from* Family Tree
Gabrielle Drake, Nick's sister, sings along on this home-recorded, harmonized version of an American folk classic; the domestic context and the circumstances of Nick's life loading the words with a bittersweet poignancy.

4 Way to Blue *from* Family Tree
This simple demo version – Nick singing at the piano – has a Satie-like delicacy that makes it more effective and to-the-point than the arrangement on *Five Leaves Left*.

5 Northern Sky *from* Bryter Later
Perhaps it's the nostalgic celeste played by John Cale that lends this listing shuffle all the charming simplicity of the Velvet Underground at their breeziest.

6 Day Is Done *from* Family Tree
Recorded directly to Robert Kirby's reel-to-reel on a battered old classical guitar, the straight-to-the-point delivery suits the lyrics, pondering the themes he obsessively returned to – the passing of time and its finality.

7 Pink Moon *from* Pink Moon
Warming strumming and piano that peals like a village church bell are the unlikely setting for portentous lyrics of impending doom.

8 Road *from* Pink Moon
As urgent as his famously mellow music gets, this is probably Nick's rootsiest song, with punchy guitar playing a gauche English blues.

9 I Was Made to Love Magic *from* Fruit Tree
A singularly elegaic "showtune" arrangement makes this defeated tango a song that would be perfect for a glum Disney musical, were they ever to make such a thing.

10 Black-Eyed Dog *from* Fruit Tree
In many ways, Nick Drake's guitar-playing grew ever simpler: this song pinwheels anxiously around the same home note like a taciturn take on Indian raga.

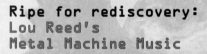

Ripe for rediscovery:
Lou Reed's
Metal Machine Music

Few records by an established major artist can ever have been greeted with such overwhelming critical hostility as that which greeted Lou Reed's *Metal Machine Music* on its release in 1975. An anti-record of anti-music with no songs, no lyrics, no hooks, no melodic themes and no voice, it's a double album of noise and overlapping loops of guitar feedback produced and played by Reed alone in his home studio. Even the creator himself admitted in the album's liner notes: "No one I know has listened to it all the way through, including myself. It's not meant to be. Start any place you like. Most of you won't like this and I don't blame you at all." Some – including Reed himself at times – have attempted to position it as an artistic statement alongside the work of experimentalists such as LaMonte Young but, in all honesty, it lacks the seriousness of intent to qualify as a significant contribution to avant-garde composition.

So what, if any, are its merits? Basically, it worked as an anarchic, two-fingered gesture, at a time when popular music had hit a trough and the word "progressive" in a rock context had come to take on the exact opposite of its intended meaning. *Metal Machine Music* was born of the same aesthetic that created the punk explosion.

It is a record that has stood the test of time, winning fans in the form of Mark E. Smith, and influencing legions of noise musicians. Most notable among them being Masami Akita, aka Merzbow, the extraordinarily prolific Japanese noisemaker. *Metal Machine Music* could convincingly be described as the template for everything he has done.

According to Reed: "It was a giant fuck you to clear the air and get rid of all those fucking assholes who show up at gigs and yell for "Vicious" and "Walk on the Wild Side". By which, of course, he meant all the people who had bought his records and made him a star. Crass and ungrateful, perhaps. But there's also something rather magnificent about such uncompromising orneriness.

NW

Jobriath

He could've been... David Bowie?

At the height of glam rock in the early 1970s, there were plenty who were coyly playing with conventions of gender, experimenting with bisexuality and transvestitism. But the first openly gay rock'n'roll icon to come out was Jobriath, a bizarre and ultimately tragic figure.

What's more he came out in the most spectacular way imaginable, in a whirlwind of hype. The apex of which was his record label Elektra erecting a giant replica of his debut album cover, featuring a crawling nude, plaster-white Jobriath, on a billboard in Times Square. A barrage of ads featuring the photo also appeared not just in the music press but in such mainstream publications as *Vogue* and *Penthouse*.

Born Bruce Wayne Campbell in rural Pennsylvania, after a stint in the US army he moved to California and adopted his new name, a contraction of "Job" and "Goliath." He landed a part in the LA production of *Hair* (from which he was allegedly sacked for his repeated attempts to upstage the rest of the cast) and joined the failed rock band Pidgeon before a solo demo tape of his caught the ear of impresario Jerry Brandt, who promised to make him a star – the world's first openly gay rock star.

Predictably enough, the hype backfired. On the release of his debut album in 1973 a suspicious music press dismissed Jobriath as nothing more than a Ziggy Stardust wannabe. His sexuality was seen as just another publicity stunt.

Listen to his debut album today, however, and it sounds like the best record David Bowie never made, a bold mix of rock'n'roll flash, proto-disco and camped-up showtunes that anticipates the music of both the Scissor Sisters and Rufus Wainwright.

A second album, *Creatures of the Street*, followed in 1974 and when it too flopped, his manager and label abandoned him. Without a record contract, he retreated to New York's Chelsea Hotel, where he lived in a pyramid-shaped room, and developed a musical alter-ego as the lounge singer Cole Berlin, playing piano in supper clubs. He also worked on a musical, *Pop Star*, that never came to fruition and supplemented his meagre earnings with prostitution. For years he was regarded as one of the music industry's most expensive blunders and his music remained unavailable until the 1990s when Morrissey, a longtime fan, released *Lonely Planet Boy*, a fifteen-song compilation of Jobriath's two LPs, on his Attack label. According to some reports, the former Smiths singer even tried to track him down to be his support act on tour, unaware that a decade earlier, in 1983, his body had been found at the Chelsea. At 37 years old, he had died from an AIDS-related illness.

NW

Jandek

Musicians such as Daft Punk have been known to disguise themselves for their entire career. Others, such as My Bloody Valentine and Scott Walker, can go for years without releasing any new songs. Jandek has somehow managed to put out over fifty albums since 1978, many of which have his face on the cover, yet still earn a deserved reputation as the most secretive man in music.

What we do know about the Houston resident relies on detective work from his handful of obsessive fans, the odd educated guess and one documentary film. There is no official website, no email address, and just two or three interviews grudgingly given in three decades. To buy a Jandek album, you must write to "Corwood Industries" at PO Box 15375, Houston TX 77220, for a catalogue. A "representative" can sell albums in bulk at an extremely cheap price. Any cheques will be endorsed by Sterling Richard Smith, believed to be Jandek's real name.

Every album cover consists of an amateur photograph, sometimes a blurry holiday snap, sometimes featuring a gaunt red-haired fellow at various stages of life. The music has simultaneously developed and regressed over the years, occasionally including electric guitar, piano, occasionally sticking to purely spoken word. But broadly speaking it is characterized by largely atonal, repetitively plucked acoustic guitar and Jandek's weak, droning, impossibly bleak voice. It is the blues played by someone with no conventional musical ability who seems to feel bluer than anyone in history.

In an interview given to *Spin* magazine in 1985, Jandek revealed that he was a machinist by trade, but gave little else away. "I'm an inordinately private person" he said, with some degree of understatement. Even the 2003 documentary, *Jandek on Corwood*, filled its ninety minutes without ever talking to the main man. "The reason people are interested in Jandek is the mystery," said director Chad Freidrichs. "If you take that mystery out, what's the point of making the movie? His non-presence in the film – that's his presence."

Suddenly, in 2004, completely unexpectedly, Jandek voluntarily became a little less mysterious, performing his first ever live show with a two-piece band at the Instal 04 music festival in Glasgow. He played for an hour although he was not on the bill and never introduced himself. Since then there have been a handful of live shows each year, all of which are gradually appearing on CD, such as *Glasgow Sunday* and *Brooklyn Wednesday*.

The live sets seem to be improvised. They sound as harsh and desolate as he ever did on his albums. He never speaks to audiences. But just seeing him in the flesh is, in its own way, a minor miracle.

DS

where to start:

1 European Jewel *from* Ready for the House
A signature song for Jandek, "European Jewel" appears in incomplete form on his debut album and pops up in four more versions on subsequent recordings *Chair Beside a Window* in 1982 and *The Rocks Crumble* in 1983.

2 Nancy Sings *from* Chair Beside a Window
Jandek's music is rather more listenable when it's the mysterious Nancy singing. Her voice is powerful and folky, somewhere in between Joan Baez and Grace Slick. She vanished as suddenly as she appeared, after 1987's *Modern Dances* album. Fans have speculated there might have been a romantic break-up at this point.

Daniel Johnston

When Kurt Cobain wore a Daniel Johnston T-shirt to the MTV awards in 1992, the singer-songwriter wasn't around to enjoy the endorsement. He was in a mental hospital in West Virginia. After Johnston had performed at the South By Southwest festival in Austin, Texas, in 1990, his father, who'd been a fighter pilot in World War II, flew him back in a small private plane. During the flight, Johnston seized the controls and crash-landed in some woods. The plane was destroyed although, astonishingly, both father and son crawled from the wreckage unscathed. Johnston had acted, he explained, upon a revelation that his father had been possessed by Satan.

There's plenty of unhinged behaviour in the world of rock'n'roll, much of it self-indulgent and infantile. Johnston's dysfunction is of a different character for he is clearly not a well man and has suffered from a bipolar disorder all of his adult life. Yet his obsessive, economical songs, which veer between child-like naïveté and something altogether more disturbing, have earned him a celebrity fan base that includes David Bowie, Johnny Depp, Tom Waits and Beck, while his paintings – primitive cartoon-like drawings made with a magic marker – are widely exhibited and now command sizeable sums. Our admiration of his strangely compelling art, however, walks a difficult, troubling tightrope. Johnston has spooked audiences by screaming "we're all going to die!" at them, has defaced the Statue of Liberty with anti-Satanist graffiti, was hospitalized after attacking his manager with a lead pipe and attacked friends he believed to be "servants of Satan". His songs, with their catalogue of personal obsessions such as Caspar the Friendly Ghost, comic-book heroes, his unrequited love for a woman named Laurie Allen (who broke his heart by marrying an undertaker), the music of The Beatles and a fixation with the number nine, offer us a rare and fascinating insight into an unbalanced mind. Is there not something voyeuristic about our enjoyment of his often disturbing songs – as if we are intruding on some private mania that is really none of our business? One British magazine, in an otherwise highly appreciative study of his work, came dangerously close to treating his affliction as freakshow entertainment by captioning a picture of him with the words "We love him, but we're also quite scared of him." On the other hand, Johnston does of course invite us into his odd world by putting his music out there.

Born in 1961 and raised in a strict Baptist family in West Virginia, Johnston's fundamentalist upbringing had a profound effect on his first recordings, which appeared on self-made cassettes in the early 1980s. Lyrics about the world "marching to hell" and denunciations of premarital sex were delivered with an unorthodox sense of timing accompanied by toy instruments and samples of TV evangelists and his mother yelling at him. Yet there was an undeniable melodic facility that one critic reckoned made his songs sound "like distant cousins of a Paul Anka tune". His lyrics often contained great insights, too. "You see, he was never really sober enough to feel the pain of being an asshole", he sang on "Don't Be Scared", the title song of his second self-released cassette. The likes of Butthole Surfers and Sonic Youth preceded Kurt Cobain in declaring themselves fans and by the end of the 1980s his underground reputation had grown to the point where the best of his dozen home-made cassettes had received commercial release on CD.

After his enforced career break following the 1990 plane crash, he was signed by Atlantic for his 1994 comeback, *Fun*.

Since then there have been sporadic recordings on various labels as he's continued to battle his inner demons. His voice has changed over the years, which may be due to the medication he is on to stabilize his condition. But his cult has continued to grow. *Discovered Covered*, a double set featuring one disc of originals and a second of covers by Tom Waits, Beck, Eels, Bright Eyes, Teenage Fanclub and The Flaming Lips, among others, appeared in 2004. The following year he was the subject of a documentary film, *The Devil and Daniel Johnston*, which won an award at the Sundance festival for its even-handed but sympathetic portrait that refused to succumb to the usual trite rock'n'roll clichés about the link between mania and genius.

NW

playlist:

1 Speeding Motorcycle *from* Yip/Jump Music
Like a brilliant and deliberately wimped-out "Born To Run".

2 Keep Punching Joe *from* Hi, How Are You
"I guess I lean towards the excessive/But that's just the way it is when you're a manic depressive."

3 Foxy Girl *from* Fun
A major-label budget allows Dan to fill out his earlier sketches; it's like Syd Barrett meeting Jimi Hendrix.

4 My Baby Cares for the Dead *from* Songs of Pain
A terrifying song about "his" girl marrying an undertaker.

5 Phantom of My Own Opera *from* Songs of Pain
Like Smokey Robinson's "Tears of a Clown" through an impenetrably black filter. You are left wondering whether to applaud or look away.

Nico

Everybody knows the voice of Nico from the first Velvet Underground album: "Femme Fatale", "All Tomorrow's Parties" and "I'll Be Your Mirror" were all sung by her and have become landmarks in rock history. Far less well-known is her complex and challenging body of work as a solo performer, which was doom-laden and stark often to the point of bleakness. However brightly lit a room was, Nico was always able to find a dark corner. That she was an intimate not only of Lou Reed but also of Dylan, Jackson Browne, the Stones, Jim Morrison and Iggy Pop, among others, has contributed to the growth of her legend. So, too, has her history of excess and her all-too-inevitable death in 1988 before she turned fifty. Fortunately such clichéd rock'n'roll headlines have also led in recent years to an upturn of interest in her post-Velvets music and recognition as the original goth-rocker with a unique, powerful and disturbing vision.

Born Christa Paffgen in Germany in 1938, she had already led a fascinating life before Andy Warhol installed her as a charismatic foil to Lou Reed in the Velvet Underground. Her early CV included modelling jobs in Paris, where she met Sartre and Hemingway, a walk-on role in Fellini's *La Dolce Vita*, giving birth to a son she claimed was fathered by Alain Delon (who has always denied this) and appearing on the cover of *Vogue*. In 1965, the Stones' manager Andrew Loog Oldham stuck her in a studio with a band that included

Jimmy Page and Brian Jones and recorded the single "I'm Not Saying", hoping to invent another Marianne Faithfull. When the record flopped, she relocated to New York and the low-rent bohemian sanctuary of the Chelsea Hotel and fell in with Warhol and his Factory crowd.

Nico's tenure with the Velvet Underground was brief. The band were never really convinced of the need for a German chanteuse and she was ousted even before their debut album reached the stores. To show that it was nothing personal, Lou Reed and John Cale both assisted on her debut solo album, *Chelsea Girls* (1968). Equally significant was the role of the teenage Jackson Browne, who in later years told hilarious stories of how he fell under her spell. He provided her with three songs for her debut and, along with covers of compositions by Bob Dylan and Tim Hardin, the result was the most conventional of her solo releases: a folk-rock record without drums or bass, embellished with chamber strings and flute and with only her deadpan Teutonic voice to distance it from dozens of similar-sounding releases.

She hated it and determined that the follow-up would be dramatically different. Moving to California to be close to Jim Morrison, with whom she made some LSD-fuelled trips into the desert, she set about crafting the songs for 1969's *The Marble Index*. There would be no more folk covers. This time she wrote the lyrics and made the bare bones of the music herself on a droning harmonium, leaving Cale to flesh out the arrangements. The sound was sombre, even desolate; the songs were morose and her singing uncompromising and brooding. It was groundbreaking, gothic and glacial European art-rock, and that it had been made under the Californian sun only contributed to the weird sense of dislocation. The album reached the bargain bins in record time.

In retrospect, it was the creative peak of her career and over her remaining nineteen years she released just four further studio albums. *Desert Shore* (1971) and *The End* (1974), both produced by Cale in London, explored similar terrain to *The Marble Index*. *The End* was particularly bleak, her harmonium-based gothic soundscapes made even scarier by the addition of Brian Eno's droning electronics and Phil Manzanera's guitar. The 1980s also saw just two studio recordings. *Drama of Exile* was more rockist and featured Middle Eastern arrangements. *Camera Obscura* (1985), her final release, was an experimental collection that oddly featured a cover of "My Funny Valentine".

Despite her studio reticence, she spent her last years touring manically, playing more than a thousand concerts between 1981 and 1988. She needed the cash to feed her heroin habit. She died in 1988 during a holiday with her son in Ibiza. Found lying in the roadside by her overturned bicycle, she had suffered a cerebral haemorrhage.

NW

playlist:

1 It Was a Pleasure Then *from* Chelsea Girls
Her only writing credit on her debut was for this eight minutes of droning guitar and violin from Reed and Cale, unsurprisingly reminiscent of the Velvets.

2 Frozen Warnings *from* The Marble Index
The trademark ice-queen vocals at their most stark and startling.

3 You Forgot to Answer *from* The End
The story of how she tried to reach Jim Morrison by phone and subsequently found out he was dead has suitably spectral accompaniment from Manzanera, Cale and Eno.

4 No One Is There *from* The Peel Sessions
A starkly chilling harmonium-and-voice rendition of one of the strongest *Marble Index* tracks, recorded in February 1971.

5 Janitor of Lunacy *from* Desert Shore
"Revive the living dream, forgive their begging scream, seal the giving of their seed, disease the breathing grief," intones the gothic high priestess. Quite what it all means is another matter.

OUTSIDER MUSIC

Behold, the weirdest of the weird…

Imagine a world where record deals are freely given to the people from the first few episodes of *The X Factor* – the ones who turn up to the audition showing off voices like wounded animals, or brandishing kazoos. There's a thin line that separates these people from "outsider" artists – the visual artists or musicians oft-labelled as "freaks" or "incompetents" who carry on their artistic pursuits no matter how many people tell them they're terrible. As with the resurgence of interest in crackpot sci-fi film director Ed Wood, a "so bad it's good" culture has arisen around a select few outsider musicians, admittedly the ones who stimulate something a little more than a strong desire to stick your fingers in your ears. Many of these musicians are genuinely compelling.

There's a disturbing beauty, for example, to the recordings of Daniel Johnston and Jandek, prominent outsiders covered elsewhere in this book. Then there are those who can kindle a smile wider than any number of chart-friendly sound-a-likes. William "Shooby" Taylor, for example, the Harlem postman whose idiosyncratic take on scat singing makes other scatters sound sensible; or the falsetto-singing ukelele-player Tiny Tim, and Texan oddball Norman Odam, aka The Legendary Stardust Cowboy. The Ledge, as fans call him, achieved minor notoriety in 1968 with his song "Paralyzed", an unholy racket featuring little more than primitive clattering drums and Odam screaming, hollering and yodelling noises that almost sound like real words. He sounds like a man whose anaesthesia has yet to wear off after serious dental surgery. It's completely unhinged but excellent fun all the same. He unwittingly invented a rock'n'roll sub-genre known as psychobilly

and gained a notable fan in the shape of David Bowie. Bowie's Ziggy Stardust's last name was inspired by the Ledge, and in recent years Bowie has programmed concerts featuring his unlikely hero in both London and New York.

Bowie seems to have a taste for this sort of stuff. In 200? he was particularly taken with a recording of his hit "Space Oddity" that was sung by a collection of Canadian schoolchildren in the late 1970s. Their innocent voices and primitive musicianship made the track even spookier than the original. It had been preserved by music teacher Hans Fenger, who had the good sense not only to get his pupils singing the greatest pop of the 1960s instead of the usual kiddie drivel, but also to record the results.

Outsider music expert Irwin Chusid discovered an LP, one of just 300 pressed for the children and their families, and reissued it as *Innocence & Despair* by The Langley Schools Music Project. Bowie recreated the album live with a local choir in a 2002 concert at London's Royal Festival Hall.

These youngsters sang wonderful, classic pop songs such as "Good Vibrations" and "God Only Knows" as part of their education, while most kids were trudging through traditional hymns. Their enjoyment is clearly audible in the pre-chorus whoops on "I'm Into Something Good" and the raucous, poorly-timed handclaps on the Bay City Rollers' "Saturday Night". The performances are charmingly ramshackle – cymbals crash seemingly at random, and flat notes thud like conkers in the playground. But when the kids really belt it out, it becomes almost impossible not to join in. It is a captivating, warm-hearted record that even makes Barry Manilow's "Mandy" sound great, overflowing with the best possible kind of nostalgia.

Equally entertaining but less good for a singalong is the 2003 compilation *The American Song-Poem Anthology: Do You Know the Difference Between Big Wood and Brush*. Song poems were the result of a 1960s scam, essentially, whereby producers advertising in the back of magazines asked for members of the public to submit "poems" to be set to music. People paid anywhere between $75 and $400 for this privilege, hoping for fame and fortune. Instead they ended up getting bizarre novelties played by jobbing hacks. The more memorable of these tracks have become popular with collectors of cult music. There's "Richard Nixon" by Rod & The MSR Singers, a glowing tribute to America's least popular president: "Al

ou Need is a Fertile Mind" by Gene Marshall, a paean to masturbation; Bobbi Blake's cute "I Like Yellow Things"; and an unknown singer sounding heartbroken on "I Lost My Girl to an Argentinian Cowboy". The disc contains country, soul and rock music … none of it particularly good.

But sounding "good" (in the traditional sense) isn't really the point of outsider music. It's the fact that these songs have been made at all, have been made with such passion and purity of vision, and that they have survived to be heard in an age when marketing men dictate our chart-toppers more than ever before. That is what's so fascinating. They could be dismissed as jokers, but there ought to be a little room in everyone's collection for music that makes you laugh – even for music that makes you question why it was made at all. And it's the fact that this stuff has never been mass produced and will never get to number one that makes it even more valuable. Long may underdogs like the Ledge bark, and howl, and roar, and gibber.

DS

Bat For Lashes' Natasha Khan on the Langley Schools Music Project

"These kids got a cool young music teacher who was really into the music of the time: The Beatles, David Bowie, Neil Diamond, the Beach Boys … all of these really classic pop artists. He decided that for what would become the *Innocence & Despair* album, he would get them all to do covers of these songs.

I found the record, in Brighton, when it first got reissued in 2001. I went along to this local shop, and they just had it in the front of the rack and I thought "Ooh – a school's project!", because I was a nursery teacher at the time. I remember when I first bought the record it was my favourite thing for about a year because there were lots of different voices. All the kids are just singing together, really joyfully, unabashed – just so free. And yet their musical interpretation sounds so incredibly cool because it was all done in a school hall, which has this breathtaking natural reverb. And there are little kids, seven-year-old kids, strumming acoustic guitars; someone is playing a wood block; someone else is hammering on a xylophone; and on a couple of the songs, such as "Mandy" by Barry Manilow, there is a little girl who sings the most beautiful solo … really inspiring.

The way this record makes me feel … I don't know how to explain it … it's just a little bit shambolic, and not all completely in time. It's just so free and beautiful that you can really feel the spirit of what music is capable of capturing in people. It's a communal thing – the communal aspects to music are really good, really powerful.

I tried to organize a children's choir for my last album, but the budget ran out and time ran out! I really hope one day to record a choir of teenage girls, perhaps in an old school hall, out in a desert or all standing on a sea shore. I would like them to try rounds like we used to sing at school. I think to capture the essence of feeling and emotion you have at that age is something that's not often done in pop music. We all inherently recognize our own inner child when we listen to children singing, and there's a sadness and loss in that along with the beauty."

Elliott Smith

Elliott Smith wrote songs about despair and self-doubt, love, loss and addiction and how they intersected. When he died at the age of 34, from a single, self-inflicted wound to the chest, the news was shockingly sad but hardly a surprise: it was as if he had been rehearsing the moment in his songs for years. His best-known song, "Miss Misery", began with the words "I will fake it through the day, with some help from Johnnie Walker Red."

Some of his fans take exception to the one-dimensional representation of him as a disturbed and doomed figure and talk up his warmth and humanity, his amiability and courteousness – although there is nothing unusual about such a dramatic combination of contrasting moods. But let us set aside the complexities of Smith's troubled soul and concentrate on what made him one of the most insightful and criminally underrated songwriters of his time. The dark, sometimes harrowing introspection of his subject matter – drug abuse, failing relationships and betrayals shot through with only the occasional glimmer of hope – may have kept him from a mainstream audience. But there is no doubting the affecting quality of his strummed melodies and the potent mix of unsettling prettiness, emotional intensity and charismatic vulnerability which characterized his songs, delivered in a deceptively casual downbeat manner. He once told an interviewer, who had asked about his unusual juxtaposition of sour words and sweet melodies, that it was his ambition to be "both John and Paul at once". It wasn't an idle rock-star boast, for what you hear in his music really does combine the pain of Lennon's primal scream with the pop jauntiness of McCartney.

Smith did not start out as an introspective troubadour but as a member of the Oregon-based indie-punk quartet Heatmiser. By 1994, however, he had started recording stripped-down songs in his basement, honing his songwriting craft by playing guitar while watching endless reruns of General Hospital. Because the style was lo-fi and acoustic, his early albums found him bracketed by critics as a folk artist. However, his chief influences were The Beatles, The Clash and Big Star's Alex Chilton, another maverick pop genius whose "Thirteen" Smith covered on the posthumous release, New Moon.

Yet it was only after Heatmiser's demise that Smith's solo muse really blossomed. "I was always disguised in this loud rock band," he noted. Either/Or (1997) sounded like a liberation, although it was a raw, bleak and at times even nihilistic freedom. "You can do what you want to, whenever you want to, though it doesn't mean a thing", he sang on "Ballad of Big Nothing". Four of the album's songs were included on the soundtrack of the film Good Will Hunting but it was a new song, "Miss Misery", that earned him an Oscar nomination and an awkward appearance in an ill-fitting white suit at the awards, sandwiched between Celine Dion and Trisha Yearwood.

The exposure earned him a deal with Dreamworks and a bigger recording budget in an LA studio. Strings, horns and piano were laid over the simple voice-and-guitar blueprint on 1998's XO, but so discreetly that his understated ethic of quiet desperation remained unsullied. His next album, 2000's Figure 8 – an image Smith claimed to like for its notion of endless motion going nowhere – was another masterpiece, many of the songs beginning with acoustic guitar before building through strings, organs, guitars and multi-tracked vocals to Beatles-esque crescendos.

What occasioned the final crisis that made him take his own life we can never know. NME once asked him what his idea of heaven was. "George Jones would be singing all the time," he replied. "It would be like New York in reverse. People would be nice to each other for no reason at all. And it would smell good." You can only hope he's finally found the perfumed contentment that eluded him in his lifetime.

NW

playlist:

1 Miss Misery *from* Good Will Hunting OST
A perfect song, which got itself an Oscar nomination. But its stark honesty didn't stand a chance against Celine Dion's overwrought theme from *Titanic.*

2 Needle in the Hay *from* Elliott Smith
Whispered guitar and voice in a masterpiece of lo-fi simplicity.

3 Last Call *from* Roman Candle
Has there ever been a more insightful analysis into the troubled aftermath of a relationship?

4 Independence Day *from* Xo
An upbeat, bouncy melody and a typically downbeat lyric, using the metaphor of a butterfly's life: "You only live a day, but it's brilliant anyway."

5 Stupidity Tries *from* Figure 8
Smith in full-on Beatles mode, trying to be both John and Paul at the same time.

Bobb Trimble

Bobb Trimble made a grand total of two albums in his early twenties, the last of which was released in 1982. He never had a record deal: the albums were privately released and he hawked them around local Massachusetts record stores and radio stations himself. He can't remember whether there were 300 or 500 copies pressed of his 1980 debut, *Iron Curtain Innocence*. But either way, there weren't many takers for his disturbingly phantasmagorical songs, and he never performed outside of his home turf in Worcester County.

A compilation on a small, specialist label in the 1990s sparked a degree of cult interest and the original albums started exchanging hands for ridiculous sums of money. Trimble himself sold his last remaining copy of one of them for $500. One of his friends claims to have sold a copy of *Iron Curtain Innocence* for $1500.

Finally, in 2007, *Iron Curtain Innocence* and its follow-up, *Harvest of Dreams*, were reissued with bonus tracks by the Secretly Canadian label. The oddball Trimble – who hasn't made any new music in years – suddenly found himself fêted in rock magazines as a lost genius and a 1980s equivalent of Syd Barrett or Arthur Lee, with Sonic Youth's Thurston Moore commenting that music "doesn't get much realer than this". Like that of his illustrious but unhinged 1960s predecessors, his music suggests that he inhabits a world all of his own making – one you're

happy to visit but that leaves you pondering the sanity of its creator.

Trimble himself was bemused by the belated recognition. "It's uncanny those records are coming out again," he told *The Guardian* newspaper. "It's eerie. The interest that has been generated is beyond what's even believable to me at this point." On the other hand, he had no self-doubts about their quality: "But I can understand why people want to hear them, because they're great records."

Even before you've heard a note, that Trimble is a singular artist is evident from the sleeve of his debut album. Out of the front cover stares a rather earnest-looking, fresh-faced young man sitting on a stool behind a microphone with an electric guitar lying across his lap. So far, so conventional. But in his right hand he's holding aloft a machine gun, like a refugee from the Baader-Meinhof gang. Inside, he's written: "Dear John, Paul, George and Ringo, If I'm a good boy and work real hard, may I please be the fifth Beatle someday? Your friend, Bobb."

The music also suggests a troubled soul born at least a decade out of time. While his Massachusetts contemporaries were in thrall to punk, metal and new wave, the influences evident in Trimble's music come from an earlier era, located somewhere in the late 1960s or early 1970s: The Beatles, Pink Floyd, David Bowie, West Coast acid-pastoralism, psychedelia at its most unhinged, classic folk-rock tropes and even the prog-rockisms of Yes and Genesis are clear influences. All are woven into spaced-out sound collages on mysterious and deranged songs of loneliness and desperation – with such disturbing titles as "Night at the Asylum", "Through My Eyes (Hopeless as Hell: DOA)" and "Killed by the Hands of an Unknown Rock Starr" (sic) – sung in a high, fragile, manically multi-tracked voice oozing with tortured passion.

On 1982's *Harvest of Dreams*, Trimble poses on the cover with what looks like a sheep dressed up with a single horn on its head to look like a unicorn. On one track, "Oh Baby", he's backed by a band called The Kidds, whose average age was twelve. When their parents grew a little wary of what their offspring were doing hanging out with a 23-year-old oddball singer-songwriter, he formed the Crippled Dog Band, whose members were older – fifteen. The Crippled Dog Band are still remembered to this day in Worcester for an appearance at a local rock festival in 1983, at which Trimble came on stage wearing top hat, green satin coat, bunny ears and bunny tail.

Harvest of Dreams is dedicated to the memory of John Lennon and sounds gentler than *Iron Curtain Innocence*. Yet at the same time the ideas are more ambitious and out-there than ever. In the original sleeve notes he wrote: "As people of world peace, we must join together and confront the Opposition of Indifference with the Spirit of Totality." A quarter of a century on, Trimble claims the record still has the same message for our own times. "It's like wow, man, they never give it a rest."

NW

playlist:

1 Glass Menagerie Fantasies *from* Iron Curtain Innocence
Brooding introspection and the clear imprint of Dark Side of the Moon.

2 Night at the Asylum *from* Iron Curtain Innocence
Strange yelps, manic witchy cackling and harmonies that sound like Abba on acid: an Hieronymus Bosch vision turned sound-picture.

3 When the Raven Calls *from* Iron Curtain Innocence
"Save the world, save a piece for me, when the raven calls that'll be world war three"; has Bobb been reading Edgar Allen Poe?

4 Killed by the Hands of an Unknown Rock Starr *from* Iron Curtain Innocence
Disarmingly gentle and melodic folk-rock and a lyric of total otherness.

5 Through My Eyes (Hopeless as Hell: DOA) *from* Iron Curtain Innocence
More lovely pastoral sounds disguising bleak despair.

6 Premonitions Boy: The Reality *from* Harvest of Dreams
Dylanesque harmonica, falsetto vocals, jangling guitars – perfect pastoral dream-pop with a deeply unsettling edge.

7 Take Me Home Vienna Taken *from* Harvest of Dreams
Haunting, ghostly and childlike. You can hear why he felt more at home in the company of twelve-year-olds than adults.

8 Another Lonely Angel *from* Harvest of Dreams
The spirit of Arthur Lee meets Tim Buckley's Starsailor.

9 Paralyzed *from* Harvest of Dreams
A 1980s psych-pop fantasia that trips like it's still 1967, man.

10 Oh Baby *from* Harvest of Dreams
Pre-teen garage rock from Bobb and The Kidds, with one of the twelve-year-olds on vocals. Bizarre doesn't even begin to describe it.

Victory for the comic muse?
Humour and music

Randy Newman, arguably the funniest man in music, was once asked why angst, misery and pain are covered so well in popular song but wit, humour and comedy seldom get a look-in. "Most songwriters want to be taken seriously and they're terrified of being humorous because they think they'll get dismissed as a novelty," he said sagely. "I got over taking myself seriously years ago." He's right, which is one reason this lot aren't household names.

Bonzo Dog Doo-Dah Band

Like a musical version of *Monty Python's Flying Circus*, the Bonzos combined satire and surreal humour with trad jazz, rock, psychedelia, old-fashioned music hall and anything else that took their fancy. The band had real musical talent, but it was the extraordinary personality of Vivian Stanshall that made them unique. To Stanshall, nothing was taboo and the Bonzos' albums fearlessly parodied anything and everything. "Jazz: Delicious Hot, Disgusting Cold", "Can Blue Men Sing the Whites?" and "Canyons of Your Mind" were among their best musical jokes but perhaps the finest example of their ability to combine genuine musicality and hip hilarity was "The Intro and the Outro", a wonderful "introducing the band" spoof that included such "guests" as Adolf Hitler on vibes ("mmm ... nice") and General De Gaulle on accordion ("really wild, General! Thank you, sir"). After the band broke up in 1972, Stanshall went on to develop his idiosyncratic *Rawlinson's End* monologues while songwriter Neil Innes created the Beatles parody The Rutles.
The Intro and the Outro *from* Gorilla

Firesign Theatre

Not a band at all, but a satirical comedy troupe who delivered a distinctly rock'n'roll brand of humour. Deriving comedic inspiration from the Goons, Lord Buckley and the Marx Brothers among others, Firesign Theatre's punning wordplay and sharp wit found favour with the same kind of audience in the late 1960s that bought into the Mothers of Invention. Specializing in studio recordings rather than live performances, their albums, which were often racked in the rock section, boasted titles such as "I Think We're All Bozos on This Bus" and "Don't Crush That Dwarf, Hand Me the Pliers", and were full of drug references and hip allusions to The Beatles, Dylan and other popular culture icons. You can also hear them providing the gunshot effects on The Byrds' song "Draft Morning".
The Adventures of Nick Danger *from* How Can You Be In Two Places at Once When You're Not Anywhere at All

Happy Flowers

A kind of musical *Beavis and Butthead*, Happy Flowers' first song was titled "Mom, I Gave the Cat Some Acid". The group was formed in Charlottesville, Virginia, in 1983 by two former members of the Landlords, John Beers (aka Mr. Horribly Charred Infant) and Charlie Kramer (aka Mr. Anus). Usually backed by a kind of improvisational punk guitar noise, their songs rejoiced in such child-like titles as "Bobby Made Me Eat a Frog" and "Mom and Dad Like the Baby More Than Me". Depending on your mood, they are side-splittingly hilarious or as irritating as hell.
I Said I Wanna Watch Cartoons *from* Too Many Bunnies (Not Enough Mittens)

King Missile

Randy Newman had a point. If you make the charts with a song called "Detachable Penis", nobody is going to believe that it's an ironic post-modernist comment on the disposability of consumer culture: it's going to be a "novelty hit". New York poet John S. Hall had been peddling his fusion of dry comic monologues and eclectic rock'n'roll over a trio of albums on the eccentric Shimmy-Disc label before he landed a major label deal with Atlantic in 1991 and made the charts. But as with most novelties, King Missile's "Detachable Penis" had no staying power. The group's audience swiftly diminished again. The major-label record deal ended. King Missile went back to Shimmy-Disc.
Detachable Penis *from* Happy Hour

Jeffrey Lewis

One of Lewis's records was called *The Only Time I Feel Right Is When I'm Drawing Comic Books*, a reference to his main occupation when not making music. Born in New York in 1975, Lewis's complex, literate and witty songs have had critics placing him in the "anti-folk" movement. Yet few others toiling in that vineyard display quite the same lightness of touch and sense of playfulness. Song titles such as "Don't Let the Record Label Take You out to Lunch" and "You Don't Have to Be a Scientist to Do Experiments on Your Own Heart" convey the general flavour. Jarvis Cocker called him "the best lyricist working in the US today", although that description cannot be applied to his most recent release, *12 Crass Songs* (2007), a collection of "anti-folk" covers of material written by the punk band Crass. Which may just be a joke too far.
The Chelsea Hotel Oral Sex *from* The Last Time I Did Acid I Went Insane

NW

Picture credits

The Publishers have made every effort to identify correctly the rights holders in respect of the images featured in this book. If despite these efforts any attribution is incorrect the Publishers will correct this error once it has been brought to their attention on a subsequent reprint.

Inside front cover Fiona Adams/Redferns; 2 Redferns; 4 josepharthur.com; 11 Redferns; 13 Redferns; 15 third; 17 Redferns; 19 Pearson Asset Library/Dorling Kindersley; 21 Pearson Asset Library/Dorling Kindersley; 22, 23 Redferns; 25 Redferns; 27 third; 30 babydee.org; 31 Pearson Asset Library/Dorling Kindersley; 33 LP Sleeve; 34 flaminglips. com; 35 saltywater.co.uk; 37 Pearson Asset Library/Dorling Kindersley; 44, 45 Carpark Records; 47 Redferns; 48 Redferns; 50 Smoosh; 51 Magnetic Fields; 54 Iron & Wine (top), Clap Your Hands Say Yeah (bottom); 55 Deerhoof; 56 Yo La Tengo; 58 vicchesnutt.com; 59 Smithsonian Institute; 61 Welk Music Group; 62 Carrot Top Records; 65 spyboy.co.uk; 68, 69 Drag City Records; 70 Redferns; 72 Redferns; 74 gillianwelch.com; 76 flowfestival.com; 78 billied.com; 79 Redferns; 80 Pearson Asset Library/Dorling Kindersley; 82 Catherine Carlson, Trylon Communications; 87 lauranyro.com; 90 Smithsonian Institute; 96 Redferns; 99 Redferns; 100, 101 Pearson Asset Library/Dorling Kindersley; 103 Redferns; 104 Redferns; 109 La Guitara/ Patty Larkin; 110, 111 Redferns; 117 crawfishfest.org; 123 Southern Records; 125 Redferns; 129 Planet Rock Booking; 134 Redferns; 137 Redferns; 138 Delmore Recordings; 140 Redferns; 141 Natasha Khan; 142 Pearson Asset Library/Dorling Kindersley; 145 Redferns; 146 Drag City; 149 lindaperhacs.com; 150 Redferns; 153 Redferns; 161 Fabric London; 163 XL Recordings; 167 scenicreflections. com; 168 Def Jam Records; 169 Thrill Jockey Records;

170 Fabric London; 175 Redferns; 178 Redferns; 181 Pearson Asset Library/Dorling Kindersley; 183 bighassle. com; 185 Redferns; 187 Redferns; 188, 189 Subpop Records; 193 Redferns; 199 Redferns; 201 Moviestore Collection; 204 hotsource.com; 207 World Circuit Records; 208 Redferns; 210 Redferns; 212 Redferns; 214 Planet Rock Booking; 217 ubuprojex.net; 227 Ruhr Triennale; 224 Bibliothèque nationale; 228 Pearson Asset Library/Dorling Kindersley; 231 NASA; 233 Redferns; 235 Redferns; 236 Redferns; 237 Wikimedia Commons; 239 space is the place; 245 Redferns; 246 Redferns; 250 Pearson Asset Library/Dorling Kindersley; 253 Jandek on Corwood; 254 Sony Pictures Entertainment Inc; 255 mininova.org; 256 Redferns; 259 batforlashes.com; 261 Richard B. Fisher Center for the Performing Arts; 263 Bobb Trimble.

Index

Rough Guides presents...

"Achieves the perfect balance between learned recommendation and needless trivia"
Uncut Magazine reviewing The Rough Guide to Cult Movies

Other Rough Guide Film & TV titles include:

American Independent Film • British Cult Comedy • Chick Flicks • Comedy Movies • Cult Movies
Film • Film Musicals • Film Noir • Gangster Movies • Horror Movies • Sci-Fi Movies • Westerns

MAKE THE MOST OF YOUR TIME ON EARTH™